Servants of the Honourable Company

Work, Discipline, and Conflict in the Hudson's Bay Company, 1770–1870

Edith I. Burley

TORONTO NEW YORK OXFORD
OXFORD UNIVERSITY PRESS
1997

Oxford University Press
70 Wynford Drive, Don Mills, Ontario M3C 1J9

Oxford   New York
Athens   Auckland   Bangkok   Bombay
Calcutta   Cape Town   Dar es Salaam   Delhi
Florence   Hong Kong   Istanbul   Karachi
Kuala Lumpur   Madras   Madrid   Melbourne
Mexico City   Nairobi   Paris   Singapore
Taipei   Tokyo   Toronto

and associated companies in
Berlin   Ibadan

Oxford is a trade mark of Oxford University Press

Canadian Cataloguing in Publication Data

Burley, Edith, 1949–
  Servants of the honourable company

(The Canadian social history series)
Includes bibliographical references and index.
ISBN 0–19–541296–6

1. Hudson's Bay Company – Employees.
2. Hudson's Bay Company – History.
3. Industrial relations – Canada – History.
4. Fur trade – Canada – History.   I. Title.   II. Series.

HD8109.N672B87   1997   338.7'613801439'0971   C97–930690–6

The licensed use of Hudson's Bay Company's coloured stripes design trademark on the cover of this textbook should not be construed in any way as the agreement or consent, tacit or otherwise, of the company or its shareholders with the facts and subject matter of the textbook. Hudson's Bay Company is proud of its heritage and its role in building Canada. It welcomes the addition this textbook will make to the ongoing study of Canadian history.

Copyright © Oxford University Press 1997

1 2 3 4 — 00 99 98 97

This book is printed on permanent (acid-free) paper ∞.

Printed in Canada

Contents

Acknowledgements / v

1 Introduction / 1

2 The View from the Top / 19

3 The Source and Supply of Labour / 64

4 The View from the Bottom / 109

5 The Denial of Duty / 156

6 Combination and Resistance / 194

7 Conclusion / 245

A Note on Sources / 249

Notes / 254

Index / 307

Acknowledgements

Since this book began as a Ph.D. dissertation, I am first of all indebted to my thesis supervisors, Nolan Reilly, of the University of Winnipeg, and Douglas Sprague, of the University of Manitoba. Doctoral fellowships from the Social Sciences and Humanities Research Council of Canada provided financial support while I carried out the research, and a grant from the John S. Ewart Memorial Fund enabled me to visit the National Archives of Canada in Ottawa. Thanks are also due to the staffs of the National Archives and of the Hudson's Bay Company Archives in Winnipeg.

I am also grateful to Greg Kealey, the editor of the series, for his suggestions and enthusiasm for the project. And last, but not least, I want to thank David for his support and encouragement.

1

Introduction

The Hudson's Bay Company tends to be seen as an organization of crafty fur traders, bold explorers, lively *voyageurs,* and dour Scots, whose control of the west protected the northern half of the continent from annexation by the United States. Historians have modified this image considerably in recent years by analysing the roles of women and Native peoples in the fur trade and demonstrating that the company's trading posts were complex communities. But, in drawing much needed attention to the social and cultural aspects of the fur trade in Canada and emphasizing that it was *more* than a business, historians have neglected the fact that the HBC *was* a business. Its posts were, after all, factories, i.e., establishments 'for traders carrying on business in a foreign country',[1] the purpose of which was to provide shareholders with a return on their investments. A governor, a deputy governor, and a committee of seven, all elected from the shareholders, ran the company from London. They hired managers, known as officers, to conduct the trade in North America and workers, known as servants, to build and maintain the posts, make and repair trade goods, and transport supplies and furs. Of the company's men, only the officers were actually fur traders. All the others—even explorers, *voyageurs,* and Scots—were workers who came not in search of adventure but of a livelihood. They were carpenters, tailors, masons, coopers, fishermen, boatbuilders, canoebuilders, sawyers, blacksmiths, tinsmiths, sloopers, boatmen, sailors, miners, and labourers.

Skilled tradesmen generally comprised 15 per cent of the HBC's employees, while 70 per cent were labourers, yet the concerns of the officers and the operations of the company as a whole have heretofore attracted the attention of historians. This is due primarily to the fact that the HBC was a conservative, paternalistic organization based on the relations of authority characteristic of pre-industrial society. Fur trade historians have observed that the company's posts resembled the pre-industrial households of seventeenth-century England, which were characterized by vertical ties and an absence of class divisions. British traders naturally replicated the relations of authority to which they were accustomed. Masters of the posts assumed the role of patriarch and, as such, claimed the right to take wives and establish families. Their subordinates resembled servants in British households. They were young, had little private life, were expected to remain unmarried, and had few opportunities to establish relationships with their peers, even fewer than their counterparts in Britain, because of the extreme isolation of fur-trading posts. As a result, HBC employees formed strong personal ties with their superiors and were quite subsumed in the company.[2] Moreover, the HBC never abandoned its hierarchical organization, always hired a proportion of its employees on long-term contracts that tied them to it in a master-servant relationship, and never ceased to believe that men from pre-industrial societies were the most desirable. Its workers tend, therefore, to appear to be little more than instruments of policy or problems of strategy as the company overcame the challenges that faced it, although finding suitable labour was an ever-present concern in the company's history and its employees frequently failed to behave as loyal servants were supposed to.

The charter of 1670 granted the HBC exclusive right to all trade and natural resources in the territory drained by waters flowing into Hudson Bay, a vast area the company named Rupert's Land. But war with France in which company posts were attacked and the unwelcoming terrain discouraged exploration during the first few years. As a result, the company's men kept to a half-dozen posts on the shores of Hudson Bay and James Bay and let the Natives and their furs come to them, an arrangement so satisfactory that there was no incentive to alter it once hostilities with the French ceased. Though perhaps unexciting, this passive way of doing business was extremely economical. The furs from which the HBC derived its profits were delivered to its posts by Natives in return for an assortment of inexpensive goods. Its establishments were manned by workers engaged on contracts that secured their labour for a specified period at a very low price, for early in the eighteenth century the HBC had discovered an excellent source of workers in the Orkney Islands, known as the Orcades in classical literature, which lay northeast of the Scottish mainland and belonged to Scotland. The Orkneys were isolated, poor, and underdeveloped and their society was traditional and hierarchical. Orcadians were therefore willing to work for low wages and eager to save as much as they could. They were also supposed to be accustomed to subordination, uncorrupted by city life, and, because of the harsh climate of their homeland, well suited to the rigours of life in the fur trade.

By the middle of the eighteenth century, however, the HBC was forced out of its inertia by the incursions of French traders and, after the Seven Years' War, by British merchants operating out of Montreal. HBC officers referred to these rivals as the Pedlars because of their mode of doing business. They sent out brigades of French-Canadian *voyageurs* who carried goods from Montreal to the main depot at the head of Lake Superior. From there parties of men headed into the North-West, where they constructed mainly small, temporary posts, from which they travelled extensively to barter and frequently live with the Natives. As a result, many Natives no longer had to trek all the way to the Bay and the HBC was forced to send its own men inland. It was not, however, until 1774 with the establishment of Cumberland House, near what is now The Pas, Manitoba, that the HBC could boast an inland trading post.

The company needed men who knew how to build, repair, and manoeuvre canoes and it required them to travel hundreds of miles, often into unknown territory, where they were expected to live off the land as much as possible. Many of the company's workers objected to these new duties and new working conditions, but the London committee was not ready for a dramatic alteration in its recruitment policy. To do so would have been to invite disorder and expense, both of which the committee always sought to avoid. Therefore, although it did recruit officers and skilled tradesmen in London, it did not want labourers from there. It had, after all, been the desire to avoid the disorderly population of that city that had led to the HBC's reliance on Orkneymen in the first place. Now, headquartered as it was in London, the committee was witnessing the breakdown of traditional social relations in England in general and the development of what E.P. Thompson has called 'the growth of a newly-won psychology of the free laborer',[3] which no member of the élite could view without trepidation, especially after the French Revolution. Workers possessing this new outlook might be serviceable for factory work, where machinery and close personal supervision enforced discipline, or for outwork, where low piece-rates and the threat of starvation ensured diligence, but they would hardly do for the HBC. Britain did, of course, possess other poor and undeveloped areas, namely, the Scottish

Highlands and Ireland, but their inhabitants were reputed to be rather wild and thus not likely to be an improvement over Orkneymen. As for Canadians, they had a reputation for unruliness and independence and demanded higher wages than the company wanted to pay. Nor did the committee consider the possibility that it should stop importing labour altogether and simply recruit from the people who already lived in its territory because it did not want to transform the local population into workers. It wanted them to remain hunters and trappers, supplying the furs that the company exported and fending for themselves as much as possible. As long as the Natives continued to follow their traditional ways of life, their labour cost the HBC nothing more than the goods they received in trade, thereby keeping the costs of the furs from which it derived its profits extremely low.

The HBC was a small enterprise, highly vulnerable to the fluctuations of the market for its furs in Europe but burdened with annual expenses that did not fluctuate in the same way. It had to purchase trade goods and provisions, hire workers, and transport everything and everyone to and from Rupert's Land, and it wanted to find the most economical sources of everything, including labour. Parsimony, therefore, won out. Although the London committee directed its officers to take on any Canadians who might offer their services, it continued to hire Orkneymen and offered gratuities to those willing to travel into the interior or to learn new skills such as canoebuilding. No doubt, it hoped that Orcadian avariciousness would eventually triumph over Orcadian stodginess.

Unfortunately for the company, however, the wars that erupted after the French Revolution did not end until 1815 and the army and navy absorbed all available British manpower, while few Canadians had any interest in joining the HBC. Thus the company was at the mercy of men who either continued to object to the duties they were asked to perform or demanded higher wages as the price of their cooperation and who could not be easily replaced. At the same time, competition increased, the price of trade goods rose, and the market for furs declined. Profits tumbled. The annual dividend dropped from 6 to 4 per cent in 1801 and remained there until 1809 when there was no dividend at all. An appeal to the government for relief on the grounds that the HBC had not sold any furs for export since 1806 and had three years' worth of stock on hand fell on deaf ears. The company was seriously in debt and the committee even contemplated abandoning active participation in the fur trade and simply outfitting independent traders who could assume the costs of dealing with the competition.

However, in March of 1810, Andrew Wedderburn (later Colvile) persuaded the committee to adopt his 'Retrenching System',[4] a plan for introducing greater economy and efficiency into all aspects of the company's operations. Imported provisions would be reduced and waste would be eliminated. Officers would be inspired to work harder by changing their remuneration from straight salaries to shares in the profits. Bonuses for the performance of new duties or for wintering inland would be abolished. The prices of supplies would be raised and payment by the task would be introduced wherever feasible. Stricter discipline would be imposed on the servants and they would be rendered more diligent by the addition to the workforce of more active elements recruited from Canada, Ireland, and the northern parts of Scotland. Retrenchment also included a long-term solution to the HBC's labour problems in the form of the Red River Colony. In 1811 the company gave the Earl of Selkirk a grant of land in what is now Manitoba, Saskatchewan, North Dakota, and Minnesota. Selkirk's goal was to provide a haven for the impoverished and dispossessed Scots of his homeland and the London committee hoped that the colony would provide a place where employees could retire and supply the company with both produce and workers. The acquisition of land was to be regulated in such a way as to ensure that only retiring officers could support themselves through agriculture alone, while the lower ranks would have to combine farming with wage labour. In this way the HBC hoped to create a traditional society of its own and eventually avoid the expense and bother of importing men altogether. Things did not work out as planned.

Competition with its rivals who had formed the North West Company (NWC) in 1804 became violent, often bloody, and attacks on the colony regularly dispersed the settlers. Payment by the task failed to increase productivity and the committee dropped the idea of extending it across the service. Old servants objected to both the new prices and the new recruits, while the newcomers' insubordination reinforced the committee's long-standing preference for Orcadians. None the less, the company's operations expanded. Prior to 1774, the HBC had had only seven posts. Between 1774 and 1821 it built 242 more, while the NWC built 342. Most of these posts lasted no more than five years, but they still involved considerable expense and resulted in the HBC's workforce increasing from fewer than 200 to just over 900 men.

When the opportunity to put a stop to this ruinous competition presented itself, the London committee was happy to take it. This came in 1821 in the form of a merger of the two companies, which promised a return to a more frugal and sedate way of doing business.

The HBC at the time of merger had 68 posts, while the NWC had 57. The new company eliminated all but 52.[5] Thrift, it was hoped, would replace extravagance and proper discipline could finally be imposed. The size of the labour force could be reduced and faithful Orcadians would again become the company's mainstay, at least until the Red River Colony fulfilled its promise. But the HBC faced a whole new situation. In the west it acquired the NWC districts known as New Caledonia, in the Upper Fraser River area, and the Columbia district, in the Columbia River system, extending into what became the state of Oregon. These two districts were consolidated into the Columbia Department in 1827, which remained under the jurisdiction of the Northern Department whose council made the decisions regarding its operations at its annual meetings. In the east, the HBC now extended its operations into Lower Canada, which was designated the Montreal Department. In between were the Northern Department, which stretched from Hudson Bay to the Rocky Mountains, and the Southern Department, which lay between the Great Lakes and James Bay. The merger thus presented the company with new challenges.

West of the Rockies, the HBC was entering unfamiliar territory. Prior to 1821 it had had no posts there and it therefore had no stable and amicable relationships with the Native peoples. Nor did it enjoy the kind of protected status that its charter had given it in Rupert's Land. In the Columbia Department it had received a licence to trade that excluded only other British companies and it thus had to contend with Russian and American traders. It also had to work out a system of transporting goods and men to the area. The NWC had supplied its post from the Pacific by way of the Columbia River, but the HBC preferred to approach from the east to avoid clashes with rival traders operating in the area.

It was soon clear, however, that the journey was far too long. In 1826 the company began to send goods by ship to Fort Vancouver, which it had established on the Columbia River near the mouth of the Willamette River in 1825. This post would serve as the depot for the new Columbia Department until 1843, when increasing American settlement and expansionism prompted the HBC to move its depot to Fort Victoria on the southern tip of Vancouver Island. Goods were brought in by ship from England around Cape Horn and taken inland by brigades of servants supplemented by men hired only for the duration of the trip, i.e., tripmen. During the 1830s the company also started to construct posts along the coast, and these were served by ships that acted as mobile trading posts. Workers assigned to the department came overland from York Factory by way of Edmonton or arrived aboard the ships. Some were also hired in the Sandwich Islands (Hawaii), where the company's ships stopped regularly and where it established a post in 1836 for the purpose of trading fish and lumber. The Columbia Department offered other opportunities for diversification as well. In 1839 the HBC formed a subsidiary, the Puget's Sound Agricultural Company, to operate two large farms in what is now the state of Washington. Ten years later it began coalmining operations at the north end of Vancouver Island. The workforce of the department thus came to include seamen of various nationalities, English agricultural labourers, and Scottish coalminers.

In the Montreal Department the company appeared to be in a more advantageous position. There its lease of the seigneury of Mingan in 1825 and the King's Posts in 1831 gave it hunting, fishing, and trading rights along the north shore of the St Lawrence from Isle-aux-Coudres to Sept-Isles and northward to the headwaters of the rivers draining that part of the coast. But rival traders and fishermen regularly ignored the HBC's privileges. Moreover, settlement and economic development meant furs were a rapidly dwindling resource at the same time as there was plenty of competition for what was left, making diversification not only desirable but necessary. Therefore, the posts along the coast of Labrador sent not only furs but such items as seal skins, seal oil, fish, feathers, and walrus teeth, while salmon-fishing stations produced substantial amounts of fish for export. The company also sold supplies to lumber camps, though its own attempts at lumbering failed.

The Northern and Southern departments covered the HBC's old territory and both continued to supply furs, but the Northern Department was the largest and most important. It included the Mackenzie River district, a major source of furs, which the HBC had just begun to penetrate when it merged with its rival. It also contained the Red River Colony, which provided the company with both provisions and workers whose services became crucial to the transport system upon which the department's business depended. Men from the colony and Natives who lived in the vicinity of HBC posts were regularly hired by the trip or by the season to take goods to wherever they were required or to help regular servants get inland. Tripmen also carried imported goods from York Factory and country produce from the Saskatchewan district and the colony to Norway House, which was now the department's depot. From here the various brigades would head into the interior with the supplies that were required at the company's establishments. These brigades might be made up of the servants heading for their winter quarters or of tripmen hired to take both servants and supplies inland and return with the proceeds of a district's trade and the workers who were leaving the service.

The most important component of this system was the Portage La Loche brigade. It took its name from its inland destination, Portage La Loche, also known as Methye Portage, the 12-mile stretch of land that separated Lake La Loche, or Methye Lake, and the Clearwater River, which runs into the Athabaska River. It was to this portage that men from the Mackenzie district would bring the furs and departing servants and exchange them for the supplies and new servants brought by the Portage La Loche brigade. The Mackenzie district was so far from Hudson Bay that getting there from York Factory before the winter set in meant having to maintain a gruelling pace. Trips to Hudson Bay in spring could be no less strenuous, since a delay could mean arriving after the ships had departed for England. The Portage La Loche brigade made it possible for the men assigned to the Mackenzie River district to travel this long distance only when they first went in and when they finally left. Also, since the brigade did not have to travel all the way to the district, it was possible for the furs to reach Hudson Bay in good time. However, since this system depended on men who belonged to a population increasingly hostile to the company's monopoly, who regularly defied it to trade for themselves, and who frequently refused to complete their journeys or carry the cargoes they were assigned, the London committee could never be sure that its goods or furs actually arrived at their destinations when they were supposed to.

The colony had indeed proved to be an important source of employees, for by the middle of the nineteenth century almost half the workers in the Northern Department had been born in Rupert's Land and by 1870 they were in the majority there. The population had not, however, lived up to expectations. It was neither docile nor loyal and could live quite well without the HBC, which could not do without them, for the merger had not permitted a return to that comfortable relationship with Orcadians that appeared to have prevailed in the last century. Orkneymen were increasingly attracted to other employment. The company had tried to compensate by recruiting men in other parts of northern Scotland and, during the 1850s, in Norway and also continued to hire Canadians, but these groups, too, had other opportunities open to them. The HBC could no longer rely on one source of labour to supply all the workers it needed. Nor did it even seem advisable to do so because no single group appeared to be so suitable as Orcadians had once been. It never occurred to the London committee that Orkneymen had appeared so reliable because prior to

INTRODUCTION 9

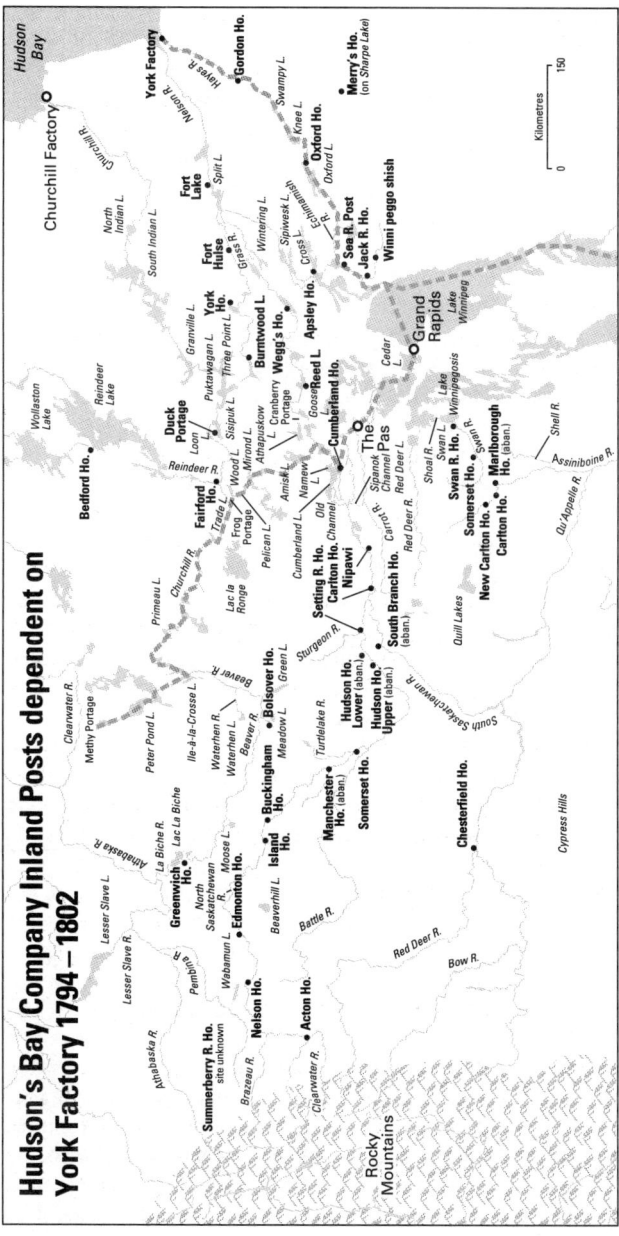

The route shown here is that of the Portage La Loche brigade, the most important component of the transport system upon which the Northern Department's business depended. From Hudson's Bay Record Society, vol. 26, map N9100. (Courtesy Hudson's Bay Company Archives, Provincial Archives of Manitoba.)

1770 its operations were small, most of the men's work was directed at their own subsistence, and profits depended more on the diligence of the Native hunters and trappers than on that of the company's labourers. It was not until Orcadians were asked to emulate their more energetic Canadian counterparts and carry out duties that would enable the HBC to expand into the interior that their disobedience became so noticeable and costly. Their disobedience frustrated the company's plans and their demands for higher wages increased its expenses at a time when frugality was vital. The London committee also failed to consider that Orkneymen might join the company in significant numbers only as long as it offered better terms and working conditions than other employers. Instead, it seemed puzzled by their lack of interest. It still hired workers in areas where pre-industrial social relations survived and it still expected to find obedient, submissive, and cheap labour, but it had come to the conclusion that no one was perfect and it was necessary to mix men of different origins so that the faults and virtues of the different groups would cancel one another out.[6]

The company's recruitment policy never succeeded in yielding a perfectly satisfactory labour force, however, because it was based on a misunderstanding of the nature of pre-industrial societies. They were not rigid hierarchies foisted from the top on a stolid, sheeplike peasantry but rather complex systems that ordinary people invested with considerable meaning. Pre-industrial social and economic relations were conducted within a 'contractual framework' in which the élite accepted certain responsibilities towards their inferiors in return for the latter's recognition of their superiority. But those at the bottom did not perceive of this relationship as deferential. It was a social contract in which the lower orders acted according to a 'moral economy', i.e., 'a consistent traditional view of social norms and obligations, of the proper economic functions of several parties within the community'. Wages might have been low, but they were expected to be high enough to supply the necessities of life, while injustice, high food prices, attempts to alter customary relations, and transgressions of popular morality aroused fierce resistance. The lower orders also possessed their own culture, which contained beliefs that not only differed from those of their superiors but were often subversive.[7] Thus, although the humble members of a pre-industrial society might have accepted their lowly place in the hierarchy, they were neither passive nor docile. The members of the London committee thought otherwise, however, because they belonged to the social élite and they assumed that submission to their authority was the norm. When its employees were not perfectly obedient, therefore, the committee blamed it on their bad character or their ethnicity.

Ethnicity in Fur Trade History

Fur trade historians tend to see the men's conduct much as the London committee did. Orcadians, for example, are described as hardy, sober, obedient, and eager to save their earnings, but cautious, stubborn, and clannish. Thus, in spite of their economic ambitions, their attempts to impose wage increases have been attributed to the fact that, once among strangers, they became more 'tribal' and 'aware of their distinctiveness and of their common interests as a group', and they therefore found solidarity 'on an ethnic basis'.[8] Their reluctance to risk their lives in the company's service has been seen not as a logical response to the dangers of venturing into an unknown wilderness but as an unreasonable display of self-interest.[9] Behaviour that conflicted with prevailing notions of Orcadian sobriety has been ascribed to isolation and boredom, without consideration of the drinking habits that might have been common in Britain at the same time or of the possibility that early Scottish writers were correct when they accused Orcadians of heavy drinking.[10]

Other groups, however, are *expected* to behave in a picturesquely undisciplined manner. Thus, Daniel Francis has called Canadian *voyageurs* 'an unruly mob' and suggests that the HBC post resembled 'a military barracks' while the NWC establishment 'had more in common with a rowdy tavern'. *Voyageurs,* he says, possessed an 'independence and pride' that gave them 'a tendency to resist the authority of their employer', while Orcadians were 'disciplined and obedient'.[11] The Métis, so defiant of the HBC's authority as an employer and its fur trade monopoly, derived their effrontery from their particular way of life. One historian has described the Métis thus:

> Unlike their European progenitors, they were not work oriented—they did not live to work. The things that were of utmost importance were their kin, their social life, and those things that allowed one to excel in the hunt—guns and horses. Most 'squatted' on their long, narrow river lots, rather than bothering to take out a formal land title, and they put little time in agriculture, except perhaps to plant a few acres of barley and a patch of potatoes.... A review of their income and expenditures would suggest that they took considerable pride in their clothing.[12]

It is true, of course, that the Métis did not behave like modern factory workers or their employers or like those HBC officers who worked hard to rise in the company. But neither did their 'European progenitors', most of the wage-labourers of industrial Britain, and most of the workers of the HBC itself. The above portrait of the Métis describes an attitude towards work, wages, and leisure characteristic of a traditional, subsistence economy. Their priorities did not include the thrift and industry that the rising middle class espoused and tried to impose. These virtues made little sense in a situation where money income was low and irregular and kinship and community were more important for survival than savings.[13] At the same time, however, one must remember that *voyageurs* did not paddle their canoes just for the fun of it; they were working, transporting trade goods and furs for their employers. Likewise, hunting was not simply a leisurely jaunt across the plains, but required effort and organization, while the proceeds of the hunt had to be processed and sold, and even small crops had to be planted, tended, and harvested. These activities were not hobbies: they were a means of subsistence. Mixing farming with paid seasonal employment was also how Orcadians supported themselves, but they are seen as hard-working and tractable while the Métis are regarded as fun-loving and insubordinate.

Ethnicity does not, therefore, provide an adequate explanation for behaviour that conflicts with assumptions that HBC servants identified with their employer. One needs instead to recognize that the relationship between the company and its men was a negotiated one and that, despite their cultural differences, their interests as workers determined how they would behave. The London committee saw them all as servants and expected them to identify themselves totally with the company because it assumed they could have no interests other than the company's. They did not perceive of the workers as a class but as individuals pledged to serve them. But, in fact, they were a class. Their status distinguished them clearly from their superiors and relegated them to subordination, while their commitment to the company was quite limited. An officer joined the HBC with a view to promotion and a lifelong career, but for a servant the HBC was only one of many employers he would have during his lifetime. He entered the company because it offered better wages and opportunities to save than those offered by other employers, but he could never save enough to allow him to retire to a life of leisure. Nor did he expect to. He saved in order to have something to tide him over during a period of unemployment or to pay rent on the family farm. Moreover, the work that the men belonging to the company's lower ranks performed not only distinguished them further from their superiors but also reduced the length of time an individual would remain in the HBC and increased the likelihood that his conduct would fail to live up to the committee's expectations.

HBC Servants as Workers

The work that HBC employees performed was pre-industrial, its routine dictated not by clocks and machines but by necessity and the season. The HBC's year was called an outfit. It started on 1 June, when the engagements of the men hired on long-term contracts began, and ended on 31 May of the following year. As soon as possible after 1 June, two or sometimes three company ships left London, carrying new employees, provisions, and trade goods to Rupert's Land. Their arrival in Hudson Bay set off a flurry of activity, with men unloading and loading the vessels as quickly as possible so that they could get out of the Bay before winter set in. Men and goods were then assigned to their posts and dispatched as early as possible to their destinations. Winter was an endless round of cutting and hauling wood, both for fuel and for construction or repairs, hunting, fishing, fetching meat and furs from Native encampments, shovelling snow, and taking packets between posts. Tradesmen repaired guns and traps, sharpened tools, made clothing and barrels, and built boats, canoes, and houses. The officers kept accounts and journals, assigned the men their duties, and dealt with Natives who visited the posts in the fall to barter for the items they wanted and returned periodically with furs and much-welcomed fresh game. In the spring, some of the men set off for the Bay with the proceeds of the winter's trade and the workers whose contracts were up. Those who stayed behind spent the summer laying in stocks of wood, planting gardens, and repairing the posts. In the fall their ranks would swell once more with the arrival of new men or old comrades, crops would be harvested, and preparations for winter completed.

Such was the routine that developed after 1770, and thus did the majority of the company's employees spend their time, even after west coast seamen, agricultural labourers, coalminers, and tripmen became part of the workforce. It was not, of course, all unrelieved drudgery. The men had Sundays off, except when they were travelling. Christmas Day, New Year's Day, and the week between them were holidays, and celebrations such as Guy Fawkes Day, St George's Day, and, once Canadians were hired regularly, All Saints' Day also provided a respite from duty. Moreover, since the men performed most of their duties without supervision, it was often possible for them to maintain a pace that suited them.

Still, the work was heavy and demanding and, as evidenced by Murdo Macleod's statement to the London committee in 1857, for some men life in the HBC was exhausting and oppressive. Macleod had joined the HBC in 1849 and after six months at York Factory was sent to Oxford House. For the journey he and his companions were equipped with snowshoes and strapped to a train carrying their clothing and provisions, which they had to drag through the snow, while only their guide had a team of dogs, even though there were plenty of dogs and sleighs at York Factory. Since the men were all new recruits, they were unaccustomed to snowshoeing and their legs became 'much swollen'. On their arrival at Oxford House, they were put right to work. Indeed, they were hardly ever allowed any rest. Men who failed to complete their daily tasks had to work on Sunday and, during the month he spent at Oxford House, Macleod was sent on trips to 'the fur Stations' on Saturday evenings, thereby requiring him to work Sundays as well. Later, after two months at Norway House under the 'charge of a Lunatic' and a fortnight at York Factory, Macleod went to New Caledonia, where he was thrashed by Donald Maclean, a clerk at Fort Alexandria, and Robert Todd, in charge at Stuart's Lake, and was starved and forced to work with a sore foot and a broken arm by Chief Factor Donald Manson.[14]

Most servants did not have to put up with such abuse, but they did have to perform tasks that required considerable exertion and submit to the authority of those set above them. Thus, for example, in the spring of 1831, 11 men arrived at Sault Ste Marie from La Cloche completely worn out from their voyage. They had faced strong winds and had been kept at their oars two nights in a row without rest, but their officers had promised them the remainder of the day of their arrival at Sault Ste Marie to recuperate before proceeding on their journey. When they were commanded to go on immediately, however, they protested that the wind was too strong for them to make any progress against it and that they had been promised a rest. Although they declared that they would be ready to leave the next morning, the officer in charge immediately told them that he no longer needed them and one of the officers who had accompanied them expressed his 'disapproval' of the men's behaviour by discharging from the service the three he considered 'most conspicuous in opposing the orders given them'.[15]

Those who were classed as servants did work that no gentleman would be required to do, thus emphasizing the difference between officers and servants, although many officers did perform some manual labour around the posts. But they were still gentlemen and their main function was to give orders and conduct the trade, while their subordinates carried out the heaviest tasks and did as they were told. This situation was not likely to guarantee that servants would build particularly strong ties with their officers or the company. Furthermore, the work itself was heavy and not suited to the old or decrepit. Therefore, not only was it impossible for most men to spend their lives in the HBC, but it also made sense for them to avoid excessive hardship and overwork to preserve their health and fitness so that they could still support themselves after they left the fur trade. What the committee might see as indolence and inactivity might, for the men, have been a reasonable pace of work and a sensible reluctance to expose themselves to hardship or danger. When men demanded higher pay or refused to engage at all, they were not being disloyal or impudently trying to extort exorbitant wages. Rather, they were trying to get a fair price for their labour or taking advantage of better opportunities. Such bargaining was due not to ethnic peculiarities but to the fact that it was a normal part of the relationship between workers and employers.

The relationship between the HBC and its employees was, to borrow Daniel Francis and Toby Morantz's description of the relationship between Natives and the HBC, a partnership in furs. As they point out, the title of their book was not intended to suggest that the fur trade was an 'equal partnership' because the traders shared neither their power nor their profits with the Natives, but it was meant to 'emphasize ... that the Indian people were crucial to all aspects of the fur trade and were responsible to a considerable degree for establishing its procedures.' Natives were 'not the defenceless, passive producers they have often been characterized as being.'[16] These statements apply with equal force to the HBC's own employees. Their relationship with the HBC was shaped both by the goals and demands of the company and by their own interests and priorities. They accepted their place in the hierarchy but were not subsumed in it. They brought with them their own notions of the proper relations of authority and were not prepared to tolerate injustice, harsh treatment, and unreasonable demands simply because they had signed a contract. They might not have possessed the class consciousness of an industrial proletariat and they organized no unions, but they knew that they had more in common with one another than they did with their officers and the London committee.

This book is a study of the HBC's employees as workers acting in their own interests and examines the ways in which they did so. It is based on the assumption that conflict was not unusual and breaches of discipline were not the result of irrational waywardness or manifestations of particular ethnic characteristics but that they were part of the struggle for control of the work process that makes every workplace 'contested terrain'.[17] The period studied is the HBC's second century of existence, 1770 to 1870, during which it abandoned passivity for expansion, acquired its empire, and finally surrendered the territory granted to it by its charter to the Dominion of Canada. It was thus a time when opportunities for conflict between the company and its employees increased and when discipline assumed new importance as the HBC sought to make its business more profitable and its workers more efficient. At the same time, however, the company's organization remained the same and its paternalistic relationship with its labour force hardly changed at all. It continued to prefer workers hired on contracts that committed them to obedience in return for benefits that other employers no longer provided. An examination of the HBC during this period thus provides an opportunity to examine how the relations between workers and a paternalistic employer operated and whether the former were as passive as has been assumed. Furthermore, because the company's workforce became increasingly diverse over the course of the century, it is also possible to see if behaviour varied according to ethnicity or race, although these do not form the basis for the examination of HBC employees in this book. Its purpose is not to explore further the ethnic mix of the HBC, but rather to rescue its workers from the stereotyping to which such an approach tends to lead and to examine them as workers who bargained with their employer, protested bad treatment, demanded higher wages, and went on strike. Such incidents are well documented in the company's records, which include correspondence, post journals, ships' logs, servants' lists, and testimony collected in the investigation of particularly serious incidents. The 'Note on Sources' at the end of the book contains a list of the primary sources used, describes them in some detail, and explains the approach taken in consulting them.

The organization of the book is not chronological. It begins with a history of the company's organization and how it changed from 1770 to 1870 as the London committee tried to make it more efficient and its employees better disciplined. As the title of Chapter 2, 'The View from the Top', suggests, its focus is primarily on the perspective of the committee and senior officers, their assumption that they were in charge, their disapproval of insubordination and disobedience, and how they tried to render their men properly submissive and make the business profitable. But even a discussion presented from the committee's perspective must concede that it was never completely in control. Its orders were often ineffective, popular opinion and economic conditions restricted its ability to exercise the authority it believed it had, and both officers and servants regularly ignored or defied its orders. Thus, the chapter also discusses the responses of the company's employees and how these responses limited what the committee could actually achieve. The following chapter examines the history of the HBC's attempts to supply itself with cheap, docile labour. To some extent, therefore, this chapter also adopts a view from the top. But the success of the company's recruitment policy, like its efforts to impose discipline, depended on the response of those at whom it was directed, for recruitment was not merely the first point of contact between the HBC and the people it hired—it was also the first point of conflict. The committee could never predict what potential recruits might do. They might simply accept the terms it offered, but they might try to negotiate better ones or turn their backs on the HBC completely.

The next three chapters deal with the ways in which the company's employees failed to conform to the ideal of the faithful servant. The danger here, of course, is to create the impression that HBC employees were so discontented and unmanageable that the company's establishments were in a constant state of chaos. Clearly, this was not the case, because the company is now over 300 years old. Since its survival depended not only on the decisions of the London committee and its officers but also on the co-operation of their subordinates, it is obvious that the majority performed their work well enough to keep the HBC in business. That the HBC endured, however, was due not to the *absence* of conflict but to the fact that the company could survive most such manifestations because these rarely attacked the relations of authority upon which the company was based. Since the men's behaviour changed so little over the course of the century under study, the discussion has not been organized chronologically. Instead, incidents of disobedience have been categorized according to how serious a threat they were to authority. Chapter 4 thus deals with what might be described as transgressions that rose out of the men's *indifference* to authority and the incompleteness of their identification with the HBC: misdemeanours such as drunkenness, neglect of duty, private trade, and desertion. It examines what I have called 'The View from the Bottom'—the habits and customs the employees brought with them, those that developed in the service, and the outlook that distinguished them from their superiors and shaped the way they approached their duties. Those in the lower ranks did not necessarily share the concerns of their officers, model themselves after them, or put the interests of the company ahead of their own. As a result, they were not always as diligent as those in charge thought they should be and at times would simply ignore the company's regulations. Such misconduct did not, however, threaten the status quo because it did not derive from an opposition to authority.

The London committee might not, of course, have agreed, since it disapproved of any form of disobedience. Furthermore, the men did not stop at behaviour that demonstrated an indifference to authority; they also challenged it when they refused outright to obey the orders they were given. This type of disobedience is the subject of the next chapter, 'The Denial of Duty'. It examines the ways in which HBC employees resisted what they considered unfair treatment, cruel officers, and excessively hard work. Chapter 6 narrows the discussion further by describing those occasions when men acted collectively to demand higher wages and better treatment. These incidents were the least common, but the most alarming. They included the Brandon House mutiny of 1810, the rebellion of a group of men known as the 'Glasgow Insurgents' in 1812, mutinies aboard several of the company's ships, and frequent strikes by the Red River tripmen. It thus appeared that the men were conspiring to seize authority for themselves. In fact, the men of the HBC never actually questioned the authority of their officers or the London committee. Their attempts to negotiate fair terms, their refusal to perform certain duties or accept certain officers, even their mutinies, were demands that an enterprise referred to respectfully by its officers as 'the Honble Company' treat those who were to consider themselves its servants in a manner worthy of this epithet.

2

The View from the Top

Oh, let us love our occupations
Bless the Co & their relations
Be content with our poor rations
And always Know our proper Stations[1]

Although composed in a facetious vein by a disgruntled officer in 1846, this verse nevertheless expressed what the London committee of the HBC had always wanted from its employees: loyalty, dedication, unquestioning obedience, and a willingness to endure whatever hardships the company's business imposed. As members of the social élite, the founders of the HBC were paternalists who possessed a social outlook based on the assumption that society should be 'authoritarian, hierarchic, organic and pluralistic'. Those at the top, as the owners of property, had both the right and the responsibility to rule and guide everyone else, whose sole obligation was to obey. They tended to favour Draconian laws to ensure obedience and prevent social disorder, but they also believed that social relations had to be governed by morality and therefore supported popular notions of a just price, fair rent, and equitable wages.[2] This outlook belonged to a time before industrialization introduced new manufacturing processes and transformed social relations in Europe and North America.

Mechanization and the division of labour revolutionized the work process in the factory and created an industrial proletariat linked to its masters strictly by a wage relationship determined by an impersonal market that was not to be tampered with, certainly not by those receiving wages. For masters, this meant freedom from any obligations towards their workers other than the payment of wages; for workers, it meant accepting that they were now nothing more than factors of production. This transformation was neither rapid nor universally accepted and not all employers welcomed the loosening of those emotional bonds that promoted deference. As defined by Patrick Joyce, this deference was 'a social relationship that converts power relations into moral ones' and cultivates among subordinates an 'emotional identification' that leads them 'to acquiesce in their own subordination'.[3]

Some nineteenth-century industrialists sought to recapture the social harmony they believed had prevailed in the past by holding communal events and providing churches, schools, and even entire villages to capture their workers' loyalty. Of course, the fact that they were less forthcoming with what their workers needed most—stable employment and steady wages—and willing to use whatever coercive measures were at their disposal to impose discipline meant that they were not very successful. Likewise, landlords and farmers, looking back nostalgically to a bygone era when rich and poor lived in harmony because everyone fulfilled the duties appropriate to his or her station, enthusiastically espoused paternalism as a way of dealing with the problems they had helped to cause by their rationalization of agriculture and pursuit of profit. But their benevolence consisted mostly of the distribution of food, fuel, and clothing and participation in popular rituals such as the dispensation of Christmas charity. As employers, they kept wages below what many considered to be the absolute minimum possible for subsistence and dismissed workers with no regard for their welfare. As landowners, they kept rents high and leases short so that tenants could be evicted easily. As magistrates, they imprisoned vagrants and sentenced thieves to transportation or the treadmill.

The Master-Servant Relationship

The HBC was different from other employers. The London committee never completely abandoned its paternalistic outlook even though its membership changed and it tried to make its business more rational and its workers more disciplined and productive. It always expected its employees, regardless of occupation or status, to consider themselves its 'Faithfull Servants'[4] whose fidelity and diligence it would reward with the wages and benefits appropriate to their stations. This term was not, however, simply a description of the personal ties that bound the company with its workers but reflected the nature of English society when the HBC was chartered in 1670. Seventeenth-century England was a pre-industrial society based on the acceptance of a hierarchy of ranks in which everyone had his or her place and where differences in status were mitigated by neighbourliness, kinship, and the fulfilment of mutual obligations. The basis of this society was the household, which was also the basic unit of production. It comprised a married couple, their children, and servants, apprentices, and journeymen. Everyone in the household was considered part of the family, there being no word in early modern English distinguishing kin from other household members. The head and master of the household was the father, who was responsible for the moral and physical well-being of his dependants, who in return owed him the filial obedience that children owed their fathers. To be a servant in a pre-industrial household was different from being a servant in a modern household. Traditionally, service, like apprenticeship, was a stage in the life cycle that marked the transition from childhood to adulthood. Young people entered service at the age of 14 or 15 and remained until they married, when they would establish their own households. Most youths in early modern England were servants and most of them were employed in husbandry. Servants did not consider themselves nor were they considered to be a distinctive labouring class and families at every level of society sent their children into service.

The institution of service played an important role in pre-industrial society. For employers, it provided a reliable source of cheap labour and made it possible for craftsmen to work farms and practise their trades as well. For young people, it provided not only wages but room and board, guaranteed employment for the term agreed upon, care in the event of illness, and the opportunity to save enough to set up their own households. It was extremely uncommon for servants to be married or for individuals to remain servants for life because service denoted dependence, which was incompatible with adulthood. Most servants became day labourers, whose meagre wages sufficed because they could supplement them by taking advantage of such traditional benefits as gleaning rights and access to common land for pasture for some livestock. For society as a whole, the institution of service was a way of maintaining order. It helped to preserve the social structure by providing a way for young people to assume a place in it and imposed on masters the responsibility of keeping their servants in line. Moreover, the masters' authority was buttressed by an extensive code of laws intended to ensure that everyone had a master.[5]

The institution of service had arisen out of efforts by the ruling élite in England to 'curb the insubordination' of the lower orders who were benefiting from the shortage of labour and the accompanying rise in wages after the plague of 1348–9. The Ordinance of Labourers enacted in 1349 and the Statute of Labourers of 1351 were intended to eliminate the fact that the relationship between master and servant had become a contractual one and restore it to a status relationship. This was accomplished by defining the rights and duties of the parties to the contract and giving masters the right to use force to capture runaway servants and rights against anyone engaging them. These laws were to provide a reliable source of labour by restricting mobility and requiring all persons to be employed at some occupation. The effect of such legislation was to establish 'the existence of a class of servants and laborers—that is, common, unskilled manual workers—categorically defined by reference to their lack of productive assets and hence penury and dependence'. As well, 'by casting them at all times as potential vagabonds in need of state-enforced discipline' to keep them from engaging in economically independent behaviour, the state 'unambiguously branded them as a proletariat'. Succeeding legislation increased the restrictions and penalties to which servants were subject and reinforced the view that manual workers were a 'readily identifiable class' apart, made up of 'impoverished perpetual quasi outlaws'. The result was a 'network of laws and institutions designed to enforce behavior in conformity with a legal status creating a liability to serve'.[6]

The master-servant relationship was thus based on the notion that emotional ties and mutual obligations united high and low and mitigated differences in status, but it was governed by laws that emphasized social differences and forced subordination. One must, therefore, beware of what E.P. Thompson has called the 'sense of emotional cosiness' that imbues the idea of a society of households headed by kindly paternalists ever solicitous of the well-being of their charges. This image makes paternalism appear to be a warm and 'mutually assenting relationship', but it is, after all, a 'concentration of economic and cultural authority' and a term applicable to the slave-owners of colonial Brazil as well as to the gentry of England. It is 'a description of social relations as they may be seen from above' and it reveals nothing about the actual relations of power.[7] Moreover, English society by the seventeenth century actually bore little resemblance to the ideal of a vertically integrated, orderly hierarchy. Improving landlords sought to make their land more profitable and ambitious yeomen enlarged their holdings, all at the expense of the less fortunate. At the same time, the population had begun to increase, the poor and landless multiplied, and the countryside seemed flooded with vagrants, tramping artisans, and itinerant labourers. Most of these 'masterless men' were looking for work, but their mobility was seen as idleness and their lack of deference deemed intolerable, particularly since some of them did preach sedition.[8] Nevertheless, the pre-industrial ideal remained and was taken for granted as normal and proper. It was, therefore, logical for a company formed at the time to be organized according to prevailing attitudes, although the London committee did not in the beginning give much thought as to exactly how its own enterprise would reproduce the relations of authority believed to exist in pre-industrial society. It had, however, every reason to believe that it had the power to do whatever was necessary to ensure proper subordination.

The charter of 1670 granted 'The Governor and Company of Adventurers of England trading into Hudson's Bay' not only the right to trade in all the waters draining into Hudson Bay but also the authority 'to make, ordain and constitute such and so many reasonable laws, constitutions, orders and ordinances as . . . shall seem necessary and convenient for the good government of the said Company, and of all governors of colonies, forts and plantations, factors, masters, mariners and other officers employed or to be employed in any of the territories and lands aforesaid, and in any of their voyages.' Furthermore, the company was authorized to 'lawfully impose, ordain, limit and provide such pains, penalties and punishments upon all offenders' as long as the penalties were not 'contrary or repugnant' to the laws of England. All 'lands, islands, territories, plantations, forts, fortifications, factories or colonies' where the company's 'factories and trade' would be were 'from henceforth under the power and command' of the company, which might appoint governors and other officers to govern them. The governors and councils of the company's establishments were also granted 'the power to judge all persons belonging to the said Governor and Company, or that shall live under them, in all causes, whether civil or criminal, according to the laws of this kingdom, and to execute justice accordingly.' Criminals could be sent to England for trial. The company could also send out to its territory such men as it considered necessary and 'govern them in such legal and reasonable manner as the said Governor and Company shall think best, and to inflict punishment for misdemeanors, or impose such fines upon them for breach of their orders, as in these presents are formerly expressed.' Anyone employed by the company would 'be liable and suffer such punishment for any offences' he committed, as the governor and council of the company considered 'fit', and could be sent to England to receive 'condign punishment as his cause shall require, and the law of this nation allow of.'[9]

During the company's first four years the London committee had no need to make much use of these powers because trade was carried out from ships during the summer. But in 1674 it decided to recruit men to stay in the country,[10] where there were far more opportunities for mischief than in the confines of a ship, and it had to ensure that they understood they were there for no purpose other than the company's business and to make the regulations that would keep them from straying from it. Company employees were to be kept 'in Military Discipline', women were barred, and daily prayers aboard ship and Sunday prayers and scriptural readings ashore would encourage 'decent decorum & peaceable demeanour'.[11]

But, as was so frequently to be the case in the company's history, the committee's orders had little effect. The posts rapidly became places of resort and residence for Native bands and many men acquired Aboriginal wives. Since these women not only performed important work around the posts but brought with them the good will and trade of their relatives, the committee had no choice but to tolerate such liaisons. Religion, meanwhile, was conspicuously absent,[12] though this did not seem to perturb the committee, possibly because it expected little from men who came from those strata of society not noted for their piety or even religious orthodoxy. As late as 1794, a minister of North Ronaldsay in the Orkneys reported that he saw 50 of the inhabitants singing and dancing in the moonlight around a standing stone.[13] Still, religious worship was too much a part of everyday life to be openly abandoned, certainly not without damaging the company's reputation as a fit employer of boys and young men, and the committee continued to send orders that could be ignored. Anyway, it had no intention of relying on moral suasion alone to maintain discipline, for it was 'sensible anough what sort of men' the officers had to 'deale with'. At the same time as it advocated 'mild and Gentile Usage' that would 'draw' the servants 'to Love & Obey' their officers, it cautioned against letting the 'Rines of Government lie too loose', lest 'mischiefe arise from thence'.[14] These exhortations expressed perfectly the essence of paternalism: the desire to be even-handed and humane, tempered by a belief in the rightness of a stable social order based on the rule of the élite and the deference of everyone else and by the assumption that the lower orders were unruly and insubordinate and needed to be controlled.

The committee's first great fear was that the men would engage in private trade. Traditionally, participants in trading ventures were paid by shares in the profits.[15] Officers, in fact, had been allowed to trade on their own accounts at first, but had lost this indulgence by 1679. In addition, both officers and servants had to swear an oath and give a 'bond with security that they [would] submit to orders', and if they 'misdemeane[d]' themselves they were to be turned out of the service or suspended until the next general court of the company was held.[16] This tightening of discipline reflected the fact that the gentry stockholders who had founded the company had by 1680 relinquished control to merchants and financiers who paid greater attention to economy and efficiency. They also restricted membership on the committee to anyone holding at least £200 in stock, prohibited committee members from revealing company business to non-members, and ruled that only committee members would henceforth be allowed to look at any of the company's records.[17]

The HBC was now firmly in the hands of a few businessmen whose decisions could not be questioned by the rest of the shareholders and who were more commercially minded and less inclined to respect traditions that interfered with profit. Private dealings were forbidden because, the committee declared in 1686, 'what comes to our servants [sic] hands, whether by the one way or the other . . . ought to be esteemed as our owne, for we are at great & vast charges there, we pay for their tyme which is not theirs but ours, & all Goods that comes to their hands is by virtue of our maintaineing them.'[18] The committee had purchased its workers' time and wanted value for its money. Consequently, it now demanded annual lists of servants with details of their employment and insisted on examining all private letters to and from Rupert's Land, though no one at the Bay was to know that his mail was subject to such perusal.[19] Still, the connection between the committee and its workers was to be based on more than simply the exchange of money for labour, as the ceremony that was to mark their arrival in North America was to make clear. A formal reading of orders, followed by stirring words, would make them mindful of the 'Dutyes' they owed to the committee 'whose Servants they are, whose breade they eate and whose wages they take.'[20] There were, however, distinctions among them.

Officers received commissions that obligated them to obey the committee's orders, but also granted them authority to command on its behalf. Together with ships' captains, when they were present, and, during the first few years, one or two senior craftsmen, they would form the councils that governed the posts. Thus, they could see themselves almost as the trusted partners of their master.[21] Everyone else was relegated to subservience. Apprentices, as was customary, committed themselves to faithful service in return for food, lodging, education, and, at the end of the term, money and clothing.[22] The servants swore 'oaths of fidelity' and signed 'Indentures'[23] that, by the 1780s, had become detailed contracts binding the committee and its employees in a master-servant relationship, in which the latter were burdened with duties and threatened with penalties and the former possessed all the power and authority. The contract obliged every servant to perform duty on the ships carrying him to Rupert's Land. Once at his destination, he swore, he would defend the company's property and rights 'with the utmost Hazard and Peril of my Life, in my Station, with Courage and Fidelity'. He promised 'in all Things' to submit 'to the Commands and Discipline of the Governor or Commander in Chief for the said Company, and all other . . . superior officers, by his Directions'. He further pledged not to trade on his own account or for anyone else and to hold all goods in his possession 'only in Trust, and for the sole Use and Benefit of the said Governor and Company and their Successors'. Moreover, he would 'endeavour to hinder' and 'detect' those who engaged in private trade, 'discover' the commodities so traded, and report all to the governor and the committee. If a servant failed to fulfil his obligations, he and his 'Executors and Administrators' would forfeit all wages or other monies due him and in addition pay the company a sum of money equal to two years' wages over and above the damages caused by his disobedience.[24] In return, the company promised wages, maintenance, and free passage to and from Rupert's Land.

Over the next century, the contract changed only slightly as the committee faced increasing competition, labour shortages, and financial crises. Thus, in 1810 when the company adopted the 'Retrenching System', it modified the contract accordingly. The recruitment of servants in Lower Canada required the HBC to design contracts in accordance with the terms to which Canadian fur trade employees were accustomed. Canadians were therefore exempted from having to pay a sum equal to two years' wages if they disobeyed orders, though they were subject to all the other penalties. Their contracts also granted each an 'equipment' consisting of specified quantities of blankets, shirts, woollen vests, handkerchiefs, tobacco, leather shoes, and collars, since they were accustomed to receiving such benefits from the NWC.[25] When war with France produced a labour shortage, the HBC tried to improve its chances of attracting European servants by reducing the term of service from five years to three and raising annual wages to £20. But, parsimony being equally important, the contract also now *explicitly* excluded clothing from the necessities that the company provided. The HBC never had supplied clothing to these workers, but it now made sure that no European laboured under the delusion that it did. The new contract also threatened both the company and the servant with a penalty of £60 sterling payable by whichever party broke the terms of the contract.[26] Since the servant's obligations were far more onerous and the law favoured the employer, the committee probably assumed it would never have to pay this fine and that its magnitude, equalling three years' pay, would deter any sensible men from misbehaving.

In 1815 the contract reverted to its old terms, minus the penalty of two years' wages for disobedience. It also added the requirement that a servant give a year's notice of his intention not to renew his contract when it expired. Failure to do so obligated him to remain another year on the same terms as his current agreement. Previously, servants had been required to give two years' notice of their intention either to leave or to renew their engagements, but this had not been stipulated by the contract.[27] In 1818, to increase discipline at a time of fierce competition, the contract was amended to differentiate between two types of negligence: 'wilful neglect' of the company's property, punishable by the deduction of the cost of damage or loss from the wages of the man in whose charge it had been; and neglect of duty or the refusal to perform it, punishable by the forfeiture of the man's wages. It now also declared that the committee could dismiss a servant at any time and stipulated that a servant remained in the service on the same terms until a vessel was available to take him back to Europe.[28] The merger of the two companies in 1821 allowed the new HBC to place Canadians on the same footing as their counterparts from elsewhere by depriving them of their equipments. Thereafter, the contract remained essentially the same, although in 1863 it was modified to require a servant to keep watch and ward and work aboard the ship taking him to and from North America and to work his passage between posts as well. The council of the Northern Department had requested this addition to deal with craftsmen who thought they ought to travel as passengers when they were transferred from post to post.[29]

The contract was an explicit statement of the London committee's view of the relationship between itself and its servants. Its permutations reflected how that relationship changed as the committee tried to improve its control over its employees of all ranks and make them more frugal, efficient, and obedient. But these alterations also demonstrated the company's inability to achieve its aims. Indeed, the contract was itself subject to negotiation—it was not unknown for servants to succeed in bargaining for privileges that were added by hand to the printed forms. Thus Thomas Wiegand, who joined as a slooper in 1824 at a salary of £18, was able to modify his contract when he re-engaged as a sloopmaster in 1852. He received permission to hunt a few days of the week when he was not employed as sloopmaster and was released from the obligation to 'perform any of the very menial duties of the place where he winters such as cleaning the Fort & other dirty work.' Instead, he would be employed at 'Sawing, Axework, or in any other capacity than that alluded to' as far as his health permitted. His last contract of 1855 granted him similar privileges. Another servant, John Rowland, who engaged in 1863 as an interpreter for two years, was at the end of his contract to be sold a cow if he wanted it. William Miller, hired as a fisherman in 1869 for a three-year term, received an annual gratuity of £2 10s. sterling because his wife would cook for the men stationed with him.[30]

Such arrangements were negotiated by the committee's recruiting agents and officers and were subject to the committee's approval. It disliked deviations from the standard agreements, but concessions such as these were not really objectionable. Permitting Wiegand to avoid work he considered beneath him acknowledged his rise in rank and his years of faithful service and would make him more contented. Furthermore, hunting and the duties he agreed to perform were all important to the well-being of the post. In Rowland's case, the promise of a cow would cost the company nothing, while providing an incentive to diligence and an opportunity for the committee to display its benevolence. The company would also benefit from the gratuity granted to Miller. His wife's labour was cheap at the price, particularly since, like most of the women who resided at the company's posts, she probably performed a variety of other essential tasks for which she was not paid. Privileges that weakened the company's control over the servants were, of course, less likely to meet the committee's approval.

In 1858, Donald McLeod, who was engaged at Stornoway as a labourer for one year, was granted a gratuity of £5 and given permission to spend the winter at Norway House rather than being sent inland. When, three years later, some former servants wished to engage on the condition that they be permitted to stay at Norway House, the foolishness of the earlier arrangement became clear. Such a request could not be granted, the committee told its agent, because men had to be at the disposal of their officers. In fact, the company's standing rules stipulated that all servants be 'disposable for general service' on their first contract.[31] The committee could not allow its hands to be tied by such agreements. After all, the contract was supposed to protect the company's interests. As Eugene Genovese has observed, paternalism grew 'out of the necessity to discipline and morally justify a system of exploitation', and it assumed a number of guises, including American slavery, which, 'like every other paternalism', had 'little to do with Ole Massa's ostensible benevolence, kindness, and good cheer.'[32] It was a means of control and, although it would be simplistic and misguided to suggest that all employers consciously and hypocritically used it to hide their true motives, one cannot ignore the fact that this ideology could conveniently legitimize greed and selfishness. Contracts were legal documents and, in the hands of many masters, also legal weapons. For the HBC, they promised to make it possible 'to discharge their servants at pleasure', and attention to detail would prevent complaints of 'irregularity' in the accounts or charges of breach of contract from discharged or retired servants.[33] In fact, however, the company was not in command of the situation.

Insubordination and Crisis

The contract defined the relations of authority upon which the company was to be based and threatened the disobedient with costly penalties, but it could not guarantee that these relations would actually prevail or that the penalties could be imposed. That the servants were not sufficiently intimidated would rapidly have become clear to the committee when it perused the journals and reports its officers submitted. Only 16 years after the HBC was chartered, the council at Fort Albany found John Cartwright and William Filpt guilty of 'stirring up Mutiny and Rebellion' aimed at 'the utter destruction of the Government and Countrey'. Cartwright had been spreading rumours that two members of the council were preparing to seize the ship and take everyone home and had declared his willingness to do so himself if no supplies arrived from England that year. Filpt had tried to 'stir up a party' to join him in breaking into the storehouse to steal the contents, a crime that, in view of the post's straitened circumstances, shocked the council. The London committee had sent no ship the previous year because war with France had ruined the market. Thus, it had wanted no furs and it had assumed, in its blissful ignorance, that the men on the Bay required nothing. The officers had not been informed of this, however, and they therefore considered it vital that the provisions Filpt wanted to steal, and probably consume as quickly as possible, be carefully husbanded in case no ship arrived that year. Cartwright was sentenced to 30 lashes, Filpt to 39, and both men were confined and kept in irons until they could be sent home.[34] Regular complaints about discontented, disobedient, and impertinent men

East view of Moose Factory, watercolour by William Richards, HBC servant born in Rupert's Land, employed as labourer, cooper, and canoeman, 1804–11. Buildings numbered: 1. dwelling flanker; 2. warehouse dock and north flanker; 3. principal gateway; 4. boatyard dock. Outbuildings include shipwrights' workshop, smith's forge, kitchen, brewhouse, and cattlesheds. HBCA Picture Collection P–117. (Courtesy Hudson's Bay Company Archives, Provincial Archives of Manitoba.)

and news of the fire that destroyed Moose Factory in 1735 during Christmas celebrations because no one was sober enough to notice the smoke[35] demonstrated that the company's posts were a great deal less orderly than the committee would have liked. And the attempts to re-establish Henley House provided further evidence that the men were far from subservient.

Henley House was first built in 1743 not as a trading post but as a showcase for the company's wares in the hope of enticing Native traders to travel the 200 miles down the river to Fort Albany on James Bay. The first master's incompetence and insensitivity prompted several Natives to ransack the house and kill five men during the winter of 1754–5. As a result, many of the men at Fort Albany, which supplied Henley House with both goods and workers, declared they would never go there again 'on any account'. Even when the post council solemnly called them before it one by one and read out their contracts and the London committee's orders to rebuild Henley

House, 20 of the 25 men refused to go, although one offered to assist in getting the boats up—18 said they were afraid of being killed, while two objected specifically to going with George Rushworth, the officer appointed to lead the expedition. A few days later, when the council again asked the men their intentions, their replies suggest that, rather than being cowed into submission, they had spent the intervening time discussing the situation and combining to turn it to their advantage. Three men agreed to obey orders, one said he would go if five others went too, and Guy Hardwick repeated his offer to help get the boats there. One of the men who had already survived a stint at Henley House refused to return there and several still objected to Rushworth, who had declared that 'he would Shoot a man as soon as look at him in case of cowardice.' Twelve men, however, said they would go if their wages were raised to £20, a sum that Rushworth himself appears to have suggested when he declared that 'a foremasthand Good God that went under .20.L P annum ought to be hang'd upon a Tree.' Six of these men also demanded that, if they were killed, their families receive £60 each.

The council did not feel authorized to grant financial concessions, but it replaced Rushworth with George Clark. Still, the servants would not concede. Three months later, when the time for departure was drawing dangerously near, the matter remained unsettled. The council summoned the men again and advised them to go to Henley House and appeal to the London committee for a gratuity. When such matters were left to the committee, the servants were assured, their honours always 'considered and rewarded handsomely'. But only two of the men changed their minds and *they* had decided to go home. Four factory men finally agreed to go and a few sloopers and three men from the ship were recruited to accompany them. Since, however, there was only one sawyer among them and the council considered it 'impracticable' to settle a post without proper sawyers, no one went. In 1757 and 1758 the water was too low for boats to travel upriver. Henley House was therefore not rebuilt until 1759, but it was almost immediately destroyed by hostile Natives. This time four men were killed, including Clark. Now even fewer men were willing to rebuild the post and, in what had become a familiar ritual, Humphrey Marten, chief of Fort Albany, assembled the men, read a contract to them, emphasizing both the duties and penalties it prescribed, and assured them of the London committee's determination to reward and punish according to each man's merits. Then he pleaded with them, telling them it was 'greatly in their Power to continue [him] in [the London committee's] Esteem' and that if his 'well being had any sway with them' it would raise his 'Gratitude to such a pitche' as would induce him to 'pinch' himself rather than allowing them to 'want for anything'. He further promised that each man who went to Henley would get a blanket, a pair of cloth stockings, and a leather toggie [a type of overcoat]. But only two of the 23 men at Albany House would agree; the rest refused without even trying to bargain for anything.

Charles Sinclair declared that he would not go 'to run his head into the hands of the Enemy', while James Thomson said 'that you may as well tye him to a post and Shoot him'. Thomas Tate observed that 'the last Corps that came from thence . . . was enough to frighten any Man from going to Henly.' Joseph Down, pointing out that he had already escaped with his life twice, said that he would 'be ware of the Third time', and John Spence, who had been with Clark when he was killed and was himself shot through the thigh, swore 'that no Money in England should cause him to go to Henly'. John Cromartie objected that he 'had enought of it already' and that his life was 'dearer to him than all the Money in the Country'. William Isbister said that if he had known he was to go to Henley House he would not have come to the country at all. Marten was reduced to throwing himself 'humbly' on the 'Humanity' of the 'Gentlemen' of the London committee, begging that they not 'be angry with [him] for the Falts of others', and had the other officers submit a declaration attesting to his unsuccessful efforts by 'Persuation, by Entreaty, and by Threats' to get the men to go to Henley House.[36] Low water levels further complicated the situation and prevented the post's re-establishment until 1766.

Clearly, the servants were not prepared to obey unquestioningly the orders they were given, as they had pledged to do by signing their agreements. To make matters worse, they were also refusing to carry out duties crucial to the company's new policy of sending men to build posts in the interior. Some officers, therefore, suggested that the servants' contracts should be altered to obligate them specifically to go inland when required, but the committee thought the terms of the agreements already bound them to do so. The servants, however, had other ideas, and in 1776 the committee decided to overcome their objections to journeying into the interior by granting bounties of 40 shillings a year to men who had been sent inland from York Factory in 1774 and 1775.[37] Then it promised this gratuity to all men who went inland. For new labourers, who were usually engaged at £6 a year, with annual increases of £2, the gratuity gave them another £2. Although the committee hoped with this measure to avoid a general wage increase, it had ended up raising the wages of everyone going inland, as well as demonstrating to the men that they were by no means the weaker party in their relationship with their employer.

At the same time, the committee's desire to control everything undermined its officers' authority, which was already limited simply because they were outnumbered. The committee insisted that officers send bad servants home instead of punishing them on the spot and that any agreements they negotiated be invalid without its approval.[38] Moreover, its concern for the company's reputation both reinforced this tendency to interfere and made it hesitate to inflict the punishments specified by the contracts. After witnesses testified before a House of Commons committee in 1749 that HBC officers abused them with impunity, the committee insisted that men sent home for misbehaviour be examined by a council of officers and the ship's captain before they left and the details of their cases submitted to the committee so that it could impose the proper penalties.[39] But it frequently ignored the officers' recommendations, which, they complained, weakened their ability to command. In 1785, the officers at Churchill protested that the committee's refusal to recall two undesirable servants as requested the year before was 'no great encouragement' to the 'promotion of diligence', and declared that 'unless your Chief has a discressionary power to rid the Factory of all those that become abusive, subordination will soon cease & anarchy & confusion take its place.'[40] But not only was the committee not prepared to surrender any of its authority, it decided, in 1792, to stop punishing disobedient servants by sending them home and to fine them instead.

The officers, sitting in council, would hear the complaint against the accused and impose a fine, which the committee promised to deduct from the offender's wages.[41] Fining, it soon became convinced, was the 'best mode for preserving due Subordination' in spite of the fact that, in the same letter, it also reprimanded the officers at Moose Factory for not finding and severely punishing the culprit who had committed 'so flagrant a Breach of good Order' as to tear down the notice posted in the guard room to announce the new measure.[42] No doubt, it hoped that men would soon develop the right attitude. But, having declared sanctimoniously that 'excessive Punishments as well as too lenient ones have their Evils', it regularly carried out its promise to 'mitigate' fines if they were 'oppressive'. As a result, reported the officers at Churchill in 1796, 'The Idea of mulcting a Man's wages in this Country is openly ridiculed by the people here, nor do we believe they will be convinced untill they feel the smart of it.' The committee's failure to back up its officers was having a 'very bad effect'.[43] But war in Europe had created a serious labour shortage and any servants returning home were likely to be pressed into the army or the navy and their services lost completely.

Fining, therefore, was a more 'eligible' form of punishment. After all, unruly men were better than none.[44] But the officers, faced with men for whom fining held no terrors, disagreed. They continued to send misbehaving servants home, even after the committee warned in 1797 that if they did so without permission except in a case of 'flagrant breach of duty' the chief officers would be charged five guineas each to cover the cost of passage to England.[45] A guinea was worth 21 shillings, one shilling more than a pound, and the penalty was thus substantial. Added to whatever deterrent effect this measure might have had was the regular re-engagement of those sent home in disgrace, which demonstrated the futility of this practice and frustrated the officers into obedience.[46]

Because labour was so scarce, the committee could not risk alienating potential recruits by forcing disobedient workers to pay the charges and damages their contracts specified, not that they were likely to have the means to do so anyway. Clearly, the contract's usefulness as a legal weapon was severely limited. But questions of discipline were becoming more pressing, not only because the servants' misbehaviour caused so much inconvenience but because it seemed to be so common. The journals were full of disquieting accounts of disobedience and insolence,[47] made doubly alarming by what was happening in Britain at the same time. By the end of the eighteenth century, British society bore even less resemblance to the traditional ideal than it had a century before. There was a growing social distance between the élite and the lower orders, which allowed the latter to develop their own norms and values, while the proliferation of small employers and outwork gave many workers complete control over their labour. Although people were losing the benefits of customary work relations, which freed employers from costly obligations, they were also being liberated from their restrictions. Social unrest was increasing and nearly a third of all labour disputes reported in Britain during the eighteenth century occurred during the last decade. There were also subversive groups interested in more than simply negotiating wages and working conditions, while the French Revolution made the whole situation all the more menacing.[48] The committee would not, therefore, have been happy to read John Sutherland's observation in 1796 that 'it really appeared as if the french Revolution has got in *People*.'[49]

The committee members did not really fear a revolution among their servants, but their perusal of the journals had convinced them that there was 'such a deficiency of the Authority in the Superiors and Consequently such a Lassitude or Indolence and Stubbornness in the inferior Servants there is no Wonder of scanty returns instead of an increasing Trade.' Servants stationed inland would do nothing unless 'bribed by Spirituous Liquors to do their duty' and, unlike their Canadian counterparts, had 'their set distances to travel daily' and could not be roused from their 'accustom'd Languor'.[50] The officers might not have agreed with the implication that they were to blame, but some of them had become convinced that the 'mutinous Disposition' that had manifested itself in the past had 'broken loose' with 'unexampled Violence' and that the company was facing 'a most important Crisis'. It was time to settle 'indisputably' who was in charge.[51]

The servants' behaviour had not really changed, but their disobedience was a greater problem than before because their unwillingness to exert themselves hindered the company's efforts to extend its trade, and their failure to identify themselves wholeheartedly with their employer meant that no officer could be certain of their support. Competition with the NWC was becoming increasingly violent and it was finally necessary for servants to risk their lives in defence of the company's property and rights, as their contracts bound them to do. Instead, an officer might find that he could not rely on them at all. Thus, one day in March of 1809, James Swain, the master of Beaver Lake House, an inland post belonging to Severn House, intercepted a Native and suddenly found himself scuffling with four Canadians for possession of the man's furs, with two more joining in when they saw their master getting the best of it. After suffering some severe blows, Swain managed to free himself, drew his pistol, and challenged his Canadian counterpart to a duel, which the latter declined. All the while, Swain's men, who outnumbered the Canadians two to one, proved themselves a 'set of poor inactive Spiritless Men'. Three of them were fishing on the ice only 300 paces away, 'as unconcern'd as could be', pretending not to hear his cries for help. Those at the house looked out, saw what was going on, sneaked back in, and sat by the fire. Swain's only support was his wife, who buckled on his dirk and came hurrying toward 'the Field of Contention boldly'. The matter was settled by the Native, who persuaded Swain to let him take his furs to the Canadians to whom he was in debt and from whom he expected a severe beating if he did not pay.[52]

Something obviously had to be done and the solution appeared the following year in the form of the 'Retrenching System', which was the first thorough attempt to rationalize the HBC. In many respects it was, of course, simply a continuation of old policies since it aimed at ensuring that the frugality and self-sufficiency that the committee had always insisted on were actually practised and that its men were actually as obedient as servants were supposed to be. But it also introduced a new orderliness to the company's organization and its records, clarified the distinctions between officers and servants, and, for the first time, explicitly laid out the company's hierarchy.

Retrenchment and Reorganization

Reorganization divided the business into the Northern and Southern departments. The former included York Factory and Fort Churchill and two new factories, as the main districts were called: Saskatchewan, which comprised all the territory on the Saskatchewan rivers above Cumberland House, and Winnipeg, which included all the country drained by waters flowing into Lake Winnipeg. The Southern Department consisted of Fort Albany, Moose Factory, Eastmain, and their outposts. Each department was governed by a superintendent. Below him were the chief factors who managed the factories of the department. Below them were the traders who managed individual posts and the districts belonging to them. Both superintendents and chief factors had the authority to suspend subordinate officers guilty of improper conduct, but chief factors had to act according to instructions from their superintendents and all cases had to be submitted to the committee for its approval. Each factory would also be assigned an accountant responsible for producing accurate accounts every year and reporting any improper practices by chief factors or traders. Moreover, these accounts were henceforth to be kept in sterling money instead of Made Beaver,[53] a unit of value based on the best beaver skins. The company would now have a tidy chain of command and properly kept books, which officers could no longer juggle with impunity and which would now resemble those of other companies and be easier to understand.

The committee was also determined, at last, to acquire a thorough and businesslike knowledge of its operations. In 1814, it ordered all chief factors and district masters to submit reports, with maps and sketches, describing the state of their districts and their trade together with suggestions for making it 'more profitable'. These reports were to include information on the topography and climate of Rupert's Land, the Native peoples, the condition and location of each post, the establishments of the NWC, and the ages, occupations, character, and physical descriptions of all employees. To prevent any future lapses into ignorance, it issued orders to ensure that proper and extensive

Southeast view of Albany Factory, showing man leading team of horses drawing wood on left; well for drawing water through ice, cattle feeding, and men cutting wood and hauling logs at centre; a figure on snowshoes, lower left; dog chasing fox, lower right. Watercolour by William Richards, HBC servant, 1804–11. HBCA Picture Collection P–118. (Courtesy Hudson's Bay Company Archives, Provincial Archives of Manitoba.)

records would henceforth be kept. The clerk stationed at each post would keep a journal, under the supervision of his master, containing a record of each day's events, the men's duties, and descriptions of the weather, flora, and fauna, unadorned by personal comments or observations. Journals were not new, of course, but the committee had never before specified what they were to contain.

Another innovation was the annual report that every district master now had to submit. This would pull together the information provided by the journals of the district's posts and include a list of all officers and servants of the district, giving their names and details of their conduct the preceding year. Each man was to be judged according to his sobriety, honesty, willingness 'in the discharge of his duty', obedience and respectfulness, activity, intelligence, skills and 'any other useful qualification', courage, and readiness to support his master 'in case of violent attacks' on the company's property. 'No anecdote' was too 'trifling' if it threw 'light upon the character of an individual', particularly of an officer with 'claims to promotion'. Indeed, withholding information was 'an important breach of duty'. The master of each district would submit his report to his chief factor for examination. Each chief factor would send evaluations of the reports he received together with his own report on the 'general conduct' of the masters under him to the superintendent of his department. The superintendent in turn reported on his department and on the accuracy of the reports of those under him, made suggestions for improving the trade, and explained the arrangements he had made for the following year. Further details would be available in waste books, men's debt books, fur books, and ledgers kept by the clerks.[54]

This paperwork constituted a significant new burden for the officers and was probably beyond the capabilities of many of them. The first set of reports certainly failed to satisfy. The committee complained that they were 'meagre and defective', that there had been no sketches, and, consequently, it had no idea where anything was.[55] Nevertheless, the committee's desire for better records altered the nature of the officers' work and distinguished them further from their inferiors. Indeed, the demand for standardized and regular information from managers placed the HBC in the forefront of the development of what would later be called 'systematic management'. This managerial philosophy has been identified with railroads and manufacturing firms, whose drive for efficiency included 'substituting managerially mandated systems for ad hoc decisions by individuals'. These systems were controlled through communication: instructions, information, and procedures were conveyed downward from those at the top of the hierarchy; data and analyses, summarized and dissected as they travelled up the hierarchy, enabled the directors to evaluate the success of their policies, monitor the individuals in the organization, and make decisions about the business; lateral communication co-ordinated and documented interactions.[56] The ideal officer was now able to bargain effectively with the Natives and also write well and understand, if not keep, accounts. He was a man of business with the 'Prudence & Zeal . . . Spirit & activity to break Thro the stumbling & wastefull habits that have pervaded the people.'[57]

Men without these virtues might find their prospects limited. Thus, in 1814, John Mannal was denied a promotion because of his unwillingness to deviate from 'old customs'.[58] Officers whose pride and egotism led them to act with too much independence would no longer do either. John Clarke, for example, a former Nor'wester who joined the HBC in 1815, was tough and energetic. But, he was also, according to James Bird,

> a Man of little or no Education, vain, pompous and so excessively fond of Shew and parade that to excel in those points would . . .

afford him the highest Gratification he is capable of feeling. It will be readily concluded that a Man of such a Taste has very little regard for Economy; and indeed he appears to have no Idea of the value of property. He may be very well calculated to force an Establishment in a Country where opposition is violent and when the Expence at which it is accomplished is not an object of Consideration, but he will never conduct a large and complicated Business advantageously. Resolution and the Art of managing Canadians are the only valuable Qualifications he possesses.

Robert Logan, on the other hand, seemed quite able 'to discharge advantageously the Duties of Store Keeper in a large Business' but was 'not calculated to thrive as an Indian Trader although he is by no means deficient in Resolution.' Aulay McAuley, with his 'rough manners', was qualified for nothing more than the charge of a single post and he was later criticized for having 'little system or management'.[59]

The acquisition of officers who could both 'force an establishment' and manage it properly became an important aspect of the Retrenching System and one of the reasons for the sharp curtailment of opportunities for promotion from below. The new system required levels of literacy higher than the average servant's and probably also beyond what officers who had risen from the ranks possessed. Young men with the requisite skills were now to be recruited as clerks and given further training in the specifics of the fur trade and the principles of economy upon which the business was henceforth to be conducted. These were the men intended for positions of responsibility, although, of course, the company still had to make do with whomever it could get. The committee's preference, however, was for officers whose training as clerks had ingrained in them 'habits of regularity & correctness in business'.[60] Clerks also offered the committee another way of extending its control, as the officers themselves realized, since it had to assure them that clerks were not intended to be 'spies' and that their memoranda would simply ensure 'greater regularity'. However, since clerks were in charge of the accounts and the books of the post and of the stores, from which they distributed goods according to the master's written orders,[61] their presence made it impossible for officers to conceal extravagance and dishonesty. The company would therefore be transformed into an efficient and economical enterprise through the importation of 'young men of good education' from England, where, the committee was happy to report, widespread unemployment rendered them abundant and, consequently, very cheap. Of course, their 'real remuneration' would 'be obtained afterwards by the advancement in the service' that those who qualified themselves for 'superior Situations' would 'assuredly receive'.[62]

The committee now looked forward to having 'respectable clerks at the Out posts who may be depended upon for activity & care of the goods' instead of 'trusting so much to the old hands among the Common men' and, in a few years, 'a succession of Experienced Traders'. But 'a great deal' depended on the 'management' of the superior officers, on the example they set, '& upon their treating the Young men in a kind & liberal manner while they conduct themselves properly & attend to their duty.' Unfortunately, 'various circumstances' had led the committee to believe that 'an injudicious & short sighted oeconomy [sic]' had 'been adopted towards the Young Clerks & the men', which tended to 'disgust them with the Country & the Service of the Company.' In particular, in many instances the principal officer at a post had not associated with the clerks and shared with them 'the little luxuries within his reach', thereby driving them 'to associate with the common men'. But clerks had to 'feel the importance' of their situation. Though they had to learn that orders were to be obeyed 'implicitly', they were to 'partake' of the 'little luxuries on the mess table' and be made 'sensible by acts of kindness that they are only considered as parts of one family.'[63] For officers, the post was a household in the traditional sense, with clerks welcomed in and tied to it with bonds of affection. The servants, however, had no place in this household. The Retrenching System relegated them more firmly to the bottom. It sharpened the distinctions between officers and servants by requiring of the former skills that the latter rarely possessed and increasing the distance between the committee and the servants through the interposition of an expanded managerial stratum.

The 'Common Men', declared the committee,

> should be impressed with a proper sense of their duty, to yield most exact obedience to the commands of the Officers sent over them. They must be made to feel, that they are not to judge for themselves what is proper to be done, but to do neither more nor less than their officers shall order them.

Discipline had been 'relaxed to the most pernicious degree'. Indeed, 'the one most important cause of the decline of the Trade' was 'the neglect' of the 'principal Officers to enforce due obedience on the part of the Men', a view that conveniently ignored the committee's frequent disregard of the punishments its officers had prescribed. Anyway, such laxness was to stop. 'No disobedience or improper behaviour' anywhere was henceforth to be overlooked.[64] Furthermore, like the officer caste, the servant ranks would be reformed by an infusion of new blood. Orcadians had been spoiled by 'indulgences & improper compliances & familiarities . . . from their Superiors' that 'would have rendered any set of men intractable.' But curing bad habits 'enfirmed by a long system of mismanagement' would require too great an effort. It was far better to introduce 'a new set of men' who would be 'order'd from the first to habits of prompt & exact obedience.' These would come from the western coast and islands of Scotland where 'a more spirited race' could be found. They would be hired on new terms and segregated from the old servants, whose bounties and too ample rations might excite discontent among the newcomers.[65] The committee hoped, however, that many of its problems would eventually be solved by its new colony.

Land grants in the settlement could be used to encourage diligence. In 1810 the committee offered 100 acres of land and the opportunity to purchase more on good terms to servants retiring with a good character. It soon added the promise that the land would be held by the men 'in perpetuity', that their families would be transported to the country at low cost, and that for every additional three years of service they would be entitled to another 100 acres. Anyone willing to engage for a five-year term would receive 200 acres at the end of the period.[66] The colony could also supply provisions, thereby reducing, if not eliminating, the need to import supplies and, once established, would produce employees with all the virtues of Orcadians but none of the drawbacks. They would be accustomed to the country and have few alternatives to employment with the HBC. Transporting them to their posts would be easy and their removal equally simple if they proved undesirable.

At the same time as it was trying to create a traditional society, however, the committee was also trying to unburden itself of some of the obligations that traditional social relations imposed on the élite. It cut back on the indulgences that everyone had taken for granted for the last century. No longer would it supply 'extravagant' imported provisions for men who came from a country 'where butchers' meat forms scarcely any part of the ordinary diet of the labouring people.' In 1811 it planned to send only a quarter as much meat and expected pemmican from the Winnipeg and Saskatchewan districts to make up the difference, while Natives would be encouraged to grow vegetables around the posts.[67] The company would no longer supply leather, except for two pairs of shoes when men were tracking boats, or brandy during journeys and it would no longer pay for furs trapped by servants. It also forbade anyone from taking a wife without permission from the superintendent of his department.[68] That the committee hoped to do away entirely with non-monetary benefits is suggested by its willingness to increase wages to compensate for their loss and to hire men on three-year contracts with no allowances at all.[69] In the past, the committee's secretary could boast to the hostile Rev. Francis Liddell that, although wages in the service were low, they were only a small part of what servants received, since their support equalled £40 a year and 'few sober men can spend any part of their wages in Hudsons Bay.'[70] Now they could not avoid it.

Retrenchment did not, however, lead to a wholesale attack on the men's amusements or customs, as was increasingly the case in Britain, though officers were not discouraged from taking steps in that direction to minimize the unprofitable use of the company's goods. Thus one officer was commended for refusing to permit his men to celebrate St George's Day, 23 May, in the usual manner by firing at a target and drinking brandy on the grounds that it was 'an unnecessary expense'.[71] The superintendents of the two departments decided to reform the expensive custom of allowing company carpenters to manufacture chests for the servants. Men cutting down timber for the posts usually kept the best wood for their chests. Blacksmiths ordered large quantities of iron and steel to make locks, hinges, and handles, in the manufacture of which they also used the HBC's tools and coal. Moreover, the servants demanded high-quality locks with 'numerous securities against picklocks'. Henceforth these chests would be made only when it could be 'conveniently done', the men would have to pay 20 shillings for them, and cheap ready-made locks would be ordered from England.[72]

Nor was the company's time to be squandered any longer. Officers and servants waiting for ships to take them home, rather than being 'kept idle', would spend the time transporting goods to the interior or performing whatever other tasks could be found for them.[73] The committee also frowned on 'the laziness of the workmen' and criticized the 'misapplication of labour'. It called the method of haymaking 'ridiculous' and deplored the fact that collecting firewood appeared to be 'the main activity' of most of the men. It decided that the 'improper construction' of fireplaces led to such enormous fuel consumption and, recommending that a lesson be taken from 'other northern countries', decided to substitute stoves. Gathering wood would now take up less time, while the workshops would be more 'comfortable' and work could continue even in the severe cold.

The committee also attacked the traditional autonomy of the artisan. To prevent the 'waste of labour', each craftsman was to keep a memorandum book in which he noted everything he and any apprentices or journeymen under him did each day and, at the 'conclusion of any work set down', the 'money price' he would be 'entitled' to charge in his native country in a column 'ruled for that purpose'. He was also to record the quantity of materials used and the 'extent of the work according to any sort of measurement' that could be applied. And all journals were to have a separate section for keeping an 'exact diary' of the employment of all the men.[74] In this way, costs could be calculated more precisely and the men's efficiency, diligence, and honesty more easily judged. Such records would make it possible, as never before, to determine who wasted the company's time or materials. Frederick Taylor, the inventor of scientific management, would have approved.

Retrenchment also introduced new systems of remuneration designed to promote diligence by making a man's pay depend on his efforts. In the case of officers, the committee hoped to ensure honesty and responsibility. Employers of the eighteenth and early nineteenth centuries generally mistrusted managers because, since they were salaried, it was assumed that they had no stake in the business. Bad management by uninterested men was seen as the ruin of many large-scale companies and as evidence that self-interest was 'the only possible driving force in industry'.[75] Of course, this force needed to be steered in the right direction. Much of the self-interest of the HBC's officers had heretofore been directed at illicit trade and self-aggrandizement.[76] Therefore, in 1806 the committee had hoped to stimulate the chief officers by supplementing their salaries with 1 per cent of the profits of each consignment of goods sent to them. In 1809 it moved to replace fixed salaries for chief factors with a premium on each fur traded at their factories and at the posts within their districts. It planned in the following year to give traders premiums on the furs they collected and grant a sum equal to their premiums to be divided among their men. Finally, in 1810, the committee decided to set aside half the profits to be divided among the officers, a third going to each of the superintendents of the two departments and the remaining third divided equally among the other officers. Since it would take time for this system to be properly established, for the next three years superintendents would receive annual salaries of £150 each plus a share of the profits amounting to at least £250. Chief factors were guaranteed salaries of £100 and £50 in profits, while traders received £50 in salaries and £20 from the profits.[77]

In 1813, the committee decided that, since 'frontier posts' were less profitable than those nearer the Bay, their profits would be combined and divided equally among the officers stationed there. Accountants would receive salaries of £60 a year instead of shares of the profits. And, because the profits had not been as high as hoped, officers' salaries would be continued for another three years.[78] In 1814 the committee decided that the fund of profits from the frontier posts would provide bonuses for their officers. The rest of the profits would be divided into 100 shares, of which superintendents would get 10 each, district masters four each, second masters two, and junior masters one. These latter three positions were chief factors, chief traders, and traders with new names. The committee also decided to introduce a second to the superintendent, now often referred to as the governor, to supervise the masters of the trading districts. He would receive two shares of the profit. The Southern Department soon had two seconds, perhaps because of a suggestion made by Thomas Vincent while he was acting governor in 1814 that a second in that department had more to do than a chief factor and there should be two.[79]

But the committee feared that giving shares to junior officers provided them with too much information about the company's affairs. Therefore, in 1815, it decided to limit shares to 'Chiefs or Officers of the First Rank' and throw the shares then assigned to seconds and masters into 'an aggregate fund' from which they would be paid salaries. Although, the committee declared, this alteration might 'weaken & confine that stimulus to exertion, which it has been the great object of the new arrangements to give', the supervision of 'seven or eight superior officers deeply interested in the success of the trade' would be enough to prevent 'any neglect' on the part of those under their command. In fact, junior officers were naturally looking to promotion and, with 'every one anxious to lay a foundation for this by shewing a good balance of profit upon the account current of the Post under his charge', they would surely behave. The annual statements submitted to superior officers by the accountants would make apparent the profits of each trading district, and anyone aspiring to promotion would try to ensure that the statement from his post reflected favourably on himself.[80] Thus, even junior officers could consider themselves partners and, although not guaranteed promotion, conduct themselves in such a way as to prove themselves worthy to ascend to whatever positions opened up.

The committee also proposed to modify how servants were paid. It had always preferred to reward men for their efforts with bonuses instead of higher wages, and by 1810 servants were receiving bounties not only for travelling inland but for performing new duties, such as building canoes, and even for renewing their contracts.[81] Now it planned to abolish bonuses entirely and hire men at 'fixed wages'.[82] A few years later, it was prepared to abandon these in favour of payment by the task.

The London committee was not alone in adopting the attitude that a system of payment by results was an effective way of remunerating and controlling workers. Piece-work, long standard in such occupations as mining where supervision was difficult, was considered 'quaint' and 'peculiar' until the second quarter of the nineteenth century when it became 'the managerial orthodoxy'. Piece-work came to dominate the putting out trades, but it was also introduced into the factory where time wages were more logical. As John Rule has observed, however, the principle that underlay the piece-work system was 'the stick', not 'the carrot'. Piece-rates were so low that workers had to work harder and longer to earn the same income as before. The purpose of piece-work was to transfer to employers the control over the pace of work that workers had traditionally enjoyed.[83] Employers' acceptance of the desirability of piece-work was a manifestation of their increasing withdrawal from the rituals and celebrations that had cemented relations between masters and workers. Sidney Pollard has pointed out that older systems of payment by results, particularly in mining, were a type of 'group piecework' in which the 'cohesion and ethos' of the group were as much a source of discipline as the wage. The new systems were aimed at individual effort and also marked 'a major change' and what he considers a 'forward step' in the employers' attitude towards labour. It signified the beginning of the notion that workers were responsive to monetary incentives and an end to the belief that workers were looking only for subsistence and that long-term contracts were effective sources of discipline.[84]

In 1814 the committee decided enthusiastically that employing men 'by the piece in lieu of fixed yearly wages ought to be adopted in wherever practicable.' It began by introducing it into the timber business, limping along near Moose Factory since 1809,[85] and in the construction of a winter road from York Factory to the outlet of Lake Winnipeg. The committee did not specify how this plan would work at the sawmill, but thought that the roadbuilders would receive low wages, buy provisions and European goods from the company, and receive a small piece of land to cultivate for themselves. These arrangements, the committee believed, would provide 'a strong motive for economy, as well as industry'. Although the workers' earnings would be lower than everyone else's and they would have to purchase all their supplies, they could feed themselves from their gardens. Once it became clear how much money could be saved under the new system, others would be 'tempted to apply for the same advantages, and this competition' would permit the reduction of payment. This beneficial effect made it worth introducing piece-work even 'where no immediate saving may arise from it'. Moreover, the committee remarked,

> The introduction of piece work may be of use collaterally in exciting some emulation in the workmen who are employed by the year and enabling the Officers to judge more correctly whether these men do fair days' work. It appears very evident that some stimulus is much wanted: & that the quantity of work done by our people both labourers & tradesmen; bears no proportion to the days' work of a man in any part of Britain. The enormous length of time employed by the Carpenters at York in making the Boats supplied to the Red River Settlement is disgraceful; and we have learnt with surprize that at some of the Southern Factories the workmen have been allowed to consider half the day as their own time.[86]

Furthermore, since the company was unable to recruit as many officers 'as advisable' to supervise the men working at the mill and on the winter road, their employment at piece-work would provide 'sufficient stimulus' to keep them at work with only a 'trusty man' to take charge of and serve out provisions and liquor.[87]

The eight Norwegians hired to build the first of the five posts that would accommodate the men and horses employed on the winter road were, however, hired on agreements that combined old and new terms. They were hired for three years at £20 a year and would not have to pay for their provisions. But they were told that any of them who cleared 15 acres of land and planted it with potatoes or grain would be considered to have performed his service of three years and receive his three years' wages. Anyone who cleared and planted more than 15 acres would receive £4 a year for the surplus. And, as an additional incentive, the company promised them a premium of one shilling for every bushel of potatoes harvested from each acre over 80 bushels per acre and 3 shillings for every bushel of grain over 15 bushels per acre. The committee expected to profit from this arrangement even though it was obliged to pay three years' worth of wages because if the men completed their tasks in two years the company would save the expense of one year's provisions and have the job done sooner than it would have been by men under the usual contract.[88] But not everyone shared the committee's optimism about the future of piece-work in the HBC.

Thomas Thomas, the superintendent of the Southern Department, doubted its 'practicability' anywhere but in the timber business. The committee disagreed. Although it realized that annual wages could not be completely abolished, it was sure that men might 'always be stimulated to industry by premiums upon the quantity of work done over and above a specified task', as in the case of the Norwegian labourers. Indeed, 'this principle' might be applied to 'every sort of work that admits of being measured, or that is paid by measurement in this and other countries', such as cutting and bringing in firewood and timber, boatbuilding, all types of carpentry, cutting and stacking hay, digging gardens, ditching, and putting up fences. Moreover, it would be 'very desirable to try its effect' where men were not employed under 'the constant supervision of their officers', which had always been the case for most servants. The committee believed that Orcadians and other Scots, who all had reputations for frugality, would be 'stimulated' to 'spirit and activity, of which at present many of them appear totally destitute'. If they had the opportunity of adding 'from sixpence to a shilling' per day to their regular wages, they might be 'induced to do two or three times as much work' as otherwise.[89] As for Alexander Christie's reservations, the committee suggested that the 'Prejudice of the Men & their Unwillingness to work by the Piece' might be 'surmounted by Firmness & Temper' on his part and by his convincing them that the plan was 'calculated as much for their Advantage as the Company's.' It also predicted that the success of the Norwegians in their piece-work would 'most likely induce others to work in the same way'.[90]

The timber business proved unprofitable, however, and was discontinued a few years later, without persuading anyone one way or the other about the benefits of payment by the task, while the Norwegians did little more than terrorize their hapless overseer.[91] The committee ended up dropping both the idea of a winter road and its efforts to extend piece-work throughout the service. Payment by the task did not, of course, disappear. The company had always employed Natives on this basis and would always hire men on similar terms for specific jobs wherever this was practical. Indeed, in the company's territory west of the Rockies, Native labour hired on a daily or seasonal basis became a significant component of the company's workforce.[92] Furthermore, when the HBC recruited colliers for its Vancouver Island mines in the 1850s, it found that it *had* to hire them on piece-work because this was the method of payment to which they were accustomed. But its first attempt in the second decade of the nineteenth century to introduce payment by the task as a way of remunerating its contracted employees was discouraging and suggested that achieving its goal would be difficult. Moreover, the next few years were so tumultuous that the committee had more pressing concerns. Competition with the NWC intensified. The HBC had to undertake costly expeditions to establish itself in the North-West and the Canadians regularly attacked the colony, while its need for manpower kept it at the mercy of men like Andrew Spence, reported as 'too independent & masterly to be a good Servant' and possessing 'a temper that sets at defiance all order & regularity that ought to be observed between master & man'.[93] The coalition of the rival companies in 1821 promised to put an end to the company's problems at last.

The Merger

The merger has tended to overshadow retrenchment as a turning point in the company's history. It is credited with making the HBC's hierarchy more rigid, eliminating the possibility of promotion for ordinary servants, and, as E.E. Rich put it, introducing 'system and certainty in place of experiment and expectation'.[94] But it was the *opportunity* not the *desire* to do so that was new in 1821. The committee had always wanted 'system and certainty'. It had always distinguished among the various ranks in the company, encouraged officers to hold themselves aloof from their inferiors, and provided only limited opportunities for advancement to common servants. What the merger did was produce new distinctions between officers and make it more difficult for qualified men to assume positions they might have occupied before 1821. The committee could now finally hire educated young men possessing commercial skills as officers instead of promoting from below. It thus added to the old hierarchy a management stratum of middle-class white-collar workers who were expected to abandon ungentlemanly conduct, which, in Rupert's Land, included excessive drinking, the use of uncouth language, and the acquisition of Aboriginal wives. George Simpson epitomized this new type of officer. Recruited from outside, promoted over the heads of older, experienced men, he ruthlessly stamped out inefficiency and waste wherever he found it. His personal life was a model of middle-class respectability: after sowing some wild oats, he acquired an ornamental wife and became a family man, a pillar of society, and eventually an important member of the 'commercial aristocracy of Montreal'.[95] But his meteoric rise was impossible for most of those who came after him. They had to progress through a more clearly defined hierarchy of ranks with less room at the top.

The merger of 1821 was a partnership agreement binding for 21 years. It divided the officers into three ranks. At the top were the commissioned gentlemen: 23 chief factors and, below them, 28 chief traders. Their remuneration consisted of shares in the profits of the trade. The profits were to be divided into 100 shares, 40 of which were further divided into 85 sub-shares. Chief factors would receive two sub-shares each and each chief trader would receive one. The remaining sub-shares would support redundant officers during the first seven years of the coalition and then be combined with 10 whole shares to provide for retiring officers. The chief factors also comprised the councils that managed the departments, with chief traders filling in for chief factors unable to attend meetings.[96] In 1821, these ranks were assigned to the officers with the most seniority and prestige and their names were listed in the Deed Poll that defined their duties and privileges. The rest became clerks, who were paid salaries rather than a share in the profits of trade and promoted only when a place at the top fell vacant. The path to a commission might now be exceedingly long. A young British man generally started his career with a five-year contract as an apprentice clerk, followed by a series of three-year contracts as a clerk. Young men of Aboriginal ancestry usually began as apprentice postmasters. Ironically, there were more places to start, but those who occupied them might find themselves spending more years than they wanted in what George Barnston called 'Paper Bondage'. It took Robert Campbell 33 years to advance from clerk to chief factor. Others never made it. Charles McKenzie, for example, had joined McTavish, Frobisher and Company, one of the firms in the NWC, in 1802 as an apprentice clerk. When he retired from the HBC in 1854, he was still a clerk—and a deeply resentful one, too.[97] Indeed, since years of service might be rewarded with nothing but the security of more years of service, it was unnecessary, even inadvisable, for all officers to have lofty ambitions. Thus, when George Simpson passed through Split Lake in August of 1824, he was impressed by its master, John Scott, whom he described as a 'plain stupid oeconomical [*sic*] Man but competent to the management of a small post in this part of the Country' and 'at the height of his ambition on a Saly of £40 p. Annum'. Moreover, he remarked,

> it is to be regretted we have so few of his description in the Service instead of Young Gentlemen of higher expectations who can never be provided for by shares in the concern and to whom the business cannot afford such Salys as their qualifications and respectability might appear to entitle them and who consequently become dissatisfied and disaffected.[98]

However, ambitious officers were unhappy not only because they had to wait so long for promotion but because they perceived the whole process as unfair.

As William Mactavish complained, 'partiality will do everything, & interest in this service is all in all, a few quarrels among the Nobs & you are done for ever let you be as useful as you may.' Even worse, the company did not need to promote a good clerk to hang onto him because after 'about 10 or 12 years engaged in the Fur Trade a man becomes totally unfit for other business, & of course feels his incapacity' and was thus 'obliged to stick by the Country'. The 'Gents' also knew that almost all the clerks had families in the country and would have to stay because most of them were 'perfectly unable to appear in society'. Importing English wives to overcome this problem would 'never do' because conditions were intolerable for British women.[99] Like their white-collar counterparts in more conventional enterprises, junior HBC officers might now have to settle for modest economic rewards and seek consolation in their distinction from the servants and whatever constituted 'the paraphernalia of gentility'[100] in Rupert's Land. They might join the fur trade gentry by marrying the refined daughters of company officers and the Red River élite, thereby adopting a cultural identity that linked them with men of superior rank and wealth. It was thus possible for clerks to achieve respectability even without a commission, if they wished to. Others, of course, cared neither about rising in the hierarchy nor about aping their betters and were as indifferent to what Simpson and his cronies thought and did as the servants were.

While the merger erected new obstacles for ambitious clerks, it promised elevation to grand heights to the chief factors and chief traders. At the same time, this actually resulted in undermining their independence. The fact that the department councils centralized and co-ordinated the operations of each department reduced their autonomy, but, since they made up the councils, they could still expect to enjoy considerable authority. Yet they were no match for the tireless and despotic George Simpson, who identified himself utterly with his employers and would stop at nothing to eliminate waste and disorder. Simpson exemplified a new type of management, appropriate to modern enterprise and illustrative of a new style of authority, which emphasized uniformity and regularity. Like the social reformers who were horrified to find that criminal subcultures, not the supervision of honest, dedicated warders, were responsible for whatever order there was in eighteenth-century prisons,[101] Simpson was determined to introduce a whole new regime to an institution he believed had

THE VIEW FROM THE TOP   51

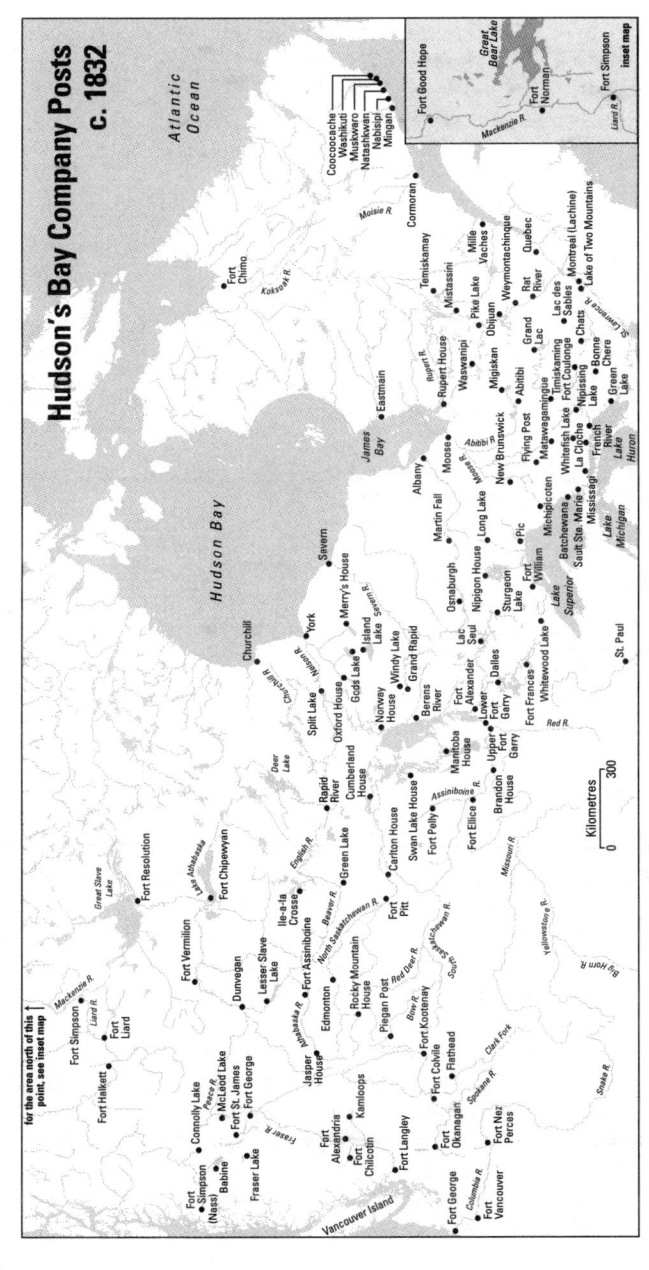

The merger of the Hudson's Bay Company and the North West Company extended the reach of the HBC from coast to coast. From Hudson's Bay Record Society, vol. 30, map N8139. (Courtesy Hudson's Bay Company Archives, Provincial Archives of Manitoba.)

become wasteful and lax. He was going to shake up the world the fur traders had made. Having been recruited from his uncle's sugar brokerage firm in 1820, Simpson possessed neither a sentimental attachment to any of the customs of the country nor an antipathy towards old NWC enemies to deter him from doing what was necessary to make the HBC an efficient, well-disciplined organization. His appointment as governor of the Northern Department in 1821 was a break with the past. It also broke a promise made by another committee in 1688 that it would never 'Send New Raw & unexperienced men to put over the heads of such as have Served us Longe & faithfully.'[102] But the times and the committee had clearly changed. A hardheaded and, if necessary, hardhearted manager was required to wrench the company's traders out of their lethargy.

Simpson was not a fur trader: he was a businessman with extensive business interests and a desire to ensure that the ventures in which he was involved, whether as manager or investor, realized a profit. He viewed the HBC not from inside a 'fur trade society' but rather from a 'world of balance sheets'.[103] Furthermore, by 1826 when he was appointed governor of the Northern, Southern, and Montreal departments, Simpson was based in Lachine, near Montreal, and although he regularly undertook expeditions through his fur trade empire and kept himself well informed about the business, he was as distant from the everyday life of his subordinates as the committee in London. He looked down on 'the Gentry of Ruperts Land' and its 'narrow constricted illiberal ideas' and did not hesitate to deal with 'Malcontents' from the lower ranks with 'a good drubbing'.[104] A.S. Morton might have thought Simpson's letters revealed 'great kindness' and a 'laughter-loving character',[105] but they often expressed a harsh disdain for those he considered inferior. In 1828 he reported that when a pilot 'was about to shew the cloven hoof . . . by arguing a point', he 'brought him to his senses . . . by compelling him to Sing in spite of Sore throat.'[106] In 1843 he warned Wemyss Simpson against trusting any servants with keys to the stores because, he observed, '99 out of 100 of our people are Thieves.'[107] Simpson's references to the native-born women he considered fit for his amusement but not for marriage are particularly repugnant. To him one officer's wife was nothing but a 'bit of Brown' and his own 'country wives' were an 'article' and a 'commodity'.[108] Simpson's prejudices were not only racial, however, for a European woman who was not also a lady was equally unworthy of his respect.

Simpson's position in the company together with his regular visits to London beginning in the 1830s entrenched his authority firmly. His enormously detailed annual letters ensured that, even when he was not there in person, it was chiefly his views and his recommendations that came before the committee. As a result, he exercised an unprecedented influence in London. Even a case as complicated and controversial as the murder of John McLoughlin Jr by his men at Fort Stikine in 1842 resulted in the committee deferring to Simpson's judgement that the incident was a case of 'justifiable homicide' even after it began to entertain doubts about his verdict.[109] His dominance prompted one unhappy officer to ask in 1854, 'Is he not the Committee and Governor as regards this Country?'[110] Another officer, John McLean, his ambitions thwarted by Simpson, observed that the governor 'combined with the prepossessing manners of a gentleman all the craft and subtlety of an intriguing courtier; while his cold and callous heart was incapable of sympathising with the woes and pains of his fellow-men.' He had won over the old Nor'Westers and acquired such influence with the London committee that he could do as he pleased. The councils had become a sham, the company was 'ruled with a rod of iron', and 'the mercantile Colony of Rupert's Land' was governed by an 'authority combining the despotism of military rule with the strict surveillance and mean parsimony of the avaricious trader.'[111]

The officers' frustrations were not all Simpson's fault, though, because they had 'misconceived' their powers, as the committee put it in 1823 after the chief factors had 'promulgated' the classification of clerks submitted to them only for their consideration and opinions. It alone, the committee reminded them, made the final decisions 'in all matters'.[112] The senior officers might have considered themselves 'wintering partners'—a term originating in the NWC where officers really *were* partners, but HBC officers were in fact very highly paid and privileged servants. They were partners only in the sense that their income depended on the profits their efforts produced. All rules and regulations, all fines levied for misbehaviour, all expulsions of officers from the councils, all dismissals of clerks, and the determination of allowances required the approval of the London committee. Once it had made its decision, officers had to abide by it. For them to believe otherwise constituted a 'misperception of their authority'.[113]

The Deed Poll of 1834 assailed their position further. The committee objected to the fact that under the current agreement chief factors and chief traders could retire whenever they wanted, but the company had 'no power' to 'dispense with the services' of any commissioned officer, however 'old, infirm or troublesome' he might be. This was 'contrary to mercantile usage and to the usage of all public or private

Services and might be productive of serious inconvenience and injury to the Concern.' The new Deed Poll thus introduced an 'alteration', the 'reasonableness and expediency' of which no one could possibly question: officers were now subject to dismissal just like ordinary workers. Furthermore, since the committee comprised the 'sole Proprietors of the Country, and of the Capital employed in the Trade', it was 'reasonable' for it to have the 'power' and 'authority' to elect those officers without being 'confined' to the 'nomination' of the councils as heretofore. Besides, it was better informed about more candidates and unlikely to be influenced by 'feelings of partiality or prejudice'.[114] In fact, of course, it was highly likely to be influenced by George Simpson and any powerful individuals who had friends or relatives for whom they wanted to find places. Thus, the merger, which made it more difficult to rise in the service and which still allowed those who did rise to think of themselves as partners, did not endow the officers with the power that seemed appropriate to their status.

As for the lower ranks, they were to be relegated even more firmly to the bottom. The committee hoped the merger would enable it at last to hire only 'efficient valuable Servants' and 'none of those, who are only useful during an opposition.' It also expected to require fewer workers and, therefore, to be able to hire them on 'much more reasonable terms', meaning severely reduced wages and benefits. New men were to be hired at 'a fixed rate of wages', with Orcadian labourers receiving £15 and Canadian middlemen 400 *livres* 'Montreal money', which equalled £20. Steersmen and bowsmen would receive £22 10s. if recruited in the Orkneys and 600 *livres* if from Canada. When stationed where work was 'more severe' and conditions harsher, a small sum would be added in compensation. Skilled workers would get no more than £40. Interpreters would receive no more than £50 and, the committee hoped, would be eliminated altogether in a few years because no apprentice would now be promoted to a clerkship until he could speak a Native language. Further savings would be derived from the elimination of 'equipments' for all but apprentices. Canadians would now have to purchase what they needed from the company like everyone else. All remuneration was to be monetary. Not only would this measure reduce the company's expenses, it would, the committee believed, also inculcate thrift and prudence in the servants. The men could count on a 'fair scale of wages' and 'moderate' prices on all goods, except spirits, which should be expensive and sold only in limited quantities, and each could 'dispose of his money' as he wanted. As a result, they would learn economy, and 'the more sober and careful of their own means' they were 'the more careful they [would] be of the company's property.' In fact, carefulness would be forced on them because they would not be allowed to accumulate debts greater than two-thirds of their wages, and in 1827 they were deprived of all gratuities and bonuses.[115]

New marriage regulations added further to a man's financial burdens. In 1824 marriage to Aboriginal women was prohibited and marriage to other women made subject to approval from the prospective groom's chief factor. If permission was granted, a man had to sign a contract obligating him to support his wife, have a marriage ceremony performed at the first opportunity, and, in some cases, pay a penalty if he failed to fulfil the latter pledge. Clerks and servants now also had to pay for their families' maintenance.[116] The relationship between the company and its servants now bore a greater resemblance to the one favoured by other employers. Although it had not abandoned yearly wages in favour of piece-rates, the committee had still managed to free itself of much of the burden that its traditional mode of hiring had imposed.

The company also stopped granting land to servants intending to retire to the Red River Settlement, which was proving to be a disappointment. By 1825 it had become overcrowded, in the opinion of William Williams, governor of the Southern Department, who recommended that the company detain in the service for a year anyone desirous of retiring to the colony.[117] News of a burgeoning population should have pleased the committee, but the reports of the officer in charge of the district suggested that it was entirely the wrong kind of population. According to Robert McKenzie, the colony harboured people who depended on the company's charity or preferred hunting, fishing, and roaming to full-time farming and were too independent to make good servants. To avoid adding to this 'expensive & vagrant class of people', he suggested that, in future, when men applied to retire there they be judged according to whether they would add to the 'prosperity' of the place or prove a burden 'to their old masters as paupers for life.'[118] It might have been this consideration that prompted the council of the Northern Department in 1834 to resolve that no servant could retire to Red River until he had purchased 50 acres, although, many years later, George Simpson alleged that the company had begun to charge servants for their land because free grants had 'occasioned an inconveniently large drainage of men from the service.'[119] It is possible that the prospect of land encouraged more men not to renew their contracts, but what really troubled the committee was that the settlement was not serving the purpose for which it had been founded.

The committee had tried to achieve what its secretary was to describe in 1849 as the 'object of every sound system of colonization': not the reorganization of 'Society on a new basis, which is simply absurd', but the 'transfer to the new country [of] whatever is most valuable and most approved in the institutions of the old, so that Society may, as far as possible, consist of the same classes, united together by the same ties, and having the same relative duties to perform in the one country as in the other.'[120] It wanted to re-create a traditional society in which wages were low because access to small amounts of land supplemented earned income. Wealthy farmers, primarily retired HBC officers whose rank entitled them to larger land grants than ordinary servants, would be the leaders of the settlement, as their designation as 'Principal Settlers' indicated.[121] The company's own hierarchy would be mirrored in the colony's social structure. The humble faced restricted opportunities for advancement so that their labour would be available for those who needed it to build an economy based on the export of agricultural products, while the HBC retained its monopoly of the fur trade. This happy state of affairs had not yet been achieved and might not be if admission to the colony was not better regulated. Charging men for their land was one way of exercising more control over the settlement's development. The committee did not object to this innovation, but, although it had once offered servants grants of 100 acres, it now believed that permitting servants to purchase as much as 50 acres would enable them to become 'small independent Farmers'. The 'great difficulty' encountered by 'Persons of capital' when 'settling in a new Country' was that everyone was in 'that situation' and 'none in that of Labourers, who find it necessary and for their advantage to give themselves to work for others.' It was preferable to establish villages with 'small lots of Five or at most Ten acres' that retiring servants would have to buy, thereby providing 'the means of cultivating exportable Produce afforded to Persons of Capital'.[122]

Nevertheless, the council of the Southern Department passed a resolution requiring men to purchase at least 50 acres of land at 7s.6d. an acre, with payment made to the officers in charge of their posts prior to their departure for the settlement.[123] Then, in 1843 servants from the Southern Department were prohibited altogether from retiring to Red River.[124] By this time, however, the company's attempts to control settlement in Red River were becoming increasingly pointless. Most of the inhabitants were squatters, who never purchased land at all, and the company did not interfere with them. It still gave grants to anyone who applied for them, but people seldom did, probably because they were required to sign an indenture prohibiting them from selling their property without the consent of the governor and the company.[125] It is not surprising, therefore, that the committee came to question the point of making retiring servants purchase land. In 1860, it observed that the purpose of this regulation had been to 'prevent the influx of pauper settlers . . . and to give every new comer, as a proprietor of Land, an interest in the Colony', but the rule had been frequently ignored and was 'felt a great hardship in cases where it was enforced'. The committee thus recommended its abolition.[126] This regulation probably appeared particularly unfair after 1857 when, at Simpson's suggestion, the company once more offered land grants to new recruits. Labourers would receive 25 acres and tradesmen 50 on the completion of five-year contracts, plus the promise of more of the same quantity of land after an additional five years.[127] But in 1862 the council of the Northern Department requested that grants to servants engaged in Europe cease until an examination of the unoccupied lands had been made. The following year, at the request of both councils, the committee abolished the custom of granting land at Red River to retiring servants.[128]

The Retention of Paternalism

The elimination of the non-monetary benefits its servants had enjoyed for so long did not mean that the committee abandoned its paternalistic outlook. When, in 1823, Simpson wanted to increase wages to attract labour and raise prices at the same time, the committee declared it 'a vicious system' to give high 'nominal wages' and 'look to seducing the men into extravagance, and imposing upon them by charging an undue price for their goods as a compensation for these high wages.' Anyway, the plan would not work with men 'possessed of sense or discretion'. The committee preferred low wages and low prices and believed that 'patient and full explanation' would eventually lead the men to see the advantages for themselves. The servants should be 'well paid and clothed' and expenses could be kept down by hiring 'really effective' men, eventually resulting in a 'great Saving and facility in provisioning the posts'.[129]

Twenty-five years later the council of the Northern Department adopted the measures that Simpson had recommended, but then had to rescind them because the committee refused to approve them. If higher wages were necessary to attract men, the committee observed, they would be raised, but to increase prices at the same time was 'not defensible in point of principle' and the men would soon see that they were no further ahead. The 'great objection' to this 'alteration' was that the men had to purchase at the company store. If they could buy elsewhere, the HBC could charge what it wanted. Clearly, the committee did not wish the company's character besmirched by insinuations that it oppressed its workers through the hated truck system. Moreover, the committee pointed out, these remarks applied 'with equal if not greater force' to the treatment of the HBC's Hawaiian labourers. It was 'far from right' that they were paid £30 a year, but were charged 140 per cent on the invoice prices of the goods they bought, while European labourers, earning £17, paid only 50 per cent. Necessary labour should be paid for 'at its full value' and the Hawaiians should not be punished for being 'more useful . . . than other servants'. No distinctions should be made in the prices of goods sold to servants on account of the wages they received.[130]

The committee still felt obliged to ensure that its servants received fair treatment, as defined by itself, of course, not by the servants. It did not approve of the overtly manipulative strategies that Simpson favoured. He possessed a more modern view of the servants, seeing them less as subordinates to be ruled and guided than as human resources to be deployed for the benefit of those who had purchased their labour. Thus, in 1844, he suggested that the company provide luxuries like tea, sugar, and a 'finer description of clothing' for the men to buy in order to prevent both 'dissatisfaction' and the accumulation of 'the large credit balances' that 'give rise to a feeling of independence, which at times may be attended with inconvenience.' He had no objection to their being able to retire 'with a little means', but it was 'unprofitable and impolitic to put them in a condition to retire while their services are required, some of the men being young and in the prime of life.'[131]

Simpson probably did not care how little those means were, but the committee did. It was disturbed that year by the 'great proportion' of men recently returned to Canada from service in HBC territory either without wages owing to them or in debt to the company even after many years in the service. As a result, they were 'disaffected' and 'so refractory' on the voyage home that their officers had 'little influence over them'. They frequently deserted along the way, consumed excessive amounts of rum, and left a trail of 'disorder'. To permit the men 'thus to get into debt', contrary to its instructions and the resolutions made by the governor and councils, was 'extremely discreditable to the management' of the gentlemen in charge 'inasmuch as it combines neglect of duty and indifference to the interests of the Concern'. Not only did the company thereby lose the sums advanced to the men when they engaged, but it also suffered a 'loss of character by the state of poverty' in which the men returned to their homes. 'Effectual measures' had to be taken to put a stop to 'a practice so injurious to the service'. The council of the Northern Department soon after resolved that servants re-engaged on the east side of the mountains to serve in the Columbia Department would not be given their freedom until they had served three years and had not less than a £50 credit balance. The councils of both the Southern and the Northern departments also passed measures designed to encourage the men to 'economise their means & . . . be prevented from indulging in extravagance of any kind as much as possible.'[132] Although intended to preserve the company's reputation, such measures did reflect a genuine concern for the welfare of the workers. Moreover, this concern extended beyond the men's periods of employment.

For officers who made a career in the HBC, retirement meant leaving paid employment and living on their savings and pensions from the fund established for that purpose. Their subordinates rarely remained in the service for life but moved on to other work. This departure was not, however, a complete break. Former servants and their families turned to the company in times of need. They saw the relationship between themselves and their employer as more than a cash transaction and the fact that the committee often provided aid both reinforced this notion and indicated that it shared this view. Indeed, the committee sometimes went to considerable effort to help, as the case of William Tomison indicates. Tomison, engaged in 1836, left the service only two years later in such bad health that he could no longer take care of himself and he was placed in an asylum in Bethnal Green at the company's expense. Documents found on him were addressed from South Ronaldsay and in 1840 the committee's secretary inquired of Edward Clouston, their agent in Stromness, whether Tomison had any friends there who could look after him. The committee was willing to transport him to an asylum there and grant him an allowance of about £10. Both a parishioner named William Bews and a sister residing in Stromness declared themselves willing to take Tomison in, and Clouston was asked to investigate and determine which of them was the fitter guardian. Clouston's judgement in favour of the sister was accepted and Tomison was sent off.[133] The committee was also willing to reward long, faithful service. William Linklater's 39 years of toil were acknowledged with an 'allowance' of £6 per annum, beginning 1 May 1856.[134] Naturally, not everyone was so fortunate.

James Johnston, after receiving £5 because of injuries sustained on the voyage to Rupert's Land in 1847, applied for a pension in the fall of 1851. His request was denied even though it was submitted by William Ross of Stromness, who testified to Johnston's disability and provided a doctor's certificate declaring that his hernia made hard labour impossible and that 'he appeared not to be possessed of robust health.'[135] David Robertson, who had injured his leg in a sawmill accident in the Columbia Department in 1835 and sought aid after his return to Britain in 1839, was informed in 1840 that the committee did not think he had 'any claim', but in consideration of his 'distressed situation' he would receive a 'donation' of £5. But he was not to expect 'any further relief' from the company. In 1845 he re-entered the service, returned home in 1851, and, on the grounds that his injury made it impossible for him to 'labour for his own support', petitioned for 'such Gratuity or Pensions' as the committee deemed appropriate until he could work again. A doctor's certificate stated that Robertson suffered from extensive ulcers, but the committee remained unconvinced of its obligation to provide assistance in this case.[136] Neither of these men was so incapacitated or had served long enough for the company to consider pensions appropriate.

Like the rest of the commercial élite, the members of the HBC's London committee intended their philanthropy to help tide individuals over difficult times, not to encourage idleness or discourage self-sufficiency. Therefore, when Peggy McLeod, having lost her husband and three sons, asked in 1861 that her brother, John, then in the company's service, be permitted to return home, the committee not only granted her request, but presented her with a 'small amount of aid' in the meantime.[137] Of course, good deeds also benefited the company's reputation. Its donation for the support of the destitute family of the recently deceased John Groat, despite his having died in debt to the company, prompted Edward Clouston in 1844 to comment that 'such acts of benevolence raise the Company in public estimation.'[138] Like other nineteenth-century employers, the HBC was expected to support good works directed at the underprivileged and needy. It donated to such worthy causes as the Destitute Sailors' Asylum and the Seaman's Hospital Society and received appeals from such organizations as the Thames Church Missionary Society, formed in 1844 to minister to 'the vast floating population on the Thames' by means of a 'Cruising Vessel of Worship and Pastoral Visitation'.[139]

Still, whatever bounty the London committee was prepared to dispense to worthy unfortunates and however willing it was to support Victorian philanthropists in their relentless search for groups upon whom to impose religion and morality, the purpose of the company was, as always, to make a profit. To do so, the committee had always been prepared not only to trade furs but to exploit whatever other resources its territories possessed. By the mid-nineteenth century, the areas where fur-bearing animals flourished had shrunk and, although the HBC still dominated the fur trade, the future seemed to lie elsewhere. The take-over of the company by a group of British financiers who organized the International Financial Society in 1863 was a step in that direction. The society purchased control of the company with the intention of developing the country's resources 'in accordance with the industrial spirit of the age', as its circular offering stock to the public put it. The fur trade would continue on lands unfit for colonization, while the southern part of the territory would be opened up under 'a liberal and systematic scheme of land settlement'. The HBC's personnel and establishments, so conveniently already present, would be the means whereby the company would 'inaugurate' the new policy.[140]

This change in direction was to bring home to the officers more forcefully than ever just how mistaken they had been to think that they were partners. They were not consulted when the members of the London committee sold their shares to the IFS and were treated, as some officers protested in 1866, 'as menials who could be transferred wholesale without explanation or notice, to different concerns'. They, not the shareholders, would be most affected by alterations in the business, but the 'home shareholders . . . received the opportunity to retire with a high premium, while the Trade was forced to chew the end in silence under the new order of things.' The accuracy of this description was demonstrated repeatedly during the next five years. Their claims for a share in the profits from the sale of the London headquarters, in the proceeds of the transfer of the territory to Canada, and in the sum paid by the American government in compensation for the loss of territory in Oregon were all denied. Much debate over the officers' status ensued. The new shareholders did not see the officers as partners and would have liked to put them on straight salaries. They also believed that the fur trade was doomed to disappear as soon as 'civilization' came to Rupert's Land and they expected to reap the benefit of this transformation in the form of enormous profits from the sale of land. But the directors did not wish to alienate those upon whom the conduct of the business depended. They therefore terminated the old Deed Poll, reimbursed the officers for their contributions to the retirement fund, and in the new Deed Poll of 1871 allowed officers to continue to receive shares in the profits until 1893. But they also introduced the rank of inspecting chief factor to visit the districts, audit the books, report on everything, and suggest improvements, tasks previously the responsibility of the chiefs of the trading districts.[141] Although they could still see themselves as 'wintering partners', the officers had learned that neither their old nor their new masters saw them in this way.

For the majority of the employees, the change in ownership made no difference, but something new *was* in the offing. When in 1863 James R. Clare complained about the 'insubordination among the servants', Thomas Fraser, the committee's secretary, did not reply with exclamations of outrage at such mutinous conduct. Instead, he remarked that the men's behaviour was 'much to be regretted', but it was 'difficult to suggest a remedy to the discontent which will occasionally occur among men who have entered upon a novel service in a Country and with occupations so different from those which they have left.'[142] A century earlier, the committee would not have shrugged off disobedience so casually. Not that discipline had lost its importance, but the committee's new scheme did not require a subservient, indentured workforce. If its plans were successful, most of its employees would be managers and the small number of fur trade employees it required could be easily recruited from those who settled on the land it was going to sell. However, its ambitions were premature. In 1869, when the opportunity came to make a fortune by selling most of its territory to Canada, while still retaining millions of acres and a right to trade in furs, it took advantage of it. Someone else would now keep order in the territories for which it had for so long been responsible, while it could attend strictly to business. But that business was still primarily the fur trade. Therefore, a change in its traditional mode of hiring was not necessary.

The relationship between the committee and its employees was not, of course, the same as it had been in 1770. It was more distant. It had also reduced the non-monetary benefits it offered to its servants so that the latter now had to bear most of the cost of their maintenance. The HBC's hierarchy had become more rigid and the lower ranks more solidly entrenched at the bottom. But the company remained a paternalistic organization. In 1870 a servant still promised to 'faithfully serve the said company as their hired Servant . . . and devote the whole of his time and labour in their Service and for their sole benefit', to serve 'by day or by night . . . as he shall be required to do', and to defend the company's property 'with courage and fidelity'. He pledged neither to 'absent himself from the said service' nor to 'engage or be concerned in any trade or employment whatsoever except for the benefit of the said Company and according to their orders.' In case of 'any wilful neglect or default' committed by him when in charge of the company's goods, the loss or damage caused thereby would be covered by a deduction from his wages. He also promised to give a year's notice of his intention to leave or to re-engage, failing which he was obliged to remain in the service for another year. Moreover, he was to remain a 'hired servant' until a ship arrived to take him home. 'Upon condition of the due and faithful service . . . in like manner as aforesaid, but not otherwise', he would receive his wages. If he deserted or neglected or refused duty, he would have to pay for his passage to Europe and forfeit his wages 'for the recovery whereof there shall be no relief either in Law or Equity'.[143] The contract that most company employees signed still described a traditional master-servant relationship, even if the committee saw that relationship in far less emotional terms than its predecessors.

3

The Source and Supply of Labour

> *I pray you to send me Some country lads, that are not acquainted, with stronge drink, that will woorke hard, and faire hard, and are not debauched with the voluptuousness of the city.... send over yearely 5 lykly country lads of 17 or 18 Years of age, and let their tyms be 7 years, so that before their Tymes be out they will be lusty Younge-men, and fit for your service both at sea, and land, and at small wages... if England can not furnish you with men, Scotland can, for that countrie is a hard country to live in, and poore-mens wages is cheap, they are hardy people both to endure hunger, and could, and are subject to obedience, and I am sure that they will serve for 6 pound pr. yeare, and be better content, with their dyet than Englishmen*[1]

This was Governor John Nixon's advice to the London committee in 1682. It was still hiring workers from the most convenient source—London and its environs—and Nixon's comments reminded it of the dangers of recruiting from urban areas, the necessity of having properly trained employees, and the existence of a pool of labour with a reputation for hardiness, docility, and cheapness. As a result, the committee soon embarked on a new policy to which it would cling for the next 200 years: it looked to areas where traditional social relations prevailed and where, therefore, the lower orders were supposed to be accustomed to hard work, low wages, and obedience. That the committee never abandoned this policy does not mean that it actually succeeded in supplying the company with the type of employees it wanted, for recruitment was not simply a matter of gathering up all the eager hands offering their services. Like the other aspects of the relationship between the HBC and its workers, recruitment was subject to negotiation. Furthermore, no single group ever became the source of infinitely loyal and dedicated servants that the HBC wanted. But, whenever the men it hired failed to work out as expected, the committee did not conclude that its assumptions were faulty. Instead, it always tried to find another, equally marginal group, which would behave as anticipated. The committee did not deliberately set out to follow this pattern. Rather, the pattern developed as the committee learned what kind of qualifications its workers needed, and this became a habit once it discovered men willing to join year after year in the Orkney Islands.

The first Scots entered the service in 1683, although the committee continued to hire London men with backgrounds strangely incongruous with the fur trade: Henry Crouch, a fishmonger; Ralph Knight, a merchant; William Bright, a haberdasher; and John Lawson, an apothecary.[2] It also began to take apprentices, but not, as Nixon had suggested, necessarily from the countryside. Nor did its approach to apprenticeship resemble that of other joint-stock companies, which offered opportunities for corruption and private trade that attracted even the younger sons of the gentry. Instead, like the early industrialists who could not persuade adult males to enter their factories, it took parish apprentices and the pupils of charity schools.[3] The HBC's recruitment of apprentices mirrored its general recruitment policy: it indentured the children of the poor, whose social marginalization promised to foster in them the same virtues that geographical isolation fostered in men from the fringes of the British Isles. Apprenticeship was the customary means by which children learned trades, but parish apprenticeships were apprenticeships for labour and were intended to prevent pauper children from being a burden on the ratepayers. Education was secondary. Overseers of the poor disposed of such children according to the provisions of the Poor Law, binding them out to anyone declaring himself willing to provide support and instruction. Normal apprenticeships were entered at the age of 14 and lasted seven years, but pauper apprentices could be bound over at a much earlier age and boys might have to serve until the age of 24 and girls until the age of 21 or until they married. It was a system in which masters frequently abused, neglected, and even abandoned their apprentices, while the latter were virtually slaves, condemned to years of drudgery and exploitation.[4] Most employers, however, were unwilling to take very young children because it might be years before they became profitable. Those with pauper children to dispose of would have found the HBC's interest most welcome. Also, since apprenticeship was one way of gaining a settlement, i.e., the right to live and receive relief in a particular parish, every child removed from a parish was one less burden for the future—and no parish was further away than Rupert's Land. For the HBC, such apprentices, though young and uneducated, promised to provide long-term, reliable workers who had grown up in the service and for whom, therefore, the HBC had become their family.

Most of the company's apprentices came from charity schools, in particular, Christ's Hospital in London, known as the Blue Coat School, and the Grey Coat Hospital of the Royal Foundation of Queen Anne in Westminster. These institutions, unlike most charity schools, which, like workhouses, were designed to prevent vagrancy, offered an education that was more than the inculcation of discipline, humility, and obedience. They taught navigation, surveying, and mathematics, which made their pupils particularly attractive to the HBC, particularly by the 1770s when it began to expand inland.[5] Hospital boys were older and better educated than the pauper apprentices and intended 'to rise to higher Stations in the Compys Service according to Merit',[6] but all apprentices, regardless of origin, had the chance to become skilled and useful and rise to whatever ranks they were qualified to fill. The HBC thus offered its apprentices opportunities that surpassed what children of their class generally faced and, no doubt, the committee assumed they would recognize their good fortune and make the most of it.

One should not, however, assume that all benefited equally or even had the same ambitions, for their situation was not necessarily conducive to success and their careers varied considerably. John Hinson, for example, was a parish apprentice bound out to the HBC in 1708 at the age of eight to serve until he was 21. His contemporary, Joseph Adams, was five years old when he was indentured in May of 1705 to serve until the age of 24. In 1719, both were 'disconsolate', but Adams learned to read and write, spent several years in charge of Albany, and retired to London in 1737 as a gentleman, while Hinson died from 'excessive hard drinking' in 1727. Samuel Hopkins, a Blue Coat boy engaged in 1715 for seven years and sent to Albany to keep accounts, ran away in October of 1722 and stayed with some Natives until the first of May. A few weeks later he tried, unsuccessfully, to run away again because, he complained, he had been forbidden to leave the fort without permission. The committee subsequently discharged him and resolved never to hire him again. William Clowes, apprenticed in May 1737, was whipped in May 1739 for 'severely cursing and damning' his master, Thomas Bird, 'wishing' Bird dead, and 'neglecting his watch'. 'Indeed for Vileness', Bird commented, 'I never saw his Fellow, and do realy believe few in any Gaole in England can of his age out do him in Wickedness.'[7]

It was obviously impossible to predict how the company's apprentices would turn out. Some of them appear to have been as unmanageable as popular opinion declared apprentices to be, although they could not participate in the riotous apprentice subculture that existed in England. One cannot presume, however, that they were unaware of it or that their behaviour was uninfluenced by it.[8] Nor should one forget that many apprentices did not join the HBC voluntarily and might have resented their situation. Besides, even if they were young and poor and had been supported by their parishes or lived in charity schools, one cannot assume that they had no ties to family or friends, or that they became as attached to the company as the committee hoped. But even if each apprentice did become a loyal, dedicated, and perfectly trained employee, the apprenticeship system alone would not have supplied the company with all the workers it needed.

The HBC and the Orkney Islands

The London committee could not staff its posts with little boys and teenagers. It needed able-bodied labourers and skilled tradesmen, adults whose characters and habits were already fully developed. For these, the committee looked northward to Scotland, as Nixon suggested, although it did not need Nixon to make it aware of the benefits of doing so. By the late seventeenth century, the 'Celtic Fringe' of Scotland, Ireland, and Wales had become what Michael Hechter has called 'internal colonies' of England, their economies subordinated to the interests of their English overlords and their populations regarded as good sources of cannon fodder and cheap labour. This unequal relationship was maintained both by force and by the denigration of indigenous cultures, resulting in 'a cultural division of labour' in which cultural distinctions were 'superimposed upon class lines'. Underdevelopment, poverty, and differences in social organization were attributed to cultural backwardness and the resulting ethnic stereotypes ensured that the people of the fringe were relegated to certain economic roles. The Irish, vilified as drunken and lazy, were unlikely to appeal to employers who wanted disciplined and diligent workers. But Scots were seen as 'dour, dogged, honest, hard-working, and superlatively thrifty', an image created by the Scottish élite to counter condescending English criticism of Scottish backwardness, though Highlanders were an exception. They were still looked down upon as 'idle predatory barbarians'.[9] The London committee probably knew little about the Orkneys, if the reference of Alexander Henry Sr in 1775 to Orcadians as 'Highlanders, from the Orkney Islands'[10] is any indication. The Orkneys actually bore no resemblance to the

Scottish Highlands, culturally or otherwise, but their location might have led Englishmen to suppose that they did. What mattered, however, was that Orcadians seemed to be Highlanders who were primitive but not barbaric and who possessed all the Scottish virtues. Furthermore, since the company's ships already stopped at Stromness in the Orkneys for supplies on their way to North America, hiring Orcadians was also convenient.

Expediency probably accounted for the first Orcadian recruits, picked up in 1702 to make up for the failure to hire sufficient men in England. That by 1722 company ships were stopping regularly for both provisions and men[11] was due to mutual satisfaction with the arrangement. A series of poor harvests from 1695 to 1702 had caused considerable hardship and meant that the HBC appeared on the scene at a critical time. Continuing crop failures ensured that service with the company remained very attractive. It offered long-term employment and wages that, at £6 a year, were low but still better than the alternatives, especially because HBC employees received the necessities of life and could save most of their wages. Agriculture was the main economic activity on the islands, but Orcadians also accepted

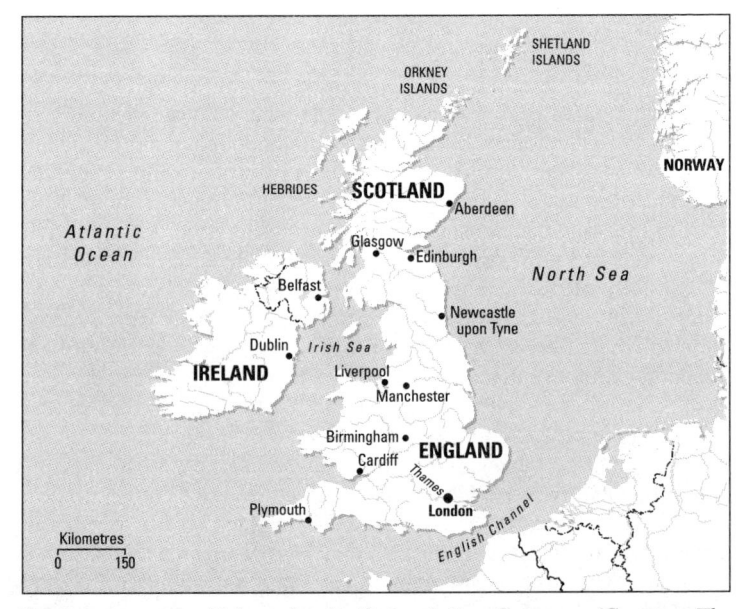

European sources of labour for the Hudson's Bay Company. (Courtesy *The Software Toolworks World Atlas* CD Rom. Copyright The Software Toolworks Inc. and Electromap Inc.)

Orkney Islands of Scotland

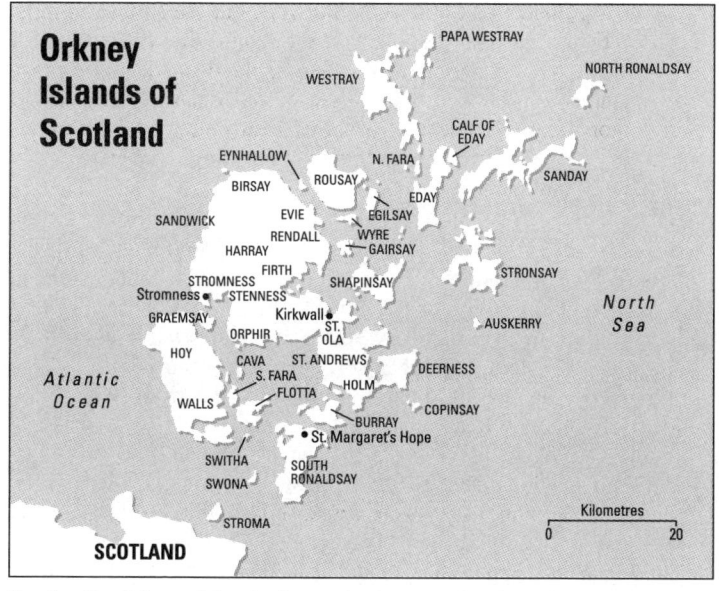

[Map showing the Orkney Islands with labels: PAPA WESTRAY, WESTRAY, NORTH RONALDSAY, EYNHALLOW, N. FARA, CALF OF EDAY, SANDAY, BIRSAY, ROUSAY, EDAY, SANDWICK, EVIE, EGILSAY, RENDALL, WYRE, HARRAY, GAIRSAY, FIRTH, STROMNESS, SHAPINSAY, STRONSAY, Stromness, STENNESS, GRAEMSAY, Kirkwall, AUSKERRY, ORPHIR, ST. OLA, HOY, CAVA, ST. ANDREWS, DEERNESS, S. FARA, HOLM, FLOTTA, COPINSAY, WALLS, BURRAY, St. Margaret's Hope, SWITHA, SOUTH RONALDSAY, SWONA, STROMA, SCOTLAND, Atlantic Ocean, North Sea]

Scotland's Orkney Islands, in particular, provided a convenient pool of cheap, hardy labourers.

seasonal employment as fishermen, whalers, and seamen. The cash income from such wage labour helped individuals set themselves up as farmers or pay the rent on the family holding. The HBC presented a better opportunity to accumulate savings than other employers, thereby making it easier for Orcadians to hold on to their land and preserve their traditional way of life. For the HBC, the Orkneys seemed to be an ideal source of labour. Not only was the population already accustomed to leaving home for extended periods, Orkney society was still a traditional, pre-industrial one. The islands appeared to be an unspoiled oasis on the northern margins of Britain where men were habituated to subordination, uncorrupted by the vices of the city, and cheap, and where, as an added bonus, a harsh climate also made them hardy and well suited to the rigours of life in the fur trade.

But Orcadians were neither as unworldly nor as passive and their islands neither as rocky nor as isolated as the London committee believed or fur trade historians tend to portray them. The Orkneys had long had international trading links and the population produced goods for trade and worked in the fishing, kelping, and whaling industries. Nor did Orcadians live in a harmonious, pre-industrial society in which, as Peter Laslett has put it, 'every relationship could be seen as a love relationship.'[12] People were poor and hungry not because the climate was harsh and their agricultural techniques were backward, but because they received only a small share of the fruits of their labour. The islands were usually self-sufficient in grain, but the majority of Orcadians were tenant farmers and most of what they grew went as rent to their landlords, who exported it and pocketed the profits.

The major landowners, descended from Scots who had flocked to the islands in the sixteenth and early seventeenth centuries in search of position and economic opportunity, had no emotional ties to the islands or their inhabitants. Their interest in their tenants extended only as far as their ability to pay rent. Failure to pay meant eviction and destitution, unless friends or relatives could provide assistance. There was no system of poor relief. Merchants and landlords also dominated the fishing and kelping industries. Far from being independent producers, Orcadian fishermen and kelpers were seasonal labourers earning meagre wages that never reflected the enormous profits their toil generated for their masters, who controlled all the conditions under which they were employed, supplied equipment and provisions, and charged their cost against the men's wages. Many Orcadians were perpetually in debt. Relations between ordinary Orcadians and their superiors were thus exploitive, the latter greedily monopolizing as many resources as they could, dividing up even the rocks and usurping the rights to the seabirds that nested upon them.[13] Such circumstances did, indeed, produce men who 'were used to working hard for not much reward, and were able to endure much without complaint',[14] but the *ability* to endure hardship without complaining is not the same as a *willingness* to do so. Nor did it blind Orcadians to the true nature of their relationship with their employers, as even commentary usually taken to support the Orcadian stereotype suggests.

In 1750 Murdoch Mackenzie, grandson of a bishop and master of the grammar school at Kirkwall, observed that Orcadians were hardy and capable of 'an abstemious and laborious life', but, 'for want of profitable employment, slow at work, and many of them inclined to idleness.' They were 'sparing of their words, reserved in their sentiments, especially of what seems to have a connection with their interests; apt to aggravate or magnify their losses, and studious to conceal or diminish their gains.' They were also 'tenacious of old customs tho' never so inconvenient' until shown the superiority of the new by their successful adoption by one of their own rank. Though 'honest in their dealings with one another', they were 'not so scrupulous with respect to the master of the ground', running up debts to him while settling speedily with everyone else, a state of affairs arising from the 'absurd and unpolitic custom of short leases, racked rents and high entries'. Other observers commented on Orcadian superstitions, such as the placing of knives in the walls of houses to protect against attacks by fairies and witches.[15] One might see in this evidence a picture of a quiet, conservative people with a tendency to indebtedness. Or one might see such descriptions as the slightly condescending remarks of members of the élite of a society in which there were economic and cultural divisions that contained at least the seeds of class conflict. The humble members of Orcadian society might not have possessed the class-consciousness of an industrial proletariat but they would have known that they had little in common with the Murdoch Mackenzies of the world, and this knowledge would have remained with them and even been strengthened when they accepted employment as fishermen, whalers, seamen, or HBC servants.

Orcadians joined the HBC for their own reasons and, like all workers, negotiated any arrangements into which they entered. Their harsh existence may have endowed them with hardiness, but it also taught them that it was necessary to make the most of the limited opportunities available to them. They joined the HBC because it offered better wages and longer terms of employment than other employers and, while fishing or kelping generally resulted only in eternal debt, a man could leave the HBC with savings. The Orkneymen's appreciation of these benefits and their willingness to engage year after year earned them a reputation for being 'strictly faithful to their employers, and sordidly avaricious'.[16] This rather smug view was not, however, an accurate one, although the ease with which the company could attract Orcadians during the first half of the eighteenth century and the success of its modest operations would lull the committee into complacency. But it was bound to lead to consternation when Orcadians demonstrated that neither their fidelity nor their avarice was limitless. Orcadians joined the HBC for economic reasons. Their earnings could help them acquire or secure a hold on the land, set up in trade on their own, or simply stave off penury. Recruits tended to be young, mostly in their early twenties, and more than 40 per cent of them were the eldest sons in their families. They came from the 'middle and lower ranks of island society' and were 'typically' the 'unmarried sons of small tenant farmers, craftsmen, and cottagers'. During the eighteenth century, the average age at marriage of a male Orcadian was slightly over 30, making it possible for a man to serve two five-year contracts before settling down.[17] Employment with the HBC thus fitted into the traditional life cycle and, in fact, helped to preserve it.

But even working for the HBC did not guarantee prosperity, as John Nicks's examination of recruits from the parish of Orphir from 1780 to 1821 suggests. Nicks concluded that 'most returning servants could have afforded to become farmers if they had wished to do so.' The figures upon which he based this statement suggest that men could accumulate savings. Nicks was able to calculate that most men served for eight years or less. In his sample, the mean savings of the three labourers who served for eight years was just over £62. Six of the 28 labourers he studied spent more than eight years in the HBC and they were able to save more. The largest sum saved was £107 19s. One labourer who served for 11 years saved £99 11s.5d. Higher-ranked servants could, of course, do better. The one tradesman employed for eight years managed to accumulate a little more than £170. Since taking up an average holding in Orphir required an investment of £40 to £60 in the first year to pay the £10 rent and buy livestock worth £30, the average servant could have established himself on a farm. In doing so, however, he would spend most of his savings, leaving little to fall back on if he became ill, his crops failed, his cow died, or he fell behind in his rent.

The absence of surviving tenancy records for the major estates made it impossible for Nicks to learn how many of the men he studied actually became farmers or how successful they were. He did determine, however, that one-third of the long-service employees and one-quarter of the career employees rejoined the company after several years at home. He accounts for this pattern by suggesting that some men missed the freedom of life in the fur trade and their friends and families in North America, while others were seeking to escape from domestic or personal problems.[18] These are reasonable conjectures, but, given Nicks's contention that economic motives drove men to join the HBC in the first place, it is odd that he would ignore the possibility that they rejoined for the same reasons. At the same time, his conclusions serve as reminders that simplistic economic explanations of the men's actions are inadequate, as do the London committee's assumptions that Orcadians kept signing on because of their desire to save money.

The committee believed that its servants had the most to gain by accepting the terms they were offered and then doing as they were told so that neither fines nor improvidence jeopardized the growth of a nest egg for the future. After all, for most labourers and craftsmen, service with the HBC was only one of a variety of employments they would pursue over the course of a lifetime and was suited only to men in their prime. The committee insisted on *'Stout, able & active'* recruits 18 to 30 years old, although it did accept men as old as 45,[19] and expected them to carry out their duties, undistracted by families or other interests and responsibilities, and then depart to make way for fresh hands. Lifelong service might well have resulted more from an individual's failure to leave at the right time or economic difficulties that forced him back than from a conscious decision to make a career in the HBC. In any case, a man's survival both during and after his stint with the HBC depended on the preservation of his health and physical fitness. Without these, money was of little benefit, since no servant could—or expected to—save enough to retire to a life of leisure. An individual's actions thus depended on calculations in which money was only one factor and his exertions on the company's behalf depended on whether the rewards outweighed the risks. Men joined the HBC when it offered better terms than other employers and, once in the service, continued to act in their own interests, which were not always best served by unquestioning obedience. As long as the company's operations were limited to a few posts along Hudson Bay, its manpower requirements were small and getting a regular supply of inexpensive men was not difficult. But once competition made it necessary for the HBC to send men inland, the service, although still on the whole an attractive proposition, now made new demands on its employees and these intensified the negotiation that had always been part of the recruitment process. Since there was also almost uninterrupted warfare until 1813, labour was in short supply and workers had the advantage. But the committee's mania for control and economy made it a poor negotiator. It refused to make small concessions that might have reaped substantial benefits.

For example, in the summer of 1788, the men at York Factory would not leave for their winter posts until the officers promised to ask the London committee to have its ships stop in the Orkneys on their way home to drop off returning servants instead of taking them to London. The expense of their journey home from there used up their savings, thereby defeating the whole purpose of joining the HBC in the first place, not to mention making the promise of free passage to and from Britain, which the contract guaranteed, a rather hollow one. William Tomison, an officer at the factory, suggested that a small wage increase might solve the problem. He also reported that the ships' captains favoured this measure as a way of attracting better men and observed that 'infirm, and Cripples constitute the whole at this place (Tradesmen excepted).'[20] The committee, however, altered neither the ships' route nor the men's wages. Instead, a few years later, it sought to impose a solution from the top by trying to find a more responsible recruiter who would, presumably, supply the company with hardier workers less given to whining. The company still relied on its ships' captains to hire Orkneymen and they seemed entirely too careless in their selection. Like other employers, the HBC gave departing servants certificates of good character if they had proven satisfactory. It would re-engage only those who could produce such certificates. But men whose 'infirmities' obliged them to leave the country also received such certificates 'as encouragement to others' and they were also being rehired. In fact, Joseph Colen reported in 1790, the previous season one captain had sworn in public 'that *if any person whatever applied to him without a limb or otherwise infirm he would have engaged them provided they brot one of the Companys printed Characters with them signed by any of their Chiefs.*' As a result, Colen complained, nearly half of the 57 men stationed at York Factory were 'objects for Hospitals & . . . a burden to the Factory'. He recommended that the certificates report both character and physical condition.[21] Accordingly, the next year the committee directed that the men's fitness and ages be reported on the certificates and also appointed an agent, David Geddes, in Stromness, to take charge of hiring in the Orkneys.[22]

The committee never liked to admit that it did not control the recruitment process, and its members saw the root of the problems not in what they were offering to recruits but in the poor quality of the men themselves. Certainly, weak and sickly men were unsuitable, but they were there not just because the captains were negligent but because fitter men had either been pressed into the army and navy during the French Revolution and the Napoleonic Wars or they simply had preferred to seek employment elsewhere. The committee's approach was unlikely to woo them back, but this would not matter if the company could reduce its dependence on Orkneymen in the first place. It therefore contemplated recruiting French Canadians. Dipping into the labour pool heretofore the preserve of the HBC's rival held out the promise of procuring more energetic workers who, moreover, came from a social milieu similar to the one that made Orcadians so attractive. Indeed, as Alan Greer's examination of the fur trade and French Canada indicates, the NWC's recruitment strategy in Canada bore a strong resemblance to the HBC's in the Orkneys: it hired in rural areas, drawing on 'land-owning peasants' who could support themselves between 'stints in the Northwest'.

Canadian recruits were young, their careers in the fur trade were short, and they used their wages to maintain their traditional way of life. For the population of Sorel, a major source of workers for the

NWC and, after the merger, the HBC, employment in the fur trade was a 'normal part' of the *habitant*'s life. Like the Orkneys, Sorel had an economy based on subsistence agriculture and temporary wage labour, but, in its case, poor soil and low productivity meant that it could not produce wheat, the only available cash crop, and fur trade wages, rather than the proceeds of wheat sales, provided the funds *habitants* needed to pay their debts. Sorel, therefore, 'remained a community dominated numerically by peasant proprietors, encouraged by fur trade wages to multiply despite the poverty of their agriculture.' Like the communities that later supplied seasonal labour in the lumber camps, Sorel was backward and poor because the domination of merchant capital prevented economic development.[23] The recruitment of 'Canadian peasants' who were 'brought up to the Service from their Infancy' thus was not an illogical step,[24] but what the committee had heard of them suggested that this was a risky proposition.

The Canadians might have been more willing to travel and live with the Natives than the Orcadians were, but they were neither deferential nor submissive. They were accustomed to setting their own pace and doing much as they pleased, and their work habits were so irregular that to some observers they hardly seemed like work habits at all. Thus, in 1779, George Sutherland, a young HBC man forced to travel inland with some Canadians, was appalled. 'Never', he declared, 'did I see such a parcel of lazey fellows as these frenchmen are and they are fit to Eat the divel and smoak his mother for they must stop and smoak and Eat at Every miels End.' They were 'lazy sons of bitches', never starting before seven, eight, or even nine o'clock in the morning, when they should have been off at four. They objected to tracking, i.e., towing canoes through shallow or rough water, saying that the 'anglois are not better then slaves and that their feet are made of stell [*sic*].' That it took four Canadians to track his canoe, which Sutherland was sure it would take only two of the HBC's men to do, convinced him 'of the truth of the common fraze that one English are always able for two french.' He wondered how they would ever get where they were going because they had 'no master to rule them so that Every wane dous as he thinks fit.' When their stock of flour began to get low, they did not, as Sutherland thought they should, prudently reduce their daily allowance and he feared that starvation would be the result. Nevertheless, they did eventually arrive at Sturgeon Lake, where he and his clerk built a hut and spent a miserable winter. Without provisions and unable to catch fish, they turned to the nearby Canadian post for whatever assistance it could render, which was slight.

Sutherland's visits provided him with small escapes from his bleak existence and further exposure to Canadian unruliness. Their Christmas celebrations convinced him that they were 'heathens'. According to their custom, they fasted all day Christmas Eve and went to prayers at midnight. Immediately thereafter 'the General call was Sacre dieu donnez nous La Sheudive nous avons un Sacre faim and Such Stuf that is god damn you give us the kettle for we are all damned hungary. . . .' Everyone then partook of the kettle of Indian corn that had been prepared for the feast, drank their drams, and then danced until two in the morning. Christmas Day was celebrated with another dram and a substantial dinner and Sundays were spent dancing, drinking, and playing cards. What Sutherland saw made him wish that he had 'only as much to doo with them' as he had with his 'old shoes'. Even their own master considered them 'a parcel of grouling Sons of bitches' and complained that, if any of them died of hunger, which was 'too often the case', the rest would 'make a terrible compleant to the ouners' that he kept some alive while he let others starve. For all their faults, however, Sutherland reported, they were tough and hardy and willing to live on fish and corn, and they understood 'the management of canoes in falls very well' and carried 'very heavy loads'. By contrast, at Fort Albany, with which he was familiar, there was no one 'capable of conducting a large canoe up one bad fall'. The company's men learned to perform only the 'Slavish and disagreeable duty' of cutting wood and tracking that 'any lumper' with enough strength could carry out:

> when the men come from the Ship the first work he does is to go to henly with the Boates. now if a man be lazier then the others the Stearsman calls out ho lo you white jacket, (perhaps he does not know his name) haul you lazy son of a whore you dont haul a pound. now he sees that he is taken notice of he mends his pace and hauls the Boat against the Currant by main Strength. this is well Enough where Strength puts it forward. but Such men as these are as incapable of working large Canoes as I am to be Bishop in the Church of Rome. . . .

Without Canadians and large canoes, Sutherland predicted, the company would 'do nothing' inland.[25]

The committee was not yet ready to introduce a large number of such unruly individuals to its service and it adopted instead a very cautious and therefore also very ineffective policy. Rather than sending recruiters to Canada, the committee directed its officers to encourage any Canadians in the neighbourhood to sign up, but only if their contracts with their former employers had expired. Instead of matching the wages paid by the NWC, the committee offered £15 a year for contracts as short as two years, confident that, once the men saw that the HBC did not charge 'exorbitant' prices for its goods, they would appreciate that they could live better and save more than on NWC wages.[26] With most Orcadians still entering the service at £6 a year, the recruitment of Canadians represented a significant increase in the cost of labour. To compensate for this, the committee planned to take advantage of the Canadians' familiarity with voyaging and living off the land to carry out the inland business with temporary outposts of log tents instead of larger, permanent establishments. This strategy would reduce both the quantity of provisions and the number of men that had to be imported. The Canadians' 'Fidelity' would be ensured by their recognition of the HBC's superior terms and by a prudent mixing of Canadians and Europeans.[27] Indeed, it thought such mixing might 'excite an emulation and in the end, tend to the more speedy Improvement, in the Knowledge of the Country'.[28] The company's British servants had other ideas.

Given Orcadians' reluctance to expose themselves to the discomforts of inland service, Joseph Colen's observation in 1788 that they considered themselves second to none in their ability to bear 'fatigue and toil' must have prompted a few snide remarks from the members of the committee. Even worse, instead of manifesting itself in enthusiastic trekking, this manly pride expressed itself in 'threats . . . not to return Inland with those of another Country'. Three years later the officers at York Factory reported that rough treatment was driving Canadians out of the service. British servants objected to getting into the same canoes with them because, they said, 'the Canadians were not from their town.' Lest this behaviour be attributed to tribalism, however, it is important to note that the men had been 'very disorderly' when their demands for wages were not met and most of them were indifferent to the company's offer of a 40 shilling bounty to build canoes. Furthermore, almost all of the inlanders were drawing for the balance of their wages, which the officers suspected was partly to prevent their wages being stopped for refusing duty.[29]

HBC servants were also quick to threaten to defect when their demands were not met. Only a few years earlier it was said of the men arriving at York Factory from the interior that 'one and all carryed things at a high hand' and with the 'most insulting and threatening Language' declared that 'if their terms were not complied with', they were 'resolved to enter into the Canadian Employ as soon as they *arrived in England* for they were determined to do all the injury they could to the Honble Company.'[30] Making Canadians feel unwelcome in order to keep them out of the service was not, therefore, necessarily a display of ethnic solidarity. It was a way of preserving a monopoly of employment with the HBC and an ability to combine to increase wages and exert control over working conditions. Faced with such hostility and the equally strong antipathy of some of the HBC's officers,[31] Canadians were unlikely to tolerate lower wages, too, not that the company's passive strategy supplied them in sufficient numbers. As a result, no significant influx of new men came to the company's rescue. Meanwhile, despite the Orcadians' resentment of newcomers, the HBC's popularity was plummeting in the Orkneys.

In 1794 the Reverend William Clouston reported that 'murmurs' had 'been excited in this Country against the Company' due to 'the small encouragement' given to men in its service.[32] Some of those murmurs may have belonged to the Reverend Francis Liddell, who complained in 1797 that Orcadians left their homes to become 'slaves in a savage land', forced to 'assume the manners and habits of beasts', dragging loads of timber 'yoked as a team, like beasts of burden' for 'the paltry sum of £6' instead of staying home and cultivating the land or 'offering an honourable service to their King and country' by joining the army or navy.[33] Rather than trying to silence its critics by increasing wages, however, the committee repeated its order to hire any Canadians who offered their services and gave 'permission' to hire the grown sons of servants.[34] In 1797, to hang on to the men it already had, it prohibited anyone from going home unless he could be replaced in the Orkneys. Such blatant disregard for its servants' wishes, not to mention ignoring the notices of intention to withdraw from the service, could only blacken the company's reputation further, while its inability to procure regular supplies of men made the order impossible to carry out.[35] Indeed, the continuing labour shortage meant that every year those whose contracts were up could demand wage increases.[36]

The committee thus found it necessary to soften its stand. It therefore followed David Geddes's suggestion to permit three-year contracts during the war instead of the five-year agreements it preferred because he asserted, erroneously as it turned out, that those engaged for these terms would not 'think of returning home' at the end of their first contracts. It also raised wages for new labourers from £6 to £8. The short-lived declaration of peace with France in March of 1802 prompted the committee to insist once more on five-year contracts, but, with so few men engaging and so many leaving, it felt compelled to continue the 'War Wages lately given' and the usual bounty of 40 shillings for inland service to persuade them to join 'freely'. The company needed 120 to 150 men, but Geddes was not to let anyone know how desperate it was.[37] The servants already possessed too great a sense of their own importance. Unfortunately, peace between Great Britain and France lasted only until May of 1803 and the HBC had to continue to allow three-year contracts. Even so, Orcadians remained reluctant to engage.

The company had done nothing to combat the grumbling that the Reverend Clouston had brought to Geddes's attention in 1794 and its reputation was subjected to new attacks. In 1802 it was rumoured 'all over the country' that the company's ships carried no provisions because during the previous two years the men had, according to William Tomison, 'been almost perished to death' on the voyage to Rupert's Land because the trips had taken longer than expected and rations had almost run out by the time they arrived in Hudson Bay. As a result, men previously set to engage had changed their minds. Tomison suspected that one of the captains was responsible for this story,[38] but there was more to Orcadian dissatisfaction than one captain's rumour-mongering, as the insolence of William Tilloch suggests. Reprimanded for negligence while unloading a ship at Churchill in August of 1804, Tilloch threatened to 'post the Character of this Factory on the doors of the Churches in Orkney', which was where the HBC's recruitment notices were affixed. It would not do to have defamatory statements alongside them, particularly one referring to Churchill, which was already one of the most unpopular posts.[39] Tilloch's threat suggests that he knew he would find a receptive audience. Indeed, by the following year there was a 'combination' among servants, former servants, their friends, and their relatives to raise the HBC's wages. But rather than legitimate discontent, the committee saw only the 'tricks' of opponents and vowed to use 'every resource by natives or foreigners' to break the conspiracy and 'thwart' its enemies. It sent recruiters to Caithness and Sutherland, considered hiring in the Shetlands, and pondered the establishment of recruitment agencies elsewhere. It also offered two guineas to each recruit, paid once he was safely aboard ship at Stromness in June. These plans came to nothing,[40] but the following year the committee drew up an elaborate system of bounties to entice men into its employ.

New hands engaging for three years would receive four to eight guineas and servants re-engaging for the same term would receive as much as 12. For those who agreed for four, five, or more years, bounties would increase in proportion. The committee was also willing to hire 'stout & active Lads' under the age of 15 and, to spur Geddes on, it raised his allowance of 10 shillings for every man he hired to one guinea. For men earning as little as £8, these bounties amounted to significant sums and the committee's willingness to spend so much testifies to its desperation, but parsimony and caution won out again. Fearing that these incentives would encourage men to 'abuse the Liberality of the Company' by leaving in order to re-engage and collect the bounties again, it insisted that these rewards would cease in 1805. When the continuing labour shortage forced it to retain them for another season, it abolished them for new recruits.[41] Henceforth, bounties would be used to encourage re-engagements. In 1808 the committee offered 12 guineas to any servant not earning more than £25 who signed a new contract for five years. It also urged its officers to 'make the best Use' they thought 'Proper' of the information that 'every Man of the King's Subjects as soon as he sets foot on British Ground according to the late Act of Parliament must be a Soldier the Local Militia Bill exempts none but the Aged & Crippled.'[42] The spectre of impressment had little effect, but the Retrenching System of 1810 promised to solve all problems and free the company of the 'very inefficient men' it had been receiving.[43]

Recruitment and Retrenchment

The committee had been toying with the idea of a more organized policy of procuring French Canadians. In 1810 Colin Robertson, a former Nor'wester, sang their praises in the hope of being appointed to recruit them in Montreal. He described their skill and love of the country while pointing out that Orcadians joined the HBC 'more from necessity than inclination', never did their duty 'but by halves', refused to endure the slightest hardship, and left as soon as they had achieved their 'darling object of gathering a few Pounds'. Of course, Canadians were accustomed to wages twice as high as those offered by the HBC, but, he was careful to point out, their pay took the form of overpriced goods and the *voyageurs* were so 'attached to the Country' that they did not complain. He predicted that the HBC's modestly priced wares together with the shortness of its summer voyages would give the company 'a preference in engaging men' and, once Canadians had come to appreciate the benefits of joining the HBC, it could reduce wages. Though it was 'determined to send no more' Orkneymen, the committee considered Robertson's plan far too expensive and opted instead to seek workers in the Western Islands (Hebrides) and along the coast of Scotland, where the people were 'of a more spirited race than in Orkney'.[44]

It engaged two recruiters in the Hebrides, another at Glasgow, and one in Ireland, while Lord Selkirk agreed, in return for his land grant, to hire men in the Highlands, hoping thereby to succeed in 'forming an extensive local connection in the Highlands of Scotland & in Ireland'.[45] This ambitious undertaking was intended to acquire men as marginal as the Orcadians but free of the bad habits they had developed in their long association with the HBC. Familiarity had bred contempt. New men, properly disciplined from the beginning and ready to promote the company's interests more vigorously than Orcadians but less expensively than Canadians, would give the company the kind of workforce it needed to set it back on the right track. In return the HBC offered tempting terms: wages as high as £18 a year for three years and grants of land.[46] Such benefits, it was hoped, would attract willing workers, guarantee their diligence, and add to the population of the colony, which would eventually supply both provisions and labour in ample quantities. Until then, however, the HBC was pinning its hopes on men who, though apparently as marginal as the Orcadians, had no reputation for or history of docility. No doubt it hoped that the proverbial ferocity of the Irish and the Highlanders could be turned against the NWC and, if the scheme worked, assure the company of a highly economical victory. Rather than incurring the expense of hiring Canadians, it would triumph by recruiting impoverished Highlanders and Irishmen, unaccustomed to high wages, and by rewarding them with land of no commercial value.

The plans went completely awry. Selkirk's grant was not formally approved until 30 May 1811. The ships, already delayed, had to wait for convoy and a favourable wind and did not arrive in Stornoway until 17 July, where the recruits waited, bored and possibly alarmed by the dire predictions of 'Highlander', really Simon MacGillivray of the NWC, in the *Inverness Journal*. Moreover, Roderick McDonald, the Glasgow agent, had hired 10 labourers for an unacceptably high £25 a year, which aroused resentment among the others. He had also promised the new writers, i.e., junior clerks, high wages, annual increments, mattresses, blankets, and accommodation as cabin passengers. When they learned that none of these benefits would be forthcoming, they joined in the general grumbling. During the last muster of passengers on the *Edward & Anne,* they were informed, in accordance with the Passengers' Act, that they were not legally bound to embark if conditions did not meet the Act's standards, which, aboard this ship, they did not. As a result, many of the men jumped overboard, some into the waiting boat of a 'Captain McKenzie', who was allegedly Donald Mackenzie, the HBC's former agent at

Stornoway turned press gangster for the army. As a result, the company lost the wages it had advanced to the deserters and hastily had to recruit some Orcadian replacements.[47]

Eighty-one men arrived at York Factory in September of 1811, of whom 66 were labourers and craftsmen to be divided between the colony and the fur trade. Miles Macdonell, the governor of the colony, demanded 31 for the settlement, leaving only 35 for the whole Northern Department, which Superintendent William Auld considered insufficient. He also objected to the men's three-year contracts because he believed they would not renew them but leave to take up their land grants, abandoning the company just as they were becoming useful. Furthermore, of the 33 Orkneymen who had arrived, all but one were 'either raw ignorant men or old & useless Servants' who were 'a dead weight'. David Geddes's list indicated that eight of them were 40 years old, but some were 'old factory mates'. One admitted to being 56, although he had first joined the HBC in 1781, while another, 'rated at 30', had first entered the service in 1784. In addition, Auld predicted, the presence of the Irish would lead only to trouble. In fact, he reported, it was 'in a great measure to the dislike of these people' that only one of the men whose contracts expired in 1811 would re-engage and then to serve exclusively at Severn House in order to 'be at a distance from the Irish Men'.[48]

As in the past, the Orcadians, as Macdonell also observed, resented 'the arrival of strangers among them' because they had 'enjoyed the exclusive advantages of the trade for a long time unmixed with any others which might induce them to suppose that no people ought to be employed but themselves.'[49] Auld's pessimism derived mainly from his dislike of Macdonell, the colony, and all the newcomers, and his reports of the winter's events were sensational enough to persuade the committee that it had made a serious mistake. On New Year's Day 1812 a drunken brawl broke out in which some of the newly recruited Irishmen inflicted a severe beating on some Orcadians. A month later a group of newcomers, some of whom were from Glasgow, rebelled and could not be forced back to work until June. William Auld, the superintendent of the newly formed Northern Department and the London committee's main source of information about these two incidents, blamed everything on the newcomers, whom he loathed. 'Every body knows', he remarked, 'a drunken Irishman is synonymous with *Devil Incarnate*.' But the Irish servants had been given liquor and left unguarded, and as a result these 'murderous fiends' had attacked defenceless Orcadians innocently getting ready for bed. This 'atrocious conduct' was 'a too fatal confirmation' that their 'brutal dispositions' made them 'utterly unfit for this Service'. As for the Glaswegians, their misbehaviour was rooted in the fact that that city and its vicinity had, he observed, 'long been notorious for the republican & levelling disposition of their inhabitants' and these 'villains' proved 'the legitimacy of their descent'. The new recruits were 'manufactours out of bread last May & . . . hired to sow their levelling & seditious principles among an ignorant & timid people as the Orkney-men always are.' In fact, four of the men, including William Finlay, were Orcadians and one was a Shetlander, but Auld saw them as 'simple thoughtless boys' led astray by their Glaswegian comrades.[50] It might, therefore, have been he who dubbed the renegades the Glasgow Insurgents, as the group came to be called.

Auld's dramatic and heated reports could not help but remind the London committee of why the company had resorted to the Orkneys in the first place. The Irishmen's behaviour accorded with the popular stereotype, while the Glaswegians possessed tendencies that the committee did not wish to see in the company. Glasgow was an important centre of dissent and its handloom weavers were at the heart of a nationwide organization. In 1812, while the Glasgow Insurgents were defying their officers, Glaswegian weavers were agitating for a minimum wage and the enforcement of apprenticeship regulations. The Scottish Court of Session would approve the weavers' wage proposals, but their employers' refusal to comply with the decision would result in a violent strike in November and December of weavers in Glasgow and 80 other Scottish towns.[51] News from Scotland would only demonstrate the veracity of Auld's version of events and thus reinforce the committee's preference for men from societies where old-fashioned master-servant relations prevailed.

Certainly, the Irish and the Scots did bring with them a potential for conflict. The American and French revolutions had found widespread sympathy in the north of Scotland and the area was inhabited by workers with a history of militancy. Furthermore, the weavers of Glasgow were finding their respectable and comfortable way of life threatened as Irish immigrants, migrants from the countryside, and the urban unemployed flooded into weaving because it was easy to learn, thereby depressing wages and strengthening the hand of their masters. The Irish also had a history of resisting oppression, and the failed revolution of 1798 and the brutal repression that followed would still have been fresh in their minds.[52] The Irish attack on the Orcadians might well have been caused by long-standing tensions that, on a day usually celebrated with excessive imbibing, erupted into violence. None of the participants left an account of the event, however, and it was blamed on Irish ferocity. Of the three Irishmen against whom charges could be made to stick, one agreed to pay £7 to two of the victims, since Macdonell thought it wise to hang on to him because of his 'numerous relatives & connections in Ireland' that might be of use for the colony, but the other two were 'notorious bad characters' who should be gotten rid of.[53]

The Irish went down in HBC history as 'mutinous' and 'addicted to quarreling and fighting', a notoriety reinforced the following year by a mutiny aboard the *Robert Taylor*, carrying men destined for the Red River Colony. According to historian J.P. Pritchett, Andrew Langston, an Irishmen, stirred up dissension by telling the passengers they were being treated tyrannically and that the Scots were being treated better than the Irish. The man in charge, Owen Keveny, one of the recruiters and 'a hotheaded Irishman' himself, was prone to violent responses to the 'most trivial offenses', clapping offenders into irons or forcing them to run the gauntlet. Langston had been subjected to the latter several times. The mutineers, apparently a group of Irishmen from the same town, planned to seize the ship, take it to a country at war with Britain, and sell the vessel and its cargo. But the conspiracy was betrayed and the three ringleaders were subjected to both of Keveny's favourite punishments and sent home on the next ship. There was nothing distinctively Irish about this mutiny. Nor should it be seen as something peculiar to the establishment of Red River or the fur trade. Mutinies were forms of resistance to oppression and bad working conditions. Langston and his followers were behaving according to the egalitarian traditions of seamen who rebelled against injustice and cruelty and sometimes became pirates, which is precisely what the *Robert Taylor* mutineers would have become had their plot succeeded.[54] For those inclined to see men in ethnic terms, however, the mutiny served to strengthen the stereotype. As for the Irish, they were as disappointed with the HBC as it was with them. On their return home, some of them regaled the company's agent in Sligo with 'miraculous storys', one man complaining that for three weeks he had had nothing to eat 'but the bark of willow trees &c.' The agent warned that neither the HBC nor Lord Selkirk 'or any one within 100 miles of' them would ever get any of 'the peasants' in Ireland to engage after the reports of the bad treatment the Irish servants had endured. Indeed, he believed that they had been 'badly used' because all of them told the same tale of being 'half Starved'.[55]

There is no evidence that the committee was unduly distressed by this news, perhaps because its enthusiasm for Irish servants had already begun to wane and it was turning its attention elsewhere. In

1812 the committee engaged the firm of Maitland, Garden, and Auldjo as its agent in Montreal to procure skilled *voyageurs* for the purpose of establishing a firm foothold in the Athabasca district. It requested 20 'Bout de canoe', i.e., men able to work as steersmen or bowsmen, and 10 middlemen, i.e., labourers, who paddled in the middle of the canoe. The middlemen would receive wages as high as £20, the new maximum for labourers in the company, while the steersmen and bowsmen were to be hired as cheaply as possible, probably for no more than the £30 allowed skilled workers and steersmen. These terms attracted no recruits that year.[56] That the committee was willing to go to this trouble suggests that it was feeling hard-pressed. Its recruitment of Scandinavians suggests that it was feeling desperate.

In 1814 it hired 20 Norwegians, two Danes, one Swede, and two Scandinavians of unspecified nationality.[57] The committee was not considering an extensive recruitment campaign in Scandinavia, as it undertook years later in 1853. The acquisition of these men was, like the recruitment policy of its first years and its first engagement of Canadians, the taking advantage of a convenient source of apparently suitable labour, in this case, prisoners of war.[58] How these men were acquired, whose idea it was to hire them, and who made the necessary arrangements are questions the HBC's archives do not answer. No doubt, however, members of the London committee had connections with the authorities who had jurisdiction over prisoners of war and took advantage of the situation to recruit men who came from a part of the world that promised to supply labour well suited to the service. Scandinavia was as isolated and underdeveloped as the northern parts of Britain. Its people were poor, practised occupational diversity, and were accustomed to conditions that made them seem as suited for life in the fur trade as the population of the Orkneys, which had once belonged to Norway. Thomas Malthus, during a six-week visit to the country, had been much impressed by the people, claiming to observe there the workings of the preventive check on population that he wished to see in England.[59] As well-read individuals, the members of the London committee might therefore have thought that Scandinavians would make good servants. They certainly appeared to think so when they assured Alexander Christie that the Norwegians' 'habits & previous employment' would render them 'more useful and expert' than any men he had ever had under his command.[60] They probably also hoped that gratitude for their release would translate into good conduct and that their unfamiliarity with the service would make them amenable to whatever terms the committee proposed. The committee was mistaken.

The Norwegians employed erecting the first station of the winter road to York Factory at what was to become Norway House were dissatisfied and insubordinate. They did nothing but build themselves 'a paltry House' and threatened to give their overseer, Enner Holte, 'a hearty Drubbing'. James Sutherland, sent to check on their progress, reported that they were 'a stubborn Set, and unanimous in their Obstinacy'. Deciding that 'harsh Measures' would be ineffective, Sutherland tried 'Persuasion' and got them to work, but 'in a very unsatisfactory manner', as they refused to be hurried or directed. 'It appears to me', he observed, 'that they never have been accustomed to Subordination or hard Labour and are very unfit for the Job.' The Norwegians, however, claimed that they had been 'deceived in their Engagement' and led to expect European provisions but had to live on fish. They all declared themselves 'completely tired of the Country' and wished 'themselves back again in an English Prison'. Sutherland suspected them of misbehaving deliberately in order to be sent off in the next ship. Holte believed that because they had 'been on an equal Footing with their Superior' while prisoners of war they had become 'so obstinate that they will hardly know any thing of Inferiority.' Thomas Thomas agreed that their imprisonment had 'erased from their Minds every Idea of their Duty as Servants'.[61] None of the other Scandinavians caused trouble, but they did not take to the service. Only one Norwegian and one Dane re-engaged when their contracts expired in 1817.[62]

The Norwegian experiment must have reinforced the committee's desire to ensure that its servants came from suitable sources and, since the war had ended and unemployment was soaring in Britain, it appeared that the HBC would be able to do so. In 1818 the committee expected to acquire men at £15 per annum for five-year terms and considered it unnecessary to offer re-engaging servants, except steersmen and tradesmen, more than £20 and insisted that renewals be for five years as well.[63] Cheapness had rendered the allegedly inactive Orcadians attractive again, but the committee had also appointed another agent in Lewis,[64] which might supply equally cheap but more active men. But the committee pinned its hopes for expansion on Canadians, the first large contingent of whom was recruited in 1815.

The expedition for which they were hired was a disaster, yet it provided valuable lessons on the management of Canadians. First, they complained of not finding their 'Necessaries in abundance' contrary to what they had been led to believe in Montreal. By HBC standards they received 'an immensity of goods', but they wanted their usual equipments and promised to be impossible to satisfy unless they got them. Then, the winter of 1815–16 revealed that, contrary to Colin Robertson's assertions, not even Canadians would continue singing when surrounded by misery. John Clarke, their commander, had established Fort Wedderburn on Lake Athabasca, as well as a number of outposts, and then dispersed most of his men to fend for themselves while he set off along the Peace River with five half-loaded canoes to winter near the NWC's Fort Vermilion. Clarke had taken no provisions with him, assuming that he could trade for them, but the local Canadian master had persuaded the Natives to have nothing to do with his rivals. As a result, 16 of Clarke's men starved to death and some of the survivors, after finding their way back to Fort Wedderburn, took an oath not to do anything else that winter and, if there were not provisions for them, to desert to the NWC.[65] Because the ships carrying the records and furs of that season were unable to leave Hudson Bay in the fall of 1816, news of what transpired during the winter of 1815–16 did not reach the committee that year; even if it had, it would have been too late to affect the preparations for the 1816–17 outfit already under way early in 1816.

As always, the committee stressed economy and control and disliked irregularities of any kind, in this case, having to hire Canadians on terms different from those of the other servants. But, realizing that without them the Athabasca trade could not be established and that 'they would only engage on the terms they were accustomed to & understood', the committee agreed to pay them more than Europeans, but it also charged them more for their purchases.[66] This was the same strategy it would condemn several years later when Simpson suggested it as a way of fooling men into joining up, but necessity, not principle, mattered now. The committee might also have assumed that Canadians, reputedly thoughtless and improvident, did not really care. In any case, the result was that the HBC was charging Canadians the same prices as the NWC, even though the committee had urged its Montreal agent to impress on the recruits 'the advantageous terms' upon which they could outfit themselves with clothing and other necessities from the company's warehouse. This benefit was supposed to compensate for lower wages.[67] But whatever the price, Canadians turned up their noses at the HBC goods. They wanted fine cloth such as calico and corduroy and slops, i.e., cheap ready-made clothing, made out of good material.[68] Clearly, the committee had been arrogant in its estimation of the quality of its goods and, if it hoped to lure Canadians away from the NWC, it would have to give as much thought to the articles it offered its workers as it did to those it offered the Natives. With provisions, on the other hand, it was 'sufficiency' that mattered.[69]

To give the Canadians what they wanted, the company would have to abandon, at least temporarily, its tradition of parsimony. But it resisted. It repeatedly reprimanded the Montreal agency for its extravagance and insisted that the men not receive large advances, since they were 'too strong a temptation to many minds to desert'.[70] The difference between the limits the committee placed on the agent's expenditure and what the agent actually spent was so huge that one suspects the committee had no idea what economic conditions in Lower Canada were. In 1817, for example, the committee ordered the agency to organize an expedition of 80 men at a cost of no more than £4,000 and was most annoyed when it received a bill for £18,056 18s.6d.[71] It was the company's officers, however, who had to live with the results of the committee's stinginess. In 1819 William Williams, appointed governor in chief the previous year, wrote to the Montreal agent himself, urging that 'a few Livres in point of Salary must not be put in competition with the importance of the expedition' and complaining that the previous year's men had been 'the refuse of those rejected from the North West Company'.[72] The committee finally included equipments in the Canadian agreements and also opened a shop at the depot for Canadian servants to spend their wages and 'supply themselves with luxuries'.[73]

Hiring Canadians also meant bearing the burden of transporting them from Montreal to Rupert's Land, the hazards of which were amply illustrated by Roderick McKenzie's journal of 1819–20, a uniquely detailed account of the 'trouble & expense' attending the company's 'business in Canada'. Departure was delayed because the officers 'were kept on the Tramp' rounding up the men, who were getting drunk in 'grog shops' or taking leave of their friends. Even then they did not stop drinking and much persuasion and a few threats were required to get them off. A gale then forced them to land, providing opportunity for more drinking, more visits to friends and taverns, and a few desertions. Once well under way, insolent guides and malingering or worn out steersmen kept the group from travelling as quickly as McKenzie thought necessary. By contrast, the transport of European servants by ship was simple and uncomplicated. Nor did the Canadians' behaviour improve once they reached their winter posts. They evaded work by whatever means they could, pleading exhaustion, broken snowshoes, tired dogs, and ignorance of where to enter the woods. On one trip, two men 'Grumbled' about travelling so late and, after being told by McKenzie that they had no right to complain, observed that 'they were not engaged to the Devil to work day & night.' The season concluded with an argument over whether the men were obliged to return to York Factory with the furs. Some of them considered their contracts finished early in May, on the dates they had engaged, not at the end of the outfit as was customary in the HBC. Dissatisfaction with this arrangement prompted one of them to say that he would neither work nor go to Hudson Bay and 'that he was not at a loss for his livelihood' and 'knew where to apply'. When threatened with forfeiture of the remainder of their wages, one replied that McKenzie 'might keep the whole & walked of[f].'[74]

McKenzie's journal could only strengthen the image of Canadians as volatile and insubordinate. Moreover, their misbehaviour was more costly than that of their British counterparts because they represented a greater investment. Their wages were higher and they insisted on ample provisions and expensive goods, which took up space that could have been occupied by trade goods. The journey inland provided plenty of opportunity for the men to abscond or indulge in behaviour that slowed the brigade's progress. A long delay could mean that the men arrived in Rupert's Land too late in the season to go inland for the winter, depriving the company of their services as well as burdening the Bayside posts with extra men. Furthermore, their skill and experience gave them considerable control over the speed with which they travelled, while their familiarity with the NWC made it easy for them to desert to the rival company whenever they became dissatisfied. As a result, as McKenzie discovered, they were not perturbed by the thought of losing their wages. They had less to lose by their desertion than the HBC did, since they would probably be welcomed by the NWC, to whom they might reveal the HBC's secrets, and would encounter no difficulty finding employment in the fur trade either in the interior or in Montreal. Canadians, like the other servants, knew their value and were prepared to take advantage of it when their contracts expired, making what the officers considered 'exorbitant' demands, which, unless sufficient replacements were sent, had to be granted. They would even hold off re-engaging until they saw how many men arrived from Canada in hope of extorting 'extravagant' wages. So serious was this problem that even Colin Robertson, once so enthusiastic about Canadians, proposed that some of them be replaced by Englishmen and boats.[75]

Cautious as ever, however, the committee was not prepared to hire enough Canadians to deprive those already in the service of their power, as its officers recommended. It ordered 40 winterers for 1820 in spite of Governor Williams's plea for at least 100 to make the company 'independent' of the men in the interior and their demands.[76] Williams's complaint that the Northern Department was undermanned met with the response that the 420 European and 350 Canadian servants on the books were quite enough. Indeed, the cost of their wages suggested that, unless returns were larger, the workforce should be reduced. In fact, the committee declared, it would send *no* Canadians for the next year and servants whose contracts were up should be re-engaged to save the expense of bringing new men from Montreal.[77]

This was a foolish economy. Any savings would probably be more than matched by the increased wages that old servants, their position strengthened, would demand, not to mention the loss of trade to the NWC, which did not skimp on manpower, provisions, or forcefulness. Perhaps a perusal of the company's records made the committee realize that its decision was unwise, since in October of 1820 it directed the Montreal agents to engage 100 men, although still with an emphasis on moderate wages.[78] It must have realized, too, that it could not overpower its servants with an influx of Scots. They were still in the majority, but their interest in the HBC appears to have been declining. Of the 591 men listed in the 1818–19 servants' list, 51 per cent of the 567 for whom birthplace is recorded came from the Orkneys and just over 18 per cent came from other parts of Scotland. But almost 79 per cent of the Orcadians had been in the service for five or more years, while only slightly more than 27 per cent of the other Scots had been there as long.[79] Though not conclusive, these statistics suggest that the company's favourites were becoming less receptive to its overtures. Certainly in 1819, the 'extraordinary wages' offered by herring curers lured away some potential recruits, while the return of many young men 'disabled by frost &c' deterred others, prompting one observer to suggest that, rather than allowing such men to make an 'unfortunate impression upon their companions and Country men', they be allowed to go to the colony instead. The company should also provide all servants with 'facilities to send home good accounts' and urge old hands to stay in the service.[80]

The difficulties involved in importing men were probably the reason for the committee's decision to turn again to apprenticeship to supply itself with 'a body of valuable attached Servants'. This time, however, these apprentices would be the 'half breed' sons of European labourers taken on in their mid-teens for seven or 10 years and trained as tradesmen or canoemen or employed hunting furs or provisions. In return they would receive £5 or £6 a year, which covered the cost of their clothes. But the proposed apprentices 'spurned the lowness of the Wages', leading Governor Williams to declare angrily that they could 'shift for themselves, this class have been too long an expensive burthen to the Posts throughout the Country.'[81] Unlike their pauper predecessors, however, the sons of HBC employees had more attractive opportunities available to them, including the defiance of the company's trade monopoly. It might have been the failure of this scheme to attract apprentices as well as the desire to free the posts of unproductive young men that prompted the council of the Southern Department to make such apprenticeship compulsory in 1839. Henceforth the sons of servants were to be separated from their families after the age of 15 and engaged as apprentice labourers or tradesmen for terms of seven years, which they would spend in the Northern Department. A parent who did not consent to this arrangement would be discharged.[82] The indifference that greeted the plan in 1819 did not alarm Williams or the committee, since its benefits were not expected to be immediate anyway. Then, in 1821 the merger promised to solve all the company's problems and raised hope that it could revert to a more sedate and less expensive mode of business.

Recruitment and the Merger

Only 'efficient valuable Servants' would be retained, those 'only useful during an opposition' would be eliminated, and Canadians were to be re-engaged for no more than a year.[83] Orcadians were available for £15,[84] which would now be the starting wage for Orcadian labourers, and presumably also other Europeans. Canadian middlemen would start at 400 *livres,* the equivalent of £20. The wage for European steersmen and bowsmen would be £22 10s., while Canadians would get 600 *livres,* with small additions when work was 'more severe' and conditions harsher. Skilled workers would receive no more than £40 and interpreters no more than £50.[85] As usual, however, the servants did not accept these innovations unquestioningly. Canadians resented the wage reductions so fiercely that George Simpson feared 'a Mutiny and other serious consequences'. As a result, their wages ranged from the equivalent of £30 to £40 for middlemen and £35 to £60 for steersmen and bowsmen, depending on where they were posted. They also continued to receive equipments of blankets, tobacco, beads, cloth, mittens, and knives. British servants were less successful in their resistance, but labourers and steersmen ended up receiving £2 more than specified.[86] By the summer of 1823, however, after one of his conspicuously strenuous expeditions in which he had managed to reach Cumberland House in record time by means of a boat and crew of exhausted Orkneymen, Simpson concluded that much of the company's transport could be conducted by boats instead of canoes, a plan that would help deprive the servants of the ability to thwart the company's plans.

Simpson introduced boats in the Athabasca district first, intending to extend their use wherever possible. Boats could carry more cargo more securely with fewer men than canoes and permit a reduction in the number of servants, particularly of costly Canadian *voyageurs,* and a more judicious mix of men. Canadian skill and activity and Orcadian cheapness and steadiness would balance one another, while Irishmen and other Scots, both of whom Simpson condemned as 'quarrelsome independent and inclined to form leagues and cabals which might be dangerous to the peace of the Country', would become scarce in the service. Under the impression that the Orkneys were suffering massive unemployment, Simpson urged that a few men under the age of 22 be procured on five-year contracts at £12 a year, thereby facilitating the reduction of wages throughout the service, for the old servants were still resisting the new terms, although half the Canadians re-engaged in 1823 had relinquished equipments, a concession that Simpson considered 'a great point gained'.[87] The committee hoped, however, to eliminate Canadians completely and resort again mainly to the Orkneys for men.[88] Now that the rivalry had ended, the company wanted to benefit again from the Orcadian virtues of steadiness and cheapness, the attractiveness of which had no doubt been enhanced by their apparent absence from the characters of Canadians, Highlanders, Irishmen, and Norwegians. But times had changed in the Orkneys.

During the next few years, most recruits were former servants who, complained Simpson, could not 'shake off their indolent and luxurious habits' instead of young men whom the company could 'mould' to its wishes. But these young men preferred the good wages that could be earned in the Greenland and Davis Strait fisheries.[89] Consequently, the company had to continue to recruit in Canada, where its popularity was in sharp decline. In 1825, McGillivrays, Thain and Co., the HBC's Montreal agent since the merger, reported that men returning from the interior were 'in such bad humour' that none would consent to return and 'they have spread their opinions over the Country.' They would 'not hear of the wages' and seemed 'to have taken an absolute disgust at the Service *tout est changé, on est regardé comm des chiens* is in every bodys mouths. . . .' Another 'dreadful cause of complaint' was the 'system of mulcting them of wages', which they complained made it 'uncertain what they have to depend upon.' Undiscouraged, the committee declared that once the new system was 'perfectly understood' and the good treatment of those hired that year eliminated 'that unpleasant feeling' about fines, the agency would have no difficulty finding 'Stout Novices'.[90]

Simpson, of course, denied that there were grounds for complaint at all. Fines were rare, he declared, and never since the beginning of the fur trade had the men been 'so well clothed, so well fed, so lightly wrought, so rarely maimed in maintaining proper discipline and subordination, in short so comfortable and happy in every sense of the word and so peaceable well behaved and well disposed' as now. The problem was the 'wretched selection of new hands' from both Canada and the Orkneys. The agents paid no attention to their instructions, he complained, but kept making promises the company could not keep and recruiting totally unfit men. The solution was to hire 'a few young Half breeds annually at Red River' on three- to five-year contracts to fill vacancies as they occurred. If brought into the service at an early age, he observed, they would become 'useful steady men' and prove 'the cheapest and best Servants we can get.' Indeed, Red River would 'from hence forward be found the best and cheapest nursery for the Company's Service.'[91] News from the colony and Simpson's own report after two lots of Red River recruits suggested, however, that he was unduly optimistic.

According to Roderick McKenzie, the settlement had become home to 'old and worn out' former servants, mainly Canadians with 'half breed' families, living off the company's 'charity' and spending their time hunting and fishing. In Britain these had, of course, by the early nineteenth century become the sports of the gentry, perquisites of their social position protected by game and land laws. Among the lower orders, such diversions were distractions from duty. As a result, McKenzie accused the Métis population of living in 'idleness' and holding 'in contempt the quiet toil of the industrious Colonist'. Like Murdoch Mackenzie noting the idleness of Orcadians in 1750, Roderick McKenzie's class bias made it impossible for him to see anything other than constant, regular toil as real work. He also held the prevailing view of the Métis as inclined by race to unsteadiness and indolence and concluded that their preference for 'a hazardous idle and roaming life' over 'independence in a settled and laborious one' meant they would become a 'permanent burden' on the company and perhaps even endanger the peace through horse stealing and 'other acts of plunder'. It was unlikely that they would ever 'be brought to support themselves in a stationary industrious course of life' or that they would make good servants, because 'at the least disgust or slightest hardship they disregard all contracts and desert to their old haunts in the plains—far beyond the reach of the Companys power.'[92]

Simpson agreed that their indolence made it difficult for them to adjust to the 'laborious duties' of the service and he deplored the ease with which they could 'escape' from the company when things were 'not exactly to their fancy'. In fact, desertions were so frequent, he claimed, that one-third of the Red River recruits were sure to disappear 'when their services are most required'. Their recapture required 'great good management and address' in order to avoid 'differences with Indian and half breed relatives, which in the present circumstances of the colony would not be politic.' Nor could the Red River men be hired for less than the standard £15 to £17, although, since they were already in Rupert's Land, hiring them eliminated the expense of bringing in Europeans or Canadians, whose trip from Montreal also led to 'not infrequent' desertions. Still, he did not despair 'of making these people useful' and believed that in a few years 'every man required to recruit our Establishments may be had from thence.'[93] Simpson was mistaken again.

Two years later, Francis Heron reported that labourers at Red River could earn as much as five shillings a day and men transporting goods to York expected £7 a trip. He had managed to persuade some to work for him at Brandon House, in spite of the measly £10 he had to offer for a nine-month term, by getting the governor of Assiniboia to agree to equip them at the Fort Garry shop from the *'Cream'* of the goods. They had insisted on large advances at the prices granted to settlers because they considered themselves 'still on the footing of Settlers, and *not regular* servants of the company, by reason of their temporary engagements'.[94] Clearly, these men possessed a sense of independence not welcome in those consigned to servant status. Of course, they *were* more independent. The HBC may have been the biggest employer in the area, but the local population had other sources of subsistence to which they could resort each time their periods of employment ended. Hiring them for short terms allowed the company to be free of their maintenance the rest of the time, but each time they were hired new negotiations over agreements ensued in a labour market that did not favour the company. Indeed, the company's terms seemed to attract mostly men who might 'be considered Boys'.[95]

The company's need for labour had been increased by the merger because it now had establishments from the Pacific Ocean to the coast of Labrador. The territories west of the Rockies presented the greatest challenges: competition from Russian and American traders; the expense and difficulties of provisioning; and the establishment of good relations with Aboriginal peoples, some of whom were hostile. Fortunately, the HBC was able to take advantage of the presence of

Sandwich Islanders, who worked aboard ships that plied the Pacific and were also regularly recruited by other traders. Sandwich Islanders were very cheap, paid only in food and clothing, until 1823, when Chief Factor John Dugald Cameron allowed them £17 a year, the same as the rest of the servants, among whom this innovation had 'occasioned much dissatisfaction'. And 'very naturally so as they are by no means such serviceable people', commented Simpson, displaying an unusual tolerance for servants who dared to question the decisions of their masters. In this case, their protest resulted not in heated denunciations of their insubordination but a reduction of the Hawaiians' wages to £10, saving the company some money and demonstrating its thoughtfulness. Because they had a reputation for honesty, submissiveness, and bravery, however, Simpson considered Sandwich Islanders 'valuable in establishing new Countries' and suitable for employment as guards or in 'common drudgery about the Establishments'. In 1824, therefore, he recommended adding 15 more to the 35 already in the service.[96] For more skilled work, Simpson recommended Canadians, whom he considered 'better adapted for Columbia voyaging' than the Orcadians, and he suggested that the former be transferred to the west while the latter served in the east,[97] thereby overlooking both the committee's desire to hire no more Canadians and the continuing reluctance of Canadians to engage. Indeed, Simpson's suggestion could not be carried out.

The agency at Lachine could never guarantee a supply of men because Canadians still objected to the reduced wages and the abolition of equipments, while new opportunities lured them away. In June of 1830, François Boucher reported that three of his four recruits had disappeared and were allegedly working as canal labourers. Another recruiter, John Crebassa, traversing the countryside in search of men, expressed surprise at finding none 'but worthless fellows' appearing to sign up at William Henry, in the parish of Sorel, once an important source of workers for the NWC. Now the young men of the parish turned to other employments and most of them had left to work in the timber industry, which, Crebassa said, they preferred to wintering in the interior. He thought that higher wages might lure them back.[98] Although it recognized that the 'improved condition of Canada' had increased the price of labour, the committee refused to offer more because to do so would be tantamount to reverting to the 'extravagant wages' of 'opposition times'.[99]

The fur trade thus ceased to be an important part of Lower Canadian life. In 1843, Simpson responded to criticisms of the quality of men sent to the Columbia Department by remarking that the recruits had been 'fair specimens' of those who had applied and that it was now 'quite impossible' to acquire bowsmen and steersmen in Canada 'as canoes have long fallen into disuse there.' They were now 'principally used' in the Columbia Department, which had become 'the great nursery for canoemen'. Of course, the chances of finding satisfactory men were not improved by rumours of 'extreme ill-usage', which had made that department 'unpopular' with Canadians and non-Canadians alike.[100] The Columbia Department could not rely on Canadians for its labour, but employing them in the Montreal Department was not wise either because this was as risky as employing men from the Red River Colony close to the colony. They were too much at home and, therefore, harder to control. In 1844, therefore, Simpson recommended that Orkneymen replace all the Canadians there,[101] though by now he should have known better.

The Search for New Sources of Labour

Since the merger, the fittest and hardiest Orcadian men had demonstrated a strong preference for other employment, particularly in fishing and whaling fleets, leaving the HBC with puny youths and worn-out old men who displayed 'a great aversion to leave the coast'. The Northern Department was supposed to supply workers for the Columbia Department, but, when ordered across the mountains, many Orcadians feigned sickness and asked to return home. Therefore, in 1830, Simpson recommended the recruitment of 20 Lewismen as labourers specifically for the Northern Department. He was confident that their clannishness could be controlled by mixing them with Orcadians and Canadians, and he warned against stationing them in the Southern Department, where the proximity of free traders and Canada would tempt them to desert. Accordingly, the following year the firm of W. and R. Morison became the company's agent in Stornoway, but it procured only 12 men. It supplied 40 the next year, but they proved 'exceedingly stubborn and difficult of management, and so clannish' that it was 'scarcely possible to deal with them singly'. As a result, the company turned again to the Orkneys only to discover that young, fit Orcadians were whaling or emigrating to Australia. Thus it was forced to resort to Lewis again, and in 1839 to Caithness and the Shetlands. But there was full employment in Caithness, and the Shetlanders and the Orcadians considered the HBC wages too low and its period of service too long. The arrival of the whaling vessels doomed the company's efforts. By the end of April its agent, Edward Clouston, had hired only six men, all Orcadians. Clouston was puzzled by such 'backwardness to engage'.[102] The committee lashed out in indignation at 'those inconsiderate people losing sight of the many advantages the Fur trade holds forth to them', particularly the ability to save most of their wages. If this attitude persisted, it would raise wages and prices and then see how the ingrates felt about the standard £17 and lower prices. Furthermore, if the Orcadians continued to be so unco-operative, the company would abandon them altogether and resort to Ireland, where labour was cheap.[103]

The failure of the whale fishery and the poor state of the cod and herring fisheries in 1841 must have raised Clouston's hopes, but that year 'some grumblers', having returned from North America, were spreading 'unfavourable accounts of the service' and undermining his efforts. In Caithness, meanwhile, there was more interest in emigration to the Canadas than in the HBC. Clouston ended up with only 11 men, three of whom changed their minds at the last minute. He warned the committee that if this case of defaulting was 'passed over', others would follow. Instead, baffled by the Orcadians' reluctance to enter its service since it had 'always heard' that they were 'well treated' and the wages were 'fully as high as they could obtain in other quarters', the committee decided to carry out its threat to pass them by. It would abandon them for a year or two, by which time they would 'feel the loss' and become as eager as ever to join. Until then, it would recruit in Lewis and the Shetlands.[104] However, of the Lewismen who arrived in Rupert's Land, three were found to be completely unfit for the service and were sent back immediately, while some of the remainder were so 'slender' and 'diminutive' that Chief Trader James Hargrave feared they might be 'too weak' for the work required of them. Nor were they sufficiently 'tractable'. The committee, therefore, abandoned its plan to snub Orkneymen and added a selection of Shetlanders to the men sent out in 1842. They proved as small and sickly as the Lewismen. Nevertheless, both of these new groups became permanent components of the HBC's workforce. In fact, Lewis became the most important source of European servants after the Orkneys—at least 500 men, by Philip Goldring's estimation, came from Lewis from 1830 to 1890.[105]

The committee's decision to seek men in the Outer Hebrides was entirely in keeping with its traditions. These islands were isolated and marginal and the population was attached to its way of life, which was based on subsistence agriculture supplemented by seasonal wage labour. But they were much poorer than the Orkneys and the population had been condemned to tiny, infertile plots of land by 'improving' landlords in search of cheap labour. By the 1840s their already bleak situation was deteriorating further. The kelping industry had collapsed and the price of cattle, whose sale had always been an important source of income, plunged. Highlanders continued to find employment in projects designed to put them to work, such as the construction of roads and canals. Some travelled south to build railroads, worked on farms and in the fishing industries developing in northeast Scotland, or joined the navy or the Greenland fishing fleets. But none of these occupations provided an income sufficient to prevent permanent indebtedness.

The crisis came in 1846, when several years of poor crops were succeeded by the potato famine, which hit the Western Islands the hardest. Those Highlanders who were not evicted in a flurry of new clearances found themselves at the mercy of the Central Board of Management of the Fund for the Relief of the Destitute Inhabitants of the Highlands, which was formed, under government pressure, in 1847 by a number of private relief organizations to deal with the crisis. The board, made up of businessmen and lawyers from Glasgow and Edinburgh, succeeded in making relief 'conducive to increased exertion', i.e., paltry for those who worked and almost non-existent for those who did not. Besides unsuccessful schemes to 'improve' the Highlands by turning its population into cheap labour for new industries or small farmers, the board also encouraged migration by arranging employment and even paying travel expenses if necessary. The proprietor of Lewis tried to find work for his tenants until 1848 when, unwilling to carry on, he asked the board to extend its authority to the island. The board ceased its activity when its funds ran out in 1850. Relief now came through the poor rates, introduced in 1846, which it was the goal of both proprietors and Poor Law authorities to keep as low as possible. They now saw emigration as the solution to Highland poverty and used their influence to ensure the passage of the Emigration Advances Act of 1851, which provided funds to assist landlords in disposing of their no longer profitable tenants.[106] For such people, employment with the HBC was a golden opportunity, although, as the poor physical condition of the recruits indicates, an impoverished population ravaged by disease and famine and shamefully exploited and uprooted by ruthless landowners might not produce a fit and hardy workforce. Still, the company had to make do with whomever it could get. This, of course, had always been the case. Now, however, the situation was further complicated because it was becoming increasingly frequent for men to sign up and then not appear for service. The company was finally to discover just how effective a legal weapon the contract was.

In 1844 two Orcadian servants sent home such bad accounts of their experiences on the coast of Labrador that their relatives petitioned for their release from their contracts and five of the nine labourers recruited for the district in 1845 deserted.[107] In 1847, no men would agree to go there at all, while the demand for labour and good wages in Britain prompted many of the men hired for the Northern and Southern departments to break their engagements.[108] Two years later, when two Shetlanders defaulted on their agreements, the committee decided that it could no longer let such incidents pass and ordered John Cowie, its Lerwick agent, to prosecute the men for breach of contract. The culprits were ordered to pay £100 in damages, but the men were too poor and were committed to debtors' prison, where, as the law required, the company was liable for their maintenance at the rate of 10 pence a day. The committee intended to hold them until they could be forced to fulfil their contracts, but the local sheriff substitute ruled that the petitions submitted for the purpose were incompetent and the matter had to be referred to the sheriff in Edinburgh. He overturned the sheriff substitute's decision, but the company's ships had in the meantime sailed for the Bay. Thus, though victorious, the company was put to considerable expense and lost its men after supporting them during the four months of their confinement.[109] Moreover, although a precedent had been set in the HBC's favour, the legal issue remained unsettled.

In 1851 Edward Clouston offered fresh contracts to some men who had broken their engagements, threatening prosecution for breach of contract if they refused. Only one took any notice of this threat, and Clouston applied to A. Bain in Kirkwall for legal advice. Bain replied that the only course open to the company was an action for damages, in which case the men could be imprisoned until they had paid, but the company would have to maintain them in jail and derive nothing from the prosecution, 'the parties being worth nothing'. However, the men could not be proceeded against and punished by fine or imprisonment as for a criminal offence. Had the action been taken immediately, he believed, they might have been compelled under a summary application to the sheriff to 'find a caution to enter the service' under the terms of their engagements. But too much time had elapsed for this action to be taken now.[110] The committee decided to go ahead with prosecution, following Clouston's advice to wait until late spring when the men were likely to be employed and 'would feel their imprisonment to be a *punishment*'. When they were 'generally idle', they would 'feel but little inconvenience' from imprisonment. The men ended up serving two months.[111] Clearly, the enforcement of the authority that a contract bestowed on an employer was a complicated and costly affair that might not even achieve the desired end. It therefore seemed preferable to solve recruitment difficulties by looking for men in more places so that shortages in one area could be made up by hiring somewhere else. As a result, during the 1850s, the workforce became more diverse than ever.

In 1852 the committee decided that it would have to find all its labourers in Canada, a conclusion that must have made Simpson wonder if anyone had been reading his letters. Only a year earlier he had pointed out that Canadians were attracted to other employment and repelled by continuing rumours of harsh treatment and bad food in the interior and that 'the condition of the lower classes in Canada' had 'improved so much of late years' that HBC rations were 'not very inviting'. Since increasing wages would lead only to 'derangement and inconvenience' and demands for higher wages from those renewing their contracts, he recommended a heavier reliance on European servants. In fact, he proposed that the company get men from Sweden, Norway, or Denmark, where wages were low and which 'a good many years ago' had supplied men 'well adapted for the Service, being easy of management, hardy and efficient'. He suggested a small selection from the 'sea side villages where boating is the principal occupation of the inhabitants'.[112] That the company should adopt this strategy is not surprising, and not only because it had hired Norwegians before. Mid-nineteenth-century Norway, like northern Scotland, was underdeveloped and poor, populated by cottars who mixed subsistence agriculture with other occupations, such as working aboard ships and in fishing and lumbering.[113] Presumably, its belief in the desirability of workers from such a society overwhelmed any memories of the unruly and insubordinate Norwegians it had hired in 1814, especially since they had been prisoners of war and, therefore, exposed to bad influences.

The committee had considered hiring Norwegians several years earlier, but the depression of 1847 and the revolutions of 1848 had resulted in so much unemployment that the measure had seemed unnecessary. Now, in 1852, Simpson wrote to Consul General J.R. Crowe, at Christiania, now Oslo, requesting 20 men to serve on the Pacific coast on five-year terms, 16 as common labourers at £17 a year and four 'superior men', at £20 to £24, to learn English and serve as leaders. He doubted, however, that these wages were high enough to attract any Norwegians worth getting and suggested that Swedes might be preferable and Finns were even better.[114] But Crowe managed to hire 20 'as fine a set of young men as the company can desire', most of whom had 'just served their military turn of servitude with excellent characters for subordination and sobriety'. Several of them were 'accustomed to river boating and shooting, and all to hard work and fatigue.' Their number soon doubled and six tradesmen were also hired for the Southern Department.[115] Unfortunately, the first group of Norwegians travelled to their destination aboard the *Colinda*, whose captain, an uncouth and drunken scoundrel, embezzled the company's stores for his own use and then tried to save himself by goading the passengers to mutiny. Although his plot failed, he pulled the ship into Valparaiso, Chile, and because his behaviour was so intolerable no one would continue as long as he was in charge. However, the *Colinda* was a chartered ship and the captain was one of its owners, so he could not be superseded. The company could order him to repay the sums he had received for the sale of its property, but it could not appoint another captain. As a result, 25 of the Norwegians and all the Scottish coalminers destined for Vancouver Island deserted.[116] Although they had nothing to do with this disaster, hints that the Norwegians might prove troublesome had appeared on the voyage.

They objected to keeping watch aboard the ship, as all HBC servants were required by their contracts to do, claiming that there was no such clause in the Norwegian version of the contract. But they relented when threatened with the loss of pay for every day they did not keep watch and with other unspecified punishments. They also objected to the length of their contracts and complained that their rations did not include tea and sugar.[117] Word of these problems had not yet reached the committee when it optimistically ordered 20 more Norwegians for the following year. This time things went wrong almost immediately. Twenty-one men were hired, brought to England, and put up in the Sailors' Home in Dover to await embarkation at Gravesend. The night before they were to leave, 15 of them ran off to join the Foreign Legion, forcing the HBC to rely on re-engaging servants and possibly Red River men for the Northern and Southern departments.[118] Fortunately, the following year, while the 'prosperous state of Canada' made the HBC's wages too low to attract Canadians and only nine Orcadians and one Shetlander could be found in the north of Scotland, 39 Norwegians signed up. Unfortunately, some of them deserted on the way to England.[119] Another crisis loomed.

Simpson considered the company's workforce defective. He believed that 'the maintenance of order and subordination' required that the servants 'should be of different races', but it had to be the right mix. Men from Red River were unsuitable because of their support for the free traders and thus they needed to be replaced with Europeans, preferably Orcadians. Canadians, even if available, would not do because their 'language and habits' made them 'prone to unite with the halfbreed population'. They also usually married into it, settled at Red River, and swelled 'the numbers of the French Halfcaste community', who 'to a man' opposed 'the Company's rule', which they considered 'adverse to their best interests—asserting and feeling that the soil, the trade and the government of the country are their birthrights', beliefs 'instilled' by the clergy and American traders.[120] 'Red River halfbreeds' had become the majority in the Saskatchewan and Swan River districts and though considered 'active, hardy & well adapted' for the service, they were also regarded as unreliable 'when opposed to their own countrymen' and were 'frequently found plotting against their employers and playing into the hands of the free traders', whom they 'almost invariably' joined when their engagements with the HBC expired. Moreover, they were 'insubordinate and difficult of management', and without 'a preponderance of Europeans' the company was entirely 'in their power'. The Norwegians, like everyone else the company had ever hired, had revealed a 'disposition to combine together in order to resist the authority of their masters'. This judgement reflected Simpson's inability to view behaviour in any terms but ethnicity and his ignorance of the social relations that prevailed in the men's country of origin. There was unrest among the lower orders in Norway and, after 1848, a radical social movement, which the government crushed. But Simpson expected deference from men with rural roots and attributed their behaviour to the fact that they appeared to be of 'the lowest description, runaway sailors, "goal birds" &c' while, 'generally speaking', they were 'not physically equal to Orkneymen, Canadians or Halfbreeds.' Furthermore, their 'mode of life' and their language made it difficult to deal with them.[121] Simpson was right about the language problem.

The Norwegians stationed at Moose Factory in 1854 were so unhappy with their rations and duties that they submitted a petition to H.W. Crowe, their recruiter, informing him that they intended to give notice of their intention to return home in 1855 but had been told that their contracts did not permit them to do so. 'We can clearly see', they complained, 'that the company does not fulfil its Contracts in any one point, but treats us Foreigners as it likes.' Crowe, they charged, had told them they could leave any time after serving two years if they gave a year's notice, as the Norwegian contracts specified.[122] The English version of the contract required a man to give notice of his intention to return home a year before the contract expired and this, of course, was the regulation the officers upheld. Nothing was done to settle the issue, however, and Norwegian discontent grew until it exploded into a strike at Norway House in the summer of 1857. It began with eight Norwegians who, upon their arrival with the Saskatchewan brigade, gave notice of their intention to leave, according to the terms of the contract as they understood it. When this request was denied, they refused to work and were joined by eight of their countrymen who were destined for the Mackenzie River district and refused to embark. These were then supported by the rest of the Saskatchewan servants of all origins, who, Simpson claimed, were motivated by 'a mere spirit of opposition, which is quite rife in the service'. Faced by 120 determined men, Simpson thought coercion both dangerous and impossible and promised to refer the disputed clause in the contract to the committee and accept the interpretation of a Norwegian lawyer. A few months later a London notary's translation supported the men's allegations: the contract had mistakenly required a year's notice if a man wanted to leave the service 'before the expiration' of his contract instead of 'at the expiration'.[123] Still, no one thought of abandoning Norwegian recruitment just yet because it was a way of keeping wages down.

Simpson warned that offering higher wages to attract men 'would probably lead to a "strike" throughout the country for a general advance in the price of labour', and he urged that the company continue to hire Norwegians or Swedes or reintroduce land grants to lure Scots back to the service.[124] The committee tried to follow these suggestions. But land in the Red River Colony had little attraction when land could be had in Australia and Canada with no obligation other than its cultivation, while the complaints of returning servants and a widespread impression that men in the service were not allowed to write to their friends and relatives had damaged the company's reputation in Norway. Also, higher wages in the Christiania area and 'extensive emigration' made it difficult to find sufficient men at the prescribed wages.[125] But the committee, like Simpson, attributed most of the trouble to Crowe's failure to investigate the men's backgrounds properly and ordered 25 to 30 men in 1858, increasing that number to 45 when the company's recruitment efforts in Scotland failed completely.[126]

News from North America, however, suggested that the second Norwegian experiment was a failure. The Norwegians hated the service and their dislike translated into what the officers saw as a general 'laziness, insolence and disobedience to orders'. Such incidents as the theft of a case of cognac, Lars Gulbransen's assault with a knife on the night guard at York Factory, and his fatal attack on another

Norwegian further damaged their reputation. Furthermore, their unruliness was doing 'Much Mischief' because the Orkney servants, seeing the officers' 'total inability effectually to punish such open mutiny', were 'already beginning to show some of the same evil spirit'. Robert Wilson at Oxford House spoke for many officers when he declared the Norwegians 'the most useless Set of Men I ever Saw' and 'a Lazy useless good for Nothing Set of jail Birds for Certainly from thence they are Come and no place else.' Simpson declared that it was better to be shorthanded than to bring to the country 'bodies of disorderly, impracticable men over whom we can experience no controul and who virtually give us law.' He must have been relieved when, in the spring of 1858, 32 Norwegians resigned and only six re-engaged. From now on, Simpson urged, no more than 12 Norwegians should be recruited at a time, and they should be split into two groups to prevent difficulties.[127] The new batch was not even allowed to land until James Hargrave boarded the ship and offered them the opportunity to cancel their contracts. Of the 34 men aboard, only seven chose to stay.[128] Finally, a drunken brawl at Moose Factory on New Year's Day in 1859, followed by a petition from 11 Norwegians complaining about their rations and the hostility of the Natives and demanding to be permitted to go home, prompted the committee to allow not only the petitioners but most of the Norwegians still in the service to leave. It then informed Crowe that it was 'determined to give higher wages to Scotchmen rather than have recourse again to foreigners.'[129]

The committee knew that if it hoped once more to attract Scots in sufficient numbers it would have to alter the terms it offered, so it decided to improve provisions and accommodations and, at long last, increase wages.[130] In the tradesmen class, it wanted boatbuilders, coopers, blacksmiths, and tinsmiths, of whom boatbuilders would receive £30 a year and the others £35. Labourers, of whom 60 or 70 were wanted that year, would receive £22 a year, £23 if they were sloopers. All men, regardless of rank, were promised increases of £5 or more if they did duty as steersmen or postmasters. Besides the usual 'ample' rations, all employees would receive tea and sugar or £2 in cash if they preferred or were stationed where these items were unavailable. For each contract they completed, tradesmen could have 50 acres at Red River, while labourers were granted 25. All recruits were to be 'able-bodied men', no older than 30, and 'of good character and properly recommended', and they were to sign five-year contracts.[131]

The addition of tea and sugar to the ordinary men's rations was due to the new importance of these items in the popular diet, which had certainly been brought home to the committee by the Norwegians' repeated objections to being deprived of them and by such petitions as that of Peter Robertson, who in 1853 had made a claim for an allowance of tea and sugar as well as bedding. He based his case on his understanding of what constituted maintenance as promised by his recruiter. Robertson had been engaged in 1850 at Dundee, where maintenance 'invariably' included tea, sugar, bedding, and ordinary rations allowed in the country. Moreover, the company's officers were sure that this alteration would 'render the people more contented and disposed to remain in the service'.[132] Simpson was also optimistic. These new terms, he declared, would induce 'able-bodied and respectable men' to engage and be 'the means of bringing to the country a trustworthy class of servants, having no interests in common with the natives and Halfbreeds'.[133] He was wrong again.

The Contract as a Legal Weapon

The new agent in Inverness, Duncan Mactavish, reported a 'stiffness of many to engage' because, although the rations and accommodations seemed satisfactory, the wages were no more than what could be earned at home and, therefore, 'not sufficient inducement to serve in a foreign country'. At the same time, emigration to New Zealand and Australia was attracting much interest.[134]

Once he overcame this 'stiffness' to engage, Mactavish faced a 'stiffness' to show up when it was time to leave for North America. He had to threaten three deserters with legal proceedings before they would appear in Inverness and then spent a day there trying to round up his recruits, some of whom had gone into hiding. Most of the deserters were men hired early in the season, and former servants travelling around the country damaging the HBC's reputation had 'prejudiced' some of the recruits against the service. He assured the committee, however, that once the people of this part of Scotland became familiar with the company, desertions would decrease. In the meantime, he had to find a way to deal with the deserters, most of whom had fled the country, and he took legal action against two defaulters, John Mackenzie and Peter Macdonald. Mackenzie was sentenced to 48 hours in prison with hard labour, which Mactavish considered too lenient, but the magistrate had never tried such a case before and Mackenzie's representative had managed to persuade him to impose that penalty. With Macdonald, however, it became apparent again that the contract did not provide for that uncomplicated enforcement of the committee's authority necessary if the contracts were to have any effectiveness at all.

Prior to Macdonald's trial all the lawyers debated the authority of the Master and Servant Act of 1823, under which Mactavish was proceeding, and he decided to get a legal opinion on the matter from his solicitors, the Inverness firm of MacPherson and MacAndrew. They informed him that Macdonald's representative had threatened a suspension if they proceeded on grounds that the Act did not apply to the contract. The Master and Servant Act for most employers was a powerful weapon for the discipline of workers, since it allowed masters to prosecute employees under criminal law, while they themselves could be prosecuted only in civil law. By the second half of the century, in fact, the law was regarded as 'an essential weapon for controlling labour'. But the HBC's situation was more complicated than that of most employers. MacPherson and MacAndrew declared that, if the Act did not apply to the company's contract, there was no way to punish Macdonald unless the HBC had special legislation empowering it to enforce its contracts. Otherwise, a 'procedure at common law' would be necessary, and it was 'so tedious and doubtful' that they recommended against it because 'an action for damages would be of no avail as nothing could be recovered.' But that seemed to be the only route open to the HBC, since consultation with several of their 'professional brethren' had led them to doubt that the Act applied to a contract to serve outside the United Kingdom, where the Act was not in force, although they had found no legal decision to that effect. The firm, therefore, suggested that, before proceeding, Mactavish find out whether the company had a special Act or whether it had been proceeding under the Master and Servant Act and with what results. They urged caution, however, since 'these quasi criminal prosecutions' were 'dangerous' and there were always 'agents ready to take advantage of the least slip and to bring suspicions'. Upon being shown a letter from Edward Clouston regarding the prosecution of deserting recruits in Stromness, they recommended that Macdonald might be sued before the sheriff under the Small Debt Act for any sum not exceeding £12. On conviction, the man could be imprisoned, although the company would have to pay for his maintenance during his incarceration. Clouston had proceeded 'at common law' against three defaulting servants and obtained a decree in each case for half a year's wages. One man escaped, but two were imprisoned for two months and then released on the committee's orders. This action had gained the company 'not a farthing' in damages and it had authorized no further prosecutions. MacPherson and MacAndrew also suggested that the company get a legal opinion regarding the applicability of the Master and Servant Act to its service, since it was the most 'summary and effectual punishment in these cases'. But the committee decided to drop the charges, a prudent move in Mactavish's opinion. Even if 'legal obstacles had not interfered', he observed, to prosecute deserters 'with great severity' would 'render the service of the Honble Company unpopular' and he had 'good reason to believe' that the service was 'likely to become more popular in this part of the Country', which would prevent desertions in future.[135]

The whole affair demonstrated that the company was at a distinct disadvantage compared to other employers when it came to enforcing its contracts. Desertions continued and the company took no further actions. They were simply 'an evil to which the company is frequently subjected and which cannot be remedied.'[136] The HBC had to fall back on the attractiveness of its benefits alone to lure and keep recruits, but they had become much harder to charm. While in the past the company's terms would have been considered 'liberal', reported Edward Clouston, it was questionable if this was still the case. A grant of land had no appeal, since few Orcadians intended to remain in Rupert's Land and would appreciate land there only if, rather than having to reside on it, it was 'placed at [their] disposal'. Reports from Inverness and Stornoway indicated that the company's wages and other benefits could not draw many men there either.[137] The committee, however, still prone to blaming its problems on its agents, severed ties with Mactavish at Inverness because of the 'generally bad character' of his recruits. But an outbreak of typhus at York Factory in 1864 made recruiting difficult that year and bad reports spread by men sent home in 1865 hindered efforts in 1866. The committee then changed its agent at Stornoway, replacing the Morisons with Roderick Millar, an 'Inspector of the Poor', in anticipation, no doubt, of benefiting from the knowledge his position gave him of that portion of the population most likely to join the HBC. Millar, however, reported that good fishing, high wages, bad reports, and an aversion to leaving home prevented him from getting any men.[138] When only 10 Scots appeared at York Factory in 1866, many of the officers, displaying a remarkably bad memory, suggested that 'men fitted for the Service might be got from Norway.' They attributed the 'failure of the last trial' to the agent's recruiting men from towns rather than the countryside, but the committee declined to take the officers' advice.[139] In 1870, the recruits reflected nicely the company's preferences: 28 from the Orkneys, 13 from Stornoway, and 10 from the Shetlands,[140] but their small number demonstrates how the composition of the company's workforce had changed since 1770. The majority were, and had been for at least a decade, native-born. The company had come to rely on the services of a population that its own efforts had created in the hope of its providing a regular supply of cheap labour, but whom George Simpson had condemned for their untrustworthiness and the officers considered unmanageable and unruly.

Native-born servants were particularly numerous at the western posts and they had also become crucial to the HBC's transport system. But they were increasingly unco-operative, frequently carrying only as much cargo as they considered appropriate or refusing to complete their trips, with the result that furs and supplies remained at depots instead of going where they were supposed to. 'Until some means are devised of avoiding the employment of these Red River scoundrels in our transport business', declared one officer in 1862, 'a ruinous waste and abuse of property must continue.'[141] The means by which this problem was to be solved was suggested in 1870, when Donald A. Smith proposed that instead of Red River 'halfbreeds' the company rely on steamboats wherever feasible. The committee agreed enthusiastically and suggested building tramways or cart roads at some of the portages. These innovations, it hoped, would reduce the capital tied up in the trade, bring furs to market more quickly, and cut the number of ships sent out.[142]

It seems rather appropriate that a committee dominated by businessmen interested in the development of resources other than furs would select a technological innovation to solve a manpower problem. The committee was now made up of men accustomed to the more modern social relations of industrial Britain. Thus, they urged caution upon their recruiters, retained traditional terms, and continued to seek men among marginal populations that possessed the deference, hardiness, and cheapness of the Scots whom Governor John Nixon had recommended in 1682. At the same time, they accepted the fact that not all recruits would turn out well. It should be 'borne in mind', their secretary remarked in 1871, 'that the number of men sent annually to the Northern Department varies from 40 to 50 and it cannot be wondered at, that a few of them prove unsuitable.'[143] For over a century, the HBC's governing committees had struggled against having to concede this point. Now, beguiled by visions of profits from the 'civilization' of Rupert's Land, a new committee was as blasé about hiring fur trade employees as it was about disciplining them. It was content to continue the old mode of recruitment but no longer felt it necessary, as Charles McKenzie put it, to 'overrun the north of Europe'[144] in search of new populations as virtuous and willing as the Orcadians were supposed to have been in the past.

4

The View from the Bottom

On 5 December 1780, Humphrey Marten, chief at York Factory, entered a room in the men's flanker and found Thomas Dunch, a carpenter, 'much in liquor', working at a planing bench he had set up there 'in disobedience to possitive orders'. Marten expressed 'resentment at his wilful disobedience', which could prove disastrous if a spark from the lamp or a coal from the stove ignited the large pile of shavings that Dunch had produced. But Dunch responded with 'taunting answers', such as: 'O Sir you are a great man in this part of the world and must be obeyed, you can send me home at Shiptime, I wish you would, I do my duty as well as any man in the Fort, Ned Loutet knows I do, you do not, because you go out a hunting.'

The next day, when Marten asked him 'if he was not ashamed' of his behaviour, Dunch replied that he had been intoxicated. Marten then asked, 'Will you behave better in future?' Dunch remarked, 'I cannot behave worse.' Marten informed Dunch that this was 'no answer' and repeated his question. Now Dunch complained, 'Why am I to be pointed out more than others, other men got drunk as well as I.' Told that 'every man is reprimanded who gets drunk', he retorted, 'Well Sir you to be sure are a great man and know every thing, and I suppose you think I know nothing but I wish you would let the Taylor make me a waistcoat.' Marten replied that he would 'readily' grant him any favour when he behaved better, whereupon Dunch 'screwed up his nose and sneeringly said,—to be sure you are Master and must be obey'd, but Ned Luitet and every man in the Factory except yourself know I do my duty as well as any man in the Fort and you may ask them.' Marten then ordered him downstairs and put him off duty. 'This old man', he observed, 'is remarkable for a jeering taunting mode of expression, which to me seems much worse than downright abuse.' But Dunch asked for forgiveness and several days later was making window shutters. Although he appears to have caused no further trouble, he was discharged for bad behaviour the following September.[1]

Thomas Dunch was by no means a typical servant, but his behaviour on this occasion demonstrated what Table 1 suggests were two of the most common offences committed by HBC employees: negligence and drunkenness. The figures in this table were obtained by counting every incident of misbehaviour mentioned in the records, mainly post journals, but, in their absence, correspondence and annual reports, of every tenth outfit, beginning with 1770–1 and ending with 1870–1. Counting and classifying create an impression of scientific accuracy, but the table is intended only as a kind of map of misbehaviour over the course of a century and should be regarded as nothing more than a rough indicator of its frequency. It does, however, make clear that disobedience occurred often enough to warrant examination and that the history of the HBC must take into consideration not only the dedicated and the faithful but also the likes of Thomas Dunch. A table also makes it possible to distinguish between kinds of misbehaviour and, for the purposes of discussion, to categorize them by the seriousness of the challenge they presented to the company's authority and the alarm with which the London committee and its officers were likely to view them. The least common, though the most threatening, were those instances when men acted collectively to demand wage increases or fair treatment or rebelled against their officers. Such behaviour on the part of men consigned to the status of servants constituted an inversion of the relations of authority that the committee considered proper. More frequent and less menacing were attempts to negotiate the conditions and pace of work by refusing to obey orders. Such incidents indicated that the men believed they had a right to bargain over such issues and were not obliged to obey unconditionally, but in doing so they were not overtly challenging their masters' authority. Most common were offences like Dunch's, which expressed an *indifference* to that authority and demonstrated how incomplete the men's identification with the company actually was.

Such incidents also suggest that an analysis of the relationship between the company and its employees must go beyond the ideal,

York Factory in 1853. Lithograph from a sketch attributed to Chief Trader Alexander Hunter Murray. HBCA Picture Collection P–114. (Courtesy Hudson's Bay Company Archives, Provincial Archives of Manitoba.)

which emphasized the ties that bound masters to servants and ignored the fact that the relationship between the HBC and its workers was constantly subject to negotiation. The view from the bottom, after all, was not the same as the view from the top. The experiences of HBC workers were quite different from those of their officers and of the London committee. Those relegated to the lower ranks possessed their own identities and interests, which they did not abandon when they entered the service. As a result, they did not always carry out their duties with the diligence and enthusiasm their masters considered appropriate, nor did they necessarily adhere strictly to the terms of their contracts.

The Collection of the Data

To determine the extent to which HBC workers failed to behave as faithful servants were supposed to, however, it is necessary to adopt, temporarily at least, the perspective of the London committee and its officers, since they made the rules and decided when they had been broken. Further bias results from the fact that quantifying information from non-quantitative records as inconsistently kept as the HBC's cannot result in an accurate or complete count. The quality of the sources depends on the literacy, diligence, honesty, and sagacity of the officers who kept them. Particularly alarming events, such as the Brandon

House mutiny of 1811, the murder of John McLoughlin Jr in 1842, or the mutiny aboard the company's steamer *Beaver* in 1838 were unlikely to be ignored and might result in thick files of evidence. But most misbehaviour involved one man or a small group engaging in acts of disobedience that not all officers would have considered worthy of notice. As Ferdinand Jacobs put it after giving '3 or 4 Cuffs' to an insolent servant who then challenged him to 'Come & Strike him again', he 'should have a fine time of it to fight every rude fellow to his Duty.'[2]

Moreover, if a man's misbehaviour accorded with popular prejudices many of his transgressions might be overlooked, as is suggested by the case of Charles Beads, a young native-born servant. In November of 1813, while stationed at Kenogamissi, he skulked out after some Natives to share their rum instead of making sleds as ordered. When his master, Richard Good, discovered the group a half-mile from the house, he threatened Beads with a fine, whereupon Beads retorted impudently that Good 'might make it Fivety Shillings'. Good had not previously noted any misbehaviour on Beads's part, but he now mentioned that this was not the first time the man had been guilty of 'the like reprehensible Conduct' and complained that 'Reproofs has no avail with him.' In the servants' list in the annual report Good reported that Beads was generally well behaved but he drank. Perhaps because he expected a man of Beads's ancestry to be both hard to manage and prone to drunkenness, he had not felt compelled to report Beads's earlier misconduct and mentioned the latest only because Beads had finally driven Good to exasperation. Or, since, according to his report, the post suffered from poor soil, the proximity of two NWC posts, bad navigation, and a scarcity of fish, while all the best Native hunters and usual visitors had died, he might have thought that the quality of the servants scarcely mattered. At any rate, Beads's love of liquor did not bar him from continuing in the service. Seven years later, on 8 October 1820, John Murphy reported that Beads was 'attending on' the Natives 'and at the same time on himself, he has been tipsy every day since they have been in, with their rum.' Unfortunately, Murphy remarked, this man, like 'most of his race (half breed)', was 'most wretchedly enslaved to this vice' and guzzled rum whenever Murphy's back was turned.[3] Clearly, an officer's failure to report disobedience was no clear indicator of its absence, but reporting only one specific incident while complaining of repeated bad behaviour supplies only one occurrence for enumeration and makes an exact count impossible.

Table 1
Types of Misbehaviour in the Hudson's Bay Company, 1770–1 to 1870–1

Incidents	1770–1	1780–1	1790–1	1800–01	1810–11	1820–1	1830–1	1840–1	1850–1	1860–1	1870–1	TOTAL
Refusal to do as ordered	4	1	4	6	3	21	2		6	4	6	57
Negligence	2	4	1	2		18		7	3	2	13	52
Desertion				1		1	2	1	9	6	7	27
Drunkenness		3	1	1	2	4	2	1	1	5	6	26
Refusal to work	1	1		1	2	1		1	3	3	5	18
Theft			1		4	2	3				1	12
Absent without leave						2		1	4	2	1	10
Insolence	2	1	1		1	2						8
Private trade	1			1		1			1			3
Combination						1	1					3
Other	4	3	1	2	2	15	4	7	1		5	44
TOTAL	14	13	9	14	14	68	14	19	28	22	45	260

SOURCES: These figures were calculated by counting every specific incident of misbehaviour for every tenth outfit starting with 1770–1. See 'A Note on Sources'. During the second half of the eighteenth century, the workforce hired on contracts grew from fewer than 150 to 587 men in 1800. Except for 1810–11, when there were 442 such employees, and 1830–1, when there were 999, the company's labour force usually numbered in the neighbourhood of 700 men. See A.30 for servants' lists until 1819 and B./d for 1820–1. For the post-merger period, see Philip Goldring, *Papers on the Labour System of the Hudson's Bay Company, 1821–1900, Volume 1*, Manuscript Report Series, no. 362, Parks Canada (Ottawa, 1979), Table 2.1, 33, Table 2.3, 45, Table 3.4, 79. Except for Table 2.1, information is for the Northern Department only.

A similar problem arises when references to misbehaviour are too general. For example, the 18 April 1821 entry in the Fort Chipewyan journal reports that some of the men had killed three dogs, an incident counted and classified as 'other' in Table 1. However, the passage also mentions, for the first time, that the company had been greatly inconvenienced during the winter by the men eating their dogs.[4] On 27 December 1870, a man refused to get ready to take a packet to Fort Albany, an obvious 'refusal to do as ordered'. But the master of the post also commented that this was not the first time the man had been 'insolent', though he had reported no previous instances.[5] In both cases, only one incident out of an unknown and unknowable number can be counted.

Sometimes officers complained about their men's habitual disregard of regulations without referring to any particular occurrences at all. In January of 1780, for example, the chief of York Factory put up a note in the men's guardroom to chide them for their frequent disregard of the rules designed to minimize the danger of fire to the fort. Despite the notices prominently displayed reminding everyone of the times when lights and fires had to be extinguished for the night, 'sundry Persons in direct defiance and willfull disobedience to such Orders' kept up 'great fires' for much of the night and refused to put out their lights or go to bed at the appointed hour. Furthermore, 'some very disorderly drunken persons' had 'at sundry times been guilty of disturbing the factory at a very late hour, and wallowing on the ground like Brutes.' Such behaviour was to cease instantly, those who persisted would 'meet with proper correction', and their names would be transmitted to the London committee.[6] This complaint was not made during one of the outfits for which statistics were assembled, but it suggests that officers repeatedly overlooked some offences until they believed the situation had gotten completely out of hand and only then took steps to restore order. Numbers can provide no indication of the extent of such disobedience.

On the other hand, officers upon whose shoulders the mantle of authority weighed most heavily or who were simply martinets were likely to record in considerable, even excessive, detail the sins of their men. Thus the journals left by the reform-minded officers at Moose Factory during the 1730s and 1740s give the impression that the post was manned by a gang of drunken rowdies commanded by paranoid officers waging a hopeless campaign against illicit trade and corruption.[7] One might also wonder if the sharp increase in disobedience that Table 1 shows for the 1820–1 outfit reflected the expansion of the workforce required to meet competition with the NWC *or* the fact that it was George Simpson's first year in the service. Twenty-eight of the 68 incidents of misbehaviour counted for that outfit were reported in the journals of Fort Chipewyan, where Simpson was relentlessly trying to stamp out extravagance and reinstate discipline. He was determined to ensure the maintenance of a 'proper and respectable distance' between the officers and their men, whom he considered 'the very dross and outcast of the human species'. They were not to be allowed 'to remain idle about the House' and every disobedience of orders, neglect of duty, dishonesty, or 'impertinence' would be severely punished. With both Simpson and his assistant, William Brown, breathing down the men's necks and recording every detail, it is not surprising that Fort Chipewyan appears to have been such a disorderly place.[8] Officers less committed to reform might not have kept such thorough records. But even thoroughness is no guarantee of precision.

Officers were not neutral when they evaluated their men's conduct. Their familiarity with, and frequently poor opinion of, the men under their command influenced their judgement, and their reports of disobedience might be based mainly on suspicion. For example, on 17 December 1860, the officer in charge of Fort Alexandria noted that a calf had died that morning and he blamed it on the negligence of their keeper, whom he considered completely untrustworthy.[9] Without additional evidence, however, it is impossible to judge whether the officer's suspicions were well founded or not and this incident was not counted. Reports of malingering servants are equally difficult to evaluate. Thus, on 25 August 1780, the armourer at Severn House was allegedly pretending to be unable to do anything. If this was the same armourer who the previous May had been 'wilfully dilatory' and 'insufferable', and given to obstinacy, lying, drinking, and the use of 'saucy Language',[10] he was no doubt capable of malingering as well. But even bad servants got sick and, even though his blemished record made his master doubt his claim, the journal provides no real proof of the man's guilt. This incident was thus not counted. On the other hand, one of the men stationed at Pic in 1840 claimed to be 'unwell' and yet ate his rations 'with a good relish'.[11] Since this contradiction might indeed indicate that the man's illness was a sham, this incident was counted as a case of malingering and classified as 'other' in Table 1.

Another problem that arises when one quantifies non-numerical information is that it is necessary to classify and label each incident, a process that treats each the same and gives no indication of its seriousness. Thus the Brandon House mutiny of 1811 has been counted as a 'refusal to do as ordered' because it was a refusal to accept the

Plan of Fort Chipewyan, 1823. HBCA Map Collection B.39/a/22, fo. 69. (Courtesy Hudson's Bay Company Archives, Provincial Archives of Manitoba.)

new prices of provisions and the new officer sent to take charge of the post. But it was also a rebellion that usurped the officer's authority and drove him out. It was thus far more serious, for example, than John Skinner's refusal in November of 1820 to look after the pigs.[12] The incident at Brandon House was the only real mutiny that occurred during an outfit for which data were collected, and the figures therefore do not conceal others. Even so, mere numbers fail to convey an event's complexity and ignore the context in which it occurred, as the case of Thomas Dunch demonstrates. He was guilty of negligence, drunkenness, and insolence, but his misbehaviour was not counted three times. It was also impossible to determine whether he became intoxicated before or after he ignored Marten's order not to set up his planing bench in the house. But he had clearly disregarded Marten's instructions, without actually refusing outright to carry them out, and his misconduct was counted as 'negligence'. Another complex case was that of William Duffle, the cook at Eastmain, who in March of 1791 was flogged for getting drunk on stolen brandy and being 'very abusive' when discovered. Since stealing had led to his drunkenness and insolence, this incident was counted as one of the thefts of 1790–1. But it also cast a new light on an earlier affair. On 28 December 1790, Duffle had sneaked out of the post and, when he was discovered quite by accident by another servant who had gone out that evening, he displayed 'all the symptons of Insanity' and refused to come back. He was found the next day with two Europeans and two Natives at a fishing place, hauled home, and put to bed, where he remained, refusing to speak until New Year's Day, when he begged pardon. Having been 'frequently seized' with 'Humours' that cast doubt on his mental health, he was forgiven.[13] His later behaviour suggests, however, that his insanity had been phony and he was really only shirking his duty, but without proof the earlier incident cannot be counted as a misdemeanour.

Another complicating factor is the context of a particular incident that might be part of a chain of events beginning prior to an outfit for which statistics are being compiled. For example, on 3 June 1850, at Norway House, John McKinnon attempted to escape from the room in which he had been imprisoned since March when he had attacked another man with a hatchet. The two men had apparently fallen out the previous fall and McKinnon had 'determined on revenge'. He was immediately fettered and confined. Sometime during the night of 2 June, he managed to get hold of the key to his manacles and unlock them. At dawn, while his guard was reading, McKinnon sprang to the door and escaped, but he was quickly apprehended. A few weeks later he was sent to York Factory and that fall he was discharged.[14] Although his escape attempt was certainly an act of disobedience, he had been confined for attacking another man and that was the real offence. But it occurred during a previous outfit and was not counted. McKinnon's escapade, therefore, is not represented in the table. In sum, the counting of offences was far from straightforward and in many instances required careful evaluation and sometimes re-evaluation.

It was also impossible to count those incidents that were never reported. Officers who themselves engaged in private trade or drank to excess were unlikely to concern themselves with their men's indulgence in such prohibited activities. Furthermore, their men usually worked without supervision and many of their duties required them to be absent from their posts, sometimes for weeks at time, when they could do much as they wanted without anyone ever finding out. The numbers in the table should therefore not be considered comprehensive, but they do provide a way of organizing the information collected and make it possible to discern the pattern of disobedience from 1770 to 1870. They suggest that there was little change in the ways that servants misbehaved and that disobedience, while certainly not of epidemic proportions, was far from uncommon. Nor did it increase significantly between 1770 and 1810. That rising tide of disorder feared by the committee and its officers was mostly a figment of their imaginations. Disobedience grew slightly from 1780–1 until 1810–11, peaked sharply in 1820–1, fell back to the pre-merger level in 1830–1, and then gradually rose again. The 1820–1 outfit, as has already been mentioned, included some officers who exercised particular vigilance, but it was also one in which the workforce was expanding, competition made the servants' existence less comfortable, and new French-Canadian recruits were not particularly happy in the service. Thereafter, however, the number of incidents of disobedience declined sharply, as the workforce was reduced after the merger, and then began to climb slowly once more as the company came to rely on more native-born employees who came from a local population increasingly opposed to the company's trade monopoly. In addition, the HBC by this time employed seamen and colliers who were unaccustomed to the subordination considered appropriate for servants, a rank to which neither group had ever belonged. Thus the company, already accustomed to refractory labourers and tradesmen, now also found itself facing stubborn tripmen, mutinous sailors, and striking coalminers.

Despite changing circumstances and changing sources of employees, however, disobedience rarely presented an overt challenge to the company's hierarchy or authority. The most common single type of

Table 2
Refusals, 1770–1 to 1870–1

Outfit	Refusal to do as ordered			Refusal to work			Total
	1 man	2 or more	All	1 man	2 or more	All	
1770–1	1	3	4	1	0	1	5
1780–1	0	1	1	1	0	1	2
1790–1	3	1	4	0	0	0	4
1800–1	4	2	6	1	0	1	7
1810–11	0	3	3	0	2	2	5
1820–1	19	2	21	0	1	1	22
1830–1	0	2	2	0	0	0	2
1840–1	0	0	0	1	0	1	1
1850–1	5	1	6	2	1	3	9
1860–1	2	2	4	1	2	3	7
1870–1	2	4	6	5	0	5	11
Total	36	21	57	12	6	18	75

SOURCE: Figures are derived from the information in Table 1.

misbehaviour was refusing to obey a specific order. The refusal to work at all was less common, but taken together, both kinds of refusals account for 75 of the 262 recorded incidents (see Table 2). Next in importance was 'negligence', which refers to cases where men ignored orders but did not actually refuse to obey them. This category includes such transgressions as delaying on journeys, carelessness or excessive slowness in the performance of a duty, or simply doing nothing at all. Since the service offered many opportunities for individuals to be negligent, it is likely that such offences occurred more frequently than the number indicates and were probably the most common type of misconduct in the service. Desertion, which the table suggests was the next most common, was probably more regularly reported, at least prior to the 1830s, simply because a man's disappearance was bound to attract attention. But as the number of native-born servants increased and their reputation for unreliability grew, complaints about the frequency with which they ran off suggest that desertion was more common than the numbers in Table 1 indicate. Officers might well have become so accustomed to it that they hardly bothered to take notice of individual incidents.

Next in frequency was 'drunkenness', a classification applied to those incidents in which drunkenness was the only offence or the cause of another, but not if it resulted from or accompanied another transgression. Likewise, theft refers only to an occasion when stealing was the only crime or led to others. Thus if a man stole liquor and got drunk, the incident was counted as theft. If, however, intoxication prompted him to steal, the incident was counted as drunkenness. Insolence, like drunkenness and theft, frequently accompanied the commission of other crimes. A drunken servant was often an impudent one and a man caught stealing or idling his time away might be extremely disrespectful. Cases counted as insolence were occasions when, for no immediately apparent reason, men responded to their master's commands with language that Marcus Rediker has called 'a kind of verbal mutiny'.[15] 'Absence without leave' refers to men leaving their assigned places, whether posts or camps, without permission. 'Private trade' and 'combination' were the least common types of misbehaviour, with only three incidents of each recorded in the relevant years. Private trade, of course, refers to men engaging in trade on their own accounts. The combinations in question refer to attempts by servants whose contracts were up to impose wage increases by refusing to re-engage until their demands for higher pay were met.[16] Officers tended to label as a combination any occasion when men acted collectively to impose particular conditions, but those incidents so labelled in the table are those that involved no work stoppage or other misbehaviour. They were simply attempts by men to take advantage of their numbers and the value of their experience to negotiate better terms. Referring to them as combinations reflects the way in which the officers viewed them and distinguishes them from other protests. It was illegal for workers in a variety of trades to attempt to improve wages and working conditions by striking; the Combination Acts of 1799 and 1800 extended this prohibition to all workers.[17] When officers reported combinations, they were therefore referring to a type of activity that had been prohibited by a law. Their application of the term to describe incidents that were not strikes suggests that they regarded all attempts to impose wage increases as subversive, but there is no indication that they believed that the Acts were in force in Rupert's Land.

Finally, there are the incidents classified as 'other', which includes a variety of offences that do not fall into any other category. The most common of these was malingering, i.e., pretending to be too ill to work, of which there were seven cases. There were also six incidents of servants squabbling among themselves. The rest include such transgressions as making unreasonable demands, disorderliness, dishonesty, killing company dogs, socializing with the employees of rival trading companies or local Natives, being absent from or disruptive at Sunday services, wasting the company's provisions, and giving liquor to the Natives. Also included are the beating in May 1821 of a Native man by some 'cowardly scoundrels' at Severn because, they claimed, he had been looking in the window, and the 1870 case of a man stationed at Nipigon waylaying and attempting, unsuccessfully, 'to take improper liberties' with a young Native woman.[18]

HBC Workers in 'Fur Trade Society'

For the London committee and its most dedicated officers, of course, all disobedience was unacceptable. It was, after all, a worker's duty to dedicate himself to his employer's business and to perform his tasks diligently and thoroughly, but HBC employees had their own perceptions and interests. Thus, although they never proposed a revolutionary overturning of the company's hierarchy or extended their rejection of an individual officer's authority to that of the HBC as a whole, their behaviour repeatedly demonstrated how limited was their dedication to their superiors' priorities. HBC servants, like other pre-industrial workers, behaved according to customary attitudes towards work and leisure. For them, time was not money and labour was carried out in spurts of intense effort alternating with equally intense idleness.[19] Their officers, however, wanted each man to report for work every morning, go promptly and willingly to his assigned job, spend all the hours assigned to labour carrying out his duties, and take no leisure except at authorized times. While diligence promised profits and promotions for an officer, it could look like overwork to a servant. Indeed, the completion of one task led only to another one. What was indolence to an officer might have been merely a sensible pace of work to a servant, although one cannot, of course, ignore the fact that there were cases when the officer was right. Either possibility, however, reflected the fact that HBC workers did not identify themselves totally with their employer.

That this should be so is not surprising. The company's employees did not come from societies characterized by close and warm ties between the élites and the lower orders because, contrary to what the London committee believed, such societies did not exist, and their relations with previous employers were not such as to dispose them towards unquestioning allegiance. Furthermore, once they were in the service, they spent most of their time with one another, not with their officers, and were thus unlikely to adopt the outlook of their superiors. Fur trade history has tended to be about the *mentalité* that united everyone in a 'fur trade society', a concept that has gone largely undefined but implies that the fur trade led to an interaction of Europeans and North American Native peoples resulting in the development of new customs and mores and, therefore, a new culture. This was certainly true, but it is important, as Carlo Ginzburg has pointed out, to distinguish between mentality and culture. Histories of the former are characterized by 'their insistence on the inert, obscure, unconscious elements in a given world view' and the inclusion of 'survivals, archaisms, the emotional, the irrational', which are thereby removed from related disciplines such as the history of ideas or the history of culture. The study of mentalities, therefore, has 'a decidedly classless character' because it emphasizes what all members of society had in common. There is a difference, however, between the culture imposed on the masses and the one produced by them. Those who belong to the 'subordinate classes' do not passively accept the culture of the dominant: they have one of their own and it is frequently oppositional. The concept of culture allows for the recognition of the existence of diverse views that make sense to those who hold them and the existence of a class structure.[20] Thus, when one considers fur trade society, one cannot assume that all members shared the same culture or that the judgements and observations of the officers and the London committee were accurate depictions of reality. Most of the company's records, being produced by and for its directors and managers, might be seen as belonging to what Ginzburg terms 'the archives of repression'.[21] Nevertheless, since they record the deeds and sometimes words, especially the impertinent ones, of the lowly, even these archives do not entirely conceal the view from the bottom. It is in this context that the misbehaviour of HBC employees must be examined.

The culture of fur trade society was more than a matter of distinctive dress and dialect, new modes of travel and survival, particular Native-European relations, new marriage customs, and an awareness that life in Rupert's Land was different from life elsewhere. The fur trade society of the majority of the company's men was not identical to the one that those who fancied themselves its leaders inhabited. The ordinary workers had always been distinguished from their superiors by rank and function. They spent only a portion of their lives in the service and lived and worked with one another. Officers were repeatedly urged to keep a proper distance and those who did so saw the servants chiefly to give orders or inflict punishment, socializing with them only to exchange formal Christmas or New Year's greetings, join in toasts to the monarch on St George's Day, and, most importantly, dispense the festive rum or brandy. Having completed these ceremonial duties, the officers would usually withdraw, leaving the men to dance, play games, drink, and squabble. The more rigid hierarchy produced by the merger of 1821 and the virtual elimination of opportunities for promotion for common servants hardened the already existing division. Moreover, officers who wished to advance were expected to demonstrate their worthiness by dedicating themselves to the company and adopting habits that increasingly resembled those of respectable, middle-class gentlemen elsewhere. The distance between many officers and their subordinates thus increased, particularly at the company's larger establishments, like York Factory, where gentlemen were numerous enough to permit those who wished to do so to avoid unnecessary contact with their inferiors. Indeed, Letitia Hargrave judged the factory to be 'by far the most respectable place in the Territory'.[22] The servants, on the other hand, had their own priorities, which were part of a culture made up of customs they brought with them and those that developed in the service. They had their own fur trade society, which did not emphasize respectability, sobriety, and forethought. Indeed, they and many of their superiors—especially the London committee—lived in different worlds.

Not everyone, for example, adhered to the standards of sexual propriety that the most respectable officers advocated. Jennifer Brown has suggested that HBC officers were 'role models' in 'familial' spheres and the tradition of marriage according to 'the custom of the country' led to the establishment of stable unions.[23] However, as elsewhere, approaches to sexual relations were diverse and not always admirable. Not everyone was willing to shoulder his responsibility as husband and father. Thus, in 1819, James Morrison, a blacksmith at Albany, having left his wife in 'distressed Circumstances' because he had not authorized her to receive some of his wages, had to be reminded that it was his duty to 'render her some support'.[24] Some men appeared to join the HBC precisely to evade such obligations. Alexander Lain, an Orcadian cooper who engaged in 1858 as a labourer, had seduced Catherine Narquay of Flotta with 'A hundred Repeated promises' of marriage. 'Deluded by His False vows', she had borne his child, which he refused to acknowledge as his. She took him to court, but the judgement she gained against him was useless since he ran off and joined the HBC.[25] In 1869, Robert Reid of Leith, once employed by the HBC on Vancouver Island, abandoned six children and his wife, who asked the company not to allow him on any of their ships.[26] Indeed, service with the HBC seemed to present so many opportunities for irresponsibility that some of the men's British relatives expressed concern that they would succumb to the charms of 'the black girls' or 'she-Indians' and abandon the children that resulted.[27] Some men lived up to such expectations.

Some attempted to smuggle women into the posts,[28] others left the factories to indulge in 'scandalous' or 'indecent' behaviour,[29] and a few went beyond mere indecency. For example, in April of 1803, three men at Hannah Bay, where the Moose Factory goose tent was located, got drunk at a nearby Canadian post. Two of them then entered a tent inhabited by some old women and 'forced them to comply with their lustfull desire', seriously injuring one of them. Their master sent one of the culprits, Peter Pearson, back to Moose Factory to be fined and sent home to the Orkneys 'for gross misbehaviour'. But his companion in crime, William Bews, appears to have escaped punishment altogether.[30] Perhaps Bews had a better record and his drunkenness seemed a mitigating circumstance. Perhaps when committed by inferiors on victims who were themselves not highly respected, rape was considered less serious and even almost to be expected from men whose sexual behaviour was viewed as less moral. Certainly, sexual licence was not uncommon.

In 1841, George Barnston at Albany disclosed another custom of the country: there were children of company men around the post and their fathers contributed nothing to their support because, a man had informed him, 'the giving of a Handkerchief to the woman suffices to exonerate a man in Law.'[31] This casual attitude to paternal responsibilities was observed several years later by Charles McKenzie, who reported that Hugh Folster, a 'Product of Old Albany', refused to admit that he was the father of a child recently born to the daughter of George Moar.[32] In 1851, remembering the bad old days, W.J. Christie observed that there used to be 'Men lying in the same bed openly before all hands with young women'.[33] However, if William Watt's ribald missive from Long Lake is any indication, lewdness was still to be found in the service:

> I have not heard any thing (this long time) of Made Boussincau; but last news was she was getting remarkably round in the waist Made Kinosh is again in the breeding . . . I hear. She is certainly the Devil at it Young Jack Wife has produced another sweet nut for the Devil to crack that little incident occurred last Spring Isabell (Fathe) Cadreant is completely Stove in, Simpson & that Young Fellow with an unpronounceable name had her 'chacun a son tour'

all last Summer; whether it is true or not I cannot Say, but one just hopped over the doorstep and took a turn on the verandah untill Such time as the other was freshed, and then took his turn at 'stretching his boot' Some Say that the Honble Companys Establishment was nothing else than a complete whore Shop, both Yankee and British Women.[34]

Even when they did select wives, as opposed to short-term companions, the men did not always go about getting them in the approved way. In 1812, William Loutit, stationed at Deers Lake, having been denied permission to marry, took another man's wife and sent her to live with some Natives until he could join her. When J.P. Holmes, master at Nelson House, learned of Loutit's disobedience, he sent two men to fetch the woman and charged the cost of this expedition to Loutit's account.[35] In 1868, Jonathan Johnson, who had been refused permission to marry two years earlier because there was no accommodation at Fort George for more married men, told his new master that he had, in fact, been given such permission. When his lie was discovered, he was told either to send the woman away to her father or to leave the service and live as a Native. Johnson left.[36] Nor did the possession of one wife necessarily preclude the taking of another. In 1851, John Cromartie informed James Hargrave that, although one John Cooper was willing to re-engage, he would rather 'be Cleare of him' because he was 'a man of Rather bad morals and has Rather Corrupted the others this two years.' If he stayed any longer he 'would turn another James Knight be wanting another wif and hase in his own Country.' Cromartie considered Cooper's behaviour 'Shamefull for a man in his Situation as well as Sinful'.[37] In 1858 a man at Edmonton House deserted to follow a woman in spite of the fact that he was 'lawfully married' to a woman in Red River.[38] Nor did servants always conduct their marriages with complete decorum or ensure that their womenfolk behaved with what their superiors considered appropriate modesty. Thus, in 1840, William Shaw at Fort Vermilion felt obliged to speak to the 'Lady' of one of his men about 'the impropriety of being too often in the Indian Lodges'. The woman's husband, however, dismissed Shaw's concern with the comment, 'Cest La Facon dans la Rabasca de visiter le Lodge.' The visits of the woman and her daughter continued and Shaw suspected they might have *'lovers',* since 'with Indians/particularly with Beaver Indians/there is no bounds or restraint on *Love Affairs.*'[39]

Clearly, not all the inhabitants of the HBC territories adopted the middle-class model of marriage, which emphasized female virtue and domesticity, was legitimized by a church wedding, and increasingly became the only acceptable one for those aspiring to respectability. That this should be the case is not surprising, since other practices did not die out in Britain either, even though middle-class reformers considered them immoral and sought to stamp them out. Many working-class people continued to regard sexual relationships as acceptable during betrothal and expected that pregnancy would lead to marriage. Moreover, marriage might still frequently take the form of a common-law partnership.[40] In Rupert's Land, pressure for change came from George Simpson and his circle. They considered Native mates unsuitable for respectable officers and believed it necessary to postpone marriage until they could establish a proper family with a pure and refined British wife. In the meantime, of course, a young, unmarried officer, like his middle-class counterparts elsewhere, might seek the company of women who would never grace middle-class households and whose chastity, therefore, needed no protection. Thus, in 1862, George Barnston reported to James Hargrave that the 'scandal' concerning himself and 'a certain loose and yet firm Piece of Furniture that came up in the Boats' with him was only half true, but he could not 'now enlarge upon it' because he intended it as his *'Dish'* at their 'next Pic Nic Tete a Tete'.[41]

Hargrave himself, determined never to marry a native of the country lest he thereby doom himself to spending his old age there, was equally determined not to do without female companionship before marriage. When the flood of 1826 prompted the departure of many of the settlers, Hargrave complained that it was 'among those' that his 'female acquaintance was entirely centred', and now 'a willing wench [was] scarcely to be found for love or money'. The women who remained were 'completely monopolized by the Righteous', i.e. the 'psalm singing Scotch & Blues', who were 'so far liberal as to practice a community of such goods' but who punished 'with the unrelenting scourge of slander every interloper from among the "Children of darkness" who dares to poach in their sacred warrens.'[42] Once married, however, a respectable officer would become a model of rectitude and seek a degree of refinement in his family life that he probably considered neither possible nor necessary among his subordinates. There was then another basis for distinguishing between high and low.

Aboriginal women remained suitable mates for the lower ranks. By the 1860s servants were frequently being allowed, and enthusiastically requesting permission, to take 'wives from Indian tents'.[43] Officers expected to marry, if not European women, then the carefully reared, Europeanized daughters of their older colleagues. Although

Simpson and his cronies believed their elevated positions required white wives and the arrival of British women in Rupert's Land did contribute to the growth of racial prejudice, most officers continued to marry women of mixed ancestry. Indeed, as Brian Gallagher's study of marriage patterns of senior HBC officers stationed at Red River after 1821 demonstrates, they chose them when they could have married Scottish women from the parish of Kildonan. Only one such officer married a Kildonan woman in the period from 1845 to 1870 and he was one of a tiny minority after 1821 who entered the HBC as servants and became officers. It was thus not race but class that divided the colony after the merger and determined whom the company's officers married.[44]

But class was defined in part by race. Officers who sought career advancement married women who were so acculturated and so far removed from their Aboriginal ancestry that they might as well have been British. Most of the wives of the officers Gallagher studied had British names and probably belonged to that group known as 'English half breeds', who were generally held to be more trustworthy and diligent than those with French forebears. The rank and file of the company's men married women whose race and class placed them outside their superiors' circle of acceptability and reflected the men's own relegation to the bottom of the social scale. They occupied the lower ranks of the company and had few expectations of promotion, and when they left the HBC they joined the lower ranks of western Canadian society. They could never aspire to the social prominence or influence of their officers. Their wives were not refined enough to grace the drawing rooms of the élite. Indeed, these women spent their lives performing varieties of drudgery that the ladies of the fur trade gentry would have considered beneath them. And, unlike company officers and prominent settlers, they would not have sent their daughters to such institutions as Miss Davis's school, where training in deportment and ornamental arts transformed them into 'perfectly accomplished' young ladies. And their response to the bigotry of the respectable would probably have been, to paraphrase James Ross's admonition to his children: 'So what if Mama is an Indian?'[45]

The company's records provide only glimpses into such private areas of the lives of most of the company's employees, but they do indicate that generalizations based on the concerns and deeds of a few HBC officers fail to illuminate the experiences of the majority. Indeed, the evidence hints that the men's sex lives were far more varied than a concentration on the establishment of family units implies. It is difficult to know what ordinary people considered appropriate or 'normal' sexual practices, and the HBC archives are not the most promising source of such information. Nevertheless, they suggest that, as in other predominantly male environments, sex between males was neither unknown nor particularly abhorred, although it was illegal and, until 1861, punishable by death. It was classed as sodomy, which referred to 'unnatural'—i.e., non-procreative—sexual acts performed between two men or a man and an animal or a man and a woman. In England, sodomy appears to have been prosecuted most vigorously during war or times of social turmoil and members of the armed forces were the most harshly punished. Being charged with sodomy did not, however, label an individual a homosexual, since there was no clearly developed concept of homosexuality as an identity until late in the nineteenth century, though a male homosexual subculture existed in some large English cities early in the eighteenth century. Despite the severity of the penalty prescribed, popular attitudes towards such behaviour remain unclear. Certainly, it aroused revulsion among social and religious reformers and had no place in the respectable, middle-class family that was increasingly held up as the norm during the nineteenth century. As with so many other matters, however, the view from the top cannot be assumed to be identical with the view from the bottom. For example, the fact that the Royal Navy prosecuted buggery with particular harshness reflects the horror with which the Admiralty regarded it. But ships' logs reveal that not all cases resulted in trials because captains imposed their own punishments on men for unspecified, immoral behaviour.[46] How seamen themselves regarded sodomy or how widespread it actually was remains open to conjecture.

One historian, B.R. Burg, has gone so far as to suggest that until the late eighteenth century, sodomy was popularly seen as a type of sexual activity rather than an unnatural act. Although not actually condoned, it was viewed with alarm only by Protestant reformers and was rarely punished to the full extent of the law. Moreover, homosexuality was prevalent among certain groups made up mainly of males with limited access to women: young vagrants; apprentices, particularly in London where homosexuality was tolerated more than elsewhere; and Caribbean pirates, who are the subject of Burg's book. He suggests that young men from a homosexual milieu on land who went to sea chose ocean-going vessels whose all-male environment they preferred. If they took to piracy, they joined a society with a sexual orientation to which they were already accustomed. Because women were scarce in the Caribbean, homosexuality was widespread and pirates ignored or rejected heterosexuality altogether. Some of Burg's conclusions are shaky. He suggests, for example, that Blackbeard's multiplicity of wives indicates a lack of success with women, though one might just as well see this as altogether too much success. Likewise, evidence that mate-swapping was common among pirates might, as Burg suggests, demonstrate an inability to sustain heterosexual relationships, but it might also indicate that they had rejected conventional marriage practices along with other social constraints when they became pirates.[47] Burg's focus on marginal groups also contradicts his assertions about society's acceptance of homosexuality, but his discussion reminds us not to overlook this aspect of the sexuality of men living in the company of other men.

The HBC's records provide few details of sexual relations between the men. Sodomy was not a subject that occupied the London committee and, if Burg is right, one it considered unworthy of attention. Nor did company officers report many incidents. They might have remained unaware of such behaviour because the men practised it secretly or they chose to ignore it because they accepted its existence. Indeed, like sea captains, HBC officers did not always name the offence clearly, perhaps to protect the culprit from the full force of the law. Thus, in 1738 the officers of Moose Factory reported that they were sending home Thomas Carr, a labourer, because he was 'Desireous to come home along with his Brother Jno Smith as he calls him'. Carr was 'so Corupted with evil examples' that he was 'not at all fitt' for the service and Smith was 'a vile Man' guilty of 'Evil practices' who had already been sent home twice for 'Misdemeanours'. The officers expressed hope that 'they do not both goe up Holbourn hill in a Cart', i.e., hang.[48] Clearly, the officers considered Carr and Smith to be bad characters on their way to a bad end, but they declined to be more precise about the nature of their offences and imposed no penalties. When a man's sexual behaviour proved disruptive, however, officers treated it as a serious offence and imposed punishments designed to expose the offender to public disapproval.

Two men found guilty of attempting to seduce others at York Factory in December of 1754 and July of 1755 were struck several times with barrel staves or willow branches by each man at the post.[49] In April 1804, James Gaddy, an Orcadian seaman stationed at Moose Factory, was discovered by way of the child on whom he had 'twice committed the diabolical act' to be 'guilty of Sodomical practices'. Gaddy was no model servant. He had joined his fellows in fraternizing with Canadians, refused to obey orders, and absented himself from divine service, but he had escaped punishment. Now, however, the chief, John Thomas, felt impelled to act. He assembled the men and told them what Gaddy had done, but this measure appears to have had little effect. Gaddy was not shunned, since he continued to live and work with the others. Nor was he chastened. In July, he was aboard one of two boats setting out for Point of the Marsh. Ordered to take a new route around an island, Gaddy replied, 'Damn the Governor's Orders' and took his boat in the opposite direction. In August, he was dismissed for 'practices shocking to human nature' and 'Mutinous Conduct' and fined the remainder of his wages, £17 12s.6d.[50] In May of 1840, Thomas Corcoran, master at Fort George on the eastern shore of James Bay, reported that a man had complained to him that his roommate, William Dearness, had committed 'a filthy act'. Dearness had been banished to Fort George from Moose Factory for refusing to work and Corcoran considered him 'a very unfit subject for this Service, as his conduct has no tendency to improve that of others.' He also considered him 'not altogether in a sound state of mind', since his behaviour 'on some occasions' was, 'if not frantick', then 'rediculous in the extreme'. Corcoran provided no details, but by describing the man's behaviour as 'filthy' Corcoran implied that it was 'morally foul'. Still, Dearness was neither whipped nor publicly reprimanded, but merely told not to repeat his act, whereupon he 'abused' his accuser 'in the grossest manner' and moved out of the room, 'swearing horribly' that he would 'never sleep another night' there with the other man. He then went to live in the woods, but returned almost immediately because of bad weather.[51]

A more comprehensive search of the records doubtless would reveal other such cases, but incidents that upset no one were unlikely to appear there. Much also depended on the officers' own attitudes, their expectations regarding their subordinates' behaviour, and their desire to change it. Officers appear to have had little interest in the regulation of their men's sexuality and were probably content to overlook their improprieties as long as they did not interfere with the company's business. After all, company officers already had their hands full trying to eliminate those habits that *did* interfere with business because it was impossible to eradicate practices that only they— and not even they agreed in all matters—considered wrong. Like conduct that diverged from the mores espoused by respectable officers, most misbehaviour was a reflection of a different outlook and not necessarily the result of bad character. HBC employees persisted in consuming alcohol, they would not abandon careless and irregular work habits, they continued to engage in private trade, and they could not be prevented from sneaking out to socialize with Natives and rival traders or disappearing completely.

The Consumption of Alcohol

As Table 1 suggests, drunkenness was one of the most common offences of which HBC employees were guilty. But one should not assume, as Frits Pannekoek has suggested, that such behaviour was a sign of mental breakdown brought on by the tedium and bleakness of life at lonely trading posts. As Michael Payne's thorough examination of the York Factory records has revealed, alcoholism in the HBC was not widespread and drinking was rarely fatal.[52] Indeed, for most servants, liquor was a pleasant part of everyday life, as it was in Britain. It was given to them to encourage hard work, to reward their diligence, and to console them for short allowances, and it was withheld when they misbehaved.[53] One officer was moved to remark that brandy 'might be justly calld the life and Soul of Work' and he praised its effectiveness in 'keeping a few dissatisfied minds quiet' and preventing mutiny.[54] It was also an important feature of holidays, when even officers might indulge in 'perhaps a too liberal quantum of w[ine]' and make themselves ridiculous, as George Barnston felt he had done in fighting a duel with Chief Trader William Todd on New Year's Day at York Factory in 1823.[55]

The consumption of alcohol was also an important part of celebrations unique to the fur trade. In 1771, the officer at Churchill promised five gallons of rum to the first man to see or hear a black whale blow at the mouth of the river. At Lac Seul, it was 'an old Custom' to give each man a quart of rum when the fish began spawning at Black Island. At Brandon House men customarily received a 'dram' of rum when they went off to fishing or hunting tents and a pint when they returned. On New Year's Day the men received 'their Engagement Pint' to celebrate the renewal of their contracts. Treats of liquor might also mark the arrival of the governor, friends from the interior, or men who had been working away from the post. At Fort Edmonton it was customary to celebrate the arrival of sleds and meat from the plains by an issue of drams all round. The passing of some places also required the observation of certain niceties. In 1793, the passage through what Donald Mackay referred to as Berens Lake was marked by three cheers from the men and a present of a pint of grog to each, which, said Mackay, was the 'customary fee' in the country, 'particularly from a Gentleman of Property for his title & claim to such a place or part of the Country'. Even George Simpson recognized that 'ancient voyaging customs' had to be 'respected' and gave the men a bottle of rum when he learned that it was the custom for an officer on his first visit to the little Rivulet portage to treat the men with 'an extra dram' or risk being shaved, as was the practice aboard ship when a man crossed the Equator for the first time. This 'sailor's baptism' was a rite of passage marking a man's initiation into the brotherhood of the sea. It was also a momentary reversal of the prevailing relations of authority and thus not very popular with captains.[56]

These rites celebrated what distinguished life in the fur trade from life elsewhere and reminded the men of what, regardless of rank, they all had in common, while the treats bestowed upon them were demonstrations of the company's benevolent paternalism. Like the nineteenth-century industrialists who introduced communal celebrations to encourage their workers to identify with them, HBC officers probably approved of the good feelings and harmony that such festivities could produce. But the drunkenness that accompanied such merrymaking frequently had undesirable consequences. The week of holidays between Christmas and New Year's Day, for example, was often followed by additional days off when carousing rendered the revellers unfit for work. Sometimes the damage was worse than a mere hangover. In the 'drinking match of new years day' of 1822 at Lesser Slave Lake, two men 'fought a Battle' in which one bit the other's hand so severely that he was likely to lose some fingers.[57] In 1861, during the New Year's 'Convivialities' at Fort Alexandria the men went across the Fraser River and 'punished themselves accordingly'. One of them 'fell down senseless' while trying to return to the fort and was found more than two hours later with his hands and feet 'frozen stiff'. After being taken inside, he was rubbed with rum for an hour, plied with 'strong doses of Rhubarb & Peppermint' when he developed cramps, had bottles of hot water rolled over his stomach, and was finally treated with a mustard poultice. Though apparently on the road to recovery by the next morning, the man suffered a series of fainting fits and was expected to be 'useless' for a long time.[58] The rum served out every Saturday night meant that many weekends were also riotous and left the men, as one officer described them in 1819, drunk and 'disfigured' from fighting and unable to carry out their assigned duties.[59] Liquor might also be necessary to ensure the performance of those duties in the first place and might be dispensed much too lavishly. For example, the stock of brandy allotted to Brandon House for the outfit of 1796–7 was used up by the end of January 1797 because so much had been served out on the journey to the post in the fall because the men had worked so hard.[60] Moreover, like the men at Fort Albany who, in April of 1812, refused to haul home boards unless they received a pint of grog,[61] the servants did not simply wait for their masters to decide that they deserved a treat. It is not surprising, therefore, that the London committee wanted to reduce, if not eliminate, the consumption of alcohol in the service, but achieving this goal was no easy matter. Attempts to eliminate unruly, plebeian rituals and replace them with celebrations that promoted deference and morality encountered strong resistance in Britain.[62] The force of custom was equally strong in the HBC and the measures taken to reduce the amount of liquor consumed in the service were largely ineffective.

In 1829, one officer, accustomed to issuing rum in drams at Christmas, found that at Fort Albany it had always been served by the pint and, wishing 'to avoid Singularity', he had to continue the practice.[63] In 1839 the council of the Southern Department stopped supplying liquor to some of the posts in the department and reduced it drastically for the rest with the intention of eventually eliminating it entirely.[64] In 1840, there was a concerted effort across the service to do away with the Christmas spirits, which annoyed the servants[65] but failed to abolish the traditional Yuletide treat. The committee hoped, in fact, to impose a greater degree of temperance in general and in 1841 went so far as to abolish regular allowances of liquor, deciding that in future the men would receive an occasional dram if they had to work in bad weather.[66] In 1842, George Simpson ordered that no more liquor be issued to any men in the service on the west coast. 'Remonstrances' based on the excuse that 'the moisture' of the climate rendered 'the modest use of Spirituous Liquors necessary to the preservation of health' were, he declared, 'totally unworthy of notice' and to be ignored. But Chief Factor John McLoughlin Sr turned to the London committee, explaining that the servants received a pint of rum when they engaged, one on New Year's Day, one when they left for their winter quarters or on a long voyage, a pint when they returned, 'and now and then a glass'. These were 'indulgences of long established Custom' and he would 'not interfere with them, without . . . positive instructions', which the committee decided against. Instead, it declared, 'It would afford us sincere satisfaction if the use of spirituous liquors could be entirely discontinued by the people in the Company's employ, but we are not prepared to advise you to take any steps towards this end that are likely to cause discontent as the quantity distributed is so small and the custom has been of long continuation.'[67] Officers appear, therefore, to have been free to do whatever they considered best, and many of them were equally unwilling to take steps that might 'cause discontent'. Thus, James Douglas, for instance, reported in February of 1851 that he had issued no spirits to anyone since New Year's Day except for a few drams he had given to the outdoor labourers when they returned from work wet and tired and a few bottles he had supplied to the officers. But other officers still found frequent infusions of alcohol necessary to get their men to work. A few years later William McNeill noted in the Fort Simpson journal, 'our men now get a dram in the morning, and we find that they are *always* on hand at bell time in the morning.'[68] Workers continued to insist on it. In 1859 the sawyers at Fort Edmonton demanded—and received—a £3 gratuity and a pint of rum per week each.[69] When the council of the Northern Department resolved to do away with the issue of spirits altogether in 1862, some officers objected because they believed that this measure would cause widespread dissatisfaction.[70] As for Christmas and New Year's, they continued to be celebrated with 'spreeing'.[71]

It was equally difficult to abolish the regale given to the crews of the Portage La Loche brigade upon the completion of their summer journey to York Factory. Not long after the brigade's establishment, George Simpson had promised the crews that if they reached the factory in August and delivered their cargoes in good condition, they would receive an eight-gallon keg of spirits instead of the usual allowance of one pint per man given to the regular servants. The crews received their rum as they were starting their return voyages from York Factory to Red River. As soon as they were out of sight they would put ashore and stay there until they had consumed all the liquor, while their boats and the company's goods lay exposed to the elements. In June of 1853, therefore, the council of the Northern Department decided that the men would receive their rewards prior to their departure and drink them at the factory. Then an opportunity to end the custom entirely presented itself.

That summer Simpson learned that the late Bishop Provencher had organized a temperance society, which now boasted 500 members, many of whom were tripmen engaged for that year's Portage La Loche brigade. At the urging of members of the Roman Catholic clergy and other concerned individuals, Simpson ordered William Mactavish, who was in charge at York Factory, to replace the regale with tea and sugar 'on a fair & liberal scale'. No doubt, the fact that by the mid-forties a significant number of tripmen had taken the pledge and had been asking for something in lieu of rum helped to persuade Simpson that the alteration could be introduced speedily and successfully. He soon learned, however, that the 'converts refused to be made sober men on compulsion' and directed that the measure be postponed until the following year and then introduced only if it could be done through 'moral persuasion' to avoid the 'difficulties' that 'compelling sudden change in this particular' might cause. John Black, chief trader at Fort Garry, probably spoke for many officers when he recommended that all brigades be deprived of 'the maddening regale' that was responsible for 'almost every remarkable instance' of 'damaged cargoes or of gross misconduct'.[72] Although a payment of 6 shillings to each man replaced the regale the following year, the alteration was not permanent and 'scenes of uproar and annoyance' continued to mark the brigade's arrival and departure.[73]

The consumption of alcohol could not be eliminated because many employees saw nothing wrong with it. Indeed, there were plenty of sottish officers on land and aboard ship[74] whose drinking rendered them unfit for command and was sometimes too much even for their subordinates. Thus, in October of 1809, the men of Osnaburgh House reported to John Hodgson that it was 'ridiculous to see' their master:

> he drinks 'till he is not able to walk nor set, and there he lies on the Floor, which it is pitifull to see, and if it was not for his Wife he would set the place on Fire, never blows out his Candle, lies in Bed, and drinks 'till he looses his Senses entirely; Sunday morning, Beastly drunk, Cursing and Blasphemy, for every person, and for you Sir in particular.—The Company must be good indeed to him.[75]

In 1844 one of the men at Rupert's River took it upon himself to inform the surgeon at Moose Factory that Robert Cowie was rarely sober and that recently he had been 'roning' after some Native women who 'noked him over in the snow', and afterwards he sat in the house drinking and telling everyone who went out to tell the women to come in. He had been 'going on this wey the whol winter' and was 'alwais getting wars [worse]'. 'The pleace' was 'going to wrak for want of a master', for he lay in bed giving 'verey strenge orders', drove the men 'from wan Job to another', and nothing was ever done properly.[76] Not only did such officers reduce themselves to figures of fun, they were also unlikely to concern themselves with the drinking habits of their men, who, left to their own devices, could indulge with impunity. It was, after all, difficult enough for temperate officers to curb their men's drinking because there was a tradition of illicit drinking that was as much a part of the routine as officially sanctioned imbibing and that, to some extent, the officers accepted.

Many servants belonged to groups assumed to be fond of drink. Thus, for example, the intemperance of James Hall, a carpenter at York Factory in 1790 had nearly destroyed his eyesight, but he was good when there was no liquor about to tempt him. He was, therefore, not dismissed, though his company was so 'disagreeable' that his request to go home in 1791 was readily granted.[77] Hall was an artisan and drinking was part of the culture of his craft—although, in his case, taken to extremes. Nevertheless, if the company wanted his services, it had to tolerate his vices. Men of Aboriginal ancestry were believed to be particularly prone to intemperance, but their skills were also too valuable to lose merely because of this flaw. Thus, John Richards, 'an excellent boatsteerer' but 'so subject to liquor' that he was completely unreliable, was never punished, not even in 1794 when his drunkenness led him to participate in the murder of a Native woman, whom he claimed to have stabbed only after her husband had already cut her throat. He was even put in charge of a trading expedition from Brandon House in the fall of 1797 because the men assigned to it refused to go under the Canadian master originally appointed to lead them. But Richards proved to be a poor leader and deserted several weeks later.[78]

Similar expectations influenced the relations between the captains and crews of the company's ships. Dissipation was part of the annual routine. Long voyages would pass uneventfully, with the men performing their duties quietly and attracting no particular notice. But once in port they became drunken sailors, going on almost daily sprees until it was time for them to leave and settle down to work again. Since it occurred in port, where both alcohol and opportunities to abscond were readily available, excessive drinking was likely to be of short duration, while too zealous attempts to curtail it might drive the men away completely. Wise officers understood the situation and avoided confrontations that might only make matters worse. Thus, for example, during the summer of 1836 and the winter of 1836–7, the captain of the *Columbia,* docked at Honolulu, dealt with the almost constant drunkenness of some of his men by hiring Islanders to replace those too intoxicated to work. One day, however, he tried to prevent Thomas Larkins, one of the regular tipplers, from leaving the ship. Larkins struck him and made use of 'a great deal of abusive language', whereupon the rest of the crew took Larkins into the forecastle and tied him up. The men's intervention, though no doubt preserving their captain from further indignity or injury, also usurped his authority by removing the culprit and preventing his punishment. Nevertheless, allowing Larkins to be restrained by his fellows would restore order and work could continue until the ship's departure put an end to the men's excesses.[79] Drinking was part of the seaman's culture and, therefore, his due. If his right to indulge in it was challenged, he fought back—with his comrades' support. An officer's tolerance of drunkenness thus was also influenced by the fact that his ability to exercise his authority depended on his men's acknowledgement of it.

In August of 1819, John Work, the chief of Severn House, investigating a racket, found John Cromartie and a clerk 'in grips' after the latter had tried to get rid of Cromartie, who had been pestering him for a glass of rum, by seizing him and forcing him outside. Work told them to separate, but Cromartie 'only took faster hold & swore with some insulting expression that he would not let go for [Work] or any one else.' When a repetition of the order proved futile, Work gave Cromartie 'a couple of boxes on the face'. Cromartie then turned on Work and tore his coat. Although Cromartie's conduct had been interfering with their work and he was alleged when drunk to be 'very quarrelsome' among the men, 'particularly those that are not a match for him', the other servants stepped in and stopped Work from hitting Cromartie again.[80] Under other circumstances the men might themselves judge an individual's behaviour as intolerable. In July of 1808, for example, George Moad, the steersman of one of the boats heading to Brandon House, was 'rather in liquor' and so 'troublesome' and 'quarrelsome' with 'his comrades' that two of them put their property on shore and refused to go any farther with him. As a result, everyone had to wait until 10 o'clock that night while a new steersman was fetched from Osnaburgh House.[81] An inebriated steersman imperilled everyone who travelled with him, as the two men who objected to Moad realized, but drunkenness itself was not objectionable. HBC employees were, in fact, prepared to get their liquor wherever they could find it.

Men were known to pilfer liquor from the cargo they were transporting[82] and to break into the company's stores.[83] They could also take advantage of the fact that they spent so much time out of sight of their superiors to drink when they should have been at work. Many such incidents probably went undiscovered because their detection tended to be fortuitous. When the eight men who left Moose Factory for their winter stations on 16 July 1814 stopped to drink up the brandy intended to last the whole journey, for example, they certainly did not expect their master, on his way to a nearby Canadian post, to turn up the next day and catch them in the act.[84] Still, although they were neglecting their duty by delaying their trip, they were at least consuming liquor that had been given to them. Others did not care where they got their rum or even try to avoid discovery. One day in May of 1816, James Clouston, master of Neisquiscow, not far from Eastmain, ordered John Norn and William

Flett to make poles for hauling wood and then went off to set fishing nets. When he returned the next morning, Clouston saw neither the poles nor the two workers and, after enlisting a servant to accompany him, went to look for them at the men's house. There he was greeted by a 'strong smell of rum' and the sight of Flett and Norn in their beds, with a puddle of vomit in front of Flett's. Clouston asked them if they were 'badly' and both replied that they were 'well enough'. He then ordered them to go and clean fish and, after they had stumbled off, searched the house and found a tumbler and some rum, with which he confronted the culprits. They now stopped denying that they had been drinking at all and blamed each other for their misconduct, although it was Norn who had broken into the desk drawer to get the warehouse key. Clouston immediately dismissed them from the service.[85] Likewise, the men at Fort Stikine who spent the night of 5 October 1841 drinking, and the next day were 'out of their senses' and unable to work,[86] appear to have been quite unconcerned that their conduct was unacceptable and subject to punishment. The fact that the HBC was not the only source of alcohol for its employees made it even more difficult to control their drinking. There were always rival traders from whom liquor could be acquired. Prior to the merger of 1821, Canadian traders had been the main source, but as the company's territories expanded new suppliers appeared. Free traders were happy to debauch Natives and servants alike.[87] On the west coast, non-HBC vessels also proved troublesome. In 1850, someone from the barque *England* sold rum to the men and Natives of Fort Victoria. Riotous drunkenness followed, particularly among the servants just arrived aboard the *Norman Morison*. Several had to be put in irons and one man drowned after he upset a canoe in a 'fit of intoxication'.[88] On Vancouver Island the presence of squatters and whisky sellers meant that the farm labourers attached to Fort Langley spent the Sabbath in dissipation and were unfit for work on Monday.[89]

Clearly, many servants did not share the London committee's opinion that the consumption of liquor in the service needed to be reduced or care if their drinking involved theft or private trade. But they were not merely indulging a vice. There were cases of drunkenness that conjure up a picture similar to the one painted by Frits Pannekoek: an intoxicated shipwright fell off a flanker and broke his leg at Fort Albany in October of 1780; in March of 1809 an Eastmain man working in the woods was left alone to cook for his companions, stole liquor, got drunk, wandered out of the tent, and was later found with frozen hands and 'in a stupid state in the snow'; in 1822 a man at Fort

Albany fell out of bed while drunk and injured his knee so severely that he could not travel; in 1830 Jacques Nance got into 'a most beastly state of intoxication' while drinking with some Natives at Weymontachingue, tried to force a clerk to give him more rum, became 'enraged' when the clerk refused, and burst into the gentleman's house declaring 'that he wished to get intoxicated so as to fight with and clear the house of all the Clerks and masters and Bourgeois.'[90] It is still necessary, however, to recognize such behaviour as a sign that the committee's view of things was by no means dominant. For the servants—and for many officers, too—business did not always come before pleasure. They welcomed festive occasions as breaks in the routine and illicit drinking was one way of adding more of them, although in the eyes of their superiors, of course, they were being disobedient and negligent.

Neglect of Duty and Control over the Work Process

By drinking, the servants were also exerting control over the pace of their work. Drinking might not generally be numbered among the methods workers used to achieve this, but when men delayed their journeys or interrupted their tasks or simply did nothing and lolled about and drank instead, they were reducing, sometimes to nothing, the number of hours they devoted to labour. That they would do so was due to both opportunity and inclination. Like pre-industrial workers elsewhere, HBC workers supervised themselves and performed their tasks according to a traditional pattern of periods of slackness alternating with steady labour. Moreover, they did not, as many of their superiors thought they should, believe in the primacy of work or the need to do it any more quickly than they themselves considered necessary. They dawdled on errands[91] and sometimes failed to complete them at all. Thus, in September of 1809, two men returned to Henley House four days after embarking on what was supposed to be a five-week hunting expedition claiming that they could find no rabbits or partridges.[92] At New Brunswick House John Murphy spent the outfit of 1820–1 faced with what he considered 'unparalleled' laziness. Parties of men sent to outposts dallied and slept away their time instead of proceeding quickly to their stations. Their efforts to procure provisions were suspiciously fruitless. When a fishing expedition produced only four kegs of salted fish in August of 1820 and a week's hunting only eight rabbits in December, Murphy believed the men were simply not exerting themselves and did not believe their claims that fish and rabbits were scarce. Of course, they might have been telling the truth, but in March a pair of servants returned from their hunting trip nine days early, empty-handed, having eaten all their supplies and, as one confessed, the game they had caught.[93] Servants also tried to avoid work by pretending to be ill or too weak or by declaring the conditions too harsh to undertake journeys or to work, particularly when heavy labour such as cutting or hauling wood was involved.[94] In 1819 one of the men at Lac La Pluie went so far as to cut himself so that he would not have to gather birch for sledges.[95] Some men simply ignored the orders they were given,[96] while others were careless or slow and became extremely impertinent when criticized.[97]

What officers saw as neglect of duty might have been, in some cases at least, simply a traditional use of time. Thus, in August of 1818, George Gladman went to see how things were going at the hay marsh near Eastmain and found the men in their tent sitting around the fire. Instead of giving them the treat of rum he had brought for their 'encouragement', he ordered them back to work, fined the two he considered 'most culpable' 10 shillings each for neglect of duty, and threatened to fine the rest if they misbehaved again. To teach everyone a lesson, he posted a notice regarding the fines, although its disappearance while he was away suggests that not everyone was properly impressed.[98] In October of 1859, two servants at Edmonton House, clearing away a pile of earth, decided to stop working and go for a ride, but their master was able to talk them into returning to their duty. This was not the first time they had misbehaved: they had already been reprimanded for 'idle ing [sic] away their time and not working as men ought to do'. In fact, the officer remarked, 'The way in which the half breeds of this Dist (especially those from Lake St Annes) work is truely miserable and tries the patience of any one who has to be over them, to see men idle ing over a job for 2 or 3 weeks which a couple of good men would do in as many days.'[99] In 1869 the master at Martins Fall, observing the men sawing beams, commented, 'they wont hurt themselves not them.'[100] From the men's point of view, however, it made no sense to rush to complete a job because there was always another one in the offing, for the drudgery that supported a post never ended. Nevertheless, it usually got done. Had Gladman not appeared when he did, his men would probably have finished their work in their own good time and to his satisfaction, but, after all, he was supposed to be in charge, not his men.

The question of control over the work process was also complicated by the fact that the company's craftsmen, like artisans elsewhere, possessed an identity based on their status as craftsmen. They were skilled workers and their superiority to common labourers did not go unrecognized. Not only were their wages higher, but during the company's early years senior tradesmen sat on post councils and were rewarded 'with a small complement of furs' to promote good behaviour and prevent private trade.[101] By the mid-nineteenth century, they had managed to become exempt from working in the boats whenever they travelled, although no formal regulation to this effect had ever been passed. So troublesome did this privilege become that in 1863, at the urging of the council of the Northern Department, the London committee directed that tradesmen's contracts mention explicitly their obligation 'to work their passages' between posts.[102]

Some craftsmen were also bringing with them the aspirations towards respectability that increasingly characterized some segments of the British working class.[103] In 1819 Edward Taylor, a shipwright, was hired to construct a decked vessel on Lake Superior. Being a 'respectable Tradesman' with two men under his immediate command, he was to be treated as one of the junior clerks 'with respect to the little luxuries allowed them when in charge of an Outpost'. He was also accompanied by his wife.[104] In the HBC, this trend was most visible among the engineers hired for its steam vessels on the west coast. Men in the engineering trade, particularly in marine engineering, enjoyed high status, which the HBC acknowledged. In 1839 Joseph Carless, hired as engineer for the *Beaver*, received a salary of £150, free passage for himself and his wife both out and home, £200 a year if he remained in the country after his five-year contract expired, and maintenance of his family as long as he was in the country. Carless had been employed by Boulton, Watt and Co. for six years, bore 'an excellent private character for steadiness and sobriety', and was 'perfectly master of his business'. That the men of this profession were a cut significantly above the usual run of HBC servants is further suggested by the secretary's description of one of the two engineers sent in 1858 to Victoria to serve aboard the company's steamer, *Laboucher*. The man was the son of a member of 'a highly respectable firm in the City of London' and 'a gentleman by birth and education'.[105]

Artisans expected consideration of their status. Thus in 1858, James Fitz Hams, a 'Master Mason' at Fort Yale, complained that he did not think he was supposed 'to serve Mr Ovid *Allord* as a servant or Slush for *Indian* Squaws' and removed himself to Fort Hope until 'Some alterations' could be made.[106] Nor could their sensibilities be disregarded, as James Hargrave discovered that same year at York Factory. John Moar, the assistant boatbuilder, was trying to spread disaffection among the servants after their rations had been reduced. Hargrave 'reproved' him 'for the carelessness and indifference' with which he performed his duty 'in comparison with the eagerness with which he urged his claims to better Rations better Cookery and other matters that he considered "his Right"'. Moar objected that Hargrave had 'injured his character as a Tradesman' and resolved to work no longer for the company and to return to Orkney in the fall even though his contract was not up for another year. When Hargrave ordered him to Churchill, Moar said he would not go 'unless sent as a prisoner'. Several days later, Hargrave pointed out to Moar the terms of his contract and the consequences of his 'present mutinous behaviour'. Moar replied that 'he was perfectly aware of both' and remained off duty for several months. He also refused to go to the Saskatchewan district even when George Simpson threatened him with the loss of his wages from the date of his initial refusal of duty. Since the presence of grumbling Norwegians made the officers hesitate to force him to fulfil his engagement, they sent Moar home.[107]

Such workers were accustomed to regulating their labour and time, although their craft pride could be expected to ensure that they were conscientious and their work was impeccable. At the same time, their independence was ill-suited to servant status and could, if their employer's expectations clashed with their own, lead to conflict. Thus, one of the complaints made by the Norwegian tradesmen at Moose Factory in 1854 was that they had done more work outside of their 'profession' than in the workshop. They objected particularly to cutting timber and sleeping in the open air because it was work to which 'Norwaymen' were not accustomed and it prevented their apprentices from learning anything. George Simpson himself accepted the principle upon which they based their protest, since he had ordered that they be employed only at their trades. But he believed that 'the turn of duty' usually taken by mechanics in the woods in the winter and on the boats in the summer was 'by them considered in the light of a favour being a relaxation from steady hard work & an agreeable change in other respects.' Instead of dealing with the Norwegians as artisans, however, he proposed to solve the problem by splitting them up and sending no more than one man and his apprentice to the same post so that they would 'more readily accommodate themselves to the habits of the country when unable to keep up a national feeling.'[108] It is probably true that many tradesmen enjoyed their sojourns at wooders' camps, where they were far less subject to the scrutiny of officers than they were in their workshops. But the fact that they had been able to free themselves of the obligation to work in the boats suggests that not all outdoor work was welcomed as 'a favour' and that Simpson was not nearly as well informed as he believed. By this time, of course, he had for many years been based at Lachine and geography had combined with his own arrogance to distance him from the majority of the men he commanded.

Some of the company's tradesmen, to be sure, adopted an altogether too leisurely tempo and standards not always reflective of the craft pride they were supposed to possess. Indeed, the HBC possibly attracted craftsmen who could find no employment in Britain and were among neither the most respectable nor the best-qualified exemplars of their crafts. Walter Bigger, for example, a carpenter at York Factory in 1779, spoiled timber and took more than five weeks to build a shoddy staircase of eighteen steps. When Humphrey Marten told him that not one of his jobs was anything but 'a scandal', Bigger replied with 'very foul and indecent language'. He also refused to take his watch, went to bed drunk, left his lamp on, and ignored Marten's repeated orders to put out the light or open his door. Marten finally broke it down and found Bigger in bed, fully dressed and wide awake. Hauled before the council, he was demoted to the rank of sawyer and labourer and required publicly to ask pardon of the officers and promise 'a due obedience to all lawful commands'.[109] In 1780 a bricklayer at York Factory, 'an ignorant saucy proud fellow' Marten suspected had never laid a brick in his life, built a chimney that had to be pulled down lest it suffocate the men. A year later he set a lime kiln 'in a very careless manner' even though he had been shown how to do it properly.[110] In 1802 the armourer at Eastmain made such a mess of the two guns he was supposed to repair that William Bolland concluded that the man was 'making a game' of him and boxed his ears, whereupon the armourer held up the butt of one of the guns in question in 'a threatening posture'. After being disarmed, he ran to the forge, seized a sledgehammer with which he made menacing gestures, and then drew a knife. He was sent home on the next ship.[111] In 1822 the master of Albany complained that the cooper knew his business, but was 'slow beyond comprehension', having taken a whole week to make a few water buckets.[112] In 1858 a cooper was allowed to retire instead of being offered a new contract because of 'his inefficiency as a tradesman and his mischief-making propensities among his fellow servants'.[113] And in 1869 the officer in charge at North West River complained of one of the men: 'for Carpenter as he pretend[s] to be I never saw such a botch of a fellow—the best thing that can be done is to send him home—the only good that I see he can do is to eat.'[114]

Obviously, many of the HBC's men did not dedicate themselves completely to their employer's business. This is not to say that they were uniformly disobedient and defiant, but they were certainly not subsumed in the company. When they signed their contracts they did not relinquish their identities or their interests, and these, not their status or the ties of the much-idealized master-servant relationship, determined how they would behave. Their diligence and loyalty, therefore, might not rise to the expectations of their superiors but still would be sufficient to allow for the performance of the necessary work. At the same time, they also engaged in activities that demonstrated even more forcefully how limited was their commitment to their employer: private trade, leaving the post without permission, and desertion. Indeed, these offences were displays of disloyalty and, in the case of private trade and desertion, also serious breaches of contract. They account for 40 of the incidents of misbehaviour included in Table 1, although it is likely that they were far more common than the numbers indicate.

Private Trade

Only three instances of private trade appear in Table 1. It was, however, a deeply entrenched custom with roots outside the company itself and by 1770 had become an elaborate system involving everyone.[115] But none of the journals of 1770–1 mentioned it. Yet, when the *Prince of Wales* arrived in London in October of 1771, a cache of illegal furs was found hidden aboard. It therefore seemed safe to count this as one case of private trade.[116] That the officers would not report it is not surprising, since the company had deprived them of the privilege of trading for themselves over a century ago, but they continued to do so anyway. And why should they stop, they might well have asked themselves, when the ships' captains were still permitted to carry goods for sale on their own accounts? In 1786, however, the committee abolished this privilege, prompting the captains to protest that this measure was 'exceeding hard' because their right to trade privately had 'been a Custom ever since the Company was established' and 'always been thought as a Perquisite' and 'part of their Agreement' with the committee. Although their petition for permission to continue 'like other Commanders of Ships, who all have Liberty to Trade a little in a fair Way',[117] was unsuccessful, they did not cease their private enterprise. Some years later, John Richards, one of the three captains politely throwing themselves on the mercy of the committee in 1786, was found to have been smuggling furs into

England.[118] Nor did the masters of the posts share the committee's view that private trade was bad. The officers at Churchill went so far as to aver 'that it is not in the power of any man living to prevent upwards of 20 poor Men that constantly live in the woods all the Winter from procuring a few Martens by their own industry' and to suggest that the committee's failure to give 'a proper acknowledgement' for them had encouraged illicit trade in the first place.[119] The council of the Northern Department found it necessary in 1822 to condemn the practice of officers' allowing 'favourite' servants to trade in provisions, leather, and other unspecified goods and in 1840 the London committee expressed surprise that the councils of the Northern and Southern departments needed to pass resolutions to the effect that all furs gathered by employees were the property of the company,[120] both of which suggest that officers did not change their opinions. In fact, private trade blossomed regardless of the regulations passed to prevent it.

In 1824 the council of the Northern Department ruled that each departing employee could take no more than two dressed skins or buffalo robes and 20 'Indian shoes'. But by the 1840s canoes headed for Canada laden with shoes, leather, robes, and even 'madeup furs', some of which officers had themselves presented to their men. Goers and comers, i.e., men hired in Lower Canada to transport goods and men into the west but not to winter there, bartered their supplies for furs with the regular servants and the Red River settlers. On the voyages back to Montreal, retiring servants and goers and comers traded their shoes, leather, and fur caps for liquor at Sault Ste Marie and the taverns they passed, endangering lives and property, 'occasioning desertions', and 'maiming each other in drunken quarrels'. The shoe allowance, which was intended to supply footwear on the trip, could not be eliminated, but in 1844 the Northern Department ordered the seizure of any leather, furs, or robes found in the men's possession. Nevertheless, the trade in leather continued to flourish, while, according to one officer, the company could not get enough leather for its own business.[121]

Rules designed to prevent trade in livestock were equally unsuccessful. Each commissioned gentleman was allowed the use of a saddle horse or a train of dogs, while the servants were allowed to purchase animals from the company, which would buy them back when the men left. The result was a thriving and profitable trade in horses. In 1855, George Simpson reported that both officers and servants, especially those born in the country or married to natives of it, frequently engaged in this business. Some even bred colts for sale, with herds of brood mares maintained at the company's expense and cared for by the company's horsekeepers, sometimes in the company's stables. The council of the Northern Department therefore resolved that any 'further infraction' would be punished by a forfeiture of the amount realized from the sale of such an animal and a fine of £5 for the first offence and £10 for every subsequent 'conviction'.[122] But officers demonstrated more initiative in seeking out new opportunities for private enterprise than in discouraging it in their subordinates.

Murdoch McPherson, an officer in the Mackenzie River district during the 1830s, sold supplies and packs of playing cards to the servants. When he left he took away the records of the district to conceal his misdeeds, although they must have been widely known and tolerated. Johnson G. King, gossiping about McPherson, mentioned that he had a bad reputation, although this might have been because he was 'a most tyranical Brute', not because he indulged in illicit trade. After all, King was not averse to this himself, having recently attended the auction of a deceased officer's effects and 'speculated largely intending to sell in the Columbia, where articles fetch an enormous price.'[123] In 1853, George Simpson informed the officers at Fort Vancouver that the HBC's surgeon was obliged to serve only the company during working hours. Outside of these, he had to be available for emergencies, but he might carry on a private practice, though he would have to pay for any medicines he used in it. That this subject required explanation suggests that the surgeon had been pursuing his own interests at the company's expense. Other western officers were also 'devoting a considerable share of their time and attention to the promotion of their private interests by breaking land and farming, building houses mills &c', and importing items on the HBC's generous terms to procure the goods with which they paid their labourers. They were thus at 'one and the same time depriving the Fur Trade of their services for their own pursuits and making it pay part of their outlay by taking goods below their actual cost.'[124]

Perhaps the most spectacular case was that of George Pelly, who managed the company's establishment in Honolulu. In October of 1850 Pelly accused some of his Hawaiian servants of stealing over $36,000 from the vault, but Arthur Bates of the office of the solicitor to the Crown became suspicious. He considered native servants too timid to have removed over a ton of specie from a place not 20 feet from Pelly's bed without his noticing. Bates's investigations revealed that on a salary of £400 a year Pelly was living in a style that required £2,000 and he advised Pelly to come clean. Pelly agreed to admit that he had spent the money, assume the debt, sell all his property to pay it, and leave the country or else face conviction for embezzlement. Bates then informed the company's secretary of what had transpired, but could not bring himself to provide 'the details of Mr Pelly's habits & recent outrages upon decency'.[125] The company's archives do not reveal the outcome of the case or supply information about Pelly's other transgressions. He might well have been involved in various dealings that, along with his extravagant habits, brought him to the brink of financial ruin and led to his desperate attempt to extricate himself. Most officers had to be content with a larceny far less grand than Pelly's, but, whatever its value, it was the very existence of private trade that really mattered. It was, after all, strictly prohibited. Furthermore, officers who engaged in it themselves were unlikely to do much to rein in their subordinates among whom the tradition was quite as firmly entrenched.

By the nineteenth century, both officers and servants imported goods aboard the company's ships expressly for purposes of sale, either to one another or to their Canadian rivals. It had even become common for servants to sell part of their rations to officers with families.[126] According to William Auld, the men had become 'shameless', trading openly with the Natives for items they had acquired from the HBC and never considering 'that similar conduct in Servants at home subjected them to the most disgraceful punishments'. He was particularly incensed by the 'insolent rapacity' of Gilbert Budge, an Orcadian cooper at Fort Edmonton who had purchased 'for some triffle' a 'fowling-piece' from a 'Chief Indian' to whom it had been sent 'expressly' as a present.[127] Budge had successfully combined two prohibited activities. Earlier incidents of servants bartering with the Indians for their weapons had led the committee to issue an order prohibiting such trade specifically, since it believed that Natives could not 'subsist' without their guns. Servants, on the other hand, were not allowed to possess them at all. Officers supplied them only when required and then recalled them.[128] Only Auld seemed to consider Budge's crime worth mentioning, since no record of it appeared in either the Fort Edmonton journal or the account book and Budge continued to serve until 1815, when he returned home with a good character.[129] The reason was not, however, that Budge's master was dishonest and disreputable. On the contrary, he was James Bird, a highly respected officer with most of a long and distinguished career behind him.[130] What distinguished him from Auld was not virtue but experience. Years spent in positions of authority gave officers a greater understanding of their men and of the limits of their authority.

Thus, in 1796, James Sutherland, another prominent and successful officer with 25 years of service behind him, commented that because his men were 'badly fitted out' he could not stop them from trading with the Canadians, which had been explicitly prohibited in 1793. In fact, he felt 'deprest on every hand by the discontents of the people' and was 'almost afraid' to order them to their ordinary duties lest they run off to join their rivals who were waiting with open arms, having constantly tried to 'debauch' the men, 'particularly the Ignorant who can't see an Inch before their nose.'[131] The company's officers had become accustomed to a degree of autonomy not entirely compatible with the committee's insistence that they subordinate themselves to its decisions, but it was certainly understandable given their greater knowledge of the men under their direction. Indeed, the relationship between the committee and the officers was mirrored in the one between them and the servants, for the latter also possessed more autonomy than they were supposed to. They transgressed the company's regulations, regardless of their officers' efforts to enforce them, and did not limit their illicit transactions to those in which their officers colluded.

HBC workers possessed their own assumptions about the right to engage in private trade. The custom of appropriating some of an employer's goods for one's own profit, generally on a small scale, had a long history and was an important perquisite for many workers. Pilferage in the workplace was so common that many employers adjusted their wages and prices rather than bothering with costly prosecutions.[132] In some instances, HBC employees appear to have brought such habits with them, as in the case of the aptly named William Paine, a tailor from London who arrived at Eastmain in 1803. The century-old London society of journeyman tailors was 'the most militant and effective trade union' in eighteenth-century England and tailors in general were well represented in labour disputes. The extent of Paine's participation in such struggles is impossible to determine, but he was 39 years old and, therefore, an experienced artisan immersed in the culture of his craft, both its noble and base aspects. As he might have done in England, he purloined cloth from the work he was assigned and made clothes to sell to the other men, threatening to 'throw himself off duty' if John Mannall, his chief, dared to mention it. As Mannall asked, 'What is to be done with such a Man?' Paine possessed a self-confidence that often overstepped the boundary into insolence. When Mannall rebuked him for repeatedly 'idling away his time' in the cook room, he retorted with 'a deal of abusive language' that he was 'neither thief nor murderer and did not require watching, &c &c.' On another occasion Mannall distributed potatoes for which everyone but Paine was 'very thankful'. When Mannall suggested that he, too, should express his gratitude, Paine declared that 'if you expect that, I've left all my manners in England. . . . 'd—n the Potatoes I would not give a d—n for them.' He then complained that he was not treated as he had been 'given to understand', that he was told he would be completely outfitted in the service and never have to wear his own clothes. Instead, he protested, 'I find I'm imposed on and d—n me if I stay.'

When he actually worked, he was intolerably slow and he would suffer no criticism. On one such occasion, he flew into 'a most violent passion, d—d his eyes if he would do any more work and went on at such a rate.' He then followed Mannall, still 'd—n—g & Swearing', threw some material on the floor, and announced that he would not finish his task. Mannall, having just conveniently gotten a gun from the armourer, 'touched' Paine's shoulder with the butt. Paine then threatened to shoot Mannall and assumed a stance that suggested he was about to strike him, but he turned away, picked up the material, and left, promising revenge. Later, when told to finish some other work, Paine replied that he would 'see [Mannall] b—d first' and flatly refused to do as he was told. He was then put to menial duties such as cutting firewood and hauling hay.

No longer employed as a tailor, Paine demanded that the other tailor make him some clothing. Mannall told him he should be ashamed to ask such a thing, but Paine insisted he had as much right to this service as any other man. Mannall told him he might make himself a jacket and trousers after he completed his current duties. The next day Paine retired to his cabin to begin making his clothing, declining to do anything else that day. At noon, Mannall served grog to the rest of the men, who had been working outdoors in the cold, but gave none to Paine, who then demanded his share, called Mannall 'the most opprobrious names he could think of', and finally took a swing at him. On the following day Paine went back to cutting wood, though not because he had reformed but because he was afraid that the other servants would not let him near the fire otherwise. His efforts were so desultory, however, that his companions refused to work with him, saying he was 'of no service whatever'. Paine finally deserted to the Canadians, who sent him back to Mannall, who discharged him and sent him home in 1804.[133]

Paine's private tailoring was only one of his misdemeanours, and this was vastly outnumbered by his other transgressions. But it and the defiance with which he responded to attempts to curb his independence demonstrated the difficulties that could arise when experienced craftsmen were engaged in subordinate roles incompatible with the status to which they were accustomed. Paine might not have been among the more respectable members of his calling, which was reputed to harbour a large number of dissolute individuals. In fact, his very engagement with the HBC might have been the result of his low standing in London's tailoring world. But he would still have considered himself an artisan, entitled to the privileges and respect due a man of this rank and therefore indignant at his treatment and assertive of his rights. Craft traditions might have been a factor in Paine's misbehaviour and accounted for the *type* of illicit trade he practised, but the rest of the servants observed similar traditions and they were able to do so because they spent most of their time away from the eyes of their superiors and were frequently entrusted with the company's property.

When servants went trapping, which the committee encouraged them to do in their spare time, they traded on their own accounts with the Natives.[134] Threats to inflict the penalties mentioned by the contract had little effect and officers sometimes resorted to more brutal measures. Thus, in 1773, when John Ewing, a labourer at Albany, admitted to trading for a marten skin with a Native, he was manacled. Since it was his second such offence, his chief decided to make a 'Publick example' of him by tying him up and inflicting 18 lashes with a 'Cat of nine tailes'.[135] But such a spectacle could have little chastening effect on the men because they continued to believe, as John Green, an Irish labourer, declared in 1820, that 'the man is a fool who wont make a little money for himself.'[136] When in 1840, James Gunn, a servant at York Factory, thanked his father in the Orkneys for sending a bundle of goods that he had sold, his matter-of-fact tone indicated that, as far as he was concerned, this breach of contract was simply a business transaction. Moreover, he was so dissatisfied with the service that he was determined to return home the following year and never come back. He also urged his parents to put his brother to 'a good Trade', the best, in his opinion, being a ship's carpenter because without a trade a man was 'nothing in this country', which was 'very bad and always getting worse every way'.[137] Gunn might well have seen private trade as compensation for the trials he had to endure in the service, and as long as men continued to see nothing wrong with trading for themselves they would continue to do so.

The extent of such trade is incalculable because of the ease with which it could be hidden. Indeed, it often came to light purely by accident. Thus Samuel Taylor, an Orcadian carpenter who joined the HBC in 1804, had an unblemished record until January 1812 when he was suddenly revealed to be 'a most wicked Scoundrel, a Thief of the worst Kind, an exciter of Mutiny among the Men'.[138] He and another man were sent from Churchill to York Factory with a packet on 30 November 1811. When they had not reappeared by the middle of January, Thomas Topping, the chief at Churchill, concluded that they had perished and took an inventory of their property in preparation for its disposal, probably by auction.[139] Among Taylor's possessions Topping found a large quantity of Canadian clothing and 'many articles which . . . could not have been very honestly come by', an impression strengthened by the fact that Taylor had been entrusted with the charge of a house inland during the summer. The two men turned up just as Topping finished his task and Taylor admitted to trading with the Canadians and to taking an oil stone, a chalk line, and a quarter pint 'jappan'd pot' from the houses where he had been stationed, though he claimed to have found the pot on a dunghill. He also asserted that the six and one-half pounds of powder and 16 pounds of shot he had were what his masters had given him for his various journeys. Since the ammunition was in suspiciously small packages, however, Topping suggested that Taylor had 'plundered' it out of the ammunition intended for the Natives to whose tents he was sent for furs or meat. When Taylor surrendered the stolen goods, as ordered, the chalk line was found to have been cut and some of the ammunition was missing. Volunteering to look for the rest, he departed and was gone so long that Topping went after him and found him hiding his mittens, filled with powder and shot, under a washtub. Hopelessly cornered, Taylor acknowledged his 'gross misconduct' and begged for lenience, which Topping was determined to deny. Taylor had already given notice of his intention to go home when his current contract ended in 1812, so sending him home was not much of a penalty. He was, therefore, fined £9 and compelled to give a bill of £10 'to the poor of his Native Parish rather than be sent home and there hanged.' These were substantial sums for a man earning £26 a year.[140]

Topping might have considered hanging justified, but dismissal, imprisonment, fines, or corporal punishment would have been Taylor's fate in Britain, unless, as was not uncommon, he was part of a complex network of trade in stolen goods involving a variety of ostensibly upright citizens. Then he would have had nothing to fear at all.[141] Within the HBC, too, a man was protected by the silence of his fellows, many of whom were equally involved in such illicit dealings. Discord, therefore, could be revealing. As the officers at Fort Albany observed in 1770, 'it is a trite addage that when Rogues fall Out, honest Men come to the Truth.'[142] Thus, at Albany in 1840, Jacob Corrigal found an altercation between two servants highly informative. When the son of William Linklater Sr knocked down and kicked the son of James Morrison and then was insolent when Morrison asked him to explain his actions, Morrison complained to Corrigal. Corrigal confronted young Linklater, who called his father. A quarrel ensued, in the course of which both Morrison and Linklater Sr called each other 'dishonest'. Challenged by Morrison to prove his allegation, Linklater replied that Morrison had made axes 'slyly' for the people. Morrison claimed that he had made them for use at work and retorted, 'that is not so bad as you did in smuggling about 40 or 50 lbs Feathers to Moose last summer;—and I could tell more of your dishonest ways if I liked', effectively silencing Linklater. When Corrigal later asked Morrison how he had found out about the feathers, the man replied that one of the sloopers had told him that he had found a missing package of feathers at Linklater's bed place. When asked what he had meant by being able to tell more, Morrison said that Linklater had packed gunpowder in small bags, hidden them in fox skins collected while at a logging camp, and then sent them home to his family. Corrigal now understood why the Natives had accused him of not giving them full measures of gunpowder when they were being fitted out for the goose hunt, for Linklater had been in charge of distributing the it.[143] Such revelations must have made the London committee wonder with trepidation how many such cases went undiscovered.

The servants were also as adept as their officers in taking advantage of new opportunities. In 1867, W.J. Christie reported that the servants of the Saskatchewan district received their supplies in the fall and then proceeded to trade them with miners, large numbers of whom were flooding into the area 'ragged', 'penniless', and 'clamouring' for work and food. Then, in spring, the servants would inform him they intended to leave, 'taking care by every artifice . . . to draw all they can from us & generally leave in Debt'. A case in point was Alexander Aitkin, a blacksmith, who had been particularly well treated, having received a gun from Red River and permission to send for his wife in Britain, a privilege rarely bestowed on common servants. Then, in March, Aitkin had given notice because, he complained, the price of goods was higher than during his first contract and he could not save. After Aitkin had departed, leaving behind a debt of £10 18s.4d. to the HBC and several bills owing to others, which the company refused to pay, Christie learned that Aitkin had been selling off everything he had, turning 'all into cash & Gold Dust & left with a heavy purse'. Meanwhile, the 'Halfbreed Servants' engaged at Red River for the Saskatchewan district regularly went off drinking with the free traders for days at a time and, when sent with goods to trade, sold them for liquor. Not only did they thus embezzle the company's property, they also wasted it by squandering their time, consuming all their rations, and then eating the food provided for their dogs, which consequently starved to death.[144] The London committee would have been far too annoyed to appreciate that such disloyalty and disobedience were also an impressive display of the servants' entrepreneurship. But private trade was also one more manifestation of the gap between the servants and their superiors.

Gerhard Ens has observed that 'the concept of the trading post as a single patriarchal household became strained' by two 'destabilizing influences' that derived from 'a systematic illegal fur trade'. First, the seasonal presence of ships' captains, whose authority made it impossible to prevent them from trading with the servants, undermined the control that the masters of the company's posts had over their men. Second, HBC employees engaged in illicit trade with local Aboriginal groups and established liaisons with Native women. The result was the formation of '"sub households" connected to the surrounding Indian bands'.[145] However, neither of these two developments would have been possible without the servants' willingness to engage in private trade in the first place in defiance of their officers and in breach of their contracts. Their identification with the company was clearly limited. They decided for themselves which rules they would obey and which they would ignore. It should not, therefore, be surprising that HBC employees also left their posts without permission and failed the ultimate test of loyalty by abandoning the company altogether when it suited them.

Unauthorized Absence and Desertion

Unauthorized absences and desertions together account for 37 incidents of misbehaviour in Table 1. Desertion alone appears to be the third most common type of misbehaviour, but since it was more likely to be noticed than negligence or illicit drinking it should probably rank lower. A man's temporary absence from his station might remain a secret because he spent most of his time out of his master's view and could sneak away and return without his knowledge, yet the many occasions when work did take a man away from his post might well have provided sufficient freedom and made truancy unnecessary. The rarity of both desertion and unapproved absences prior to 1821 and their subsequent increase suggest that their incidence depended to a large extent on the availability of desirable places to go. Before the merger of 1821, HBC men generally deserted to the nearest North West Company posts. For Canadian servants, whose language, origins, religion, and, in many cases, previous work experience linked them to the rival company, it was both easy and logical to cross over when the HBC displeased them. But non-Canadians were just as likely to do so, and their frequent disobedience of the orders against fraternization meant that they were not venturing into alien territory.[146] As competition heated up in the 1790s, the companies built hundreds of new posts, frequently within sight of one another, facilitating illicit fraternization and private trade and providing even more convenient refuges for deserters. Servants knew how to make the most of this situation, and more than one officer was afraid to ask his men to do anything lest they desert. The Canadians, reported James Sutherland in 1797, were 'gaping with open mouths to receive any... discontented Servants' and he could 'scarcely get the domestic duties of the place done by the people in general all casting up that the Canadian Service [was] become preferable.' For the past year, he had had, in fact, considerable difficulty hanging onto his men.[147] It was a worrisome trend, which, as usual, was attributed to outside influence. In 1816, Thomas Vincent, governor of the Southern Department, blamed the 'unprecedented Number' of desertions during the past season on the officers' neglecting their orders to prevent 'communication' between their men and the Canadians, 'therefore affording frequent opportunities to the Canadian Traders of tampering with the men, and rendering them dissatisfied with their situation.'[148] Desertions do appear to have increased, but not necessarily because the men were being lured away. The HBC, after all, was sending them further inland, where, starving and freezing, some of them were tempted to escape,[149] while disgruntled servants elsewhere simply had more places to desert to.[150]

The merger, which left the HBC as the only large employer in Rupert's Land, did not solve the problem because new opportunities far more attractive than anything the NWC had ever offered presented themselves. In the east the same employments that drew away potential recruits prompted contracted servants to abscond.[151] On the west coast, deserters were able to disappear to Oregon or California. Like other sailors, the seamen of the HBC ships could easily sign onto one of the many other vessels that put into company ports. They were particularly prone to deserting in Honolulu.[152] From there they hoped to get to California, where gold and high wages beckoned. In fact, according to Captain Weynton of the *Cowlitz,* vessels in Honolulu had been burned by their crews so that they might be free to go to

California.[153] Gold fever struck elsewhere, too. In 1849 it was necessary to give some of the servants in the western interior six months' leave of absence 'to visit the Californian El Dorado' or, Simpson feared, there would have been a general desertion. In September of 1850, Johnson G. King reported from Edmonton that 50 men had 'bolted' to the mines. Ten years later, John Saunders at Fort Alexandria reported that a gold strike at Antler Creek had caused discontentment among the men, especially because their rations consisted almost completely of flour, and they readily succumbed to the blandishments of miners and packers who loafed around the men and sneered at them for keeping their contracts when they might have better wages elsewhere. Packers could earn as much as $30 a month with board and clothing.

There was little the company could do about the situation. Its only legal recourse was to produce evidence of a man's desertion and then have him imprisoned for from one to three months with a reduction in wages during his confinement or dismissal from the service. Neither was much of a penalty. Saunders likened the latter to 'plunging a man under water to avoid a shower of rain'. Because they were convinced that the company *'had no means of punishing deserters',* men were not afraid to run away, and Saunders feared that if men at Red River got the same idea into their heads they would sign up in order to be transported free to the 'Gold Country' and desert as soon as they arrived.[154] Indeed, the general disregard for the company's authority and, according to Robert Campbell, the 'rascally lawless state of things now in the Country' meant that deserters could find refuge anywhere in Rupert's Land, including the Red River Colony through which they were easily able to pass to the United States.[155]

Like such transgressions as private trade, drunkenness, and negligence, desertion was a sign that the relationship between the company and its workers was not controlled by the former. Just as the Aboriginal traders influenced the shape of their relations with the HBC, so the company's own employees shaped theirs. They possessed their own interests and identities, which they did not abandon when they joined the HBC. Nor was the fur trade society they thereby entered free of class and cultural division. Most of the men who performed the work of the fur trade were relegated to the bottom of that society and, although they shared in the mores unique to it, they also practised customs their superiors disapproved of and tried to stamp out. This conflict was part of fur trade society and also at the heart of the company's relationship with its workers.

5

The Denial of Duty

Your Honor's Servants now a days takes great Libertys to what they used to do When I first know'd this country they was more under Subjection and was afraid of denighing any duty their Superior thought fit to put them to and now they think nothing of it but will denigh with a face of brass. . . . They tell you if you dont use them well that they never will come with you again . . . has for my part I never desired men that was under me to work Longer then 3 or 4 hours in the day Except when they was Occasion for it such as buildings &c. For I know their passages up and Down is very hard and trying to what it is staying below. . . .[1]

Thus William Walker bewailed the loss of subordination among the HBC's servants in 1789, though after 21 years in the service he should have known that its workers had never been afraid of 'denighing' duty. Perhaps, like the London committee, he envisioned the company as a kind of one-sided partnership in furs, in which, as H. Clare Pentland put it, 'the Company's dependence on its men was great: but the dependence of the men, in their isolated posts, upon the good faith and wisdom of the Company, was still greater.'[2] This view implies a negotiated relationship, but it is one negotiated by unequal partners, one of whom is deferential and submissive. In fact, of course, this was not the case, as Walker's disclosure that he never made his men work more than three or four hours a day suggests. He might have seen himself as a considerate master cursed with ungrateful underlings who repaid his thoughtfulness with insubordination and insolence. To the London committee, however, it might have appeared that Walker's men enjoyed far too much leisure and that he had relinquished his authority to set the pace of work in the service and allowed his men's indolent tendencies to prevail. But the situation was not so simple as it appeared from London, thousands of miles away. Walker understood the men he had to contend with far better than his employers did, and it was he who had to deal with servants who, as his journals of 1789–90 and 1790–91 revealed, did not behave as servants were supposed to.

He had difficulty persuading some of them to winter among the Natives in October of 1789, when it should never have been a matter for persuasion at all. In December he complained about the servants' laziness in gathering bark. In April of 1790, a man refused to turn canoe timbers because, he claimed, he was not paid to do so. On 4 May, Walker reported that only three men were at work while the rest were 'doing as they pleased'. In June, on the way back to the Bay, when some of his canoes went on in the night without anyone telling him where, Walker grumbled, 'a Master upon this Road is regarded as Nothing', and attributed the wrecking of one canoe to the fact that 'a great many' of the servants 'will not obey a Master when he does order him.' In March 1791, Walker mentioned that George Short had twice declared that he would do only what he thought 'requisit' unless everyone else did it, too, and another man announced that it was not in Walker's power 'for to hurt him, and he did not Care a dam' for him. 'I think a master is come to afine pass when inferior persons is to take command to himself and upBraid a master in that manner', Walker sniffed, and warned, 'It still will be Wors and Worse untill such time there is an example made of one or two, and then their ambition might be Lowered.'[3]

Most of the transgressions that Walker reported were like those discussed in the previous chapter: expressions of an indifference to authority rather than overt challenges to it. But his journals also describe behaviour that went further and that he believed indicated a crisis in discipline. Of course, Walker was bitter since Humphrey Marten and the York Factory council had overruled his promotion to assistant to the chief at the factory because they disliked him.[4] This slight probably made him over-sensitive to his men's insubordination and prone to exaggerating it. At the same time, the HBC's efforts to expand into the interior were being frustrated by the servants' unwillingness to perform the duties now required of them and Walker's complaints, like those of other officers, drew attention to misbehaviour that was bolder and more confrontational than the majority of the servants' offences. Coming at a time of fierce competition, a labour shortage, revolution in France, and social transformation in Britain, such conduct was bound to convince the London committee that discipline in the service was collapsing. But there was no sudden epidemic of disobedience. The company's workers were really only attempting to control the pace and conditions of their work, as they had always done, although when they denied duty, as Walker put it, they were not only refusing to perform a particular task, they were also denying their duty as servants to obey unquestioningly their master's orders.

It should not be surprising that more than one man should turn out to be what John Murphy referred to as a 'lawyer', i.e., 'one who discusses the propriety of an order before he obeys it'.[5] After all, HBC employees neglected their duty, engaged in private trade, and even deserted the HBC altogether. That same attention to their own interests prompted them, like workers elsewhere, to object to what they considered excessive hardship, unreasonable orders, and cruel or incompetent officers. As far as their superiors were concerned, of course, there was nothing legitimate about a servant's refusal to carry out whatever duties were asked of him: it was sheer insubordination and it could not be permitted. This is not to deny that, in some cases, this view was correct. After all, not every case of disobedience constituted a struggle against oppression. John Miles, for example, who would not bring some newly brewed beer into Moose Factory in July of 1771, was not being asked to perform a difficult or dangerous task.[6] Nor was Jacob Henderson, when he refused to get his watch wood at Brandon House in November of 1796 and 'dam'd' his master into the bargain.[7] An even worse case was Henderson's contemporary, Charles Seymour, a joiner at Churchill, who refused to remove a ladder from the side of the house and replied with 'insolent language' when William Auld insisted. Seymour's punishment was to keep the first watch for the rest of the week, but he would not do this either, whereupon the council fined him £1 10s. He then proceeded to demonstrate the extent to which the committee had overestimated the effectiveness of this form of punishment. A month and a half later he declared that he would not grind two hatchets 'for all the *Devils in Hell'*, thereby earning himself a fine of £3. A few months later he split the joints and broke the back of a chair he was supposed to repair and announced that it was now stronger than ever. He was not dismissed from the service, though, and in the fall was fined another £3 for 'maliciously & wantonly' ruining a new sled.[8]

At Eastmain in June of 1802, Caesar Linklater objected to boiling seal blubber, but then deliberately overfilled the kettle, which began to boil over. When told to remove some of the blubber because fat was running into the fire, Linklater refused and let the kettle continue to overflow. William Bolland then told him to take the fire away and when Linklater would not do this either, Bolland 'gave him a kick on the breech' and did the job himself. Linklater was then told to do something else, but declined, saying he had not come out 'to be used like a dog &c.' Bolland put him on half allowance and Linklater continued to refuse duty for the next five days, whereupon Bolland fined him £3 'by way of example to others'.[9] Another bad character was Samuel Flaws, a labourer at Moose Factory, who in August of 1812 would not accept his appointment as cook. Even being twice hauled before the council and threatened with a heavy fine did not change his mind. Indeed, he declared 'himself ... assured' that any fine imposed there would be remitted in England. Considering him in breach of his contract and his conduct subversive of discipline, the council argued that he had forfeited all money due him, as, of course, the contract itself stipulated. But Flaws returned to duty the next day and 'expressed much Contrition for his Offence', prompting the council to decide that the above penalty was now excessive. Still, deeming it necessary to impose a penalty 'for the Support of due Subordination', the council fined him 20 shillings.[10]

An even poorer addition to the company was Palm Saunders, who was sent to spend the spring of 1847 at Oxford House. Only a few weeks after his arrival he struck an inoffensive lad with his fist and threatened 'murder & vengeance' against some men who would not agree to return home from cutting wood at an 'unlawful hour of the forenoon'. When not pretending to be sick, Saunders spent his work hours urging his companions to 'lay down & sleep' as he did, calling them a 'parcel of fools' for being afraid that the company might dismiss them. 'Look at me', he said, 'I dont work & I shant work, I dont mind no Master or the Governor or Company a damn.' He also began 'sending to the Tents & collected Indian Wives at an unlawful hour at night ... for unlawful purposes.' Laurence Robertson, the officer in charge, was willing to put up with Saunders's behaviour because he was leaving the service that year, but found that his 'sayings & examples' were a bad influence on the other servants and the Natives. It was not until he was denied some powder and shot, however, that Saunders actually refused to work. 'I am going off', he declared. 'I will see you McTavish Governor & Company at Hell, I dont mind the Company or their work ... I'll work no more I'll obey no more orders I am intending to be off.' Robertson told him he could go where he liked, but if he stayed he had to obey orders and work.

Despite his threats, Saunders remained, and, since it was Saturday night, the question of whether he would work or not remained unsettled until Monday morning, when he would not get out of bed. Robertson threatened punishment, but Saunders replied, 'I do not mind you or any master the Governor can go to hell I do not mind him he cannot kill me, he never did much good for me.' Robertson then left. A few hours later he returned and was able to persuade Saunders to go to work by promising he would not report his conduct if he obeyed. But Saunders did not mend his ways. He tried to lead the other men astray and deliberately damaged the seed potatoes. When another servant chided him, he retorted, 'That is the way I will work I will be nothing the better for doing the work well.' After once more finding Saunders in bed after the others had gone to work, Robertson observed that if all the Oxford House servants were like him the place would be 'in a fine Mess' and left the room. Unchagrined, Saunders followed Robertson outside, saying, 'You the Oxford Servants & the Company's work, can go to hell I dont value any of you.' Robertson told him to get to work and 'give no insolence', to which Saunders replied, 'Damn your soul to hell, say one word & I will come & Knock your bloody brains out.' But Robertson 'reasoned' with him and Saunders returned to duty. None the less, he was soon up to his old tricks, quitting early in the morning and going to bed and calling the obedient servants 'fools' when they returned to the house at the proper hour. After Saunders spent a Monday sleeping on the pickets he was supposed to be pointing, Robertson ejected him from the post.[11]

At Fort Yukon in August of 1850 the man assigned to cook for the officers, having been 'told times without number to Keep the dishes clean and sweep the Kitchen floor', in response to yet another demand that he tidy up the 'abominable mess', did as he was told, but announced that he would cook no more. He also told A.H. Murray, the master of the fort, that 'as a clerk [he] had no right to have a cook & that all cooks had to receive £3 extra wages &c. &c.' Murray therefore assigned him other 'and harder' duties and the next day appointed John Ewing, whom he considered 'unfit for general work', to replace him. Ewing refused with 'some very insolent language without the slightest provocation'. When Murray reminded him that his wages would be stopped and he would be put on half rations if he disobeyed, Ewing told him he could not do so and he *would* have his regular rations, and then proceeded to spend the day at leisure. The following morning Murray appointed another cook, who also rejected the assignment. Murray now discovered, although he did not record how, that the three men's misbehaviour was an 'arrangement amongst themselves' instigated by the first cook, and Ewing agreed to assume the culinary responsibilities on the following Monday.[12] In May of 1851, at Fort St James, one of the men, having repeatedly disobeyed orders, having been 'generally backward & apparently not willing to work', and having refused to reform, simply left after his officer 'had some words' with him.[13] In August of 1870, two of the men at Fort Edmonton refused to work 'at the carts' and spent a day doing virtually nothing.[14]

Men could, of course, attach a tinge of legitimacy to their misbehaviour by refusing to work on the Sabbath,[15] although piety had little to do with it. Thus, in August of 1810, some of the crew of the schooner at Albany virtuously declined to help unload the vessel because it was Sunday, 'though at the same time they thought it no sin to curse and swear during the day most heartily against the irreligion of others.'[16] Sabbatarianism was not widespread in the HBC, the men's attendance at the mandatory divine services was always highly irregular, and by the 1840s many officers failed to hold them at all.[17] Indeed, a man of a truly pious bent was out of place. Poor Laurence Bain, having attended revival meetings in Scotland, was driven to 'insanity' when 'his religious sensibilities' were 'wounded by the very wicked conduct of some of the men among whom he was placed in Hudsons Bay.'[18] Ron Bourgeault has suggested that during the 1840s the 'class interests of the Half-Breed working class' were 'taking form' and the *voyageurs* fought for a day of rest on Sunday, among other things. As a result, 'many a strike and mutiny occurred over this issue.' Unfortunately, his evidence consists of only one such incident in the summer of 1846 at Portage La Loche.[19] Sunday was, however, traditionally a holiday in the service, except when travelling, a situation that the servants accepted. When, in 1802, for example, François Snoddy, who had been appointed to go inland from Churchill, declared that he would not work in the boats on Sundays, the other men threatened to abandon him along the way. He then refused to work at all and was replaced.[20] Former servants making formal complaints to the committee did include working on Sunday among their grievances, not because they had to travel but because they were not allowed a break from their duties at their posts, which, they complained, were run by tyrants who overworked them. Disputes also erupted when Methodist missionaries urged their mostly Native flocks not to voyage on the Sabbath.[21] For most servants, however, Sunday remained a day of rest and recreation and was recognized as such by their superiors. When men refused to work on

Sunday, they were justifying their misbehaviour by referring to a firmly established custom, not necessarily expressing a new class consciousness. Nor were their motives always noble or idealistic.

The Refusal To Be Imposed Upon

Nevertheless, the misconduct of some should not divert attention from those occasions when disobedience was not due to bad character but to a reluctance, as the expression went, to be imposed upon, in spite of the fact that it was not a servant's place to consider the orders he was given an imposition. Incidents of misbehaviour, therefore, must be examined from the perspectives of the men themselves in order to appreciate the rationale that motivated them. Thus, Caesar Linklater, who had refused to boil blubber and whose consequent provocative behaviour could have caused a conflagration, was nevertheless assigned a messy and unpleasant task that he might have considered so disagreeable that he felt justified in refusing to do it. Likewise, William Walker's men were not always simply being excessively lazy and disobedient. Objections to wintering with Natives were not at all unusual and reflected a widespread dislike of the hazards and hardships that working for the HBC entailed. Indeed, Manchester House, situated on the North Saskatchewan River, was at the time one of the furthest inland of the company's posts. The men stationed there were in precisely the sort of situation most likely to lead to discontentment, for, of all the duties that servants were obliged to perform, venturing into the interior to establish or occupy posts was the most frequently refused. Almost every year, when assigned to their winter stations or ordered to embark on exploratory expeditions, some men objected to going. This was the case in 22 of the 57 incidents counted as refusals to do as ordered (Table 1). In 11 of these, men were refusing to go to specific places, in six they were refusing to proceed until certain demands had been met, and in five they were refusing to go inland at all.[22]

Although such refusals were a constant source of inconvenience to the HBC, they were particularly troublesome during the years of competition with the Canadian traders before 1821. The annals of the fur trade may celebrate the journeys of Henry Kelsey, Samuel Hearne, and David Thompson, but most servants had no desire to be explorers. It was their unwillingness to undertake expeditions into the interior as much as the HBC's lack of interest that encouraged the company to keep to the shores of Hudson Bay.[23] The servants' resistance, certainly, was to a large extent due to the company's ineptness in carrying out its expansionary policy. The London committee wanted its men to explore the country, living off its resources instead of imported provisions, acquainting themselves with the Native peoples and their languages, and establishing trade relations, as the Canadians were doing. But while the Canadians journeyed inland in large, well-equipped parties and established posts from which men would take assortments of goods to Native encampments, the HBC expeditions were usually individuals sent out to live with Aboriginal bands, find out what their competitors were doing, and return to the Bayside posts with plenty of Native traders and their furs.[24] This mode of exploration increased the committee's knowledge of its territory, but its stinginess—due no doubt to the same ignorance that had led it to believe that it needed to send no supplies to the Bay in 1695—exposed the men to hardship and deprivation beyond what they considered reasonable. Not that provisions were always ample or even good at the well-established Bayside posts, but scarcity there did not seem to excite the same clamour as elsewhere, perhaps because everyone knew that new supplies would arrive with the next ship. Going inland meant relying on the resources of an unfamiliar environment with no assurance that those resources would prove adequate, and when the worst happened it strengthened the servants' resistance to suffering the same fate.

In 1777, for example, the men at Gloucester House were reduced to eating tree bark in the summertime when the living should have been easy. Then, in October, the local Natives informed the master, John Kipling, that they could not stay for the winter because there were no victuals and offered to guide the Europeans to Henley House. Since, as was the case with most of its posts, the company was relying on local Aboriginal bands to provision Gloucester House, the Natives' inability to do so alarmed the men. They begged Kipling to accept the Natives' offer to take them away, declaring that 'they had suffered Enough in the Summer to undergo the same as in all Likelihood they will if they stay for there is not any thing to be got by Englishmen.' Kipling felt obliged to give in. The following June, when Thomas Hutchins appointed men to Gloucester House, three of them refused to go without a wage increase and would not give in even when Hutchins reminded them of the terms of their contracts and the penalties for disobedience specified therein.[25]

A few years later George Sutherland's disastrous expedition had a similar effect. Sutherland had spent 1777–8 tenting with Natives and was no greenhorn when assigned to do so again in 1779–80, but this time the adventure almost killed him. Once inland, he and his clerk learned that the Natives with whom they were supposed to live did not have the resources to support them. As a result, the two men and one of the Canadians with whom they had travelled inland built themselves a house and spent a winter of 'unparalleled distress'. Under the assumption that the Natives would feed them, they had not been adequately provisioned and they could catch no fish. They had been told to go to Gloucester House if they got into trouble, but they could not do so because they had nothing to travel on or anyone to accompany them. Sutherland resorted to the nearby Canadian post for company and whatever assistance it could render, but that was so meagre that he ended up eating dogs, mice, his leather breeches, shoes, and mittens, and returned to Albany 'reduced . . . from one of the most sprightly Men to a perfect Cripple', unable to 'stand upright nor walk without a stick'.[26]

Although it is not certain that Sutherland's ordeal caused the men of York Factory to extort a wage increase in excess of what the rules permitted as the price of their going inland,[27] it caused serious difficulties at Fort Albany. There the most capable canoeists left or declared their intention to return home the following year, while the men just landed there were, reported Thomas Hutchins, 'crying . . . that they may not be sent Inland, they declare they will die first.' To allay these fears, he stored up eight months' worth of provisions, but somebody 'had infused into their Minds' that, although there might be plenty of provisions that year, 'it was only a trick to get them to go' and next year there would again be nothing. Some of the men swore they would 'rather go on board a Man of War and die at once, than suffer a lingering Death inland'. 'Your Honours will perceive from hence', observed Hutchins, 'that the Men remember they have been often at short allowance and how *absolutely necessary* it is to send an *ample* supply of Provisions', a memory kept fresh by news that John Buchan, wintering inland with Natives, had starved to death in January.[28] There was also trouble at Henley House, where six men refused to go inland, although one offered to do so if his wages were raised to £15 a year. Another, however, insisted he would not, even 'at the peril of losing his Wages and going on board a Man of War'.[29] News of what awaited them if they left the comparative safety of the Bayside posts came from outside the company, too. In 1790, Joseph Colen reported that the Canadians had 'made it public that they are often driven to great extremities, wintering so far to the Northward; which has deterred the principal part of your Honors Servants from venturing.' As a result, when Malcolm Ross offered to undertake expeditions to the north from York Factory if a capable man accompanied him, all the men declared that they would rather go home than go on 'so dangerous an Expedition' without a gratuity 'beyond the common wages allowed' by the company.[30]

The committee's perennial mania for economy, as well as its fear of private trade, ensured that it would heed no demands for higher wages or more provisions or the advice of experienced officers like Eusebius Bacchus Kitchen, who warned in 1779 that its settlements would never grow 'advantageous' unless it first set about 'satisfying' the servants.[31] Instead, the committee insisted on low wages, reprimanded the officers for requesting too many goods and medicines, and reminded them to order no more supplies than 'absolutely needed'. At the same time, it asked its officers what luxury goods the servants might wish to purchase. The council at Churchill replied that it was fine to furnish 'menial servants' with good slops, but there was no market for tea, chocolate, and coffee at the prices suggested.[32] Probably both officers and servants would have been happier if the committee had simply sent more of the necessities, but the gentlemen of the committee had no personal experience of what their employees faced, whether camping with Natives, hauling logs out of the woods, paddling down rivers, or eking out an existence on an Orcadian farm. Besides, had not the committee ensured that its workers were drawn from populations accustomed to poverty and endowed with a hardiness that fitted them for the duties required of them? Still, it did not want its servants to suffer needlessly. It paid bounties to those going inland and in 1799 sent a 'digester' to make 'portable soup', i.e., a pot that reduced soup to cakes that could be carried on journeys and diluted with water for consumption.[33]

The servants, however, preferred wages that compensated them fairly for their efforts and working conditions that did not expose them to inordinate hardship. They therefore took advantage of the company's need for their services by demanding wage increases with distressing frequency.[34] But money was not everything, although it might have appeared that way to the London committee. Higher wages did permit the accumulation of more savings, but these could never be sufficient for a man to retire from work. A few more pounds a year might, of course, enable servants to purchase more clothing or rum, but the company was neither willing nor equipped to sell its men unlimited quantities of either. Indeed, for those who found themselves in the middle of nowhere at a post with modest supplies of trade goods and few imported provisions, there was even less to buy. This situation was certainly ideal for saving, but a large sum entered to a servant's credit in the company ledger neither released him from

Sleighs and dogs used for hauling firewood, 1870s. HBCA Photograph Collection 1987/363–C–55/71. (Courtesy Hudson's Bay Company Archives, Provincial Archives of Manitoba.)

toil nor kept him from starvation. Thomas Saunders, on his way from Fort Albany to Lac La Pluie in July of 1818, certainly entertained such thoughts. Threatened with a fine for taking rum from the cargo, he replied, 'I dont velou [value] what youle fine me what is the goud of money to me I am only starving while I Serve you and if you fine me by god I shall leave you at OH and perhaps before.' His equally disgruntled companions complained that they could not work as hard as they were expected to because they were starving.[35] HBC servants wanted due consideration of their comfort and well-being. In July of 1791, for example, when the men assigned to Swan River found out how far from the house their supplies would be left, there was 'universal discontent and Murmuring' and they demanded, though without success, that the goods be transported for them over the portage.[36] In 1802 William Bolland ordered some of the men to undertake a voyage northward from Eastmain aboard the shallop. Sam Irvine, an Orcadian sailor, whose contract was up that year, replied 'in his dirty offensive language before all the people, he would be B—d before he step'd on board her.' Bolland immediately put him off duty and on half-allowance. The rest of the men also objected to the voyage, though more politely, and would not go until Bolland promised them 'the proper encouragement', presumably bounties, and gave them clothes to replace those damaged from working with oil.[37]

Even when wages were an issue they were not necessarily the main one, as the situation at Fort Albany in 1800 and 1801 demonstrates. In August of 1800 none of the 13 men whose times were up would agree to return inland, despite the bounties they could expect. Nor did they take advantage of the fact that the post was facing a severe labour shortage to try to force the company to raise their pay. John Hodgson had received no new hands the previous year and only one carpenter and three labourers now, a situation that he expected to be 'a very great check to' his plans. To make matters worse, the ship had brought no tracking line and there was none at the factory. As a result, the men set off for Martins Fall, about 300 miles upriver, with much 'Grumbling . . . even almost to Refusing the Journey' because they had no line 'they can trust their Lives to among the Falls and Strong Currents.' The following year the contracts of more than 30 servants expired. A few could be re-engaged only at increased wages, while 24 refused to stay on any terms because they were 'obliged to be on Foot all the Winter sometimes Night and Day, and obliged frequently to live with the Indians and many times their living is very miserable.'[38]

Sending men to live with Native bands was an important part of the company's strategy because it provided information, helped build a skilled labour force, established amicable relations with Aboriginal hunters and secured their furs, and freed the posts of a few mouths to feed. But many servants felt like James Houston, who declared in 1796 that he would 'rather stay home and starve like a dog'.[39] In 1819 one of the servants at Point Meuron went so far as to declare that 'no servant could be obliged to remain along with the Indians', a logical observation since one of his fellow workers had already returned twice from thence without suffering any punishment.[40] At the same time, though, it is important to remember that some men's objections to living with Natives had as little to do with suffering as refusals to work on Sunday had with devoutness. James Corston, for example, who turned up at Nipigon House late in February of 1803, had been sent out earlier that winter with another servant and several Native men. He had abandoned them and accompanied Thomas Richards to the latter's father-in-law's tent, where he had fallen in with two Canadians and gone with them to their house. He had then proceeded to spend his time tracking down Natives for his hosts, but was now unwilling to suffer the 'fortig' (fatigue) of returning to them. Corston claimed that starvation had driven him to the Canadian post, but

William Corrigal, the master of Nipigon House, did not believe him. The Natives and the servant with whom Corston had originally set out had arrived a month before and he knew that the Natives had taken the two HBC men to a good fishing place and helped them set up their tent. Corston had also left a blanket and a shirt at the Canadian house, a sure sign of his intention to return there. Nor was his response to Corrigal's reprimand what one might expect from a dutiful servant forced by circumstance to disobey his orders. He said, reported Corrigal, 'I might doo my worst, and helpe my self and be d—d.'[41]

Corston's case serves as a reminder that duties that took men away from their posts also offered welcome opportunities for independence. Many servants were happy to spend time at fishing and wooders' camps, where, far away from the eyes of their superiors and in the company of like-minded co-workers, they could engage in a wide variety of prohibited activity. Indeed, when a post's provisions ran out or turned bad, a man could live far better in a hunting tent. Nevertheless, although transporting packets between posts and hauling home wood, fish, or meat were assignments that removed men from the supervision of their superiors, such tasks were still hard work. Robert Dudley probably spoke for many of his fellows when, refusing to accompany one of the officers to trade with some Natives, he declared 'that he was not going to be worked about all the Year lik a pack Horse—He was not paid for it and he would be damned if he should do it any longer.'[42] Furthermore, such trips could be risky. In January of 1812, for example, two members of a party returning to Moose Factory after delivering some goods to Eastmain had frozen feet. The two men had refused to complete the journey to Eastmain, had been left along the way, and, unable to start a fire, had spent the night freezing at minus 43 degrees.[43] Although resulting from their own disobedience, the men's injuries were still clear reminders of the dangers of such duties. Even more unfortunate was John Malcolm, who was sent to Gloucester House late in 1817. When John Daniel, an experienced steersman, refused to conduct Malcolm to his destination, he went alone, lost his way, and froze his feet, which had to be amputated. Daniel was fined £10.[44]

Such disasters not only crippled some men for life, they also helped to strengthen others' determination not to tempt fate.[45] Of course, most men survived these experiences, but there were enough cases of frostbite and exhaustion to demonstrate that travelling in the company's service could be dangerous. Servants were therefore not always ready to undertake duties that required them to leave their posts. In fact, of the 57 refusals to do as ordered (Table 1), 14 were

'Coast Indians' at Rupert's House, 20 April 1868. HBCA Photograph Collection 1987/363–R–37/19. (Courtesy Hudson's Bay Company Archives, Provincial Archives of Manitoba.)

refusals to perform such jobs. Of these, nine occurred in 1820–1, six of them at Fort Chipewyan. There was one incident each in 1770–1 and 1800–1, one in 1860–1, and two in 1870–1. These numbers suggest that servants were most likely to object to such duties during the years when the company was attempting to establish itself in the interior. Once it had succeeded in doing so, few men needed to fear the privations of their predecessors.

In later years wintering with Native bands ceased to be necessary, supply lines became well established, a large proportion of the company's workforce was native-born and accustomed to the country, posts were less isolated, and the proximity of free traders and settlers increased opportunities for private trade and reduced the servants' dependence on the HBC. Nevertheless, travelling to and residing at inland posts were still rigorous enough to raise objections among servants who found the conditions unacceptable. This was particularly true of European recruits, whose numbers decreased because they were attracted by new employment opportunities and disturbed by news of ill-treatment or harsh conditions in the most remote parts of the company's territories, particularly the Columbia Department and the coast of Labrador. But not only the most extreme deprivation caused those who did engage to balk when they were assigned to their posts. Robert Gunn, for example, declared in 1850 that he would 'rather forfeit every penny he is worth to return to his native country' than go to Martins Fall, though he did eventually change his mind.[46] Martins Fall was an old, well-established post where there was no danger of starvation and the work was not particularly onerous. Expectations had changed, however, and European workers now judged the quality of their maintenance according to standards that applied elsewhere. The absence of tea and sugar and the sparsity of imported provisions sparked complaints that the room and board offered by the HBC were inadequate. One of the causes of the Norwegians' discontentment during the 1850s was the absence from their rations of tea, sugar, and fresh beef, which they believed they had been promised. A number of them applied for compensation because they had to supply themselves with the goods the company would not provide. J.C. Arnesen, for example, petitioned the London committee for repayment of what he had spent on 'the necessaries of Life', which he claimed he had been forced to buy. The contract promised free board and lodging, but these, he declared, were 'in such bad style' that they were 'equal to nothing'. Seven pounds of flour, three and a half of pork, and seven ounces of grease in seven days were not 'to be called good Board'.[47]

Faced with a labour shortage that could only be worsened by such charges, the committee decided in 1860 to provide tea and sugar or a monetary compensation if these could not be supplied, plus items such as beef and pork that would appeal to British recruits. But it failed to make clear to all recruits that these rations would not be available at all posts, so the issue remained unsettled. Men continued to refuse to serve where it appeared that conditions were not what the company's agents had said they would be. In 1860, five of the new hands destined for the Mackenzie River district 'rebelled', prompting William Sinclair to punish them by sending them to posts where no European provisions were served out.[48] In 1864, several servants would not return to the English River district, east of Lake Winnipeg, because their rations consisted chiefly of fish, the 'common' food at posts in the interior. They insisted on beef, pork, potatoes, and a pound of flour a day, as their recruiters had promised, and declared themselves willing to serve anywhere else, foolishly assuming that they would get what they wanted at any other post and that their request would be considered reasonable. But Samuel McKenzie, an officer at York Factory, thought they should be dismissed for their insubordination because to permit them to choose where they went would only encourage everyone else to try to do the same.[49] It is unlikely, however, that their example had anything to do with the problems of 1865, when three new servants refused to go inland, seven old servants refused to return there, and none of those who did go 'went without difficulty'.[50] Whatever their officers might have thought, men refused to go where they were told not simply because they were bad, but because they objected to what *they* considered poor working conditions and inferior provisions, neither of which they felt compelled to endure.

The Refusal to Tolerate Cruelty

The quantity and quality of provisions and the arduousness of the work were not all that determined whether conditions were acceptable or not. Much also depended on the quality of the officers, of whom both the London committee and the servants expected appropriate behaviour. The committee wanted officers who were honest, diligent, abstemious, responsible, and dedicated. The servants, though no doubt aware of the value of these virtues, also wanted their officers to treat them humanely. They might have been relegated to a subordinate status in a hierarchy they rarely questioned, but, as the Fort Albany servants demonstrated by refusing to accompany George Rushworth to Henley House in 1757 and the Manchester House men made clear to William Walker in 1789, they would not go with masters who did not 'use them well'. Thus, at the conclusion of the outfit of 1780–1, 15 of the 21 men of Hudson House on the North Saskatchewan River submitted to William Tomison their 'complent in Bad Wesage [usage]':

> the men all Decleares that ther is not wons Neam marked Hiear that will hever go allong with Robert Longmoar a day nor an owr for him to be master for thear is nothing But Noking pipeal about and put to short alouns by His falt and not your Orders Sir When farder inqurie is mead you may Knou mor about it sir Morover ther is not a man in sefety that goes wher he is when Indens Comes for He was allwies Drunk sir you aer our master and to you we are mead our Complent first For Either he or Els won or all of us Never comes from the Factray for him to be master for we all wies thought that He Head mend but in pleas of Better it is wors[51]

The officers at York Factory concluded that the dispute was the result of 'a misunderstanding' between Longmoor and his men, and although they did replace him they declared their firm belief in his innocence.[52] Leaving Longmoor in charge could have interfered with business, but removing him without defending him would have strengthened the servants' belief in their right to reject their officers, an assumption that the men's actions demonstrated repeatedly.

Thus, the 'spirited Efforts' of Donald Mackay, a former Nor'wester, might have pleased the London committee, but the conduct of his men made him lament that it would 'require the philosophy of Sir Isaac Newton to deal with' them. His preference for forceful managerial methods made him so unpopular. When some of the men at Fort Albany in 1796 learned that they were to accompany Mackay to Brandon House, they refused to go because he had beaten some of them 'without occasion' when they had wintered with him before. They remained 'inflexible' even after John McNab resorted to the tradition of calling them before the council and pointing out the consequences of their actions. Five men, one of whom had already served with Mackay, finally set off with him in September and made his life miserable, even, according to Mackay, twice trying to drown him. At Osnaburgh House the men stopped and refused to continue, in obedience to secret orders from McNab, who wanted to sabotage Mackay's plans. Mackay was forced to spend a lonely and comfortless winter in the woods and in the spring had to proceed to York Factory alone. None of the men appointed to accompany him would do so, 'on account they said, of his Violent Disposition, and bad will towards them.'[53]

John McKay, probably Donald's brother despite the difference in the spelling of their names, appears to have had similar tendencies, although his biographer saw in his journals 'a man of even temperament and humane disposition, with a sound understanding of the men who opposed him and the Indians with whom he traded'. Predictably, the servants are absent from this historical assessment. They might not have considered McKay so even-tempered. In May of 1801, Jasper Corrigal, employed as cooper and sawyer, arrived at Fort Albany, probably from Martins Fall, bearing evidence of 'a most severe Beating', including two black eyes. McKay's violent temper 'had rendered the man desperate' and he had refused to stay with him, although McKay claimed that he was sending Corrigal down for misbehaviour. The absence in the HBC Archives of a Martins Fall journal for 1800–1 makes it impossible to clarify this situation, but John Hodgson attributed the animosity between McKay and Corrigal to 'an old dispute' that had occurred when they were both at Osnaburgh House. That post's journal for the year 1798–99, however, contains no evidence of a serious altercation, although it reported that, while tenting, Corrigal had proved a 'Great . . . Gormandizer', consuming as many as 40 rabbits, eight pounds of pork, and 12 pounds of flour a week. He had also neglected to come home when ordered, but when he had finally arrived McKay appears to have neither reprimanded nor punished him. In 1801, McKay took command of Brandon House and remained in charge there until his death in July of 1810, except for 1806–7 because in July of 1806 the men refused to return inland with him as their master. They gave no reason and McKay's journals shed no light on the situation, but the servants' intransigence forced the master of Martins Fall to put Thomas Vincent in charge that year.[54]

John Charles was another officer whose bad temper caused difficulty. In July of 1798, one of a group of men who did not want to spend another winter with him threatened him with an axe, calling to the rest to assist him. None of them accepted this invitation, but they remained firm in their refusal and William Auld had to find others to go in their place. Some years later, George Simpson, in his famous 'Character Book', described Charles as so 'irritable and violent at times, that 'tis feared he will some Day get into trouble' with the Natives. As usual, Simpson took no notice of what this irascibility might mean to the servants.[55]

An officer who did not treat his men with the consideration they considered their due could not expect them to treat him with the respect he considered his due, as Robert Jones, a clerk, discovered in 1818 on the journey to Lac La Pluie. Jones started the trip on the wrong foot by informing the men that he intended to make them start earlier every morning, stop later in the evening, and get to their destination 10 days sooner than the previous year. Instead, progress was slow and another officer warned him that they would arrive 10 days later than ever if he continued to get the men up at two o'clock in the morning and make them travel until sunset. The usual practice was to start at sunrise and stop an hour before sunset so that the men could cook by daylight. Thus, when one of the Canadian servants announced his intention to shave Jones upon their arrival at Lac La Pluie, it is unlikely that his declaration to observe this traditional *bourgeois* baptism was made in a spirit of lighthearted fun. Jones certainly did not think so. He responded by swearing that if anyone laid a hand on him or complained about their rations, 'By the eternal God he would blow their braines out.' The men then assembled and challenged him 'if he was brave enough to do that now'. They also told him that he was to blame for the slow progress of their journey 'by chastising them late and early and fining them at different times for Singing after they had put up.'

Violence finally erupted while the party was stopped at Osnaburgh House. One of the men, Hugh Cameron, demanded more rum, and when Jones refused to give it to him he threatened to break a window. The next morning Cameron would not embark because Jones had fined him £22 for his misbehaviour. Jones, who was drunk, had Cameron forced into the boat, but the man refused to do any work, whereupon Jones hit him on the head and hands with a piece of iron 'until Blood painted the Oars and Covering' and he himself fell overboard. This was the last straw for the other Lac La Pluie men and they jumped out of the boats, declaring they would go no further with Jones unless he 'used them better'. Two of the other officers present advised the men to proceed on their journey, which they did, and Jones followed later. The men were still grumbling when they arrived at Lac La Pluie, where Jones proved no more popular with the officers than he was with his men.[56]

The case of Owen Keveny demonstrated even more dramatically the wages of cruelty. It became clear that Keveny's career in the HBC would be a rocky one while he was still on his way to Rupert's Land aboard the *Robert Taylor* in 1812—his frequent application of corporal punishment provoked a mutiny. Ashore, Keveny's regime was the same as it had been afloat, and his tyranny finally proved fatal in 1816. He was so harsh on the journey from Fort Albany to Red River that two of his men, Patrick Cavinough, or Cavinor, and James Corrigal, deserted at Osnaburgh House. Keveny continued without them, but left orders that they be delivered to him when they were found. After the deserters had been handed over, Keveny made them run the gauntlet while he stood by with loaded pistols in his hands and a sword by his side. Cavinough and Corrigal were then put into irons and obliged to work. Cavinough deserted again soon after and the group went on without him. Keveny's regular resort to whipping with willow branches for the smallest and, according to one of the men, imaginary offences resulted in regular desertions until, in a fit of rage, he ordered the four remaining men to go to a nearby NWC post, which they did. The Canadians took advantage of the opportunity to arrest Keveny and carry him off to Fort William for trial, which never took place because he was murdered along the way.[57]

Although the London committee did not approve of servants threatening their officers, it had always deplored cruelty. 'Use your Men with proper kindness', it had urged John Thomas in 1786, 'so that their Obedience to your Commands may proceed rather from an affection to your Person than dread of your Authority.'[58] Not that corporal punishment was unknown in the HBC. There had always been and always would be officers who, when confronted by insolence, intransigence, or carelessness, in the heat of the moment would give a servant a swift kick or a box on the ears or whack him with whatever object was at hand,[59] to which servants might respond in kind. Corporal punishment was also doled out more formally. HBC employees were whipped when the crime seemed to merit it, as in the already mentioned cases of John Cartwright and William Filpt in 1696, John Ewing in 1773, and William Duffle in 1791. Whipping, after all, was what the law of England prescribed for a variety of misdemeanours, particularly petty larceny, i.e., the theft of goods worth less than a shilling, and after 1750 also grand larceny. Its effectiveness derived not only from the physical pain but from the fact that it was usually carried out in public to humiliate the criminal and to act as a deterrent. It was therefore considered too harsh for gentlemen, because their loss of honour constituted a more severe punishment than the law intended, but appropriate for the vulgar, among whom the employees of the HBC would surely have been numbered. Towards the end of the eighteenth century, however, corporal punishment was falling into disfavour and public opinion was beginning to consider it preferable to try to reform and rehabilitate criminals.[60]

Flogging had never been universally regarded as acceptable. It was, observed E.P. Thompson, next to the press gang, 'perhaps the most hated of the institutions of Old England'. The Levellers, seventeenth-century radicals who advocated a classless society, considered it fit only for 'slaves and bondmen'. By the end of the eighteenth century, radical reformers were attacking it as inappropriate for an army, which they saw as made up of citizen-soldiers, and during the first half of the nineteenth century they campaigned to eliminate the practice. But they had no success until 1881 because their opponents did not see the army in quite the same way. The argument that the elimination of corporal punishment in the American, French, and Prussian armies had not damaged them usually met with the response that those armies were conscripted and, therefore, contained a cross-section of society. The British army, on the other hand, was drawn from, as the Duke of Wellington put it, 'the scum of the earth', the 'lowest and most thoughtless', who joined the army to 'extricate themselves from some scrape'. Such men needed a strong hand to restrain them, and that hand, apparently, needed to wield a cat-o'-nine-tails. Nevertheless, although popular opinion was unable to overcome the government's fear of indiscipline, flogging in the army did diminish.[61]

In the HBC, changing attitudes manifested themselves in several ways. The committee became convinced that fines were the most effective form of punishment.[62] Fines were a better penalty than sending men home, where many other employers competed for their labour and might deprive the company of men altogether. Fining was also more humane than whipping, which could only damage the company's good name and make recruitment difficult. The incidence of flogging decreased, at least in the eastern part of the HBC's territory. The last flogging administered for theft at York Factory occurred in 1797. In 1798 at Churchill, Peter Baikie, found guilty of theft from the cook room, was fined £2 and flogged by the men of the factory.[63] Thereafter, corporal punishment was applied mainly to those deemed in some way inferior. For a few years it continued to be inflicted on apprentices,[64] whose age and status defined them as completely subordinate and in need of discipline. Others, considered inferior by virtue of their culture or race, which tended to be seen as the same thing, also continued for a short time to be subjected to such indignities. In 1812, two of the recently recruited Irishmen were punished by running the gauntlet, one for theft and the other for 'impertinent language'. Running the gauntlet was a form of flogging carried out not by an officer or his deputy but by all the men and was an expression of communal disapproval of certain crimes, usually theft. Thus, the men might not have objected to punishing a thief, who had stolen some of their provisions. Impertinence, on the other hand, had never aroused popular disapproval, but no one objected to beating the other Irishman. Perhaps they saw it as an opportunity to exact retribution for the New Year's Day attack by the Irishmen on some Orcadian servants.

William Auld, superintendent of the Northern Department, feared the effects of 'this new trial of punishment without the sanction of the law or authority' and remarked that he would not be surprised if every old servant 'positively' objected and refused to serve 'under those who can outrage every right however they might be justified had they legal sanction for their proceedings.' At the same time, he did not consider such treatment inappropriate for some of the newcomers, remarking that 'from perpetual thefts which running the Gantlet and severe flogging repeatedly inflicted had no influence in preventing— one would rather have thought them intended for Botany than for Hudsons Bay.' As for the rest of the servants, he observed, 'we must use all our own influence over the old hands who will confide in us sufficiently to screen them ... from that summary mode of treatment so new and discouraging.'[65] The results of Owen Keveny's frequent resort to this 'mode of treatment' demonstrated that Auld's concern was justified, but flogging did not become common in his part of the country.

In the Mackenzie River, Columbia, and New Caledonia districts, the situation was quite different. There, servants believed, they would be bullied and starved, and the complaints and reports that reached the London committee revealed that their employees' fears were not groundless. In 1836, William Burris, a seaman aboard the company's steamer *Beaver,* protested that mariners in the HBC were treated differently from those on other ships and, 'being promised that our Vessel will be made a Hell of', appealed to the London committee for 'deliverance'. Burris objected to serving under a man 'who damns the Law, and says there is none here he will make Law himself.' He did not name the individual in question, but described the wickedness of several likely candidates. One, William Heath, the chief officer, had recently challenged a man to a fight and, being 'drunk as a Beast', had not cared that his victim had recently been flogged and his back was a sight 'which would make humanity shudder'. This, remarked Burris, 'is what they call due subordination and we are compelled to put up with it, I suppose they think we have no better understanding.' Moreover, unlike Heath, the men were not receiving grog. 'We have signed to defend Your Property with bravery', Burris wrote, 'how can we do so with cheerfulness or in fact at all, when instead of encouragement we get descouragement, such as stopping our Grog and telling us that we have signed for no Grog.' Captain Home, who would face a mutiny aboard the *Nereide* in 1838, had reduced the ration to 'a glass to a man once in a week', a measure, complained Burris, that was 'making either fools or children of us'. Burris had already sent details of the cruelty to which the crew was subjected, including the whipping of two men, one of whom was the unfortunate man harassed by Heath. Home had 'made himself a flagilator . . . to Messrs Finlayson & McLouglin', two of the HBC's officers, and had wielded a sword, cutting one man on the forehead and stabbing another 'clean thro' the Shoulders'. Burris also objected that Home had appointed him steward although he had engaged to work as a cook.

More than a year later the London committee informed Chief Factor James Douglas of Burris's complaints. It took a dim view of the incidents mentioned and insisted that in all cases where it was necessary 'to inflict summary punishment either afloat or ashore', a formal report 'duly authenticated [must] be prepared and transmitted' for its information. But such cases were to be kept to a minimum, lest they 'involve the Company in difficulties and lead to investigations' and 'expose the concern to much inconvenience'. Soon after composing this reprimand, the committee received news of another disturbing case. An employee named William Brown had wanted to leave the service in 1837 when his engagement ended, but had not been allowed to do so. When he had refused to return to the post where he had been stationed he was imprisoned, then tied to a cannon and flogged, and finally forced back to his duty, a story corroborated by a company blacksmith. The committee was also annoyed that the incident had not been mentioned in Chief Factor John McLoughlin Sr's correspondence. Brown had written to his father, asking him to seek assistance from the Reverend Clouston, the son-in-law of Edward Clouston, the company's recruiting agent in the Orkneys. Clouston had then written to the committee to apprise them of this matter, which had 'made a great noise here, which may be productive of very unpleasant consequences'. 'Such an occurrence as this if passed over unnoticed', warned Clouston, '... will be very detrimental to the ... Service.' McLoughlin claimed, however, that Brown had agreed to stay for an additional £3 a year and had been flogged because he had refused to return to Fort Langley to retrieve his child, who McLoughlin said was in mortal danger because it was not being properly cared for. James Douglas declared that Brown had wanted to leave the service, but because his child was less than a year old and unable to make such a trip, he was asked to stay on his former terms until the infant could be safely removed. But Brown resisted every argument 'for voluntary compliance'. These explanations failed to satisfy the committee. It replied that the case left the company's 'management open to vexatious inquiries', and if it had gone to court would have caused 'disagreeable exposure'. Brown should have been discharged immediately and simply not given a passage home, 'which would have brought him to his senses'. But the 'corporal punishment inflicted was decidedly illegal' and, to 'guard against the consequences that might have arisen from an investigation of the case in a Court of Law', George Simpson, 'acting privately', gave Brown 'a pecuniary consideration of £20' to settle the matter. By this time, Brown was already back in the Orkneys and had petitioned the committee for 'pecuniary compensation or pension as may enable him to support himself and his child as he is in very poor circumstances.'[66]

These cases, despite their gravity, would have attracted little of the London committee's attention if Burris had not sent his petitions, if its own agent had not informed it of Brown's complaints, and if the Reverend Herbert Beaver had not pounced on it to help discredit the HBC officers he had come to hate. Beaver had arrived at Fort Vancouver in 1836 and spent more time social climbing, complaining about his accommodations, and condemning the unsanctified unions of the company's men than he did carrying out his pastoral duties. His obsession with sexual irregularities, however, led him to cast one aspersion too many and earned him a beating from John McLoughlin Sr, whose wife he had defamed. Beaver thus had no affection for the HBC and he set about gathering information with which he could ruin its reputation. To the Aborigines' Protection Society he reported that the company had corrupted the Natives by encouraging its disease-ridden and heathenish men to consort with the women.

Though he clearly had no high regard for the company's servants, his attack on the HBC also included exposing the tyranny to which they were subject. He sent sensational letters to Benjamin Harrison, a member of the London committee and of the Clapham sect, which advocated moral reform, the establishment of foreign missions, and the abolition of slavery. Choosing language guaranteed to catch Harrison's eye, Beaver wrote, 'I have seen more real slavery in the short time I have been here than in the eight years and a half I was in the West Indies.' Discipline was maintained 'by the use of the lash and the cutlass, supported by the presence of the pistol'. He provided a lurid description of William Brown's whipping, an account of a Sandwich Islander flogged and then kept in irons for five months and four days, and reports of trouble among the seamen, always making sure to point out the poor quality of the officers involved. He also ensured that James Logie, a labourer at Fort Vancouver, submitted a statement describing the beating William Rae gave him for not feeding Rae's cat. Beaver witnessed the declaration and testified to Logie's 'remarkable peaceable, meek and Christian disposition' with which he had become familiar during the many evenings they had spent together preparing Logie for his baptism. After his return to Britain in 1838, Beaver continued to collect evidence for a book in which he planned to expose all the 'atrocities and inequities' he had encountered while at Fort Vancouver. He wrote to Logie and Brown asking for information about others who had suffered as they had and urged them to 'Speak very freely upon all these things that they may be known throughout the Orkneys, and others may be deterred from entering such a vile service.'[67] This, of course, was precisely the situation that the London committee wished to avoid, and it probably increased the shock value of the murder a few years later of John McLoughlin Jr at Fort Stikine on the Pacific coast.

McLoughlin, the son of one of the company's chief factors, after a misspent youth and a failed application to the HBC, had arrived at Red River in 1836 with the remains of James Dickson's expedition on its way to set up an Indian kingdom in California. George Simpson lured him away from it with the offer of a place in the company and he entered the service in June of 1837 as a surgeon and went to Fort Vancouver as a clerk. In 1840 he went to Fort Stikine to act as assistant to William Glen Rae and took over when Rae left in March of 1841. According to W. Kaye Lamb, McLoughlin was left in charge of this post and 'its turbulent staff' because he had a 'reputation for being a good disciplinarian',[68] though Lamb provided no evidence to prove that this was actually the case. In fact, the relevant records create an entirely different impression. When McLoughlin found a man in possession of some salted salmon, he 'used means which soon made him confess' that he had been stealing it regularly from the casks. Another servant, having helped himself 'rather too plentifully' to some spirits, received a 'few well merited cuffs from Mr John'. But these methods do not appear to have had the desired effect.

After Rae's departure, McLoughlin complained, it was 'impossible' to get anything done if the men were unsupervised.[69] The transfer of his assistant, Roderick Finlayson, to Fort Simpson in September of 1841 left McLoughlin feeling 'destitute'. He was suspicious of his subordinates and afraid of the Natives, who had threatened to kill him and his men if he did not reduce his prices. He was also convinced that, had someone other than himself been in charge of the post, it would not have been subject to such neglect. Furthermore, he was ready, if Finlayson's replacement was merely someone who 'cannot give satisfaction at the Depot but will be good for Stikine', to 'take his passage on board the steamer and leave the one to his own fate.'[70] He did not, however, have a chance to carry out this threat because early in the morning of 21 April 1842 one of his men shot him dead.

According to the last entries of the Fort Stikine journal, kept by Thomas McPherson and George Blenkinsop, McLoughlin and his men spent 20 April in drunken revelry, with McLoughlin becoming the most intoxicated. At one o'clock the next morning, alleging that one of the men had threatened him, McLoughlin took his rifle and went in search of him and another servant, both of whom were hiding. McPherson saw McLoughlin run down into the fort, heard four shots, and rushed out to find the officer dead.[71] Governor George Simpson arrived on 25 April and immediately questioned the men, who told him that McLoughlin frequently got drunk and flogged them mercilessly. Since the deceased had joined the company under a cloud and was a 'half breed', Simpson was inclined to believe the worst and quickly concluded that the officer had become 'a slave to licentiousness and dissipation, that his treatment of the people was exceedingly cruel in the extreme, and that the business entrusted to his charge was entirely neglected.' The men had acted 'under the influence of Terror as a measure of self preservation' and if the case were tried the verdict would be 'Justifiable Homicide'.[72]

McLoughlin Sr, however, was sure that his son had been murdered in cold blood and believed he had proof when Pierre Kanaquassé, one of the Fort Stikine men, volunteered a confession to James Douglas in July of 1842. Kanaquassé testified that all but one of the men had signed an agreement to murder their officer because he would not allow them to leave the fort at night or have anything to do with the Native women, and he had flogged two men for giving their clothing to some of them. Simpson had not questioned Kanaquassé because he considered him a 'worthless character' upon whose testimony 'no reliance could be placed', but McLoughlin believed the confession. He therefore dispatched Chief Trader Donald Manson to take new depositions and collect evidence of this conspiracy, which only added to the confusion. Thomas McPherson said he knew nothing of an agreement to murder McLoughlin but testified that he had drawn up a petition to present to Simpson, 'representing Mr John's misconduct & his ill usage of the men & begging that he might be removed.' Everyone had signed or put his mark on the document, but it was 'so badly written' that he had destroyed it out of embarrassment. The Sandwich Islanders, who could neither read nor write English, said they had signed a paper they believed had something to do with advances in wages. Another man declared that Kanaquassé had suggested that they shoot McLoughlin, but no one would agree to do it.[73] Nevertheless, McLoughlin Sr was convinced that the alleged petition was really the agreement mentioned by Kanaquassé and that McPherson had destroyed it to eliminate incriminating evidence. But Simpson wondered why he chose to take the word of a scoundrel like Kanaquassé when there was so much contradictory testimony and held to his original conclusions.

The absence of the crucial piece of evidence makes it impossible to determine whether there was a conspiracy or not.[74] The men certainly had reason to dislike the dead man. He had refused to permit them to take Native wives or bring women into the post, no doubt to improve security, but this prohibition clashed with the permission to take Native wives that George Simpson himself had given to more than 12 of the men when he visited Fort Stikine late in 1841.[75] Furthermore, even the testimony of sympathetic fellow officers suggested that McLoughlin had a violent temper. William Glen Rae declared that he had seen him intoxicated only once, on a Christmas night when he had struck one of the men, though with his fists, not with a stick as the servants had claimed. He also admitted that McLoughlin had become 'very violent' and had to be restrained and kept in his room until he calmed down. Rae had allowed him to speak to the two men who had guarded him after he promised he would only ask a few questions, but he 'began to ask them how they dared to hold him' and 'got so excited' that he hit each of them once. He immediately regained control of himself and 'was extremely sorry for what he had done'. As a mitigating circumstance, Rae observed that they had been obliged to be 'very strict' with the men there because they 'were great scamps generally'. Still, he thought that McLoughlin was no more severe than he had been himself and never, except on the night mentioned, punished the men unless they deserved it. Roderick Finlayson said that McLoughlin rarely got drunk, but that he had 'frequently' been so 'excited by anger' that he appeared drunk. He also reported that McLoughlin Jr had used his fist on a servant for stealing rum, struck Pierre Kanaquassé with his fist and a stick for stealing salmon, and flogged Captain Cole, a Sandwich Islander, with a cat-o'-nine-tails made from chalk line for sleeping on his watch.[76]

McLoughlin Sr's campaign to clear his son's name with long letters describing the depravity of the men in the department succeeded in persuading the London committee that there had indeed been a conspiracy. Learning of this change of opinion 'by a few private lines' from the committee's secretary, Simpson quickly had prepared 'an Analysis of the Depositions' taken by Manson, demonstrating that they contradicted the story told by Kanaquassé, whose character rendered him completely untrustworthy. He urged the committee to drop the affair, since any proceedings taken against the implicated men 'would fall to the ground' and be 'attended with much serious expense & inconvenience to the business'. The committee, though still sympathetic to McLoughlin, knew that, without the written pact that proved a conspiracy, legal action would be costly and fruitless. It therefore declined to take the matter any further,[77] but the affair sent shock waves throughout the service. The officers were divided over who was to blame[78] and at least one servant was inspired to contemplate doing what McLoughlin Sr was convinced the Fort Stikine men had done. In the summer of 1842, Narcisse Mousette, stationed at Cowlitz Farm, near what is today Toledo, Washington, mentioned McLoughlin's death to his two companions and said that 'if his comrades would agree' to support him, 'he would assist in murdering' Charles Forrest, the clerk in charge of the farm. One of the men, Hilair Gibeault, 'rejected the proposal with horror and reproved' Mousette 'for his wicked designs' and reported the incident to Forrest. McLoughlin Sr's investigation revealed that Forrest had scolded Mousette and two other men for failing to perform a full day's work. When questioned, Mousette said that he had 'meant it only as a joke'. McLoughlin Sr told him 'it was not language to be used', confined him, and sent him back to Canada 'to go about his business' because it would not be worthwhile trying to prosecute him.[79]

Mousette's joke confirmed John McLoughlin Sr's fear that the company's failure to punish his son's killers would encourage other servants to follow their example, a thought that occurred to others as well. At York Factory, Letitia Hargrave wrote her mother that since McLoughlin Jr had been 'in the condition of a maniac' when he was killed, the murderers would be 'acquitted' because their crime would be judged 'justifiable homicide'. But 'how are ignorant men to be taught the distinction between that and murder', she wondered, and reported, 'it is now feared that in every petty quarrel the servant will think himself justified in killing his master.' The 'gentlemen here are too apt to thrash & indeed point their guns at their men', she observed. One of the officers who came from Vancouver in 1842 was 'so detested' that the men 'confessed that if he had fallen into the river not one wd have held out a stick to him.' A less fortunate gentleman was drowned 'when he might easily have been saved without a man wetting his foot'. It was 'a hideous country for man to live', she lamented, '& . . . it is yearly getting worse . . . I pity every gentleman in it.'[80] It is not surprising that snooty Letitia Hargrave, who commented with such condescension on those she considered her social inferiors, would give little thought to what grubby labourers might have to endure. But the London committee and its officers could not avoid the subject.

Unfortunately for the HBC, McLoughlin Jr had not been all that unusual. Indeed, McLoughlin Sr himself did not have a very good record in this regard, having placed the London committee in the awkward position of having to pay off a former servant seeking compensation for a punishment McLoughlin had administered.[81] Peter Skene Ogden, who was placed in charge of New Caledonia in 1835 and was appointed to the board of management for the Columbia district ten years later, was so violent that he had been excluded from the new HBC in 1821. He had finally been allowed in only because his opposition could do more damage than his presence, and so he was dispatched to the west where his bad temper could be vented on Americans, Russians, and hostile Natives. But he was just as rough with his men, such as François Lacourse, whom Ogden had knocked down and kicked, injuring him so severely that he was henceforth 'subject to epileptic fits'. Ogden's associate, Donald Manson, who spent the last 13 years of his career in New Caledonia, blighted his chances for promotion to chief factor by acquiring an equally bad reputation. He had attacked the unfortunate Lacourse with an axe, although he had missed and only cut open Lacourse's coat, which the man had displayed at Norway House when he made his complaints. In his petition of 1857, Murdo Macleod recalled seeing Manson striking his men, two of them so severely that they 'lay upon the ground bleeding much and crying out murder'. Although he never hit Macleod, he did call him 'a damned son of a bitch' one day when Macleod was confined to bed and made him work with a sore foot and broken arm. According to the other men, Manson's sons were even worse. Macleod also suffered under Robert Todd, who struck him and William Yeats with the butt end of his pistol.[82] In 1847 Paul Kane, in the account of his travels in North America, described the punishment of two Sandwich Islanders for deserting the New Caledonia brigade as 'knocking the men down, kicking them until they got up, and knocking them down again until they could not get up any more, when they finished them off with a few kicks.'[83]

With such publicity and complaints of 'extreme ill-usage' and of 'being ... starved, beaten and maimed by the Company's Officers in the Columbia' making recruitment difficult, even George Simpson became, as John McLoughlin Sr remarked, 'all at once very sensitive about striking the men'. McLoughlin emphasized this transformation by recounting some of Simpson's exploits: the time he had 'tickled' a guide's shoulders 'with a canoe pole'; flogging a man coming up the Grand River in 1830; and knocking a man down at Fort Vancouver. 'I never saw a man get a neater blow', McLoughlin commented, 'the wall of the house, gave the mans head another, and he bled from his nose & mouth, as if he had been struck with a knife.'[84]

Actually, Simpson had not really abandoned his belief in the salutary effect of a good thrashing. When Johnson G. King, on the voyage to Edmonton in 1850, felt 'obliged to give one of the Men a good hiding for refusing to do what he was told & for general Lazyness', Simpson 'fully approved', although he had ordered King not to beat his crewmen so that they would 'write a good account of the north to their friends'.[85] Moreover, Simpson thought corporal punishment was particularly effective in disciplining Canadians. Europeans, he believed, could be controlled only by the threat of fines because they were unaccustomed to 'corporal chastisement' and 'it would not be proper to introduce it'. Canadians, on the other hand, stood 'more in awe of a blow than a fine' and, therefore, Simpson sanctimoniously informed the committee, 'altho' we reprobate this mode of discipline generally and discountenance it as much as possible it is nonetheless highly necessary on extraordinary occasions.'[86]

But the committee believed that reports of bad treatment, whether true or not, deterred 'respectable labourers' from engaging. Officers therefore had to eschew any behaviour that might provide grounds for such rumours. Corporal punishment was certainly necessary when good and bad men were mixed together, but it was never to be inflicted 'under the influence of passion or caprice'. To 'produce any good effect it should be administered with coolness temper and moderation, and at the same time with as much solemnity as circumstances will admit.' Simpson thus cautioned the officers that the charges made against them—even if false—increased the unpopularity of service in New Caledonia and provided 'ample evidence of the existence of a system of "club law"', which Simpson declared 'must not be allowed to prevail'. Discipline and obedience could not be enforced 'by a display of violent passion and the infliction of severe & arbitrary punishment in hot blood'. Disobedient or refractory servants were to receive a proper hearing and, if found guilty, subjected to arrest or short rations, 'in fact almost any punishment rather than knocking about or flogging'. Individual officers did not even have the authority to inflict fines on servants. When they believed such were deserved, they had to report the case to the board of officers who managed the Western Department.[87] Nevertheless, the London committee continued to receive sworn statements from former servants describing the starvation, beatings, and overwork they had had to endure in the service.[88] Naturally, the officers submitted their own accounts maintaining that the complainants were scoundrels, that their own conduct was as good as could be expected under such trying circumstances, and that their fellow officers were all even-tempered and universally respected. But the company's reputation had been sullied. Potential employees, already attracted by new opportunities, turned their backs on it, while new recruits balked at the prospect of suffering the ill-treatment of which they had heard.

Most HBC employees did not, of course, have to suffer such tribulations. Most officers were not cruel, few servants actually starved, and most were able to avoid overwork, usually by simply moderating their pace or, in the absence of supervision, doing nothing. Nevertheless, just as events as extreme and unusual as the McLoughlin case should not be allowed to suggest that HBC officers were excessively violent, neither should they be allowed to suggest that conflict between officers and servants erupted only under unusual circumstances. Indeed, that the London committee was willing to conclude

Men and dogs at Fort Carlton, 1871. HBCA Photograph Collection 1987/363–F–22/1. (Courtesy Hudson's Bay Company Archives, Provincial Archives of Manitoba.)

that the men of one of its posts had conspired to murder their officer with no proof other than the testimony of one disreputable servant suggests that it harboured some serious doubts about the nature of its employees and the degree of loyalty it could expect from them. It appears to have seen the relationship between its servants and their officers as one based on a hostility that might at any time erupt into violence and bloodshed. This view was no doubt due in part to the social unrest the members of the committee saw in Britain and was probably also influenced by the prejudices inspired by the racial and ethnic mix of the workforce. But it also reflected the frequency with which company servants disobeyed the orders they were given, although they were not by any means constantly on the verge of rebellion. Most of the time their refusals to obey orders were not responses to unreasonable demands or cruelty but rather attempts to exert control over the pace of their work.

Controlling the Pace of Work

Maintaining some control over their work, how quickly it was done, and what in fact was to be done was a central tenet of pre-industrial craft guilds, as it often has been for labourers generally. In the HBC, attempts at controlling the work pace took various forms. Servants refused, for example, to perform tasks that they claimed were not part of the job for which they had been hired. Thus, John, actually Johannes, Smith, a Norwegian stationed at Moose Factory, refused in April of 1815 to work 'at the New Vessel' on the grounds that, like 'all of his countrymen (except 2 or 3 engaged as Sailors)', he had been hired exclusively to fell timber for the sawmill. He offered to do anything other than work at the vessel, but he had misunderstood his status. Apart from the fact that the seamen were also expected to do whatever they were assigned, Smith himself had been hired for the Moose Factory general service. Joseph Beioley told Smith that he could not choose his own employment and that he would lose his wages. Also, since he had removed himself from the company's service by refusing to obey orders, he had lost his right to maintenance. Smith simply left and Beioley immediately directed that the rations he had received the previous Saturday be confiscated, but Smith managed to hang on to them. The next day Beioley told Smith that as long as he persisted in his obstinacy, he would be charged an additional three shillings and four pence a day and be thrown into debtors' prison when he returned to England. Smith, however, said that as long as Beioley 'did not take his life away he did not much mind about a *Prison*' and that he knew the company could not keep him there for long anyway. He held out until 6 May when his flour was gone, and then he returned to work. Unfortunately for Smith, the ships were trapped in the Bay that fall, placing a great strain on the posts' resources, and he perished 'from Fatigue & want of Sustenance' in December.[89]

Those members of the company's workforce whose occupations distinguished them from ordinary labourers had a stronger basis upon which to claim exemptions. Craftsmen might justify their refusals of particular duties by referring to their contracts. Charles Marshall, for example, who was engaged as a tinsmith in 1835, refused to do plumber's work as well without an increase in wages.[90] In 1855, the blacksmith at Fort Simpson objected to working because he had not *engaged* as a blacksmith. He spent several days working as a labourer and agreed to return to smithing once he was promised higher pay.[91] Seamen could be particularly troublesome in this regard. In 1812 John Thomas found it impossible to get sailors to do anything 'but what they please themselves'. They refused to work before breakfast, as everyone else did, and their notion of what constituted a full day's work was quite different from Thomas's. One day their efforts were limited to helping to get some sails out to dry and later helping to take them in again.[92] In May of 1837, three of the seamen aboard the company's steamer *Beaver* refused to stow the coal boxes because, they said, this was stokers' work. Led by William Willson, a 'forecastle lawyer' with 'a great deal to say', they declared they would stow wood but not coal boxes unless they got extra pay, thereby arousing suspicions that they were actually trying to extort a wage increase. Moreover, since the sails, rigging, and spars had all been landed, there was little seaman's work to be done aboard the vessel and unless the men performed whatever duties they were assigned, they would be idle. If the officers conceded that the men could reject duties they considered outside their sphere, they might soon find something else that was not part of their duty as seamen and finally do nothing at all. The conflict ended in an impasse, with Captain William Henry McNeill vowing that, next time, they would be made to obey. The men also seemed to have a particular dislike for the chief engineer, apparently because he was able to explain to the newly appointed McNeill what duties the men were accustomed to performing, which prompted Willson to call him a liar. Willson was manacled and removed to Fort Simpson, from which he was released when he promised to behave himself.[93] In 1862, James Brown refused to do labourer's work because he was engaged as a sailor and informed his master that 'God Almighty' would not persuade him to change his mind.[94]

Such incidents had a degree of logic that even an unsympathetic employer could understand. Men with specialized skills did not want to place them at someone else's disposal at prices they considered unfair or work at something other than their trades. Likewise, Hendrich Swainson might be forgiven for refusing to haul the seine because he had 'been at work all night and all week'.[95] Other men were likely to elicit nothing but disapproval, as was the case at Northwest River in August of 1840 when one of the men enlarging the sawpit simply refused to work past noon.[96] Some workers, however, resorted to much sneakier ways of limiting what they would do. William Garrioch, for example, a carpenter employed at Fort Simpson in 1802, asked to become an agricultural labourer and was duly ordered to hoe potatoes.[97] He seemed to be exchanging an interesting job for boring drudgery, but toiling in the fields probably exposed him to less supervision and therefore allowed him to work more slowly and irregularly. Honeyman Hay, a carpenter at Martins Fall in 1818, may have had a similar motive when he refused to continue making kegs, although he had no objection to peeling bark off logs or repairing a boat.[98] In 1814, at Red River, Peter Fidler suspected Archibald Curry of plotting to conceal his indolence when he refused to dig sod by himself but insisted on working with another man, thereby making it impossible to know how much labour each had done. Fidler put Curry off duty for his insolence.[99]

Such struggles for control could become running battles, as Fidler himself learned a few years later when he and his men disagreed over the number of sledges each should take when fetching meat. In January of 1816 Fidler ordered Richard Cunningham and John Flett to take three sledges of dogs. Since it was not unusual for one man to take two sledges by himself, Fidler did not consider his request unreasonable, but Cunningham refused to take more than one and Fidler fined him 10 shillings. In February, Cunningham brought home two sledges carrying only the amount of meat normally carried on one. This time Fidler only lamented that Cunningham was a 'very refractory fellow'. The next day, John Favel refused to take more than one sledge, while another man, ordered to go off with two sledges, simply left for the Qu'appelle River without saying anything.[100]

Likewise, in 1818–19 John Peter Pruden found the men at Carlton House determined to thwart him at every turn, although the struggle was due at least partly to the fact that the men had not been happy to begin with and Pruden's management only made them more ornery. When the men complained that they did not have enough to eat, Pruden was unsympathetic, since he considered six pounds of fresh buffalo meat a day enough, though he had to admit it was not of the best quality. He also refused to sell them rum on New Year's Eve because he had sold each a quart on Christmas Eve and the ensuing dissipation had rendered them unfit for work the day after Christmas, which the men probably thought should have been a holiday anyway. To prevent a repeat of such intemperance, Pruden decided to give them only the customary dram in the morning and a pint in the evening, offending all but two of the men so severely that they refused to come for the morning treat. Pruden retaliated by withholding the evening drink. Relations subsequently deteriorated. When sent out to get meat, the men repeatedly refused to haul home a whole animal on each sled, as Pruden said was the norm. He finally threatened them with five-shilling fines if they persisted, whereupon one man replied 'that if he was fined he would shoot [h]is dogs'. Nevertheless, the men began to drag the requisite loads, but their performance of other tasks became irregular. On 8 February some of the men refused to bring home firewood and sat around doing nothing while three boys performed the work. A few weeks later a group of men hauling wood quit work early, and when ordered to get what they had left behind they refused, saying it was too heavy, although any one of them, observed Pruden, could have carried any of the pieces on his shoulder. On 19 March, Pruden ordered a man, who had been idle for a week because his friends were visiting, to go and cut firewood. He refused and insolently remarked that he 'was not hired to be Mr Pruden's woodcutter', although the next day he was out cutting wood.[101] Pruden's unwillingness to increase the meat ration and his failure to allow proper celebrations and leisure at Christmas and New Year's were sure to alienate his men, who would now feel little inclination to obey him. They could not stop their work altogether, of course, because they needed the meat and wood to survive, but they could bring back less than Pruden demanded. Taking it easy while Pruden's two sons and another boy dragged wood had the added benefit of driving Pruden crazy. Indeed, if an officer mishandled a situation and somehow offended his men, they might resort to behaviour designed specifically to vex him. This certainly appears to have been the strategy the crew of the *Norman Morison* adopted in February of 1850.

Until 10 February, only William Petty, 'Ordy Seaman', had attracted unfavourable notice for his carelessness and for threatening to drop something on the boatswain's head when the latter reprimanded him. The day in question was a Sunday and, as was mandatory aboard merchant vessels, Captain Wishart held morning prayers, but none of the ship's company would attend. Asked why they were unwilling to devote a mere half-hour a week to prayers, 'some said that they had too much to do others that they got no sleep and others made the rediculous excuse that all the week the Carpenter was working over their heads.' Wishart remarked that they did not really work all that hard and reminded them that the company's orders specifically obliged him to read prayers every Sunday, weather permitting, and that when they refused to attend the men were disobeying the company's orders as well as his. This argument had no effect and Wishart told them that if they would not come to prayers, when they had been doing so regularly for the last three months, he would give them more to do. He then asked each sailor in turn whether he would attend or not. Only one agreed. The rest refused on the grounds that their comrades were refusing and they would do the same. After holding a service for the passengers, Wishart called his first and second officers to his cabin, read them the company's orders regarding Sunday prayers, and asked them if such services were customary in the HBC service. They declared that they were. He also asked them if they thought the men aboard this ship were worked harder than those on others. The officers dutifully replied that they were not. Wishart then asked them whether the provisions were good and sufficient. The officers assured him that they were. Finally, Wishart asked whether there was cause for any discontent among the seamen. The officers answered that there was none whatever. Having formally established that the crew's behaviour was entirely unjustified, Wishart decided to keep the men well occupied during the afternoon and stop their grog, which was, after all, 'given them as an encouragement of good behavior'.

Three days later, the forenoon watch was called as usual at eight a.m. and the port watch refused to appear for duty, claiming that they had not yet had breakfast.[102] Wishart would not accept this excuse, since it was the standing rule for the watch below to get breakfast at seven and relieve the other watch at eight. Wishart therefore mustered the men and spoke to them, but to no avail. One of them said that he knew the 'Law of England' and he could not be made to stay on deck during his watch below. Another said the captain could not call on all hands unless the ship was in distress. Another vowed he would not come up, 'he was up day and night as it was.' And another 'amidst much profane language and oaths said that he would not be treated as a bloody slave.' Wishart told them they were simply being required to continue the standing orders that had been acted on since the ship left England and they had no grounds for complaint. Accordingly, he informed them, he was going to put them to work, and he ordered them to haul the mainsail up. They refused and went below 'against repeated calls' from Wishart, while the other watch went aloft 'with great howlings and shouting' that continued all morning and intensified while they hauled the foretopsail. In fact, they worked 'with such noisy songs' that the mate's orders could not be heard. When Wishart himself told them that these songs would not be allowed, they replied that they could not hoist without them and continued their 'insubordinate noises shouting as loud as they could'.

The next day the forenoon watch again refused to appear, saying they had not had their breakfast, and the other watch was kept on deck until its replacement arrived. The following Sunday the port watch refused to attend prayers. On the next Sunday everyone showed up for prayers, but 11 of the men, seven of whom belonged to the port watch, refused to accept grog and lime juice when it was served out at 11:30 a.m. Wishart then ordered that henceforth only those who had accepted the grog on that day would receive it in future, though, because of the bad weather, he gave them all another chance to take the grog the next day. Only one of the men changed his mind.[103] But the rebellion was over and the situation reverted to what it had been prior to 10 February.

A good officer had to know more than how to keep books and deal with Aboriginal traders. He also had to know how to manage his men, whose response to his authority was not at all predictable. Indeed, an HBC servant could be highly sensitive to slights from his officer. In 1853, John Smith, gatekeeper at Fort Simpson, abandoned his post to chat with some men near the Native shop door. His master tracked him down, asked why he was not in his place, and gave him 'a slight tap . . . over the Shoulders' with his cane. This tap, which was probably less slight than the officer wanted the London committee to believe, aroused resentment rather than obedience. Although Smith returned to the gate, several hours later he declared he would no longer act as gatekeeper. He was then handcuffed and confined in the bastion. That evening he refused to be released and spent the night locked up and in irons, emerging several days later when he agreed to do whatever he was told. To ensure that the incident was seen entirely from his own perspective, the officer pointed out that Smith was 'an old offender' who had already run away twice and had been 'Transported' to Fort Simpson where he had been of little use because he had 'the Venereal'.[104] In 1866 one of the men at Osnaburgh House, reprimanded for his increasing laziness, responded by declaring he would work there no longer and would leave, which he did early one morning before his master was up.[105]

Clearly, officers had little real power. They were constrained from above by the committee's concern for the HBC's reputation and from below by the men's indifference and defiance, not to mention their numbers. Both the committee and the workers also regularly reminded the officers of their position, the committee with words of caution and advice, the workers in far more colourful terms as well as with acts of disobedience. Of course, the company's men were not supposed to decide what they would or would not do, nor were they expected to choose their posts, their officers, or their duties, but they did anyway because they did not consider themselves obligated to unwavering subservience. They objected to being exposed to what appeared to them, rightly or wrongly, to be excessive hardship. They demanded that the company supply what its recruitment agents promised and considered themselves justified in protesting if promises were broken. They rejected officers who were cruel and found ways of thwarting those who merely annoyed them. They also refused to perform work that, in their opinion, their contracts did not require them to do. After all, they had joined the company for their own benefit, and even though they had signed contracts demanding—and committing them to—exactly the opposite, their obedience was not absolute and their loyalty was not limitless. As Bryan Palmer has pointed out, paternalism rested on the notion that authority belonged to those who had inherited or earned the right to rule, but it also entailed a recognition of 'the humanity' of those upon whom paternalists relied for labour and whom they protected from 'unpredictable misfortune' or 'natural calamity'. Thus, although workers rarely challenged paternalism itself, their belief that their masters were responsible for them could lead to 'resistance and demand, as well as accommodation'.[106]

6

Combination and Resistance

The London committee of the Hudson's Bay Company and its officers did not see the company's workers simply as servants. They also saw them as members of particular ethnic groups, each with its own virtues and weaknesses rendering it more or less suited to the company. The ideal servant was someone like John Clouston, whom John Murphy dubbed the best he had ever seen, for in him were 'united the sagacity of the native, the activity, and almost the ambition of the real Canadian, and the obedient and docile spirit of the Orkneyman'. Even he, however, was 'beginning to fall into the common view of drunkenness and to open his ears to the insidious and discontented'.[1] Clouston belonged to that 'quiet, well disposed and easily managed race of people'[2] the committee never ceased to believe made the best servants, although their lack of enthusiasm for voyaging and their periodic preference for other employment had prompted the company to recruit men from groups reputed to be bolder and more energetic. Since each group was deemed unique and its cultural characteristics were seen as almost immutable racial traits, the conduct of the men belonging to it was judged through a filter of preconceptions about its particular propensities, even when the conduct in question was so common that other explanations ought to have suggested themselves. Consequently, collective action was regarded as the result of a tendency to band together to which certain ethnic groups were particularly prone, despite the fact that tendency appears to have been almost universal.

According to William Auld, Orcadians were 'never to be complained against except in cases where a great number of them happen to have their contracts expiring at the same time', when they united to 'reduce' the company 'to their terms'.[3] Some years later, Donald Ross observed that 'good fellows as the Orkneymen generally are, a mixture of the Celtic and Gaulish breed amongst them is very necessary: for when they have got what they term "the Ball under their foot" there is not to be found any where a more difficult set of fellows to be Kept in due subordination—of this the good olden days of Hudson's Bay have furnished many many proofs, some of which indeed came under my own observation.'[4]

The Celts and the Gauls presented their own challenges, however. Highlanders, when 'numerous' at a post, were 'disposed to be clannish and troublesome'.[5] James Sutherland, after nearly causing 'a revolution among all Hands' by fining one man, complained that 'all these Highlanders hangs together the same as the links of a Chain.'[6] The Lewismen were 'exceedingly stubborn and difficult of management, and so clannish that it is scarcely possible to deal with them singly'.[7] In fact, the Scots and the Irish were both 'quarrelsome independent and inclined to form leagues and cabals which might be dangerous to the peace of the Country' and should be avoided 'in any considerable numbers'. Orcadians and Canadians were preferable, observed George Simpson, even though the former 'when not awed by force [were] obstinate to an extreme and so guarded that it is a difficult matter to discover any plots or determinations they may form until ready to be acted upon.' Hiring an 'equal proportion' of each would encourage a 'spirit of competition' and enable the HBC 'to deal with them on such terms as may be considered necessary and proper'.[8] But 'combinations' among the Canadians made it difficult to engage them,[9] while Orcadian interest in the HBC had declined by the middle of the nineteenth century, forcing the company to hire Lewismen who were still 'very clannish and intractable'.[10] As for the Norwegians, they turned out to be 'a body of dangerous, insubordinate, useless men, who are bound together by strong national ties; and who by their union in every step they adopt, are enabled to give law to the country.'[11] The native-born population, meanwhile, had developed its own national identity and was opposed to the company's monopoly and its rule.[12]

Of course, ethnicity played a part in the men's behaviour. It was easier for men who came from the same places and spoke the same languages to join in common efforts. Norwegians, Hawaiians, and those Irishmen who spoke no English were likely to be excluded from the plots hatched by those who did, although they could hatch their own. Thus, in 1859, the Norwegians at Moose Factory were able to arrange a day off work for themselves by persuading the officer in charge that it was one of their national holidays. A second attempt failed, however, when the officer decided that 'the whole [was] a got up scheme between them' and punished them by putting them off duty, i.e., releasing them from work and giving them half-rations.[13] There was also some tension between groups, as the fights between the Norwegians and the rest of the men at Moose Factory in 1859 and the attack of the Irishmen on the Orkneymen in 1812 indicate. But collective behaviour had other bases as well. Orcadian objections to the presence of Canadians or Irishmen might have been motivated by a fear of being replaced and losing the most lucrative employment available to them. Their officers saw only further evidence of the Orcadian proclivity for combination, without considering that, since for so many years Orkneymen had comprised the vast majority of servants, if they were going to combine with anyone it would have to be with other Orkneymen. Furthermore, although they were by no means a proletariat engaged in a class struggle with ruthless industrialists, they were aware of what distinguished them from their employers, as were the rest of the company's workers. Nor, as the workforce became more diverse, did ethnic differences prevent them from acting together to bargain over wages and working conditions. Combinations rose not out of ethnicity but rather out of that desire for fair treatment that also caused individuals to refuse to obey the orders they were given or to serve under masters who failed to 'use them well'.

Combination was a means by which HBC workers negotiated the terms of their employment. It frequently took the form of what would later be called a strike, but the term 'combination' possessed subversive overtones that no longer cling to the word 'strike'. To be seen as prone to combination was to be seen as inclined to behaviour that the Combination Acts made illegal in England and that the social élite had identified as inappropriate for those of lower rank. As Reinhard Bendix has observed, 'ideologies of management are attempts by leaders of enterprises to justify the privilege of voluntary action and association for themselves, while imposing upon subordinates the duty of obedience and the obligation to serve their employers to the best of their ability.'[14] It was the worker's place to identify himself wholly with his master, defer to his decisions, and refrain from plotting against him. It was the master's place to command and when necessary to combine with his peers to preserve their authority and the status quo.

Those relegated to subordination saw things differently. They rarely questioned the social hierarchy itself, but they still regarded their relationship with their employers as subject to negotiation. Furthermore, they knew that their social position differentiated them from their superiors and they acted collectively to bargain for proper treatment and reasonable wages. HBC servants were no different. They understood that their status distinguished them from the owners and managers of the company. They entered the company knowing that they had more in common with one another than they had with their officers, and their contracts further emphasized the distinction. Nor did they require the experience of factory work to provide them with an outlook that enabled them to act together. The nature of the company itself made collective action possible, albeit on a small scale, since the men were scattered across the country. They spent most of their time with other individuals of their own rank, not with their officers, whom they outnumbered. It was certainly possible for officers and servants to establish close and amicable relationships, but these were not necessarily more important than the bonds that formed between the servants or as meaningful as their own personal desires or ambitions. In addition, the tripmen of the company's brigades, the seamen aboard its ships, and the coalminers on Vancouver Island had their own identities and bases for collective action, which influenced their relationships with the HBC.

Like the company's organization, the purposes for which company employees acted together were conservative. However threatening their actions might have seemed to their superiors, HBC workers never demanded a reversal of the company's hierarchy, even on those rare occasions when they actually usurped the authority of those placed in charge of them. Rather, they combined to bargain for higher wages and better provisions and to resist what they considered unfair treatment. Collective action, however, was less common than individual protest. As Table 2 (p. 118) indicates, in only 27 of the 75 occasions when men refused to do as they were told or refused to work did the incident involve more than one man. Individual protest also remained more common. The frequency of collective action did not increase during the century under examination. There is also no indication that the company's workers were developing what one might term a 'modern' view of employment relations and starting to behave like modern workers bargaining over pay and benefits in a capitalist system whose economic laws they had come to accept. Instead, they continued to operate within a traditional framework and to see their relationship with their employer as a moral one that was no mere monetary transaction.

Bargaining for Fair Wages

The price of labour, like the price of food, had to be fair, i.e., determined not by the market but by 'customary expectations and "normal" human needs'. Craftsmen's wages customarily equalled about twice those of common labourers and wage differentials among and within trades depended on social status. An artisan expected wages high enough to permit him to maintain himself and his family in respectable independence with sufficient leisure to rest from his labours. The desire that wages and other conditions of work be regulated to preserve 'certain minimum standards of subsistence' motivated the protests of eighteenth-century industrial workers and did not diminish until well into the nineteenth century when workers began to learn the rules of wage bargaining in a market economy. As a result, skilled labour actually cost less than it should have and workers' demands were modest while their pride in their crafts ensured diligence, at least as defined by customary notions of a fair day's work. Rural labourers possessed similar attitudes even in the early nineteenth century. More than high wages, they valued good relations with their masters, the opportunity to live in, access to land, year-round employment, the freedom to leave if their situations proved unsatisfactory, and the well-being of their families. High wages were unnecessary so long as service permitted the accumulation of savings and wages were supplemented by customary benefits, such as gleaning rights, pasturage for livestock on common land, and secure tenure of a cottage. Once agricultural 'improvements' eliminated these customs and farmers found it cheaper to pay wages than to provide room and board, labourers faced a precarious existence.

These changes confirmed what everyone had long believed: those dependent on wages alone could achieve neither independence nor a reasonable level of subsistence. It had traditionally been assumed that even day labourers had access to land to grow food or keep some livestock, without which they might sink low indeed, swelling the numbers of paupers and vagrants and thereby becoming subject to the forced labour provided for in the statutes enacted to control them. Servants' wages had not fluctuated according to the market either, but were determined by law and enforced by justices of the peace. They also depended on age. Servants did not customarily receive adult wages until their late teens, and very young servants might receive no wages at all.[15]

Workers thus saw the wage, as Marcus Rediker has put it, 'in broad terms that stressed their right to a life of decent quality'. It was with this perspective that they entered a 'world of negotiation' that 'revolved around two inherently antagonistic sets of interests'. In the merchant shipping industry, merchants, captains, and shipowners sought to enhance the accumulation of capital by controlling wages and the conditions of work and to shift the burdens and risks onto the seamen. The concern of the latter was 'the quality of life as defined by the social wage', and they tried both to maximize wages and to protect their non-monetary benefits.[16] In the fur trade, the two sets of interests were the London committee and those officers who identified most closely with it, on the one hand, and the rest of the workforce, on the other, even though the company's hierarchical structure, its paternalism, and the master-servant relationship embodied in the contracts implied otherwise. Like their maritime counterparts, HBC workers accepted their place but insisted that lowliness not be synonymous with destitution and demanded fair treatment. Money was only one consideration. Men more in tune with market forces would have demanded higher wages in return for continued service under unpopular officers instead of asking for masters who would exercise their authority in the proper manner. By appealing for redress to their officers' superiors, the men were asking for the paternalistic sympathy that the élite had traditionally been expected to show for the lower orders.

Servants of the company continued to entertain such expectations well into the nineteenth century. Thus, in 1857, Murdo Macleod blamed his sufferings in New Caledonia on 'subordinates at a distance from the Seat of Government'. Likewise, J.C. Arnesen, when he complained in 1859 that the company's board and lodging did not meet the standards of the time, absolved the London committee of responsibility. The company in London did not know what was 'passing in their Territory in North America' and it was his 'purpose to inform [them] of some [of] it'. And his request for compensation for his expenditures was 'a Request, which is corresponding to all Rights of Law or Equity'.[17] Of course, Macleod and Arnesen were also trying to ingratiate themselves with the committee, but that former servants submitted such petitions, when they probably knew that the officers would discredit them, suggests that they continued to operate according to traditional paternalistic ideals. Indeed, petitions, even those followed by riots or mutinies, were expressions of a belief that there was a 'natural order of society protecting the interests of rich and poor alike'. Petitions constituted a recognition of authority and were a common means of seeking redress.[18] But that authority was not absolute and workers did not hesitate to protest if their superiors failed to fulfil the obligations that came with rank. HBC employees, therefore, did not simply accept whatever terms were handed to them, but tried to take advantage of the company's need for their services by extracting higher wages, better provisions, and greater control over the conditions of their work. These goals were aspects of one overarching issue, namely, the question of fair treatment, and conflict was most severe when that issue was most clearly discernible.

Wage disputes in the HBC more closely resembled the labour disputes that erupted in industrial settings than the conflicts over other issues because HBC workers, regardless of their backgrounds, knew how to manipulate the labour market. They knew that, although the HBC preferred new contracts to be for five years and renewals for three, it had to agree to shorter terms or be short of men. When they tried to impose wage increases, they knew when to make their demands: when it was time to inform their officers whether they were going to renew their contracts or after their arrival at the Bay to meet the ships when their officers begged them to stay on because too few replacements had arrived. Their tactics were not always successful, of course. The Cumberland House men who combined to raise their wages from the normal £6 to £15 in 1777 were discharged.[19] Still, the London committee could not send home everyone who demanded higher wages, particularly during wartime. Thus, in 1779 most of the men whose times were up were able to negotiate pay increases, and in 1780 the York Factory men were able to force their officer to raise their wages or abandon all hope of sending anyone inland that year. Even then, the general shortage of labour made it necessary to transport goods to Cumberland House with the help of Natives, who were 'exceedingly exorbitant . . . in their demands'.[20]

Combinations to impose wage increases became almost annual affairs, especially as competition with the North West Company strengthened the servants' hands. Officers reported them in 1787 and 1788. In 1791, the steersmen at York Factory not only swore an oath to hold out for higher wages but agreed to re-engage *'for two years only'* so that their contracts would all expire at the same time. Since they knew that their expertise was crucial to the company's inland operations, they were confident that they would get what they wanted.[21] In 1799 most of the steersmen ordered to Beaver River refused to go and the rest, recognizing a golden opportunity, demanded higher wages before they would proceed. In this case, however, the men were in breach of their contracts because they had already signed their agreements. Six canoes and two boats were finally dispatched, but the three ringleaders were sent to York Factory.

Their master hoped they would be fined as an example to others, a particularly important consideration in view of the recently uncovered 'combination' not to go 'higher' than Edmonton House. The York Factory council fined them £10 each, but the London committee reduced the penalty to £4 because 'excessive Punishments as well as too lenient ones have their Evils.'[22] But lenience did not help. In 1800, combinations were reported at Martins Fall, York Factory, and Churchill.[23] The following year, William Tomison reported that when he tried to re-engage men for Cumberland House for three years at £10 for the first year and £12 for each of the last two, they 'looked upon' him 'with disdain' and said they would go home first. They wanted £14, which he refused to give. To use their remaining time profitably, he ordered them to help get the boats to Cumberland House, but they objected to this 'imposition' and refused to go without assurance that they would be back at York Factory in time to catch the ship. Tomison told them it was up to 'providence' and their own activity. Fifteen of them finally agreed to go, but only one would stay in the service, leaving Tomison shorthanded.[24]

In the spring of 1803, Peter Fidler found that none of the seven men he selected to go to Lake Athabasca for the summer would agree to stay without higher wages. They had already objected to the trip because of the fish diet, the distances they would have to travel, and the number of carrying places. They had also cleverly renewed their engagements for only one year in 1802 and now were in a strong position to demand wage increases as well as to re-engage only for another year. Three held out long enough and, rather than lose them, Fidler allowed each an additional £2 and humbly submitted his decision for the committee's approval, declaring his willingness to pay these sums himself. Of course, he would have to whether he wanted to or not. The committee did not consider the officers knowledgeable enough about the price of provisions and labour to determine how much servants should be paid and insisted that no wage increases be granted without its approval. Officers who raised men's pay and then found their decisions rejected would have the sums deducted from their own accounts.[25] This measure only made life more difficult for officers like John Hodgson, at Fort Albany, faced with men who refused to re-engage on 'reasonable' terms because of the 'fatigue' they suffered from 'running after' the Natives and the hunger they endured if their fishing failed, and with 'half-Breed or Creole' steersmen who believed that they deserved higher wages than ordinary labourers.[26]

By 1805 the situation was critical. A combination of current servants, retired servants, and friends and relatives in the Orkneys was plotting to prevent the company from acquiring a supply of men until the wages of those in the service were increased.[27] The extent or effect of this conspiracy cannot be determined from information available in the HBC's records, but, no doubt, the London committee hoped that the Retrenching System would reduce the company's dependence on Orcadians and make itself immune to any such plots in future. Not only was the HBC unable to do without Orkneymen, however; in 1811, letters from the Orkneys led to such dissatisfaction among the inland servants belonging to Churchill that they insisted on 'extravagant' wage increases, although all but three eventually agreed to the terms they were offered.[28] Competition with the NWC also worsened the situation and the destruction of the Red River Colony in 1816 made everyone 'disgusted with the Country altogether'. With so many determined to leave, some of those who stayed shrewdly 'set a higher value on their services' and 'extraordinary Wages' had to be given or some posts would have had to be abandoned. The solution, suggested James Bird, was to cease the current practice of hiring only the same number of servants as were leaving and send 150 men as soon as possible. It was also necessary to make them sign up for five, not three, years, as had become common, because short contracts meant that experienced steersmen and bowsmen were always in demand and these had it in their power to set the price of their services.[29] But the company was unable to make these changes and its employees continued to take advantage of the situation.[30] Indeed, reported Francis Heron from Fort Edmonton in 1821, years of success at doing so had the men 'overvalue their services' and rendered them 'disinterested and refractory'. The men of his district whose contracts were now expiring had entered into a combination not to re-engage unless they got even more 'enormous' wage increases than the year before. Unless these men were let go, he warned, there would 'be no managing of them'.[31] The merger presented the committee with the opportunity to do precisely as Heron recommended and, by reducing the company's manpower requirements, promised to make it easy to find a regular and plentiful supply of men willing to sign up on whatever terms the company offered. Thereby, the committee hoped, the power of its servants to extort higher wages every year would be destroyed.

Combinations of servants to increase wages became rare, but not because the merger deprived them of their bargaining position. Rather, men considering service at the company's trading posts increasingly expressed their dissatisfaction with the company's wages *before* they signed up, either by trying to negotiate higher pay or by rejecting the HBC altogether. Britons and Canadians could take advantage of more attractive economic opportunities elsewhere, while the population of the company's own territories was able to live off the land and defy the company's monopoly with impunity. In 1858 the people of the colony went so far as to combine to raise the wages for transporting goods from York Factory to Red River, forcing George Simpson to get soldiers to man the boats.[32] Moreover, if the HBC's terms were not attractive enough to persuade men to renew their contracts, alternatives were frequently so close at hand that holding out for better terms was no longer worth the effort, particularly since the HBC was as parsimonious as ever. Thus, when in 1830 the men of the Sault Ste Marie district demanded and failed to get wage increases ranging from £8 to £13, they simply departed, leaving John McBean without servants for La Cloche.[33] Wage disputes between the company and the men already in the service did not disappear, however, but they now tended to occur among groups hired as a result of the acquisition of the NWC possessions on the west coast: seamen and colliers whose customs and traditions clashed with those of the HBC.

There was nothing new about the presence of sailors in the HBC. They had always manned the vessels that visited Hudson Bay, but now they became more numerous as the HBC began to use ships to transport goods and men to and from its territory and up and down the Pacific coast. The crews of the company's ocean-going ships always had been distinct from the rest of the company's workers and from the sloopers and shallopers who were regular servants attached to the Bayside posts. Seamen signed on for the duration of the voyages, which lasted a few months if their destination was Hudson Bay and might take several years if it was the Pacific. Unlike the company's other workers, the sailors were recruited in London, where the navy and merchant marine acquired their men, and therefore comprised a far more mixed bag of nationalities than was present elsewhere in the HBC.[34]

The west coast was quite different from Hudson Bay. Forts Vancouver and Victoria rapidly became bustling ports visited by ships that neither belonged to nor were chartered by the HBC, and its own ships also docked at Honolulu and San Francisco. The HBC was thus perforce exposed to the forces of a vast labour market in which it was at a definite disadvantage. The wages offered in the ports of the Pacific Northwest were among the highest in North America.[35] Men were also eager to get aboard vessels going to California simply to desert and head for the gold-fields when they arrived.[36] Since it was customary to pay sailors monthly, they did not need to fear losing the whole of their wages if they ran away, though it was so easy to find another berth that a man did not need to remain unemployed for long. Jumping ship or otherwise escaping from the area was therefore both tempting and easy, and when the HBC's sailors bargained over pay they frequently did so with their feet. Dealing with mariners on the west coast was thus far more difficult than it ever was in Hudson Bay, where desertion had little attraction and most officers had to contend with nothing more serious than drunkenness or a refusal to do anything but strictly seaman's duty.

Thus, in May of 1849, James Douglas agreed to give the men of the *Columbia* double pay when they demanded their discharge upon their arrival at Fort Vancouver. But the second officer and eight sailors deserted and headed for California, as Douglas feared the rest were planning to do. He therefore gave the remaining men an additional $100 each and replaced the deserters with Sandwich Islanders. In September, eight seamen and a stoker deserted from the *Beaver* and the *Mary Dare* and could not be found. 'We live', wrote Douglas, 'in hourly apprehension of seeing the Company's vessels altogether deserted in consequence of the enormous pay given to seamen, in Calefornia.' On offer in San Francisco was $140 a month, while the HBC had recently raised its seamen's wages to £4, the equivalent of $16.[37] In January of 1850 five sailors deserted from the *Cowlitz* while it was docked in Honolulu. The 10 remaining seamen and their three apprentices then refused to put out to sea until the deserters had been replaced. Since the size of the crew still met the requirements of the law, Captain Weynton tried to convince the men that they had no grounds for complaint, but he did so without success. He then asked the British consul general, William Miller, to be present during the investigation of the matter. The men were duly mustered again and Miller appeared and questioned them. Concluding that they had no grounds for complaint, he provided a declaration to the effect that Weynton was entitled to assistance from the local authorities. Weynton then mustered the men again. Now they agreed to return to work even if no more seamen were hired if their pay was raised to the new £4 a month. This having been granted, they then demanded a month's pay in advance in cash. This was refused, however, because they were suspected of planning to desert as soon as they had received it, so the men remained on strike.

Meanwhile, the local police authorities found that there was no law by which they could interfere, and Miller appealed to the Minister of Foreign Relations and asked to have the disobedient seamen imprisoned. The matter was then taken up by the King's Privy Council, which resolved that His Majesty should direct the marshal of the

Hawaiian Islands to arrest and detain the men pointed out to him. Weynton confined the apprentices aboard ship, while the seamen were imprisoned at the fort ashore, where they were to be kept until they could be transferred to a British naval vessel. The resolution of the conflict was thus far from satisfactory and, like the company's attempts to prosecute deserters in Scotland, demonstrated how difficult it was for it to resort to legal means to impose discipline. The company had to pay the costs of maintaining the prisoners, while Weynton was left without a crew and had to hire 14 Sandwich Islanders who were completely unacquainted with the duties required of them. Six of the imprisoned seamen were finally persuaded to go aboard the *Mary Dare,* which had lost most of its crew at Honolulu, but they deserted while the ship was in the Columbia River, making it necessary to hire more men at a rate of £25 a month in Victoria.[38] Two men were also transferred to the *Cowlitz* from the *Norman Morison,* which had itself been the scene of some turbulence.

The boatswain of the *Norman Morison,* Edward Edwards, having been reprimanded for carelessness and accused of incompetence, had refused to do any more duty and demanded his discharge. Captain Wishart disrated him instead. Edwards refused this demotion to the rank of common seaman and demanded to go ashore and present his case to Richard Blanshard, the recently arrived governor of Vancouver Island. Edwards might have believed that, as the first colonial governor with no connection to the HBC, Blanshard would have had more sympathy for him than the company. But Blanshard had not yet become its opponent and, upon due consideration, had Edwards locked up. During the next few weeks, four sailors ran off and seven green hands were added to the crew. When Wishart ordered the men to weigh anchor and head out of the harbour, 10 of them refused, insisting that four more seamen be hired to replace the deserters. Wishart told them that he had no intention of going to sea four hands short, but it was necessary to get out of the harbour while conditions permitted. Anyway, he observed, 30 men were enough. He also pointed out that by their disobedience they had broken their articles and forfeited all money due to them. The men would not be swayed and Wishart notified James Douglas, who came aboard and twice tried to persuade them to return to duty without success. He finally imprisoned them in the forecastle, intending to transfer them ashore when he found a place to put them.

Meanwhile, because the ship was now in 'a state of mutiny', the officers armed themselves, but after four seamen joined the crew several days later, the 10 prisoners were satisfied and returned to work. Douglas generously told them that their misbehaviour would be overlooked if they behaved better in future and promised them double wages from 20 April 1850 to the termination of the voyage and a gratuity of £25 to each. The London committee considered this excessive, since only four of the men had actually deserted and the boatswain, 'the active person in exciting the men to such misconduct', had been punished. Moreover, according to decisions in previous cases where 'extravagant wages had been extorted', the men had no legal claim to the wages and gratuities they had been promised. The *Norman Morison* men themselves admitted this, but insisted that their case was different since Douglas had made his offer 'voluntarily'. Reluctantly, the committee gave in, complaining that it would increase expenses but believing 'it best not to throw any doubt on the faith which might be safely reposed in Mr Douglas's promises.' In future, however, it suggested, the company's officer should leave the settlement of conflicts to the captain and his crew, who would appeal to him only as a last resort if they could not arrange matters themselves.[39]

Douglas had probably believed that the committee would approve his actions. It had, after all, ordered him to keep the ships in an 'efficient' state, especially with regard to men, and observed that 'while wages continue high the Company must submit as others do to the additional expence in the hope that a supply of seamen equal to the demand may soon take place.'[40] But, as always, the committee was uncomfortable with such profligacy and it probably hoped that an experienced ship's master would know better how to keep a vessel properly manned without making unnecessary promises. In January of 1852, however, Douglas again became involved in shipboard conflicts. Seven men deserted from the *Norman Morison* and four others refused to work until they received 'high wages' for the voyage home. Douglas kept a 'well manned canoe' circling the ship at night to prevent further desertions and was forced to secure 'the fidelity' of the remaining men by increasing wages by £2 a month for able seamen and £1 10s. for ordinary seamen, the latter term being the common designation for sailors with less than two years' experience. These wages would be retroactive to the date of the ship's arrival. To compensate them for the ship's being shorthanded on the way home, each man was promised a gratuity of £12 10s. Douglas pointed out that the sum of the gratuities for the 15 men was less than the cost of the wages of the 11 missing men would have been and fewer men also meant a reduction in provisions.[41] But a dangerous precedent had been set.

The following year the men of the *Norman Morison* 'came to a strike' at the last moment and 'in the most shameless manner demanded' the same gratuity that had been granted in 1852 before they would move the ship, which was aground in the entrance of the harbour. Douglas had to submit to their demands because he could not replace them and did not want to risk delaying the ship's departure.[42] Double pay while at anchor at Vancouver Island became the rule and was not abolished until 1864, when the committee also limited the men's advances to one month's wages and eliminated monthly payments. It now became possible for the committee to carry out its determination that deserters would forfeit all wages owed to them, as the provisions of the Merchant Shipping Act of 1854 allowed.[43] Of course, for men bedazzled by the opportunities of the Pacific coast, these regulations were not much of a deterrent and did nothing to reduce their ability to desert and disappear.

Equally difficult to satisfy were the miners hired for the company's coal operations on Vancouver Island. These began in 1849 with the arrival from Ayrshire of John Muir, who was to be the oversman, his wife, their four sons, and a daughter, Muir's two nephews, one of whom brought his family, and John Smith and his family. Scottish coalminers, though serfs until 1799, regarded themselves as 'independent colliers', not 'company hands'. Hewers, i.e., men who worked at the coal face, considered themselves skilled tradesmen and exercised control over the pace of their work, free of intrusive supervision from mine owners or managers. Moreover, their earnings were based on piece-work, which, by tying remuneration to effort and expertise, reinforced their 'sense of skill'.[44] The committee did not take these factors into consideration when it arranged for their recruitment, though it took the advice of its agent, David Landale, a mining engineer, to base their pay on the 'darg', i.e., what a man could produce in a day, and also to allow a bonus of two shillings and six pence for every ton of coal over 30 produced in a month.

The resulting contracts promised the miners £50 in wages plus the bonus, as well as materials and assistance to build dwellings. Nevertheless, as Keith Ralston has pointed out, the London committee appears to have assumed that the miners would be on the same footing as the rest of the company's tradesmen, but the contradiction between this status and the special terms in their contracts led to conflict. The company's ignorance of the men it had hired is aptly demonstrated by the sole surviving and undated indenture in the HBC Archives. It bound a man to serve as a 'Working Collier or Labourer', a phrase that was meaningless in the coal industry. It also stipulated a

10-hour workday, although it was customary for miners to work an eight-hour day when at the coal face, and obligated them to work as labourers if the coal turned out not to be worth mining.[45]

The committee's failure to appreciate the difference between colliers and ordinary labourers was further demonstrated by the fact that the miners spent their first three months ashore working in the dockyard at Esquimalt. Once they reached Fort Rupert they had to build houses, work for which they were unskilled, and the promised assistance was only grudgingly granted. They also feared the Natives, who had hitherto gathered coal for their own trade and who therefore resented the newcomers. Worst of all, there was no workable seam of coal ready for them and their first job at the mine was to sink a shaft. The pit filled with water every night and it took until nearly 10 a.m. to drain it every morning. Because the miners were guaranteed an eight-hour day if they toiled underground, it was necessary for the regular servants to do the draining to ensure that the miners worked only the specified number of hours. The company's officers resented this diversion of their men's labour,[46] while the miners resented having to dig shafts at all. They had engaged under the impression that they were going to a fully functioning mine where they would extract coal. Instead, they were set to digging pits, which they declared was 'neither connected with coal digging as a branch, nor with labourers work, but stands by itself.' Moreover, the bonus, which was 'the only inducement' that had lured them 'to this comfortless place', could not be earned if they were digging shafts. They therefore petitioned for daily compensation equal to the bonus and threatened to stop mining and work out their contracts as labourers if their request was not granted.

Landale considered their demand excessive, since he believed that sinking was less productive than coal working and should be less remunerative. He also thought that if they were too well paid for sinking pits they would continue to do so even after finding a workable seam of coal if that seam did not provide enough coal to earn them a bonus as great as they could get by sinking shafts. He recommended a bonus for every fathom dug, an agreement he was sure the miners would find acceptable, and suggested that the company's officers and John Muir should work out the details of such an arrangement. But, he warned, 'Colliers are as a class selfish & lazy' and their emoluments should depend on the quantity of work performed, *'not on days wages alone'*.[47] The miners would have been grossly insulted to hear themselves described thus. If Landale failed to appreciate the significance of piece-work among miners, seeing it only as a way to keep slackers at work, it is no wonder that the London committee did not understand just whom it was recruiting.

The committee finally decided to grant the miners two shillings a day in compensation, but while their request was still under consideration the colliers left the mine. According to John Muir, the company's continued failure to provide assistance and protection prompted him to bring his men to the fort and offer their services wherever they might be needed. Two of them, Andrew Muir and John McGregor, were sent to cut a drain through the fort below the Sandwich Islanders' house, which they considered 'a place not fit for a pig to go through, let alone a man to work in'. On their fourth day of work, 26 April 1850, George Blenkinsop, the officer left in charge in the absence of his father-in-law, the irascible William Henry McNeill, came and 'in an abusive manner' charged them with breach of contract, fined them £50, and put them off duty. When McNeill returned he sent for the men and 'in the most abusive manner possible to describe' threatened that they would 'be shot like dogs' and had them 'thrust' into the bastion, 'with Irons on their hands', and kept there for six days, shackled day and night for two days and two nights, and fed on bread and water. On 9 May they were freed from their chains and on 11 May permitted to return to their own houses, though they were not allowed outside the fort until 13 June. Having received no satisfaction from James Douglas, they would not return to work and demanded a 'public hearing'. Although the London committee asked for an explanation and an investigation into Blenkinsop's management, it took a stern view of the miners' actions. Not only had Muir not been specific enough about the assistance he needed, though the committee presumed he wanted carpenters and protection from Natives, he should have limited himself to an appeal to James Douglas 'to see that justice be done'. But by refusing to work, the miners had 'taken the law into their own hands' and 'caused great loss to the Company thereby'. Douglas would investigate, but the miners would have to fulfil their contracts or suffer the penalties inflicted therein.[48]

Douglas informed the committee that the miners' complaints were groundless, that their request for a stockade was unreasonable, and the fact that they hunted along the coast was proof that they really had no fear of the Natives. Furthermore, Muir and McGregor had brought their punishment upon themselves. They had refused to dig a drain, and Blenkinsop had told them they were 'idle fellows' and a bad example to his men and that if the company chose it could fine them £50, which they had forfeited by breach of contract. At that point they threw down their tools and said they would not do another day's work for the company. The rest of the miners had soon joined in the strike, refusing to return to work until they received 2s.6d. per day for shanking. Muir and McGregor had been locked up as described, but remained 'refractory' after their release and would not work, though they still received their full allowance of provisions. Their confinement had indeed been illegal, Douglas admitted, but an example had to be made or there would be 'an end to all subordination'. He and the London committee also suspected that the miners' real object had been to get to California,[49] although there is little evidence for this. Nevertheless, all the miners but John Muir, his wife, and their youngest son left for California aboard the *England* along with a blacksmith and six men from the *Norman Morison*. Muir was dismissed and mining carried on with local recruits and regular servants.

Douglas soon concluded that the coal business should be left to an independent joint stock company, since the venture could not be carried out without investing heavily in tools and machinery and satisfying the miners who objected to living on fish and whose wages would have to keep pace with those offered in California. The committee, however, decided to recruit new miners, though this proved difficult. Douglas had advised Blenkinsop to avoid intemperate language because the miners' complaints of threats that they would be shot or knocked down gave 'a ruffianly character to the Service', but he had been too late. Reports of 'severities practised on the men under John Muir' and rumours that the Natives had massacred the miners at Fort Rupert frightened some of the new recruits into defaulting on their contracts. It was thus vital, the recruiter warned, that their replacements be 'treated with more than usual Kindness' in order to 'reconcile them to the new state of things upon which they are about to enter'. Being 'superior to the ordinary class of Servants', they deserved such indulgence. But this new group was no happier than the first, complaining about their provisions, both aboard ship and at Fort Rupert, and the state of the coal operations.[50] Douglas was able to improve their temper by increasing the bonus to 4s.6d. per ton in 1853, but the committee still clung to a belief in the utility of poverty. People of this 'class', presumably the irresponsible working class, it declared, 'when they get very high wages' are 'often disposed to work less, and to be content to earn only a little more than they had earned before'. It recommended raising their quota of coal from 30 to 50 tons a month, but Douglas reported that 30 tons, a large rate of production, had become the accepted rate and that the extra wages were actually spurring the miners on.[51]

By the time the committee read Douglas's letter the third group of Scottish miners, travelling aboard the *Colinda,* had been deposited in Valparaiso and efforts were under way to recruit English colliers to go to Nanaimo, where promising coal deposits had been discovered. This time the company proposed to hire families, in the hope that they would be more stable than their predecessors, although the group was to include as many useful hands as possible with 'a good proportion' of single men and only a few children 'unavailable' for work. Only four of the 36 men hired had no families. The committee also accepted Landale's advice to modify the contract to oblige the engagee to serve as a 'Working Collier, Miner, Sinker or Labourer'. The use of the term 'Working Collier' suggests that the committee was still ignorant of coalmining, but the contract would now at least clarify what duties a man was expected to perform. The committee also ordered Douglas to have houses ready, all designed so as 'to encourage decent habits of living among them'. Ten 'collier labourers' were also to be hired on five-year contracts at the rate of £17 a year with provisions and lodging and a gratuity of £25 in land at 20 shillings an acre if they conducted themselves satisfactorily. When the company failed to get these men, it planned to use labourers drawn from its ordinary servants and local Natives.[52]

The new miners, who were from Staffordshire, added a disgruntled element to an already discontented lot. The voyage to Vancouver Island was wretched, marked by the deaths of several children and a woman in childbirth, bad weather, and dreadful rations that prompted a one-day mutiny by the miners.[53] When in 1854 Douglas went to re-engage miners at Nanaimo, he was annoyed by their extravagant demands, although he did not record the details, probably because he absolutely refused to make any concessions beyond raising their bonus from 4s. to 4s.6d. He was able, however, to hire two new miners on terms that included no fixed wage, only 4s.6d. per ton produced, victuals for one person, and tools. When sick or otherwise off duty, they would receive neither food nor pay from the company. Later that year the miners struck for higher pay. According to Douglas, 'missionaries' from the American collieries at Bellingham Bay were promising them high wages, but he managed to persuade them that the HBC would pay as much and they returned to work. Although seven miners deserted in April of 1855, Douglas still felt that with 'good training' and 'the influence of proper discipline' the newcomers would become satisfactory employees. Also, the fact that some of them had asked him if their miner friends could come here by the company's ships led him to believe that the recruits would soon be very easy to come by. He observed, as well, that miners who were paid by the ton, with no other pay or allowances of any kind, produced the most coal and were the least troublesome, and proposed that fixed yearly wages for miners be abolished.

The committee liked Douglas's suggestion. It directed that those who broke their contracts not be readmitted on their old terms and that when the contracts of the rest expired that they be employed strictly on piece-rates. In addition, if they stopped work they would be ejected from their houses. But the miners remained 'restive and untractable'. There were frequent disputes between them and their manager, often ending in a 'general strik[e]'. Six of the deserters who had returned to the fold were 'idle and disorderly' and careless about the quality of the coal they produced. Another party of eight had deserted to the nearby gold diggings. On their return they were admitted on new terms: four shillings for every ton of coal and no rations. Their objections were fruitless and the committee pressed on with its alterations. It even ordered Douglas to sell small lots around Nanaimo to encourage a permanent settlement of miners in the area,[54] a plan reminiscent of the HBC's establishment of the Red River Colony.

During the next few years the company eliminated the last remnants of paternalism in its relationship with the colliers. By December of 1856 the miners were supporting themselves and being paid nine shillings a ton, though they still received free housing. The following year Douglas hired three Cornish miners from California and concluded that it would no longer be necessary to send miners from England. In July of 1858 he reported that it was easy to replace deserting miners with men from the colony, though some of them were 'not the best characters'. In 1859 he decided to sell the miners their houses along with the lots on which they were situated, thereby relieving the company of all expense except wages. As a result, the strike for higher pay that took place in 1860 did not lead to the intervention that previous incidents had. But mining was not profitable and wages were high because their level was regulated by those in California and Oregon,[55] and the company sold its coal operations in 1862.

Miners could not be transformed into servants. Colliers would not be relegated to a status that clashed with their traditions of independence and craft pride, nor would they accept a mode of payment to which they were unaccustomed. They did not find piece-work objectionable because they considered themselves skilled craftsmen and expected to regulate their earnings by applying their skill and knowledge without outside interference. For them, battles over wages were thus also struggles for autonomy and recognition. The wages of the rest of the company's employees reflected a different status, one which was supposed to be inferior and subordinate, and had little to do with the intensity or duration of a particular task. Nevertheless, although the men relinquished their autonomy when they signed their contracts, they still demanded that they be recognized for who *they* were, namely, men to whom the company owed fair treatment. They accepted the gap between their pay and their officers' and they never demanded a share of the profits that their labour made possible. Indeed, their wage demands were quite modest, despite their superiors' regular complaints. After all, when employers speak of reasonable wages, they really mean wages just high enough to keep their workers alive and able to work. For those further up the hierarchy, of course, remuneration ranges from the generous to the outrageous, but no manager and few workers question the inequity of this situation. HBC employees did not question it either, even when they struck for wage increases. They did, however, demand fair treatment, and this, not wages, was the issue that provoked the most serious discord.

Demanding Fair Treatment

Like armies, HBC men travelled on their stomachs. According to Donald Mackay, the 'custom of the men' was 'if their Belly is not full they can do nothing.'[56] Collective action was therefore sometimes collective grumbling about the quality or quantity of provisions,[57] though the men did not limit themselves to 'murmuring and disagreeable mopings'. They also refused to accept the food served out if it was something they disliked, such as potatoes or fish, or if it was so bad that they considered it inedible.[58] Their officers were not always unsympathetic, either. When provisions were scarce at York Factory in 1789, Joseph Colen recognized that 'examples are far beyond precepts when driven to extremities', and 'to prevent murmurs' he reduced his own rations after Christmas.[59] In 1802, William Tomison commented that experience had taught him that 'if their be anything bad at York its good enough for the Inlanders'. The cheese and bacon he had received were so bad they put him off these victuals permanently, and his inspection of the oatmeal at York Factory confirmed the servants' charges that it was nothing but husks. When he informed the chief of the state of the meal, he was told not to complain because he 'was not served with such'. Tomison replied that since he was 'a fellow servant and working as they did' his 'wish was that they should be served with as good provisions' as he had. Otherwise, he asked, 'how could I expect they would obey my orders in taking care of the

Company's property?'[60] At Fort Halkett, on the Liard River, December of 1830 found its residents almost reduced to 'absolute want' without hope of more provisions and almost out of firewood. John Hutchinson put his men on half-allowance, equipped them with snares so that they could fend for themselves, and decided to 'exact no duty' from them.[61] In June of 1850 a party of men encamped at Lac La Pluie protested that dried sturgeon weakened them and refused to proceed if they had to continue living on it. A promise of sugar and grease to accompany the fish persuaded them to go on and left them in a much better humour, which even the cramps induced by a feast of wild strawberries a few days later did not spoil.[62] In November of 1867 Robert Campbell expressed concern that the company's determination to prevent its servants from becoming indebted had resulted in unreasonable deprivation. Because they were not permitted advances equal to more than two-thirds of their wages, the servants' orders, particularly those of the inland men, had been reduced 'so indiscriminately' the past season that most of them were 'far short of their requirements for winter' and had to be supplied out of the trade goods. There was thus both added expense and 'much discontent.'[63] Most officers were genuinely concerned for their servants' wellbeing, but, as they were fully aware, discontentment could also lead to disorder, for the men did not simply wait for their masters to intercede for them or limit themselves to respectful entreaties.

In September 1780, as their officers were closing the packet at Fort Albany, the men gathered to demand something to make up for their short allowance of flour. One of them threatened to 'deny Duty' and was immediately discharged. The others went back to work.[64] In December of 1796, James Sutherland tried to adopt at Brandon House the standard of allowances laid out for the inland posts belonging to York Factory, but had to abandon his plan when the men threatened to withdraw their labour if he made this alteration.[65] In October of 1799, while on the expedition that established Greenwich House on Lac La Biche, Peter Fidler wanted to follow a group of Canadians to the mouth of the Lesser Slave River, but he had no provisions for such an undertaking and his men refused to go. Indeed, he complained, 'of late they have become nearly their own Masters', for it was almost impossible to get them to go anywhere but where they thought 'Proper' and they would not go where they had to live on fish.[66] In April of 1812 the men of Brandon House refused to work until they got fat with their meat, complaining that they were 'used worse than Slaves' and that 'it was not the company's orders'. Their master told them they could have fat if they paid for it, which most of them agreed to do.[67] On this occasion, of course, the men were not really suffering and their histrionics were a device to make a point, but real deprivation did exist in the service.

In March of 1816, for example, the sawyers and wooders belonging to Great Whale River, on the east coast of Hudson Bay, returned to camp from their labours and presented their master, Thomas Alder, with a petition. They had not received their usual rations during the past week, they protested, and were not fed enough to work on. They therefore requested the normal allowance of half a pint of oatmeal per day per man or flour instead. According to Alder, the petition, of which no copy survives, suggested that his compliance would 'preserve tranquillity' while his refusal would 'breed discontent'. The stocks of flour and oatmeal were too low for Alder to comply and the men dropped the issue, but in April they complained again that their allowances were inadequate. This time Alder was able to give each man two pounds of flour to make up for the bad meat and lack of oatmeal and continued to augment their rations with an extra pound of flour a week. Great Whale River was a bad place for provisions and almost no fresh food was available over the winter. The men had to subsist on flour, oatmeal, preserved meat, which they and Alder considered inedible, and exceedingly rare additions of fresh fish. This diet took its toll and scurvy appeared in July. One man was unable to leave his bed and his legs were so swollen his clothes had to be cut off him. Another suffered severe pain in his legs and all his teeth were loose. Fortunately, two Natives brought fish and venison, which saved the day.[68]

The winters of 1815–16 and 1816–17 were also difficult for the men further south. In the fall of 1815, the company's ships *Eddystone* and *Hadlow* were trapped in the Bay by an early winter. The servants who had been headed home were divided among the Bayside posts. But the sailors were kept together on Charlton Island under deplorable conditions, confined for most of the day in a house that was much too small, without exercise or the opportunity to clean themselves or their dwelling. Dirtiness and inactivity being considered the primary causes of scurvy, Thomas Vincent, the governor of the Southern Department, was not surprised that the disease 'soon began its dreadful ravages'. The surgeons did what they could, but, Vincent complained, the ships' officers would not force their men to follow medical advice and 12 sailors died. The seamen's lack of submissiveness, however, ensured that they would receive little sympathy. As far as James Russell, the master of Eastmain, was concerned, they were 'a reprobate refractory set' who did 'not deserve any pity than what extends to humanity'. In November they instituted their own biscuit ration of four pounds a week. When their officers reduced it to three in January, the men objected so ferociously that Russell ordered the captains to resort to arms if the men tried to take anything by force, but no confrontation occurred.[69]

Unfortunately, that fall the *Emerald* and *Prince of Wales* were marooned and an even worse winter loomed. The posts' resources had been exhausted, and when 40 returned passengers arrived at Eastmain the people there 'put on a look of Despair'. By January, they had had enough and complained that they could not work on four barrels of flour a week and a piece of pork for 10 days. It was also unfair, they observed, that they had been forced to work harder than the men at the other Bayside posts the previous year but that the latter got better provisions. Russell agreed and rewarded their 'irreproachable good behaviour on all occasions' with a half-pint of flour per day with their half-allowance of meat. At Fort Albany there was trouble among the returned passengers. The post's population had risen to 67 with the arrival of 31 men from the ships and Jacob Corrigal had sent 29 of them to Capusco, where he hoped they could support themselves by hunting geese in the marsh. But geese were few and far between and the rations so meagre that the men constantly threatened to return to the fort and take food by force. By April discontentment had reached critical proportions, so Corrigal summoned all but those too sick to travel back to the factory and sent John Cromartie and William Saunders with flour and beef for those left behind. On their second day out they met the people returning to Fort Albany, gave them the supplies to take to Capusco, headed back to Albany for more provisions, and set off once more for the marsh. To their surprise, they found the men from Capusco exactly where they had left them and all the provisions except for two pieces of beef eaten. The beef became that evening's meal and grain was sent to Capusco in the morning.

Disaffection was also building aboard the *Prince of Wales*. In April the crew complained to Captain Hanwell that they could not 'exist' on the weekly ration of three pieces of meat and 18 pounds of flour for five men and he appealed to Eastmain for some geese. But Hanwell had disobeyed Joseph Beioley's order to share his stock of meat with the posts because he feared that the sailors would mutiny if they saw food being sent away, and his request now prompted James Russell to observe that Hanwell cared only for those under his immediate command and lived 'in Luxury and Affluence' while others starved. The captain of the *Emerald* reported that he had been forced to increase his crew's weekly allowance.

Serious trouble finally erupted on 19 August when the men of the *Prince of Wales* refused to weigh anchor. The next day they went to Moose Factory to demand more provisions for the voyage home and declared themselves in a 'State of Mutiny'. The officers at Moose Factory had seen them coming and closed the gate. Some hours later seven of the seamen took a letter to Hanwell and four came back with a letter from him asking for provisions, which were handed over to his gunner. A few hours later they all returned to the ship.[70] HBC officers tended to see mariners, who were normally present at the posts only during shiptime, as the popular stereotype depicted them: turbulent, improvident creatures of little use on land.[71] As a result, the officers disapproved of the fact that their captains refused to bully their crews into submission; at the same time, they recognized the justice of their own men's complaints although they could be equally turbulent.

In 1820 meagre allowances rendered the men destined for the Peace River so 'mutinous' that even George Simpson thought it necessary to 'try to coax them' into a better mood with a modest concession. Despite Simpson's entreaty, 'a ringleader' refused to depart for his post. Deciding he could not risk permitting such 'flagrant misconduct', Simpson gave one of the officers 'a hint' and the officer gave the culprit 'a shaking he is not likely to forget', dragged him into the canoe, and fined him 300 *livres*. Grumbling resumed inland, however, when there proved to be almost no provisions at Fort Chipewyan.[72] In 1831 four men belonging to the Montreal Department did not even arrive at their destination, but abandoned their officer along the way because, they said, he half-starved them.[73] When in November of 1852 most of the men at Fort Simpson plotted to 'strike work' if their allowances were not doubled, one of the conspirators informed the master, who then made some unspecified 'preparations', perhaps for the application of corporal punishment, which apparently 'intimidated' the men sufficiently to stop them from carrying out their plans, though not to pacify them permanently. The following July, 11 of them demanded more salt pork and flour, threatening to appeal to the captain of HBC *Virago* currently undergoing repairs on the beach. The officers consulted the captain and followed his advice to give additional rations.[74] But sometimes the men's protests aroused only indifference, as was the case at Fort Alexandria in November of 1860 when the men objected to eating the remains of a horse that had frozen to death. They wanted a full ration of flour, which was running low, and refused to work until they got it. The master told them to suit themselves and set a good example by breakfasting on the meat himself. Some of the men returned to work and were rewarded with full measures of flour, while the rest received only half-rations.[75]

Situations thus varied, depending on the men's readiness to take action, the degree of hardship they were actually suffering, and their officers' responses to their demands. Not all confrontations were battles and some officers at least came to accept that complaining was an HBC tradition. Thus, when Simpson's successor, Alexander Grant Dallas, reported in 1862 that the men at Fort Edmonton had gone 'on strike', he mentioned that this appeared 'to be the Custom' when they could not be supplied with full rations.[76]

Cries of misery and starvation were, of course, frequently part of the ritual of negotiation rather than descriptions of reality. Still, being adequately fed was vital if the men were to survive their stint in the service, and their refusal to expose themselves to excessive hardship of any kind was quite reasonable. This led to most of the difficulties in the company's transport service. HBC servants disliked the long voyages so much that by the 1830s it had become common to hire Natives to assist the men coming to the Bay from the Athabasca and the Mackenzie River districts. Simpson wanted to eliminate this practice because of its cost and the danger that servants in other districts would want to adopt it, though he reconsidered because the Natives would work for 'very moderate pay'. They could not be acquired in sufficient numbers, however.[77] The solution to the problem was to hire tripmen at Red River, a measure, it was also hoped, that would render the service more attractive because regular servants would no longer have to make the arduous annual journeys to and from York Factory. But by the 1850s the 'Red River halfbreeds' upon whom the company had come to rely had 'also conceived a distaste for such employment'. Indeed, observed William Christie in 1864, 'The ole hardy Voyageur is an article not to be found now a days and other means of transport must be ... devised or we will be in a fix.'[78] To some extent, the company was already 'in a fix', however, because the Portage La Loche brigade, which had become central to its operations, was made up of Red River tripmen and when they refused to accept employment with the HBC or, having signed on, refused to do as they were told, they threw everything into disarray.

The men were engaged for the brigade in the winter and their tour of duty began the first week of June when they departed from Red River. Their first destination was Norway House, where they picked up the supplies for the Mackenzie River district, which had been stored there the previous autumn. They then headed west across Lake Winnipeg, through Cedar Lake, and along the Saskatchewan River to

Cumberland House. From there they followed the Sturgeon-Weir River north to the Churchill River and along it to Ile-à-la-Crosse. Then they turned north again, travelled through Peter Pond Lake, along the La Loche River, and through Lake La Loche to the portage. There a brigade of men belonging to the Mackenzie River district would be waiting for them with the proceeds of the winter's trade and the workers who were leaving the district. The two groups would exchange cargo and the departing servants would be replaced by the new servants who had accompanied the brigade inland. The inland crews would then head back to their respective posts and the Portage La Loche brigade would head for York Factory with the furs, which would be loaded aboard ship immediately upon their arrival. The brigade would then return to Red River with that district's supplies, pausing to deposit the following year's inland cargo at Norway House. The whole trip was supposed to take about four months.

To ensure a smooth flow of goods, the council of the Northern Department ruled in 1843 that boats carry 65 pieces from Norway House, leave five at Oxford House, and deliver 60 to York Factory. A piece, actually *pièce*, was a bundle of goods and weighed 90 pounds. In years of very low water, the ladings might be reduced, with 55 pieces to be delivered at the factory. In 1849 the council established the office of superintendent of transport to regulate this traffic and decided that crews were to number one man for every 10 or 12 pieces. Nine pieces per man down and 11 up would be allowed when water levels were low. A crew of eight had to carry at least 75 pieces of cargo, while a crew of seven could carry no fewer than 70. No inland boat was to have a crew of more than seven men, except with the superintendent's special authorization. Such was the procedure—at least when the system was 'in perfect working order'. By 1870 the brigade comprised 18 boats, each with a crew of seven men, who seemed possessed by an 'increasing spirit of mutiny'.[79]

As usual, the company's regulations were no match for its employees' determination to control the pace and conditions of their work and their willingness to take advantage of the value of their services to exert such control. Like the rest of the HBC employees, tripmen wanted to be properly provisioned and not overworked. Thus, in 1857 when the officers tried to decrease the consumption of pemmican by giving the brigade's flour instead, the men simply helped themselves to pemmican from the cargo and when told they might be charged for it, the men replied that, in that case 'they would return with empty boats to the place from whence they had come.'[80] In August of that year, some of the Portage La Loche men asked William L. Hardisty to request that they be allowed some warm clothing over and above their wages so that they would have protection from the cold if winter set in before they got home. Because they were setting off so late in the season, Hardisty was sympathetic and urged that their wishes 'be favorably considered'.[81] Such requests were not unreasonable. Tripmen spent an even smaller proportion of their lives in the HBC than contracted servants. They were seasonal employees and their service as boatmen could not be allowed to jeopardize their ability to support themselves the rest of the year. Nourishing food and protection against the elements ensured that working for the HBC did not damage their health. Even more important was timing, because the men spent the fall hunting on the plains to lay up a stock of food for the winter and they regularly tried to ensure that their voyages would be completed in good time.

Thus, in 1855, two brigades of Portage La Loche boats refused to wait at York Factory for the ship, which was late, because, they said, they had been engaged to remain only as long as it took to have their boats repaired.[82] Anything that might delay the brigade's progress could lead to objections. In 1856, for example, desertions along the way left each boat short a man and the remaining men refused to leave Norway House undermanned. On this occasion they were bribed to continue to the portage with the promise that each crew would share a bonus equal to the pay of a middleman for a trip to and from the portage.[83] Usually, however, more money could not overcome the men's determination not to lose a season's hunting. In 1857 George Barnston proposed to one brigade that each boat carry 20 extra pieces besides the 50 required by the contract from York Factory, in return for which each man would receive an addition to his wages. They declined because the additional cargo would slow their return and perhaps prevent their getting to the plains to procure winter provisions. When he made the same offer to another brigade, the voyagers refused to commit themselves until they had seen the state of the water.[84] In 1862 one of the brigades would carry only 30 pieces per boat.[85] In 1863, the crews of the boats from Red River refused to complete the fall voyage to York Factory because their long journey on Lake Winnipeg had delayed their arrival at Norway House so seriously that they were afraid they would be 'set fast' on their homeward trip if they went to the Bay.[86]

As far as the company's officers were concerned, however, the men's demands and their refusal to be delayed were simply the result of their bad character and poor quality. James A. Grahame complained in 1865 that immediately upon their arrival at Norway House, the men of the brigade showed 'the cloven hoof'. They plagued him with requests for advances in the form of blankets, shirts, or trousers and some of them refused to proceed until they got them. Others would not embark at all. As a result, 131 packs had to be left at Norway House. Those who did proceed to York Factory refused to carry away more than 30 packs per boat, although their contract stipulated 45. Moreover, from the 'numberless applications' to be sent back 'on account of all sorts of ailments', he observed, 'one would suppose the Brigades were manned by hospital patients.'[87] The following year was no better. One of the boats was made up of men so unfit they got no further than Norway House in the spring. In the fall two of the brigades refused to carry more than 45 pieces per boat from York Factory and some of the other crews returned to Red River without going to York Factory at all.[88] In 1867 most of the crews of the Portage La Loche brigade refused to make the trip to the coast. As a result, most of the Mackenzie River returns remained inland and of the four boats that made the trip, two did not reach York Factory until after the ship had left for England. Six tripmen refused to go further than Norway House because of the lateness of the season, the bad summer they had endured, a scarcity of provisions, and their own weakness.

James Stewart considered their refusal the result of a combination entered into at Portage La Loche and the fact that the brigade was composed of 'the worst set of men' he had ever seen. Many of them, he claimed, were mere boys, easily led astray by the 'proposers of the affair'. He did concede, though, that they had received few supplies of very poor quality at Cumberland House and Ile-à-la-Crosse and that they were on 'short rations' most of the way. Still, he suggested, not only should the brigades leave earlier in the season, they should be made up of men 'who do care something for their Character' and the guides and steersmen should be made 'more responsible' for what occurred on the trip. But the fact that the brigades behaved much better the following year after leaving Red River earlier in the season suggests that the men really were concerned about the dangers of travelling too late in the year and they were not the scoundrels that Stewart considered them. Peace might also have prevailed because not all the crews had contracted to travel all the way to the factory.[89] Likewise, the following year one of the Portage La Loche brigades was engaged to return to Red River after coming back from the portage to Norway House. Presumably, the officers hoped that this arrangement would ensure that those who did not want to go to the factory signed up for this brigade.[90]

Nevertheless, the 'spirit of insubordination' continued to spread and the situation was particularly bad in 1870. Recruitment was difficult, but five boats were finally manned by members of the 'French halfbreed population lately in arms' and four by 'English halfbreeds' and Natives from the Christianized settlement of St Peter's. Three boats returned from Norway House, their crews pleading illness, and the rest set off, accompanied by five supplementary boats manned by Natives engaged at Norway House. At Grand Rapid on the Saskatchewan River there was a 'general mutiny' among the men from Red River—the crews of four of the boats abandoned their cargoes and returned to the settlement, keeping the boats. The remaining two Red River boats and the five from Norway House continued on their way, but the officers had to make complicated arrangements to get supplies to the Mackenzie River district. Other tripmen added to the disorder by getting drunk on stolen liquor at Norway House and when they arrived at York Factory they demanded a regale of rum because they had travelled to Portage La Loche. Since they did not belong to that brigade, their request was denied, whereupon they refused to take any new hands aboard their boats, claiming that they were acting in accordance with a promise made them at Norway House. Finally, William Parson had to bribe them to take the newly arrived recruits by giving each man six shillings on account at Norway House, but they would not accept another six to take 10 extra pieces of cargo. Then, just after loading their boats, one of the crews threatened to remove five pieces from each of the boats belonging to their brigade unless they received an extra glass of grog. Although he had recently granted the same to another brigade, Parson refused, whereupon the men unloaded the pieces and left. The company's relationship with its tripmen had reached its nadir and its adoption of steamboats allowed it to avoid having to rebuild whatever ties had once existed.[91]

Mutiny in the HBC

By this time, of course, the HBC had turned Rupert's Land over to the Canadian government, treating the population who manned its boats as cavalierly as it had treated the officers who managed its posts when the company was sold to the International Financial Society in 1863. Neither group went quietly: the officers had petitioned and protested and the men of Red River had rebelled. That the Red River Rebellion of 1869–70 would make it difficult for the company to recruit tripmen and that its relations with them were so bad that they rebelled against it should not, therefore, be surprising. Moreover, in labelling the incident at Grand Rapid in 1870 a mutiny, HBC officers were not simply resorting to their usual habit of referring to ordinary disturbances and work stoppages as mutinies. Unfortunately, the company's records provide no further detail, since the officers, as was their wont, indulged in vigorous condemnation without analysis and left no descriptions of the event. Perhaps because the incident involved tripmen whose unruliness was no longer surprising, especially after the rebellion, no one considered it necessary or possible to make further inquiries. But the tripmen had rejected their superiors' authority and departed with their employer's boats. They were thus behaving very much like mutinying seamen. The word 'mutiny' is usually associated with the armed forces or seamen and involves the curtailment or overturning of constituted authority and, in the case of sailors, might include the seizure of the ship. In an organization like the HBC, in which workers occupied the status of servants and were defined by their contracts and the law as totally subordinate, disobedience constituted a breach of contract and a defiance of the authority legally set over them. Moreover, given the reciprocal responsibilities that defined the master-servant relationship, such misbehaviour also smacked of gross ingratitude and disloyalty. Thus, although officers did occasionally refer to strikes, they were likely to see them not simply as 'job actions' but as mutinies.

At the same time, however, officers also appear to have assumed that mutiny was a particular type of misbehaviour that could be punished by particular penalties. Thus in 1815 Thomas Vincent, governor of the Southern Department, issued a notice that all the masters of posts were to read to their men. The servants of the department had been guilty of 'disobedience, neglect of duty, Combinations, and desertion' and the notice was to ensure that no one could plead ignorance of the penalties for these offences. It cautioned 'all Artisans, tradesmen, Sailors, and labourers, and all servants of every denomination in the pay of the ... Honble. Company' that all such transgressions would be punished according to the laws of England. Furthermore, since there were now 'foreigners and other persons unacquainted with the Laws of England in the service of the said Honble. Company', there was an appendix listing the 'leading offences' and their 'probable' punishments. The first such offence was 'Mutiny and desertion', for which 'the same Punishment [would] be inflicted as in the Army and Navy besides loss of pay'. 'Disobedience, insolence or disrespect' were also to be punished as 'similar offences' were in the army and navy. Combination was punishable by fines and imprisonment in irons or whatever the governor and his council might decide. Anyone found guilty of assaulting an officer would receive corporal punishment, lose his pay, and be imprisoned in irons. An accomplice to such an assault would be punished according to what the governor and council might decide. In addition, neglect of duty or carelessness in its performance would be punished with a fine.[92]

The HBC charter had granted it the authority to discipline its employees in accordance with English law, but it had not granted it the authority to hang men for mutiny and desertion, as the army and navy could. Vincent was not specific in what he meant by the same kind of punishment as in the armed forces. He might simply have been implying that mutineers would be flogged, as John Cartwright and William Filpt had been in 1696 after they were found guilty of attempting to organize a mutiny. He must have known, however, that the company could not actually impose military discipline, although referring to it certainly created an impression of severity and strictness. It is not clear where Vincent got the information he appended to his notice. Nor did he define what he meant by mutiny, probably because he assumed that everyone would know what he meant. He also appears to have assumed that it was possible for workers to commit mutiny and to be found guilty of it. But workers were not soldiers or seamen who had sworn loyalty to king and country, and mutiny had no legal significance in a commercial organization. Nevertheless, Vincent's notice implied that it did, perhaps because circumstances rendered it necessary to make the servants believe that they owed their employer the same obedience as a soldier owed his monarch and that their employer could resort to extreme measures in dealing with insubordination. The newcomers, among whom were riotous Irishmen and disobedient Norwegians, needed to be made aware of the regulations to which they were subject, while those familiar with the service had to be reminded of them, particularly in view of two incidents that had occurred only a few years earlier and that did indeed appear to be mutinies.

Genuine mutinies were rare in the HBC. Unlike combinations, in which men acted collectively to achieve specific ends and settle particular grievances, mutinies erupted after a period of what men regarded as genuine oppression. Perhaps the most famous mutiny in the English-speaking world is the one that occurred on the *Bounty* in 1789. It is what tends to be expected in a mutiny: sailors driven beyond endurance by a cruel captain to rise up, seize the ship, and eject the offending master. The mutinies that occurred in the HBC did not follow this pattern. Rather, they resembled another well-known mutiny, the naval mutiny of 1797 in which the seamen refused to sail until their complaints regarding low pay, poor food, and bad officers had been dealt with. The sailors did take over their ships and deposed their officers—one of whom was William Bligh, formerly of the *Bounty* and now the highly unpopular master of the *Director*, one of the last ships to return to duty. But they were orderly and disciplined and violence was uncommon. In their petitions the men emphasized their loyalty to king and country, appealed to the benevolence of the Lords of the Admiralty, and pointed out the justice of their demands.[93] The seamen were not revolutionaries. They were demanding fair treatment, as were the HBC men when they engaged in what their officers regarded as mutiny. There were two mutinies of fur trade servants. The first took place at Brandon House in February of 1811. The second occurred a year later near York Factory.

The Brandon House Mutiny

At Brandon House the combination of higher prices instituted by the Retrenching System and the arrival of Hugh Heney, formerly of the North West Company, to succeed John McKay proved explosive. Signs of trouble appeared on 30 October 1810 when Heney reached the forks of the Red and Assiniboine rivers where Thomas Mason waited with horses and carts to transport Heney and his belongings to Brandon House. When Heney told Mason to stay and wait for William Auld, who was supposed to winter at Brandon House, Mason replied that he could not do so since he had neither the provisions nor the clothes for such a sojourn. Heney, however, had instructed William Yorston, who was temporarily in charge of the post, to station a properly equipped party at the forks until Auld appeared. Auld later concluded that Yorston's disregard of this order indicated that the Brandon House servants had already begun to plot against Heney and were trying to ensure their success by preventing Auld's arrival. Whatever the truth of these allegations, the result of Yorston's failure to do as he had been told caused immediate discord. Heney angrily dismissed Mason from the service, but the latter insisted that, having brought the horses from Brandon House, he would return there with them. According to Mason, Heney then armed himself with pistols and they set off. A few days after Heney's arrival, the men threatened to stop work until the price of slops was reduced to the old scale. Heney replied that anyone who refused duty would receive no victuals and could take to the plains to support himself. The men pointed out that they were not refusing duty, that they were simply asking for the old prices, which Heney finally allowed on goods they had purchased before he got there. Thereafter the situation went rapidly downhill. According to William Yorston, who took charge after the mutiny, Heney 'imposed on' the men, 'put extravagant prices on all goods & went amongst them always with his arms on, which they were not accustomed to.' Moreover, he never spoke to them, although he must have done so at least once, since he called them 'Orkney Hogs'. The crisis finally occurred on 24 February 1811.

Heney had recently returned from Pembina to find that Yorston, whom he had left in charge, had disobeyed orders not to sell the men anything from the warehouse. He therefore took the keys away from Yorston, who departed with angry words. Although relations between Heney and his men were clearly poor, he was to place most of the blame for what happened on Archibald Mason, who had accompanied him from Pembina. Mason appears to have been hired for his knowledge of agriculture but not assigned any particular occupation. According to Heney, he was masquerading as an agent of the London committee sent to spy on the officers and he set about turning everyone against Heney. On the evening of 24 February, Heney accepted Mason's invitation to join him and two other gentlemen for a friendly drink. Conversation soon turned to the men's misbehaviour and then to William Yorston, whom Mason defended. Then, suddenly, Mason jumped up, opened the door, and challenged Heney, who turned him out of the room, whereupon Mason ran down the stairs calling for help. When Heney went to investigate, one of his drinking companions and another man urged him to return to his room. Heney told them that unless they chose to support him they should 'Hold their tongues', and he threatened to blow out the brains of the first man who got in his way. Shortly after, he went in search of Mason and found the men gathered in 'a grand Council'. They told him Mason was asleep, then 'jumped' on him, disarmed him, abused him, took his keys, robbed his room, and finally released him. According to the servants, Heney and Mason were drunk that night, they quarrelled, and Heney, armed with pistols and a cutlass, searched the men's houses for Mason. The men then disarmed him, and Mason declared himself an agent of the company and took Heney's keys. Heney fled to some nearby freemen's tents, but after learning that some of the mutineers were going to Pembina he headed there, too.

John Isbister claimed that the men who raced Heney to Pembina were going in order to prevent Heney from avenging himself on the people there with a gun he had acquired from a Canadian. Some of the others said the party had gone to fetch two kegs of salt. But the letter that Mason and Yorston sent to Pembina suggests otherwise. In it they reported that Heney was up to 'some curious Capers . . . with regard to Prices of Goods, &c.' They also accused him of having gotten drunk to lift his spirits after the failure of his plan to marry the late John McKay's daughter in order to get his hands on the deceased's money, for the purpose of which he had sent off his 'Wedded Wife'. They wanted Heney seized and held so that he could be taken to London. The mutineers reached Pembina before Heney did and succeeded in turning everyone against him. He was forced to surrender his gun and was subjected to 'vulgar' abuse from Mason, who declared that he would make Heney go 'in his Indian Coat & Britch Cloath as he had done before at the Rocky Mountains'. Heney said, 'You Cannot prove that', to which Mason replied, 'I can and plenty more.' When Heney referred to the London committee and the rest of the company, Mason retorted that they were a 'parcel of Damnd Raskals together' and 'that the Company was aparcel of Jack Asses for agreeing such Damnd Raskals'. Heney considered knocking him down, but changed his mind because he was outnumbered. He spent the night under guard and in the morning confronted Mason before all the men, calling him an impostor and them 'a set of fools' for believing him when he had shown them no proof of his authority. He grabbed Mason's lapels, but the men made him withdraw. The next few days were peaceful, but on 9 March Heney demanded to know the basis of Mason's authority, to which Mason responded, 'what the Devel is Your Business you damnd Scavenger' and 'so on'. Heney then struck him once, whereupon the Brandon House men grabbed Heney and told him he would not strike Mason. Heney and the men then talked for a short time, though the deponent who reported this incident, William Plowman, gave no details, and then Heney left the room. Soon after, he found refuge with some Canadians.

When William Kennedy arrived on 13 May to escort the men to York Factory to answer Heney's charges, he found William Yorston in charge and in complete control of the men. They paid no attention to Kennedy, and Yorston would do nothing to help him because Kennedy had hurt Yorston's feelings by not presenting him with the company's papers. Yorston declared 'that he was looked upon as nobody', that he would answer to the HBC alone, that no man in the country was his master, and that he would go to Fort Albany. He finally relented, though, and assured Kennedy that the men would go wherever they were ordered, although four of them had to go to Albany to act as witnesses for Mason. He was himself willing to go, but preferred to stay inland. Kennedy therefore organized three boat crews to go to York Factory, but the mutiny was by no means over. When Kennedy told the men that he was 'glad to see them so far come to a sense of their duty' and would 'interest' himself on their behalf, George Henderson, a labourer, speaking for all the men, declared that they would answer for themselves. Moreover, they would go to York Factory only on the condition that they received the same allowances as at Fort Albany and would return to Brandon House. They also vowed never to serve under Heney again. Kennedy replied that only his superiors could grant their requests. He was at last able to get off on 23 June. They arrived at Red River five days later and Heney arrived on 5 July.

William Auld expressed surprise that any HBC servants 'should take upon themselves to act without any authority from their superiors or to resist the orders of those appointed by the Honble Committee themselves', and was concerned that Orcadians, 'hitherto so remarkable for propriety of conduct & faithfull obedience to whosoever was placed over them', would participate in such a shocking affair. Auld blamed that 'Rascal' Archibald Mason, who had 'stimulated & directed the brutal men there to disobedience, insolence & mutiny'. Mason, Auld had heard, had misrepresented himself to the servants and told them that the price increase was the 'fabrication' of Auld, Heney, and Thomas Vincent. Nevertheless, the men were guilty of acting 'in direct opposition to their own solemn engagements by which they bound themselves to obey all orders from their Chief Factor and from such Officers as he shall appoint to direct them'. As 'faithful Servants' they should have 'quietly and obediently submitted to' Heney's commands for the duration of their contracts or at least for a year, after which they would 'have it in their power to state their grievances if they had any in a becoming manner to the Chief'. The men must be 'convinced', Auld wrote to Yorston, 'that to *reject* or *even hesitate* to accept for their Master such person or persons as the Chief appoints must be productive of the most awful consequences for which yourselves will have to answer in this world as well as the next.'[94] Auld should not have been so surprised, however, for William Yorston and the men of the Red River district had already demonstrated their readiness to usurp authority.

Yorston had joined the HBC in 1796 and in the fall of 1797 had with others refused to go up the Red River with a Canadian master, whom they said they did not know and could not understand. Even when John McKay pointed out that John Richards, a native of the country who understood French, would be second in command and, therefore, giving them their orders, the men would not be swayed. Knowing that ordering was 'out of the question', McKay asked them to reconsider, but finally appointed Richards to lead them. Richards, however, spent his time drinking and grumbling about the company and deserted in October. The men then wrote to McKay, describing Richards's drunkenness and carelessness, and complained that they were badly off 'for want of a head'. Then, according to Yorston, they met, with all the oldest servants present, and chose a new master, though who this was is not clear. It might have been Magnus Murray, an Orcadian labourer, in the service since 1791, who composed two of the three letters the men sent to McKay. The five men who signed the first letter and who may well have been the leaders of the group were all labourers. Four of them were Orcadians, three of them in the service since 1793. The senior member of the group was John Easter, an 'Esquemaux' who had joined the company in 1784 and whose expiry date was recorded in the servants' list as 'Life'. Easter, described by James Sutherland, master of Brandon House in 1796–97, as 'the Company Slave', had been very unhappy the year before because he received no wages and was 'used lik a Slave &c.' He had even refused to work for two days in April of 1797. Sutherland believed that 'The People, together with the Canadians', were 'Poisoning the morals of this simple fellow' and, fearing Easter would desert, bribed him back to work with a present.

McKay was not much more sympathetic to John Richards's subordinates. He sent Thomas Miller to take charge. In spite of Richards's record of intoxication and disobedience and the evidence Miller discovered of Richards's wastefulness, McKay believed that it was not as serious as the disobedience of the 'rascally men' charged and that, in fact, 'if the truth was known' it would prove that 'his Men was the cause of his leaving his Post.' Yorston, however, presented this incident as one in which the men's responsible actions contrasted sharply with their leader's dereliction of duty. Likewise, the mutiny of 1811 was justified by the master's drunkenness and irresponsibility. Heney, he declared, had left the Canadians because he had quarrelled with them and was 'more Tyrannical' at Brandon House than he had been before.[95]

Archibald Mason, judged the ringleader, was dismissed from the service and fined the full amount of his wages, a punishment Auld regarded as 'astonishing forgiveness'. He also decided that if the *'Principal* in a ruinous *Mutiny* joined with a *capital felony'* escaped 'the Gallows', Yorston, 'who was only the *Second',* could not be punished according to the 'unanimous resolutions' of the officers, who had recommended sending him home in irons.[96] Auld's forbearance might also have been due to the man's good record. Yorston had acted as summer master at Brandon House for several years and John McKay had praised him as the 'most usefull Hand he had.'[97] Yorston therefore returned to Brandon House along with all the mutineers who had renewed their engagements.

Things were quiet until January of 1812, when 'another revolution' almost broke out. William Kennedy, who was now in charge, suspected Yorston of trying to 'throw obstacles' in the way of a proposed trading expedition short of actually refusing to go. His 'insulting' language provoked Kennedy into giving him 'a slap or two' in the face, which Yorston tried to return. Kennedy then insisted that Yorston say whether he would go or not so that Kennedy could punish him for an outright refusal of orders, but Yorston said that Kennedy himself had prevented him from going by disabling him. Kennedy declared this answer unsatisfactory and invited Yorston outdoors. Yorston retorted that he would not give a more satisfactory answer and would not go outdoors until he wanted to. Kennedy then ran to the next room, returned with a pair of tongs, ordered Yorston to the men's house, where he was to remain on half-allowance until spring, and threatened to 'break his head' if he did not obey. When Yorston proved 'as obstinate as a mule', Kennedy hit him on the arm with the tongs. Yorston then tried to hit Kennedy and disarm him. At this point Thomas Favel entered the room. Favel, an erstwhile mutineer, had begged forgiveness with tears in his eyes and 'most pathetically promised' that since he had been 'born & brought up in the Service he would spend the remainder of his life in the discharge of his duty & in Support of the authority of such officers as were placed over him.' Favel took the tongs away, enabling Yorston to knock Kennedy down, sit on him, pound him for 10 minutes, and twist a handkerchief around his neck until he was almost strangled. Kennedy called for help, but the men all ran away, saying they would have nothing to do with the situation. Kennedy was not surprised that the 'rascals who served Mr Heney so ill last winter' would behave thus, 'notwithstanding some of them had made very fair promises last summer.' Finally, Yorston let Kennedy up and, while the latter ran to arm himself in order 'to enforce obedience', Yorston fled to the NWC fort. The Canadian master came over but refused to help put Yorston in irons. From his sanctuary, Yorston sent word that he would go on the expedition that had caused the dispute in the first place. Since he was the only one who knew the way and the relevant Native language, his offer was accepted and he escaped punishment.[98]

Yorston's petition to the committee told a different story, however. Kennedy, he charged, was always intent on harassing him and asked him to go on a hazardous journey, for which service he had not been engaged. When Yorston protested that the trip was too dangerous and the goods with which he was supposed to initiate trade were unsuitable, Kennedy beat him. Still, in spite of this 'outrageous conduct', Yorston went on the journey, which turned out just as badly as he had predicted. Kennedy was also so unpopular with the Natives that Yorston had to act as master of the post. Finally, Yorston decided he wanted to return to Britain to seek redress for his injuries, a plan that met with many obstacles. First, Kennedy would not let him take his property with him. Then, when he arrived at York Factory in July, William Auld informed him that he and all the other officers 'had resolved to make him an Example', no doubt because they had just finished dealing with the 'Glasgow Insurgents' and were in no mood to be lenient with one of the Brandon House mutineers. Yorston thus found himself banished six miles into the woods for 15 days, with only two gills of unsifted oatmeal and a quarter-pound of rotten bacon per day. While so exiled, he contracted a 'distemper' from which he still suffered, and upon his return to York Factory he asked to be 'bleeded'. But Auld, a surgeon, would neither perform this procedure nor let another surgeon do so and Yorston had to bleed himself.

Yorston considered his departure aboard the *King George* an escape from his 'prosecutors'. Now he laid his case before the committee, protesting the treatment he had received from Heney and Kennedy and the cruelty he had suffered at the hands of Auld, which 'no Master appointed by the Company had a right to inflict, without Trial, even on the basest Criminal', certainly not on 'a most meritorious Servant of the Company who had constantly laboured in their Service for Sixteen Years'. Should he not receive redress, Yorston warned, the company's reputation would suffer and Orcadians would shun it. However, far from regarding Yorston as 'a good Servant worthy of reward', the committee judged him 'most unruly and mutinous, and rather deserving of Punishment than of any remuneration'.[99] Clearly, years of faithful service and a record of responsibility could not redeem a man who had so grossly subverted the natural order.

As for the rest of the Brandon House men, Kennedy considered them 'such a set of dam'd, careless, uninterested fellows' that he had 'never met before in the Country'. This outburst was prompted by their return in April of 1812 from the hunting tent with only part of the meat they were supposed to fetch. Refusing to believe their assertion that there was no more, Kennedy observed that they were utterly indifferent to the company's interests and would not improve until they were dispersed and 'some examples made of them'. They had been 'so long accustomed to do & say as they please' that they had 'entirely forgot (that is to say if were they even possessed of the properties) that belong to good Servants'. Furthermore, a complaint from another master alerted him to the fact that signs of 'the infection' that 'began or rather broke out' at Brandon House had appeared in the Swan River area.[100] Kennedy's fears must have been further heightened by news of the mutiny of the Glasgow Insurgents, 14 of the men assigned to Miles Macdonell, the first governor of the Red River Colony.

The Glasgow Insurgents

The first Red River colonists were men hired as company employees and assigned to begin building the settlement in anticipation of its colonization by families.[101] They arrived too late in the fall of 1811 to head inland and the ships that brought them could not leave the Bay. To relieve the overcrowding at York Factory, Miles Macdonell, the colony's governor, and William Hillier, a new HBC officer, and their men were sent to spend the winter up the Hayes River not far from the factory. Relations between Macdonell and his men deteriorated rapidly and he blamed it on the presence of Orcadian servants, who had already been in the country and 'whose habits of idleness and inactivity' it was going to be 'very difficult to eradicate'. It took only a few of the old hands to 'poison any party' by telling the newcomers 'that they ought to have this thing & that other thing & make the whole discontented & keep themselves in the back ground.' In December, Macdonell complained to Auld that the clerk, William Finlay, had 'already occasioned a little difficulty laying down factory-law (as he explained it)' and vowed that more misconduct would 'occasion further steps to be taken with him'. Early in February, when Finlay refused to drink a concoction made from pine needles that Macdonell had ordered everyone to take as an antiscorbutic, Macdonell immediately put him off duty. When he ordered him back to work several days later, Finlay declared that he would do nothing.

A week later, Finlay was tried before William Hillier, who, along with Macdonell and a number of the company's other officers, had been made a justice of the peace in December 1811 under the Canada Jurisdiction Act of 1803. This Act was not, however, actually in force in Rupert's Land. It extended the jurisdiction of the courts of Upper and Lower Canada over the so-called 'Indian Territories' and was intended to deal with conflicts between the HBC and its rivals. Rupert's Land was governed by the company's charter, which gave it civil and criminal jurisdiction over the territory it had been granted. Still, as both a company officer and a justice of the peace, Hillier could assume that he had considerable authority behind him. He found Finlay guilty of being 'a refractory servant' and sentenced him to confinement in a hut constructed for the purpose.

On the evening of Finlay's incarceration, 13 men, a 'party he had formed among the people', gathered and burned the hut to the ground, 'triumphantly shouting in the most audacious manner when they had got it in flames'. Macdonell and Hillier then dragged the whole lot before them, but the men refused 'to submit' to their authority, 'walked away', and took up residence in the woods. Unwilling to provide them with supplies, Macdonell warned William Hemmings Cook at York Factory that the mutineers would probably come there for provisions. Also, because he suspected that the insurgents had 'private advisors & abetters' among the rest of the men, he cautioned Cook against allowing any of the rebels access to their boxes at York Factory without an officer present because they had 'Pistols &c' in them. Cook was alarmed. The reduction in rations imposed the previous fall had 'occasioned a general ferment' that would require 'nothing . . . but time & strength of Party to ripen . . . into open Rebellion.' In fact, he had 'long expected something of this kind' and the 'daily murmurings & discontent' caused him to wonder what might happen come spring. He wanted Macdonell to look after the insurgents himself and urged him to give them sufficient provisions, 'for Hunger is a strong incentive to moral turpitude', and if the rebels visited the factory 'in an irritated state of Mind', who knew 'what Mischiefs might not ensue?' Macdonell accordingly supplied the men with the usual half-rations given men who were off duty, but he did not prevent them from visiting the factory, where, of course, they could buy whatever they needed. Therefore, in March, at Auld's direction, Macdonell ordered that the men be allowed no more purchases, no matter what they needed.[102]

The insurgents refused to give in. They charged that putting Finlay into a hut in February was 'inhuman' and complained about their allowance of oatmeal, bacon, and fat. Auld, however, observed that 'a more determined set of mutinous insolent miscreants at no time has appeared any where' and remarked that Finlay would have been better off in his hut than many of the servants who had to travel with no shelter at all. Had 'humanity' actually been 'so abundant in their bosoms', the gratitude and respect they felt for their master would have made them mindful that his 'zeal for their comfort' entitled him to 'a petition' asking for 'the liberation of their guilty companion'. Had a petition been unsuccessful, 'still no hidden attribute of humanity required their setting the hut on fire' or 'such demonstrations of respect as the loud huzzas & cheerings' with which they concluded the 'scene'. Still less did humanity require 'them in agitation of their plan to propose rising on their Officer', as a witness had testified. No, it was not humanity that motivated them; it was the 'republican & levelling disposition' for which the inhabitants of 'Glasgow & its neighbourhood have long been notorious'. Nor had they any business complaining about their rations, for they were no worse off than the men at York Factory who were eating 'Rusty Bacon', the same food that Macdonell considered fit only for his mutineers. Indeed, Auld remarked sourly, Macdonell's people were feasting on venison, which was in very short supply, and he and his officers 'were like a Committee of Common council-men, sleek & shining in all the splendours of Rubicundity.'

To make matters worse, disloyal clerks were regularly visiting the insurgents and keeping them apprised of everything their superiors were doing and saying, and someone, probably the same clerks, had supplied guns and ammunition so that they could hunt, thereby making it impossible to bring the rebels to heel. Finally, in May, Macdonell suggested that the insurgents be transferred from the colony to the company's regular service. But Auld feared that their presence at York Factory would 'only fan the half-smothered discontent which glows more or less in every European bosom.' Indeed, all was not well at York Factory, where the men had recently refused to drink the table beer brewed 'as a preservative to health'. William Hemmings Cook believed that they were 'determined to resist the adoption of every new regulation . . . however salutary or advisable', and he feared that there would be no end to the 'Murmurings & Dissatisfaction' until all the old hands had been replaced. The insurgents, however, refused to do anything until assured that they would receive wages for the time they were off duty and not be fined. Auld insisted they return to the fold entirely on the company's terms, but not as 'eye sores' at York Factory. They were going to cut firewood outside the post.[103]

After several meetings between Macdonell and the insurgents, the latter submitted a letter, which has not survived. It set terms that Auld judged 'so inadmissible that nothing is or can be meant by them but to continue to defy us' and sent Macdonell into a tirade against the 'miscreants' who had 'spurned' his and Auld's 'good intentions'. Macdonell would not agree to the men's conditions and advised them to 'take their chance & strive to conduct themselves in a manner to merit forgiveness'. But they would 'acknowledge no fault'.[104] Finally, on 13 May, Auld ordered Macdonell and Hillier to summon all the officers and servants and have a message read to the insurgents, who would be compelled to decide on the spot whether they would submit to terms or 'take the consequences'. Before the insurgents were allowed to leave, 'a most strict search' was to be made for all guns, ostensibly as a precaution against accidents. All firearms and ammunition, especially those belonging to the clerks, were to be secured and 'strictly' accounted for with no distinction made between 'public & private' articles. Furthermore, the clerks who had been visiting the insurgents were to be threatened with demotion if they continued this practice. Auld's letter to the insurgents reprimanded them for 'their obstinate refusal to return to their duty' after Macdonell and Auld had taken 'so much pains' to 'lead them to a proper line of conduct'. Now, 'finally', here was an ultimatum. If they returned to work immediately, they would be taken on the books and their punishment would be left to the company, though they would lose the wages for the time they 'continued in defiance of their chief factor's authority'. If they rejected these terms, they would go home as prisoners aboard the company's ship to be turned over to 'the civil power' or kept aboard a royal ship until demanded for trial.[105]

The men duly assembled on 15 May, the document was read and presented to them, and the insurgents 'absolutely rejected' its terms. One of them, William Brown, refused even to hear the paper read and left, passing three officers on their way to seize the arms at the insurgents' camp. As soon as the rest of the insurgents left, Macdonell, Hillier, and some of the other gentlemen armed themselves and followed 'to prevent insult being offered' to the first three officers, but they were too late. The trio was returning, having confiscated no weapons '& having suffered gross abuse with threats of violence'. All the officers then proceeded to the insurgents' house only to find that the guns had been hidden in the woods. The rebels were then ordered to surrender their arms immediately, Auld's edict to that effect was read, and the consequences of refusal were described. The insurgents remained 'inflexible' and one of them, John Walker, 'went so far as to say that the country did not belong to the HBC but to the French'. Much alarmed, Macdonell and Hillier declared that these men 'must be treated as people in open hostility who set all order at defiance'.[106]

The insurgents saw things differently. Their response to the events of 15 May was a letter to William Auld, describing 'the most cowardly usage' they had received from 'the Chiefs' according to Auld's orders. They had been 'decoyed up' by 'the Chiefs', who, as soon as the men had arrived, sent three officers 'to rob the house in a most dastardly manner'. Fortunately, the insurgents had 'timely interposed and prevented an action so base that no Gentleman who had any feelings of honour would ever have countenanced.' 'We are happy Sir to find you all out in your tru colours', they declared; 'this shews us what kind of men you are and we tell you once for all that we will never come to your terms.' As for Auld's threat to send them home for trial or imprisonment, they considered this 'a menace so silly that we scarce think it worth the trouble of writing'. They were right, too. Macdonell had wanted the insurgents sent home for trial, but Auld had informed him that an earlier attempt to try a Canadian servant for robbery in England had failed because Rupert's Land fell under the jurisdiction of Canadian courts and the London committee had dropped the case rather than pursue it through 'such a circuitous route'. Besides, if the culprits were sent home, they might harm the 'cause' of the colony in Scotland. Indeed, they declared themselves 'happy to get home in any form where as Britons' they had 'a right to an impartial trial by the laws of [their] Country'. They signed themselves 'the highly injured and unjustly styled Insurgents'. There were 10 signatures and three X's, and none of either belonged to William Finlay.[107]

The mutiny now entered its final stage. Hillier and Macdonell blamed the failure of negotiations on the baneful influence of three of their clerks, one of whom had dined with the insurgents a few days before and who Macdonell suspected of composing their letter because he thought it resembled 'his diction'. The 'countenance' given by this constant fraternization had, he believed, been 'the means of keeping them hitherto closely linked together'. Two of these clerks would now be sent to camp by themselves and one would remain with Hillier. The other rebels would be subdued with 'Army or Navy discipline', which Macdonell considered 'the only thing fit to manage such fierce spirits'. He would issue no more orders for their provisions. The insurgents had 'gone too far to be yielded to now' unless they were 'very submissive'.

Macdonell forwarded their letter to Auld, claiming that he had not even deigned to read it, though one might well ask how he had managed to judge its diction if he had not read it. Auld was also determined to get tough. As long as the insurgents refused to surrender their arms, he considered it 'justified' to withhold all provisions, although he entertained doubts about the loyalty of the servants at York Factory if the insurgents attempted to take supplies by force, in which case he thought he could count on three officers and several Natives over whom he believed he exercised influence.[108] On 22 May the insurgents came to Macdonell for provisions, which he denied them because they had not surrendered their arms. They said that they had returned them to their owners, but Macdonell wanted to know exactly where they were. The next day the insurgents, minus Finlay, whom Macdonell kept with him, set off for York Factory, where Auld also refused to give them provisions until they had surrendered their weapons. When they declared that they had no firearms but would not reveal who now had them or who had given them the guns in the first place, Auld ordered them into the woods to fend for themselves. Even then, they would not tell, saying they wanted 'to prevent mischief ... to the innocent'. However, 'one of the best servants ever in the service', who had been away erecting a beacon, now came and revealed that he had sold his two guns to the insurgents because he was going home and no longer needed them. He was very sorry, but no one had told him that 'such bargaining' was forbidden.

Further investigation disclosed that one of the insurgents' guns had burst and another had been confiscated, leaving one to be accounted for. Auld concluded that it had been returned and the next day gave the insurgents three-quarters of the usual allowance at York Factory. Several days later, Auld informed them that they would get rations only if they worked, and on 3 June they gave in. Having been, as Cook put it, 'scowered into obedience by a Regimen of Bacon & Oatmeal & not a little chastized by the muskitoos' while leading 'a Sylvan life', they petitioned to be taken back in and promised 'exemplary behaviour in future'. The insurgents were then dispersed among the company's posts, where they demonstrated no more of that 'levelling' disposition which had so distressed Auld. Seven of them, including four Orcadians and Hugh Carswell, one of the treasonous clerks, were still in the service three years later. In fact, in 1816 James Bird described Carswell as 'the most promising young man' in the Edmonton district.[109]

Auld's handling of the situation was influenced as much by his dislike of the innovations that accompanied retrenchment as by his disapproval of insubordinate employees. He had no fondness for the colony or for Macdonell. He even excused the misbehaviour of the clerks who had been involved with the Glasgow Insurgents by remarking that it was unfair to punish young men for faults caused by the mismanagement of their officers, in this case Macdonell's favouritism towards his Catholic subordinates, which alienated everyone else.[110] Auld thus underestimated the depths of the insurgents' disaffection, perhaps deliberately. Certainly William Hemmings Cook, who considered Macdonell 'a *spoony* fellow' and *'a flat'*,[111] recognized that there was more to the situation than Auld admitted. But for Auld the disorders that marred the first years of retrenchment were the fault of the new men introduced to the service. Thus Irish brutishness was responsible for the New Year's attack on inoffensive Orkneymen, the malevolent Highlander Archibald Mason had led gullible Orkneymen to mutiny at Brandon House, and subversive Glaswegians had persuaded naïve Orkneymen to join them in rebellion. Auld thus resembled the British government, which searched in vain for evidence of foreign agitators to blame for the naval mutiny. Although such an explanation absolves the men of responsibility for their actions by portraying them as the pawns of crafty villains intent on achieving their own secret designs, it also allows their masters to deny that there are grounds for complaint, thereby absolving themselves of responsibility, too. The London committee and most of the company's officers would not, however, have agreed with Auld's opinion of Orcadians, for that would have meant ignoring the many occasions when they had defied the authority of those placed over them.

Mutiny Aboard Ship

The peace of the company was never again disturbed by an uprising at one of its posts, although the murder of John McLoughlin Jr in 1842 might have led the committee and many of its officers to suspect that one had taken place at Fort Stikine. Mutinies did occur, however, among the company's seamen, though they never went so far as to make off with a ship. Their mutinies were strikes motivated by an intense dislike of their officers. As James Douglas observed, the seamen's obedience proceeded 'from a high degree of respect for their Officers', which he seems to have believed was based on fear, since he suggested, erroneously, that sailors were indifferent to 'upright principle'.[112] In fact, a captain bereft of 'upright principle' received no respect. Thus, on 15 May 1837 the men of *Nereide* sent John McLoughlin Sr a letter accusing Captain David Home of severity and assigning excessive duty, apparently regulating watches not in accordance with custom. The details remain unknown, but Home seems to have required more hours of work than the men considered fair. McLoughlin ignored the letter and the one that followed three days later. Finally, on 31 May the crew arrived in person, but he told them to return to the ship and promised to come next morning to hear them.

Home objected to McLoughlin's interference, though he was probably happy when McLoughlin told the men to obey their captain and ordered them to set sail. But the men refused to weigh anchor, remaining adamant even after being read the ship's articles and asked individually to state their intentions. McLoughlin then had them manacled, confined, and fed on bread and water, but five days later they informed him that they would not serve under Home. McLoughlin then reduced the grog ration to a glass a day and threatened punishment, presumably of the corporal variety. The crew's unity began to dissolve and within several days only John Lucas and John Jarvis still held out, refusing duty even after receiving a dozen lashes each. McLoughlin returned again the following morning and summoned all the men on deck. They then asked him 'in a way between pleading and menacing' if he was going to flog the men again. McLoughlin told them they were here to see what was done, that the HBC did not bring men to the country to flog them but to have them perform certain duties, and that, if 'fair means' did not persuade them to perform them, 'other means' would have to be tried. Meanwhile, Lucas and Jarvis were being taken to the rigging, and when they saw that they were about to be tied up they immediately agreed to return to duty and gave no more trouble.

McLoughlin, wanting to get the ship off as quickly as possible, ordered it to go and agreed that the watches aboard the *Nereide* would be arranged like those aboard the rest of the company's ships. But this concession no longer sufficed and the crew refused to sail with Home under any circumstances. McLoughlin was now convinced that the men's real intention had been 'to Dictate who should be their commander', which was, of course, true. The men objected to a master whose arrangements broke with a tradition that ensured a fair division of labour. They also objected to physical abuse. Indeed, the boatswain had refused to make a cat-o'-nine-tails when the chief mate ordered him to, saying that he had never done such a thing and never would, for which disobedience McLoughlin demoted him. Further applications of corporal punishment finally overcame the men's resistance,[113] but did little for McLoughlin's reputation.

Another unpopular shipmaster was Captain William Henry McNeill, master of the steamer *Beaver*. McNeill had joined the HBC in 1832 and was, like John McKay, one of those officers more beloved by his biographer than his men. As G.R. Newell concluded, McNeill did indeed enjoy a 'long and distinguished career', overcoming 'tricky navigational problems' and establishing profitable trading relationships with the Natives in the vicinity of Fort Simpson. But the mutiny on the *Beaver* needs to be seen as more than merely an incident that 'marred his record', and his relations with his subordinates at Fort Simpson cannot be seen as problems arising from the fact that his men were 'difficult to manage'—particularly if he was that 'Monster' and 'Vile Wretch' with 'a terrible account to settle for so Torturing Mankind' referred to in a letter of commiseration to George Gordon, one of the crew.[114] One must, of course, allow for exaggeration in the account that elicited such a response. After all, William Bligh was not an especially harsh disciplinarian, given the standards of his time. Even a man as distressed by flogging and as sympathetic to common seamen as Richard Henry Dana Jr considered it vital that the captain's power be not 'diminished an iota' and thought that the seaman's best defence against tyranny was an improvement in his 'intellectual and religious character'. Then his captain would respect him and, if his master was prosecuted for cruelty, his testimony would 'carry that weight which an intelligent and respectable man of the lower class almost always does with a jury.'[115] McNeill probably would have concurred with Dana, a fellow New Englander whose stint as sailor began the same year the London committee's approval of McNeill's appointment reached John McLoughlin Sr. Dana's shipmates, however, had a strong tradition of resistance to authority behind them[116] and a long-term commitment to the sea that he, a Harvard University student taking a two-year break to allow his eyesight to recover from the effects of measles, could not have. They might have entertained a different view of things. McNeill's men certainly found his brand of discipline objectionable and appear to have decided to rid themselves of him.

One day towards the end of January 1838, William Willson and James Starling, who were filling small casks with rum, took advantage of the opportunity to get drunk. McNeill ordered their grog stopped for a month and told them to be off. When they persisted in behaving 'like all drunken Sailors' and talked back, he gave them a caning, telling them they had brought it on themselves for not obeying him. Several days later, when McNeill ordered everyone to carry wood to the water's edge for loading aboard the steamer, the four stokers refused, declaring that it was not their duty. Two relented, but two remained firm and McNeill tied them up and gave each two dozen lashes, not an unusual number but sufficient to do serious damage. The other men objected and the next morning the sailors sent a petition to John Work, the HBC officer in charge of Fort Simpson, stating the 'illegality' of having a foreigner in command of a British vessel, enclosing what they called an 'Abstract of an act of Parliament to that effect', and pointing out that the vessel was liable to seizure. Considering this issue none of their business and realizing that their raising of it was an attempt to have McNeill 'unshipped', Work would not send the reply the men had requested. The next day the seamen and the stokers, now united, refused duty and sent another letter. This time Work told them that it was their duty to obey whoever was set over them and that the legal issues were not their affair. He also asked how, 'if they Knew the laws so well', they had come 'to overlook that relative to Mutiny' and commanded them to return to their work. The men immediately sent another letter and the engineers now submitted a note of their own, wherein they stated that they 'could not continue' their duty under McNeill.

Work then took Donald Manson and went to confront the mutineers in person. The seven seamen 'man by man absolutely refused' to sail under McNeill. So did the engineers, whom Work considered the main obstacle because as long as they were on strike the vessel would be 'at a stand still'. Therefore he focused his attention on them, brought them ashore, and tried, without success, to sway them. He then asked them to submit a written reply informing him whether they would work the engines under McNeill if the rest of the men returned to duty. They declared that they would not work under McNeill, but did not mention his citizenship. With all but the mate, the carpenter, the cook, and six woodcutters on strike, Work feared that an attempt to overwhelm the strikers and get them into irons would lead to bloodshed without restoring the *Beaver* to service. It was also vital that Fort Simpson communicate with Fort Vancouver before the York Factory express left. Work therefore took command of the steamer himself and kept McNeill aboard as a passenger so that his expertise would be available.[117]

Later Work and McNeill found evidence that two of the engineers, Peter Arthur and John Donald, were the instigators. One wonders, however, how Arthur was able to exercise influence over men who had harboured such great dislike for him several months earlier when he had been called 'a liar' by William Willson for outlining the men's duties to McNeill. Apparently Arthur had been overheard saying to the seamen, 'Now men stick to your Text and we will gain the day, I have given them my final answer or, words to that effect.' The engineers did prove the key to breaking the strike. After the ship docked at Nisqually and the officers had taken care of business at Fort Vancouver, Work told the crew that McNeill was going to be reinstated. The seamen and three stokers objected immediately, but the engineers remained silent because, while at Fort Vancouver, Arthur had been promised complete authority in the engine room. Since the crew's co-operation was still necessary, Work isolated three of them, presumably the least determined, and advised them to return to duty, warning them of the consequences of 'being led into a Mutiny by Scoundrels'. They gave in, but the others held out, going so far as to tell Arthur that 'he had got them into the scrape and backed out himself, but that they meant to stick to what he and themselves had agreed to at first.'

Arthur then confessed that the mutiny was a conspiracy of all the men and First Officer James Scarborough to get rid of McNeill so that Scarborough could replace him, and he alleged that it was all Scarborough's idea. Peter Duncan, the carpenter, testified that he had heard Scarborough declare that he would replace McNeill and then 'work up' the deposed master as McNeill 'had often worked him up'. 'Working up' meant deliberately assigning disagreeable or dangerous tasks to a particular man to settle a grudge. Duncan also knew that Arthur had furnished the men with the book, *Ship Master's Assistant,* out of which they got the law to which they referred in their petition. James Starling, George Gordon, William Willson, and William Burris, the steward, refused to give in and were replaced.[118]

To regard the mutiny as the manipulation by an ambitious officer and a member of the labour aristocracy of foolish and naturally unruly seamen is to view it through the eyes of the officers. Scarborough and Arthur, like Archibald Mason and William Finlay, may have had ulterior motives, but their plot required them to tap into a disaffection that already existed, as the steadfastness of the four who were replaced suggests. Moreover, Starling, Gordon, and Willson appealed directly to the London committee. They were sent home later that year as members of the crew of the *Columbia* and petitioned the London committee together, declaring that they had been 'very much oppressed and tyranized over' in the service, 'most especially under Captain McNeill'. They claimed he 'as often wished that he should like to see a bloody Row fore and aft so that he might blow some of our brains out.' For 'not the slightest reason' he had 'constantly advised' Scarborough to knock their 'bloody brains out' with a handspike if they looked 'black'. Moreover, he had beaten Willson and Starling 'in a most brutal manner'. For this reason they were 'obliged to refuse his Command for the safety of [their] lives' and were therefore put off duty, imprisoned, and sent home. They then called on the company's secretary for their wages, who told them he was not authorized to pay them but advised them to lay the matter before the committee. The committee, sensitive to criticism and alarmed by reports of cruelty in its western territories, appears to have been sympathetic. Instead of fining them the whole of their wages, as the company's officers in Victoria had decided to do, the committee ruled that, because they expressed 'great contrition' and it was their first offence, they would lose only the wages for the time they were off duty. McLoughlin was told, however, to make it clear to all the seamen that such 'lenity' would not be repeated. Arthur's punishment amounted to a refusal of his rather cheeky request for a wage increase and his dismissal when he objected.[119]

Other officers in the company's marine department also aroused strong opposition from the men. In March of 1845, when the barque *Vancouver* arrived at Fort Vancouver, the crew refused to work until they received a new second mate. George Simpson considered their complaints 'frivolous' and restored order by removing the men from the ship.[120] In June of 1847 the men of the *Mary Dare* objected to the man appointed to replace the chief officer who had been dismissed for drunkenness and neglect of duty and refused to work. The captain and the company's officers were able to restore discipline, but they determined to send both defective officers home the next year, the old one being disqualified by his 'unfortunate habits' and his successor by his 'unhappy temper', which had 'driven every Ships Company with which he served in this Country into a state of mutiny'.[121] In 1855 seven of the crew of the *Princess Royal,* which had lost six others to desertion, refused to obey the 'lawful commands' of their master and were imprisoned at Fort Vancouver. Four managed to escape into the woods and were not recovered until after the ship had sailed. Douglas attributed the men's disaffection to their officer's 'very disagreeable manner of carrying on the duty of the ship, arising probably from an excess of zeal, which however ought to be more temperately exercised.'[122] A ship's crew may have been hierarchical and the ship's master ensconced at its top with the authority of a despot, but both the laws, however much they were intended to enforce discipline, and custom recognized the right to fair treatment and, implicitly, the right to resist injustice.

The ship, like the household, was a model of paternalistic authority, with the captain fulfilling the roles of father and master and, more than other workplaces, it was a 'total institution'. Yet, its subordinate inhabitants were neither subsumed in it nor incapable of uniting with one another to oppose their master. On the contrary, common seamen possessed their own culture which, in opposition to those set above them, was egalitarian and anti-authoritarian and formed the basis upon which pirate ships were organized. Pirates elected their captains, shared their booty, and, like maritime Robin Hoods, saw to it that cruel captains of captured vessels got their just deserts.[123] This combination of subordinate status with insubordinate behaviour was characteristic of miners, too. They also possessed a tradition of independence and collective action that developed in spite of the fact that they had once been serfs.

If being enmeshed in such relations of authority did not produce deferential sailors or miners, why assume that it produced deferential HBC servants? Those whose authority was under attack, of course, did not accept that this should be the case. They saw only disobedience, insubordination, and a perversion of the social order. The London committee, therefore, thought the answer to its disciplinary problems lay in finding appropriate recruits, but it never found servants who would not shirk their duty, engage in private trade, refuse to do as they were told, and combine to raise wages, demand sufficient provisions, and overthrow unpopular officers. What the committee failed to realize was that the lower orders of pre-industrial societies were neither tractable nor submissive. It took its own authority for granted and saw its workers not as a class with different interests but as ethnic groups with particular characteristics. But whatever their origins, the men shared a willingness to 'combine' to negotiate a fair deal or protest the absence of one. Nor was that fair deal always a matter of wages. The most serious conflicts erupted when superiors transgressed the 'moral economy' that was supposed to regulate their behaviour. The assumption that men would meekly submit to what they perceived as injustice merely because they occupied a lowly place on the social scale was, and is, an erroneous supposition based on the wishful thinking of those at the top.

7

Conclusion

It has not been my purpose to propose that the Hudson's Bay Company was a hotbed of unrest, or that its employees hated their work or the company, or that the HBC was a particularly mean-spirited master. On the contrary, the servants accepted their subordinate position in the hierarchy. They never demanded a more equitable share of the profits or a narrowing of the gap that yawned between their own meagre wages and the salaries of their officers. The London committee was stern, but no harsher than other employers. It demanded absolute obedience, but had no desire to be either cruel or unreasonable. Had this been the situation, the company would have collapsed centuries ago.

It is my purpose, however, to suggest that this stability was due not to an absence of conflict but rather to the fact that the conflict that did occur rarely called into question the relations of authority upon which the company was based. The HBC was a mercantile enterprise organized according to traditional, paternalistic principles. The master-servant relationship that was the norm between employers and workers when the HBC was chartered in 1670 was the basis for its organization. Its employees were servants who signed contracts obligating them to fidelity and obedience in return for wages, board, lodging, and the opportunity to accumulate modest savings. Breach of contract was subject to severe penalties. To procure workers who knew their place and responded appropriately to the HBC's rewards, the company recruited men from places where traditional social relations prevailed. Although men from such places valued the benefits offered by the company and the way of life they supported, they were neither as deferential nor as tractable as was expected of them because their societies, like pre-industrial societies in general, were not as harmonious as the ideal suggested. Pre-industrial social relations were not imposed from the top; they were negotiated, and those at the bottom were prepared to defend themselves against injustice and oppression from their superiors. As a result, the London committee never achieved exactly what it had set out to do.

The HBC was not sufficiently in control of the situation to impose the five-year contracts it desired, to keep wages as low as it wanted, to enforce the contract strictly, or to alter its business strategies. The efficacy of its policies depended on the behaviour of the men it hired. They resisted five-year contracts, tried, often successfully, to impose wage increases, broke the terms of their engagements with relative impunity, and resisted changes that affected them. They did so because they had their own interests and ambitions, which, although modest and conservative, determined how they dealt with their employer. They did not accept unquestioningly the terms offered them, and when the HBC's benefits and remuneration no longer suited them they went elsewhere. Once in the service, they sought to control the pace and conditions of their work in a variety of ways, which the nature of the work itself made possible. HBC servants did not live in cosy households with their officers. They had their own houses, dined at their own tables, and socialized with one another.

Joining the HBC reinforced that awareness of the differences between themselves and their superiors that they brought with them. Their contracts provided an explicit definition of their lowly status, and while the ideal to which their officers were supposed to aspire increasingly resembled the respectable middle-class gentleman, the servants remained plebeian. At work, they usually supervised themselves and frequently took advantage of the opportunities so provided to neglect their duty or engage in private trade. They also refused dangerous or excessively hard work, demanded better provisions and higher wages, and resisted what they considered cruel treatment. The HBC was not, therefore, characterized by strong vertical relationships that inhibited collective action, even though the workforce was too scattered to combine in a way that workers in other large organizations could. Moreover, such action did not depend on ethnicity. It grew out of a common experience and a common culture that distinguished HBC workers from their masters. A similar sense of identity underlay the actions of Red River tripmen, sailors, and coalminers.

However, HBC employees were conservative. They resisted innovations rather than trying to impose new conditions on their employer. As a result, although the servants did not threaten the relations of authority within the company, they undermined the ability of the committee to use its authority effectively. The committee and its officers were outnumbered and there were too many opportunities for servants to indulge in illicit behaviour in secret. If their misbehaviour became known or was confrontational, their importance to the company's operations made it difficult to punish them. Most of the time it was not easy to lure servants into the service, and when the committee finally resorted to using the contract as a legal weapon it discovered that it was a very ineffective instrument indeed. Thus the committee also had to guard against inflicting penalties that gave the HBC a bad reputation, repelled potential recruits, and roused the ire of old servants. Instead, it had to try to make the service more attractive by offering land grants and eventually raising wages and adding tea and sugar to the provisions. These failed to have the desired effects, since they either came too late or could not satisfy the raised expectations of the recruits. Unpopular new measures, such as payment by the task, the reduction of imported provisions, and higher prices set off ripples of discontent that threatened disorder and loss. Both the servants' rejection of such innovations and the costs of persisting in their implementation tended to reinforce the committee's own conservatism and caused it to jump back from the brink of change.

Although the company survived, it did not survive on terms determined by the London committee alone. The success, such as it was, of its recruitment strategy depended on the willingness of men to engage and their satisfaction with the conditions they found. The HBC attempt to found a colony to supply it with tractable labour did provide the tripmen upon whom its transport system came to depend, but they controlled the conditions under which they carried out their duties. The success of its business depended on the fact that the servants did their work well enough to ensure its survival, but the workers did not necessarily throw aside all personal and private interest to subsume themselves in this organization. HBC servants had an identity of their own that distinguished them from their superiors and led them to act in ways that fur trade historians have either ignored or attributed to ethnicity. As a result, disobedience and resistance in the HBC have been considered unusual, even aberrant, and therefore have been relegated to the margins of both fur trade and labour history.

In fact, conduct that clashes with the harmonious image of the household model that dominates the history of the HBC was actually an important part of the master-servant relationship both in the preindustrial household and in the HBC. To accept this is not to suggest that disobedience and dissension were dominant, but rather to submit that HBC servants were more complex than the cardboard figures that appear in the history books, that they had their own view of their work and their world, and that they acted according to it. The disobedience and discontentment of the William Paines, the Pierre Kanaquassés, the William Browns, the Palm Saunderses, the William Yorstons, and the John Muirs are as important a part of HBC history as the voyages of David Thompson, the imperium of George Simpson, and the plans and pronouncements of the London committee.

A Note on Sources

To undertake a study covering a century is challenging enough, but to undertake one that depends on the records of the Hudson's Bay Company is particularly daunting. The HBC headquarters were in London and the governing committee demanded accounts, journals, and correspondence from all posts annually. As these increased so did the volume of material sent to London, particularly after the merger of 1821. As a result, the HBC Archives are vast and it is impossible to examine all the material for the period from 1770 to 1870. One might overcome this problem by reducing the scope of the study and focusing on one or two posts or one district. But this method does not provide a broad enough base of information to allow generalizations about the company as a whole. The alternative, sampling at specified intervals, a technique regularly used by quantitative historians, seemed preferable. All extant records relevant to every tenth outfit were read, beginning with 1770–1 and ending with 1870–1. Because an outfit began on 1 June of one year and ended on the following 31 May, to get the most complete picture of each outfit it was necessary to read two years' worth of material for each. For 1770–1, for example, it was necessary to read documents from both 1770 and 1771.

The documents most amenable to this method are the post journals, found in the B./a series, and the ships' logs, found in the C.1 series. The journals are also the best source of information about the servants' behaviour. Officers were required to make daily entries in which they described the weather, trade with the Natives, the duties performed by the men, and any unusual occurrences. The journals thus provide a record of both the routine and the exceptional, and it is there that officers first reported their men's misbehaviour and their insolent language, usually in more detail than anywhere else. Most officers carried out their clerical duties faithfully and, even though editorial comments were not wanted, frequently gave their opinions on the quality of the servants. Naturally, the journals reflect the officers' interpretation of events and all forms of disobedience are condemned equally, but enough information is given to provide some idea of the men's motives. The ships' logs provide equivalent information for the company's seamen. The miscellaneous ships' papers, which are in the C.7 series, supplement the logs, while the B./z series, which contains miscellaneous papers from the posts, supplements the journals, as do the annual post reports found in the B./e series. The logs of ships known to have had disciplinary problems were also examined for years other than the ones specified above.

Correspondence comprises an even larger proportion of the company's records. Officers frequently copied letters into the post journals, but they also kept separate correspondence books, which are found in the B./b series. These were approached in the same way as the journals and ships' logs. Other collections of correspondence were examined more intensively, thereby providing extensive coverage of the whole century under examination. One of these, the A.5 series, comprises the company's general correspondence outward. It contains the London committee's letters to its recruiting agents and provides information about manpower needs, recruitment, and action taken against men for breach of contract. This series also deals with requests from former servants or their families for assistance, complaints by servants of bad treatment, and applications for employment. It was necessary, and fortunately possible, to read all the correspondence in this collection from the first book, which covered the years 1753 to 1776, to those for 1870–1. The A.10 series is the companion collection, containing the incoming general correspondence. Except for the years 1712 to 1837, for which the correspondence was manageable, it was necessary to read the material at ten-year intervals and rely on material from the A.5 series and other collections to determine what further use of A.10 needed to be made. Together, these two series provide a comprehensive source of information on the company's concerns about hiring, its willingness or lack thereof to fulfil its paternalistic responsibilities to ex-servants, and the views of disgruntled servants. The A.6 series comprises the company's official correspondence and is the major collection of the HBC's letters to its officers. It provides information on the company's policies, their effects, cases of misbehaviour among servants, and the state of the trade in general. All of this collection from A.6/11 (1767–73) to A.6/44 (1870–1) was read. Its companion collection, A.11, which is made up of correspondence from the company's posts, was also read in its entirety up to 1870–1.

Two particularly interesting collections of correspondence are the B./c series and the E. series. The former is made up of the correspondence sent to the company's posts. It contains the originals of some letters duplicated elsewhere, usually official ones, but also includes a variety of personal correspondence, such as letters between officers and letters from servants' families back home. This collection, amounting to over 100 files, was also read in its entirety. E.31/2 is a box of undelivered letters, mostly to servants from family members. They provide much insight into the family backgrounds of their recipients, suggesting that in some cases men joined the HBC to escape the responsibilities that family life imposed. Some, complete with locks of hair, are from sweethearts who express fears that their men will marry Native women, and others are from wives who wish to know why they have not heard from their husbands for so long or received any financial support. E.13/1 contains depositions and papers relating to the murder of John McLoughlin Jr. Other collections in E. contain private papers and letters, all of which provide information about life in the HBC as discussed by officers among themselves and not necessarily revealed to the committee.

The A.12 and D. series are also important. These contain correspondence from the company's governors to the London committee, the former covering the years from 1823 to 1870 and the latter 1818 to 1870. The D.4 series is made up entirely of George Simpson's correspondence. Because letters to and from Simpson appear in all the collections of correspondence and in some of the journals it was thought best to rely on other collections for Simpson's letters and refer to the D.4 series as necessary in regard to specific incidents or policies. An index makes it possible to locate letters by correspondent and source. His annual reports to the committee, which appear in the A.12 series, are long and detailed, and these and the letters scattered throughout other collections provide adequate coverage of his opinions and decisions for the purposes of this study.

Specific information about individuals appears in A.30, which comprises the surviving servants' lists from 1774 to 1841, with those after 1819 providing little information. Not until 1788 are the parishes of residence given and not until 1793 are ages given. However, all give occupations, wages and bounties, length of contracts, and reports on character and behaviour. By 1815 the need for fit, active men to meet often bloody competition and an increased emphasis on good record-keeping are reflected by the addition of two new columns to the printed forms to be used for servants' lists: one to record a man's height and the other his physical condition. The keeping of such lists appears to have ended by 1821. The B./f series, which is made up of servants' lists kept at the posts from which the larger lists seem to have been compiled, duplicates to a large extent the earlier lists and continues beyond 1821 but is incomplete, with only a few major posts, such as York Factory, being well represented. Other lists, however, appear in the account books, B./d, although not every year. But they are extensive and, in addition to the personal statistics contained in A.30 and B./f, record each man's debt at the end of the outfit, whether he was fined for misbehaviour, and the amount of the fine. Further information on individuals can be obtained in A.32, the servants' contracts. This series contains contracts from 1780 to the twentieth century. Although far from complete, it describes the basis upon which servants were hired by specifying the duties, wages, and benefits a man would receive and the penalties for disobedience. The contracts also provide information about the literacy of the HBC workforce, since servants signed their engagements or put their marks on them.

Several collections in the National Archives of Canada were also consulted, the most important of these being the Hargrave Papers. James Hargrave was an officer of the HBC for 38 years, for 15 of those years as a chief factor. His papers are extensive and include not only letters to him but also notebooks into which he copied letters he sent to others. Unfortunately, these notebooks are almost illegible, but many of the originals of these letters ended up in other collections of correspondence in the HBC Archives and could be consulted there. What is most striking, although not surprising, about Hargrave's letters is the infrequency with which servants are mentioned in them. Like most people, Hargrave and his family were primarily interested in the affairs of themselves, their relatives, and their friends, and servants were rarely included in these groups. Nevertheless, the letters of Hargrave and other officers do underline the extent to which officers and servants lived in different worlds, and reading them helps to explain how fur trade historians' heavy reliance on the personal papers of HBC officers has pushed the servants to the margins of Canadian history.

Primary Sources

Provincial Archives of Manitoba, Hudson's Bay Company Archives (HBCA)

A.1	London Minute Books
A.5	London Correspondence Books Outwards—General Series

A NOTE ON SOURCES 253

A.6	London Correspondence Books Outwards—HBC Official
A.10	London Inward Correspondence—General
A.11	London Inward Correspondence—From Posts
A.12	London Inward Correspondence—From Governors of the HBC Territory
A.30	Servants' Lists
A.32	Servants' Contracts
A.34/1	Servants' Characters and Staff Records, 1822–30
A.67/1	Miscellaneous Papers, 1719–1870
A.67/8	Characters and Accounts of Servants Retiring to Europe, 1818–84
B./a	Post Journals
B./b	Post Correspondence Books
B./c	Correspondence Inward—Posts
B./d	Post Account Books
B./f	Servants' Lists
B./k	Minutes of Councils of Northern and Southern Departments
C.1	Ships' Logs
C.7	Ships' Miscellaneous Items
D.1	Governor William Williams Correspondence
D.2/1	Governor William Williams Correspondence Inward and Miscellaneous Items
E.13/1	John McLoughlin Jr—Depositions and Papers, 1842–3
E.31/2	Employees' Private Letters—Undelivered
E.37	Chief Factor James Anderson (a) Papers
E.61	McGowan Collection. William McMurray Correspondence
F.27/1	International Financial Society—Correspondence, etc.
PP 1810–1	Instructions for Conducting the Trade in Hudson's Bay, 31 May 1810
PP 1859–1	Engagement of Mechanics, 1859
PP 1859–2	Engagement of Labourers, 1859

National Archives of Canada (NAC)

MG19	A21	Hargrave Family Papers
MG19	A23	John McLeod Papers
MG19	A25	Robert Campbell Papers
MG19	A44	Charles McKenzie and Hector Aeneas McKenzie Correspondence, 1828–55
MG31	G4	Geddes, David. 'David Geddes, Whom You Pronounced a Dunce . . .' 1970 (typescript)

Notes

Chapter 1

1. *The Shorter Oxford English Dictionary on Historical Principles,* 3rd ed. (Oxford, 1973), s.v. 'Factory'. This meaning of the word was well established in 1670 when the HBC was chartered.
2. Fur trade historians rely for their notions of pre-industrial society on Peter Laslett's *The World We Have Lost,* rev. ed. (London, 1975). See Jennifer S.H. Brown, *Strangers in Blood: Fur Trade Company Families in Indian Country* (Vancouver, 1980), 20–22, 32, 47; Gerhard Ens, 'The Political Economy of the "Private Trade" on Hudson Bay: The Example of Moose Factory, 1741–1744', in Bruce G. Trigger et al., eds, *Le Castor Fait Tout: Selected Papers of the Fifth North American Fur Trade Conference, 1985* (Montreal, 1987), 383–4, 396–7; John E. Foster, 'The Indian-Trader in the Hudson Bay Fur Trade Tradition', in *Proceedings of the Second Congress,* Canadian Ethnology Society, vol. 2, National Museum of Man, Mercury Series No. 28 (Ottawa, 1975), 571–85; Frits Pannekoek, *A Snug Little Flock: The Social Origins of the Riel Resistance of 1869–70* (Winnipeg, 1991), 21–2, n. 249; Sylvia Van Kirk, *'Many Tender Ties': Women in Fur-Trade Society, 1670–1870* (Winnipeg, [1980]), 5, 231–42. For alternative views, see Ron G. Bourgeault, 'The Indian, the Métis and the Fur Trade: Class, Sexism and Racism in the Transition from "Communism" to Capitalism', *Studies in Political Economy: A Socialist Review* 12 (Fall 1983), 45–86; Glen Makahonuk, 'Wage-labour in the Northwest Fur Trade Economy, 1760–1849', *Saskatchewan History* 41, 1 (Winter 1988), 1–18. For a more detailed historiographical analysis, see Edith I. Burley, 'Work, Discipline, and Conflict in the Hudson's Bay Company, 1770–1870', Ph.D. dissertation (University of Manitoba, 1993), ch. 1.
3. E.P. Thompson, 'Patrician Society, Plebeian Culture', *Journal of Social History* 7 (Winter 1974), 384.
4. E.E. Rich, *The History of the Hudson's Bay Company 1670–1870,* II, *1763–1870* (London, 1959), 264–7, 283–4; HBCA, A.1/49, Minutes of the Governor and Committee, 1805–10, 7 Mar. 1810, fo. 115.

5. See R. Cole Harris, ed., *Historical Atlas of Canada,* I, *From the Beginning to 1800* (Toronto, 1987), plates 62, 65. The chapter entitled 'The Northwest' is an excellent source of information on the organization of the fur trade until 1821.
6. This brief account of the company's history relies primarily on Rich, *The History of the Hudson's Bay Company, 1670–1870,* 2 vols (London, 1958, 1959); and Glyndwr Williams, 'The Hudson's Bay Company and the Fur Trade: 1670–1870', *The Beaver* Outfit 314, 2 (Autumn 1983). This special issue covers the whole history of the HBC and is an excellent introduction to the subject, incorporating the most recent scholarship and including suggested further reading, a useful compendium of the most important work in fur trade history.
7. Bob Bushaway, *By Rite: Custom, Ceremony and Community in England 1700–1880* (London, 1982), 22; E.P. Thompson, 'The Moral Economy of the English Crowd in the Eighteenth Century', *Past and Present* 50 (Feb. 1971), 79. For examinations of popular culture and its oppositional, sometimes subversive nature, see R.S. Neale, *Class in English History 1680–1850* (Oxford, 1981), 68–96; Keith Thomas, *Religion and the Decline of Magic: Studies in Popular Beliefs in Sixteenth- and Seventeenth-Century England* (Harmondsworth, 1971); Christopher Hill, *The World Turned Upside Down: Radical Ideas During the English Revolution* (Harmondsworth, 1972); David Underdown, *Revel, Riot, and Rebellion: Popular Politics and Culture in England 1603–1660* (Oxford, 1985); Carlo Ginzburg, *The Cheese and the Worms: The Cosmos of a Sixteenth-Century Miller,* trans. John and Anne Tedeschi (Harmondsworth, 1980); Ginzburg, *Night Battles: Witchcraft & Agrarian Cults in the Sixteenth & Seventeenth Centuries,* trans. John and Anne Tedeschi (Harmondsworth, 1983); Emmanuel Le Roy Ladurie, *Carnival in Romans,* trans. Mary Feeney (New York, 1979).
8. Brown, *Strangers in Blood,* 31; Brown, '"A Parcel of Upstart Scotchmen"', *The Beaver* 68, 1 (Feb.-Mar. 1988), 5–6.
9. See Richard Glover, 'The Difficulties of the Hudson's Bay Company's Penetration of the West', *Canadian Historical Review* 29 (Sept. 1948), 240–54.
10. Frits Pannekoek, '"Corruption" at Moose', *The Beaver* Outfit 309 (Spring 1979), 4–11; Hugh Marwick, *Orkney* (London, 1951), 242.
11. Daniel Francis, *Battle for the West: Fur Traders and the Birth of Western Canada* (Edmonton, 1982), 51, 61.
12. Frits Pannekoek, *The Fur Trade and Western Canadian Society 1670–1870,* Canadian Historical Association Historical Booklet no. 43. (Ottawa, 1987), 20.

13. See Hans Medick, 'Plebeian Culture in the Transition to Capitalism', in Raphael Samuel and Gareth Stedman Jones, eds, *Culture, Ideology and Politics* (London, 1982), 84–113.
14. HBCA, A.67/1, statement of Murdo Macleod, 30 Nov. 1857, fos. 398–9.
15. HBCA, B.109/a/4, La Cloche journal, 1830–1, John McBean to George Simpson, 5 May 1831, 25–6.
16. Daniel Francis and Toby Morantz, *Partners in Furs: A History of the Fur Trade in Eastern James Bay, 1600–1870* (Montreal, 1983), xi.
17. Richard Edwards, *Contested Terrain: The Transformation of the Workplace in the Twentieth Century* (New York, 1979).

Chapter 2

1. NAC, MG19 A25, Robert Campbell Papers, Journal, 1 May 1846–29 Apr. 1847, 31 July 1846. No doubt, a sarcastic paraphrase of 'God bless the squire and his relations/And keep us in our proper stations.' See Roy Porter, *English Society in the Eighteenth Century,* rev. ed. (Markham, Ont., 1990), 15.
2. David Roberts, *Paternalism in Early Victorian England* (London, 1979), 2–7.
3. Patrick Joyce, *Work, Society and Politics: The Culture of the Factory in Later Victorian England* (New Brunswick, N.J., 1980), 90–2. See H.I. Dutton and J.E. King, 'The Limits of Paternalism: the Cotton Tyrants of North Lancashire, 1836–54', *Social History* 7 (Jan. 1982), 59–74; Roberts, *Paternalism in Early Victorian England,* 108–22.
4. HBCA, A.6/2, London committee to Governor Geyer and council, 2 June 1688, 8.
5. A. Kussmaul, *Servants in Husbandry in Early Modern England* (Cambridge, 1981), 1–10, 22–6, 33–4, 70–83; Underdown, *Revel, Riot, and Rebellion,* 9–17; Gordon J. Schochet, *Patriarchalism in Political Thought: The Authoritarian Family and Political Speculation and Attitudes Especially in Seventeenth-Century England* (Oxford, 1975), 64–7.
6. Marc Linder, *The Employment Relationship in Anglo-American Law: A Historical Perspective,* Contributions in Legal Studies, 54 (Westport, Conn., 1989), 45–61.
7. E.P. Thompson, 'Eighteenth-century English Society: Class Struggle without Class?' *Social History* 3 (1978), 134–6. For an excellent example of what Thompson is warning against, see Laslett, *The World We Have Lost.* For a critical review of Laslett, see Christopher Hill, review in *History and Theory* 6, 1 (1967), 117–27.

8. See Underdown, *Revel, Riot, and Rebellion,* 20–43; Hill, *The World Turned Upside Down;* Christopher Hill, *A Tinker and a Poor Man: John Bunyan and His Church 1628–1688* (New York, 1988); A.L. Beier, 'Vagrants and the Social Order in Elizabethan England', *Past & Present* 64 (Aug. 1974), 3–29; Roger B. Manning, *Village Revolts: Social Protest and Popular Disturbances in England, 1509–1640* (Oxford, 1988), 158–70.
9. E.H. Oliver, ed., *The Canadian North-West: Its Early Development and Legislative Records. Minutes of the Councils of the Red River Colony and the Northern Department of Rupert's Land,* vol. 1 (Ottawa, 1914), 135–53, 'Royal Charter Incorporating the Hudson's Bay Company, 1670'.
10. E.E. Rich, ed., *Minutes of the Hudson's Bay Company 1671–1674* (Toronto, 1942), 14, 16 May 1674, 107–9.
11. E.E. Rich, ed., *Copy-Book of Letters Outward &c Begins 29th May, 1680 Ends 5 July, 1685* (Toronto, 1948), London committee to Governor Nixon, 15 May 1682, 40–4; Rich, ed., *Minutes of the Hudson's Bay Company 1679–1684: Second Part, 1682–84* (Toronto, 1946), 12, 25 Apr. 1684, 224, 229; Rich, ed., *Hudson's Bay Copy Booke of Letters Commissions Instructions Outward, 1688–1696* (London, 1957), committee to Governor Geyer and council, 2 June 1688, 8; Rich, ed., *Letters Outward 1679–1694* (Toronto, 1948), committee to Capt. Walsall Cobby, 21 May 1680, 15, committee to John Nixon, 29 May 1680, 24.
12. Great Britain, House of Commons Select Committee, *Report from the Committee appointed to inquire into the State and Condition of the Countries Adjoining to Hudson's Bay and of the Trade carried on there (24 April 1749),* testimony of Edward Thompson, 244.
13. Hugh Marwick, *Orkney* (London, 1961), 186.
14. Rich, ed., *Letters Outward 1679–1694,* London committee to John Nixon, 15 May 1682, 39.
15. K.G. Davies, *The Royal African Company* (New York, 1970), 109–13. Both the Royal African Company and the East India Company permitted their ships' captains and officers a degree of private trade and found that not only was this privilege regularly abused, but when they tried to abolish it the practice continued anyway.
16. Rich, ed., *Minutes of the Hudson's Bay Company 1671–1674,* 17 May 1672, 38; 22 Dec. 1673, 67; 8 May 1674, 103; 28 Nov. 1674, 3, 5.
17. Rich, *History of the Hudson's Bay Company,* I, 169–71.
18. Rich, ed., *Letters Outward 1679–1694,* London committee to Henry Sergeant, 20 May 1686, 185.

19. Rich, ed., *Minutes of the Hudson's Bay Company 1679–1684: First Part, 1679–82,* 21, 29 May 1680, 72, 77; Rich, ed., *Letters Outward 1679–1694,* London committee to John Nixon, 29 May 1680, 8, 21.
20. Rich, ed., *Hudson's Bay Copy Booke,* 'Instructions for Capt. John Marsh', 18 June 1688, 39.
21. For example, George Geyer's commission of 2 June 1688. Ibid., 23–4.
22. K.G. Davies, ed., *Letters from Hudson Bay 1703–40* (London, 1965), 308, 356, 413; Rich, ed., *Minutes of the Hudson's Bay Company, 1679–1684: First Part, 1679–82,* 47–8; Rich, ed., *Minutes of the Hudson's Bay Company, 1679–84: Second Part, 1682–84* (Toronto, 1946), 234.
23. Rich, ed., *Minutes of the Hudson's Bay Company 1679–84: Second Part, 1682–84,* 16 Mar. 1683, 84; Rich, ed., *Hudson's Bay Copy Booke,* London committee to George Geyer, 2 June 1688, 20; ibid., 134.
24. HBCA, A.32/7, contract of John Best, 14 July 1795, fo. 1.
25. HBCA, A.32/59, contract of Joseph Wittman, 1819, fo. 163.
26. HBCA, A.32/56, contract of James Toomey, 3 June 1811.
27. HBCA, A.5/2, London committee to William Tomison, 24 May 1786, fo. 148d; A.32/18, contract of Thomas Garrioch, 24 June 1815, fo. 140.
28. HBCA, A.32/19, contract of James Leask, 8 April 1818, fo. 151.
29. HBCA, B.239/k/3, minutes of the council of the Northern Department, 1851–70, 21 June 1862, 239; B.239/c/14, London committee to Alexander Grant Dallas and officers, 15 Apr. 1863, fo. 117d.
30. HBCA, A.32/59, contracts of Thomas Wiegand, 1824, 1830, 1852, 1855, fos. 1, 3, 12, 14; A.32/51, contract of John Rowland, 1863, fo. 353; A.32/45, contract of William Miller, 1869, fo. 139.
31. HBCA, A.32/43, contract of Donald McLeod A, 1858, fos. 59–59d; A.5/24, Thomas Fraser to W. and R. Morrison, 23 Apr. 1861, 228; B.239/k/21, Standing Rules and Regulations, 1835, No. 21.
32. Eugene D. Genovese, *Roll, Jordan, Roll: The World the Slaves Made* (New York, 1972), 4.
33. HBCA, B.153/c/1, George Simpson to William Nourse, 1 Mar. 1844, fo. 67d; B.17/c/1, Simpson to Benjamine Batson, 31 July 1860, fos. 185d–186.
34. HBCA, B.3/z/2, Decisions of council regarding John Cartwright and William Filpt, Aug. 1696; Arthur S. Morton, *A History of the Canadian West to 1870–71,* 2nd ed., Lewis G. Thomas, ed. (Toronto, 1973), 116–17.
35. See HBCA, A.11/43, fos. 13, 26d, 108d, 140.

36. HBCA, A.11/3, Albany council to London committee, 30 May 1757, fos. 17–18; 6 June 1757, fos. 18–19d; 15 Aug. 1757, fo. 20; 18 Aug. 1757, fo. 21; 19 Aug. 1757, fo. 21; Robert Temple to committee, Aug. 1763, fos. 65–6; Temple, John Horner, William Richards to committee, 15 Aug. 1764, fo. 67; Humphrey Marten to committee, 17 Aug. 1764, fo. 68.
37. HBCA, A.6/12, London committee to Humphrey Marten, 15 May 1776, fo. 54.
38. Rich, ed., *Hudson's Bay Copy Booke,* London committee to governor and council, 17 June 1693, 189; HBCA, A.6/14, committee to William Tomison and council at York Factory, 15 May 1788, fo. 39.
39. HBCA, A.5/1, London committee to James Isham, 22 May 1754, fo. 3; committee to Moses Norton, 15 May 1765, fo. 68.
40. HBCA, B.42/b/44, Samuel Hearne and council to London committee, 28 Aug. 1785, fos. 15d–16.
41. HBCA, B.42/b/44, London committee to council at Churchill, 25 May 1792, fos. 43–43d.
42. HBCA, A.6/15, London committee to council at Moose Factory, 29 May 1794, fos. 101–101d.
43. HBCA, B.42/b/44, London committee to council at Churchill, 29 May 1794, fo. 49d; council at Churchill to committee, 29 August 1796, fo. 60; A.6/16, committee to council at York Factory, 20 May 1801, fo. 126d; B.239/b/79, council at York to committee, 21 Sept. 1801, fo. 36d.
44. HBCA, B.42/b/44, London committee to council at Churchill, 30 May 1793, fo. 46; committee to council at Churchill, 31 May 1797, fo. 61d.
45. HBCA, A.6/16, London committee to officers at York, 31 May 1797, fo. 42.
46. HBCA, B.239/b/79, officers at York to London committee, Sept. 1804, fo. 45d.
47. See, for example, HBCA, B.3/a/100, Albany journal, 1796–7; B.22/a/1 and 4, Brandon House journals, 1793–4 and 1796–7; B.42/a/123, Churchill journal, 1796–7; B.59/a/78 and 79, Eastmain journals, 1800–1 and 1801–2; B.104/a/1, Lac La Biche journal, 1799–1800; B.121/a/4 and 6, Manchester House journals, 1789–90 and 1790–1; B.166/a/1, Portage de l'Ile journal, 1793–4; B.192/a/3, Sandy Lake journal, 1800–1.
48. Thompson, 'Patrician Society, Plebeian Culture', 384–5; C.R. Dobson, *Masters and Journeymen: A Prehistory of Industrial Relations 1717–1800* (London, 1980), 26; Malcolm I. Thomis and Peter Holt, *Threats of Revolution in Britain 1789–1848* (Hamden, Conn., 1977).
49. HBCA, B.159/a/3, Fort Pelly journal and correspondence, 1796–7, 9 July 1796, fo. 1.

50. HBCA, A.6/15, London committee to officers at Albany, 30 May 1795, fo. 129d–130; A.5/3, committee to John McNab, 30 May 1795, fos. 153–153d.
51. HBCA, B.239/b/63, Peter Fidler, James Bird, Joseph Howse, and Henry Hallett to John Ballenden, 5 Aug. 1799, fos. 13d–14d.
52. HBCA, B.250/a/1, Beaver Lake House journal, 1808–9, fos. 18A, 26d–27.
53. HBCA, PP 1810–1, Instructions for Conducting the Trade in Hudson's Bay, 31 May 1810, 3–4.
54. HBCA, A.6/18, London committee to Thomas Thomas, 9 Apr. 1814, 149–213; B.3/a/118, Albany journal, 1814–15, Thomas Vincent to Jacob Corrigal, n.d., 1814, fo. 4.
55. HBCA, A.6/18, London committee to Thomas Vincent, 29 Mar. 1815, fo. 271.
56. JoAnne Yates, *Control through Communication: The Rise of System in American Management* (Baltimore, 1989), xvii.
57. HBCA, A.6/18, London committee to Thomas Thomas, 26 May 1813, 91.
58. HBCA, A.6/18, London committee to Thomas Thomas, 9 Apr. 1814, 170.
59. HBCA, A.10/1, James Bird to London committee, 27 Aug. 1816, fos. 442–3; A.34/1, Servants' Characters and Staff Records, 1822–30, 5. Clarke's management was also regularly criticized by Roderick McKenzie in the Fort Chipewyan journals from 1815–16 until 1816–17. B.39/a/6, 8.
60. HBCA, A.6/18, London committee to Robert Semple, 27 May 1815, 284.
61. HBCA, A.6/18, London committee to Thomas Thomas, 9 Apr. 1814, fo. 153; A.6/19, committee to Thomas Vincent, 18 May 1816, fo. 14.
62. HBCA, A.6/19, London committee to Thomas Vincent, 14 May 1817, fos. 25d–27; A.5/6, Andrew Colvile to John McDonald, 25 April 1818, fo. 18.
63. HBCA, A.6/19, London committee to James Bird, 20 May 1818, fos. 49–49d; committee to Thomas Vincent, 20 May 1818, fo. 59d.
64. HBCA, PP 1810–1, Instructions, 31 May 1810, 9.
65. HBCA, A.6/18, London committee to Thomas Thomas, 9 April 1814, 175–6; A.5/5, A. Lean to D. Geddes, 8 Dec. 1810, fo. 31; PP 1810–1, Instructions, 31 May 1810, 9; A.6/18, committee to Thomas Vincent, 31 May 1810, 27–8.
66. HBCA, A.5/5, Secretary to Charles McLean, 4 Dec. 1810, fos. 32–32d; Secretary to McLean, 10 Jan. 1811, fo. 35d.
67. HBCA, PP 1810–1, Instructions, 31 May 1810, 6–7.

68. HBCA, A.5/5, A. Lean to Alexander Kennedy, 16 Apr. 1811, fo. 44; B.3/a/118, Albany journal, 1814–15, Thomas Vincent to Jacob Corrigal, n.d., fos. 3d–4.
69. HBCA, A.1/50, Minutes of the London committee, 1810–14, 5 Dec. 1810, fo. 11.
70. HBCA, A.5/3, A. Lean to Rev. Francis Liddell, 17 May 1794, fo. 132d.
71. HBCA, B.145/a/26, New Brunswick House journal, 1811–12, 23 May 1812, fo. 14.
72. HBCA, B.42/a/136a, Churchill journal, 1810–11, 'Mr Aulds Memorandum Book', fos. 8–8d.
73. HBCA, A.6/18, London committee to Robert Semple, 27 May 1815, 288.
74. HBCA, A.6/18, London committee to Thomas Thomas, 9 Apr. 1814, 195–9.
75. Sidney Pollard, *The Genesis of Modern Management: A Study of the Industrial Revolution in Great Britain* (London, 1965), 12–23.
76. HBCA, A.6/16, London committee to Albany, 25 May 1803, fo. 159d; A.5/3, committee to John McNab, 30 May 1795, fo. 152d.
77. HBCA, A.6/17, London committee to officers at Albany, 26 May 1809, fos. 157–157d; A.6/18, committee to William Auld, 31 May 1810, 1–2; Rich, *History of the Hudson's Bay Company,* 291–2.
78. HBCA, A.6/18, London committee to Thomas Thomas, 26 May 1813, 94–5, 101.
79. Rich, *History of the Hudson's Bay Company,* II, 313; HBCA, A.6/18, London committee to Thomas Thomas, 9 Apr. 1814, 157–8; B.239/b/85, Thomas Vincent to Thomas, 3 Dec. 1814, fo. 11.
80. HBCA, A.6/18, London committee to Robert Semple, 31 May 1815, 312–14.
81. See HBCA, A.5/2, London committee to Humphrey Marten, 14 May 1777, fo. 27; committee to Thomas Hutchins, 12 May 1779, fo. 40; B.135/c/1, committee to council at Moose, 21 May 1788, fo. 195d; B.42/b/44, council at Churchill to committee, n.d. 1794, fo. 51d; A.5/4, Alex Lean to David Geddes, 16 May 1798, fo. 35; B.135/c/1, committee to council at Moose, 21 May 1788, fo. 195d; B.42/b/44, council at Churchill to committee, n.d. 1794, fo. 51d; A.6/15, committee to council at Albany, 30 May 1795; A.6/17, committee to William Auld, 30 May 1804, fo. 27d; A.6/17, committee to council at Albany, 20 May 1808, fos. 124d–125, and 31 May 1806, fo. 68; A.5/3, Lean to Geddes, 2 Feb. 1795, fo. 146; A.5/4, Lean to Geddes, 25 May 1807, fos. 170d–171, and 27 May 1807, fo. 174d.
82. HBCA, A.5/5, A. Lean to D. Geddes, 8 Dec. 1810, fo. 31.
83. John Rule, *The Labouring Classes in Early Industrial England, 1750–1850* (London, 1986), 120–6; Bushaway, *By Rite*, 111–18.

84. Pollard, *The Genesis of Modern Management*, 190–1.
85. HBCA, A.6/18, London committee to Alexander Christie, 25 May 1814, 217–18.
86. HBCA, A.6/18, London committee to Thomas Thomas, 9 Apr. 1814, 193–5.
87. HBCA, A.6/18, London committee to Thomas Thomas, 28 May 1814, 230–1.
88. HBCA, B.239/b/85, Thomas Thomas to Peter Fidler, 8 Sept. 1814, fos. 1–1d; A.6/18, London committee to Thomas, 28 May 1814, 231–2.
89. HBCA, A.6/18, London committee to Thomas Thomas, 4 Jan. 1815, 252–3.
90. HBCA, A.6/18, London committee to Alexander Christie, 27 May 1815, 304–5.
91. HBCA, B.239/b/85, James Sutherland to Thomas Thomas, 28 Feb. 1815, fos. 29d–30.
92. See Richard Mackie, 'Colonial Land, Indian Labour and Company Capital: The Economy of Vancouver Island, 1849–1858', MA thesis, (University of Victoria, 1985); John Lutz, 'After the Fur Trade: the Aboriginal Labouring Class of British Columbia, 1849–1890', *Journal of the Canadian Historical Association*, New Series, 3 (1992), 69–93.
93. HBCA, B.159/a/7, Fort Pelly journal, 1818–19, 13 Dec. 1818, fo. 8d; 23 Mar. 1819, fo. 16d.
94. Brown, *Strangers in Blood*, 205–6; Michael Payne, 'Daily Life on Western Hudson Bay 1714 to 1870: A Social History of York Factory and Churchill', Ph.D. dissertation (Carleton University, 1989), 52, 79–80, 484; Rich, *History of the Hudson's Bay Company*, II, 406.
95. John S. Galbraith, *The Little Emperor: Governor Simpson of the Hudson's Bay Company* (Toronto, 1976), 90, 171–86.
96. Rich, *History of the Hudson's Bay Company*, I, 406–7.
97. NAC, MG19 A21, Hargrave Family Papers, George Barnston to James Hargrave, 22 Mar. 1829, fo. 157; Kenneth Stephen Coates, 'Robert Campbell', *Dictionary of Canadian Biography*, XII (Toronto, 1990), 155–66; Charles A. Bishop, 'Charles McKenzie', *Dictionary of Canadian Biography*, VIII (Toronto, 1985), 556–7; Philip Goldring, 'Governor Simpson's Officers: Elite Recruitment in a British Overseas Enterprise, 1834–1870', *Prairie Forum* 10 (Fall 1985), 251–81.
98. Frederick Merk, ed., *Fur Trade and Empire: George Simpson's Journal Entitled Remarks Connected with the Fur Trade in the Course of a Voyage from York Factory to Fort George and Back to York Factory 1824–25 With Related Documents*, rev. ed. (Cambridge, Mass., 1968), 6.
99. NAC, MG19 A21, Hargrave Papers, series 4, William Mactavish Correspondence, William Mactavish to Mary Mactavish, 17 Sept. 1837, 262–3.

100. J.A. Banks, *Prosperity and Parenthood: A Study of Family Planning among the Victorian Middle Class* (London, 1954), 87.
101. Michael Ignatieff, *A Just Measure of Pain: The Penitentiary in the Industrial Revolution 1750–1850* (London, 1978), 29–43.
102. HBCA, A.6/2, London committee to Governor Geyer and council, 2 June 1688, 8.
103. Galbraith, *The Little Emperor*, 17.
104. HBCA, B.239/c/1, George Simpson to John George McTavish, 1 Jan. 1822, fo. 66.
105. Arthur S. Morton, *Sir George Simpson, Overseas Governor of the Hudson's Bay Company: A Pen Picture of a Man of Action* (Toronto, 1944), x, 163.
106. HBCA, B.239/c/1, George Simpson to John George McTavish, 4 Aug. 1828, fo. 360.
107. HBCA, B.46/c/1, George Simpson to Wemyss Simpson, 22 Oct. 1843, fo. 5.
108. Van Kirk, '*Many Tender Ties*', 161–3.
109. Glyndwr Williams, ed., *London Correspondence Inward from Sir George Simpson 1841–2* (London, 1973), George Simpson to the London committee, 6 July 1842, 162.
110. NAC, MG19 A44, Charles and Hector Aeneas McKenzie Correspondence, 1828–88, Charles McKenzie to Hector A. McKenzie, 1 May 1854.
111. John McLean, *Notes of a Twenty-Five Years' Service in the Hudson's Bay Territory*, W.S. Wallace, ed. (Toronto, 1932), 333–4, 383–6.
112. HBCA, D.2/1, London committee to William Williams, 13 Mar. 1823, fos. 45d–46.
113. HBCA, D.2/1, London committee to William Williams, 12 Mar. 1824, fos. 52–55d.
114. HBCA, A.6/23, London committee to George Simpson, 3 Mar. 1834, fo. 76.
115. HBCA, D.2/1, London committee to William Williams, 26 Feb. 1821, fo. 18; A.6/20, committee to George Simpson, 27 Feb. 1822, fos. 16–16d; B.239/k/2, minutes of the council of the Northern Department, 1832–50, 3 June 1835, fo. 57.
116. HBCA, B.135/k/2, minutes of the council of the Southern Department, 1822–34, 6 Sept. 1824, fo. 13; B.49/z/1, marriage contract of William Rowland and Betsey Ballenden, 1825, fo. 1; marriage contract of George Ballendine and Jeanny Black, 17 July 1829, fo. 3d; B.135/k/2, minutes of the council of the Southern Department, 1822–34, 5, 6 Aug. 1822, fo. 4.
117. HBCA, D.1/7, William Williams to London committee, 11 Sept. 1825, fos. 1d–2.

264   NOTES

118. HBCA, B.235/e/3, Red River District Report, 1826–7, fos. 6–6d.
119. HBCA, B.239/K/2, minutes of the council of the Northern Department, 1832–50, 1 July 1834, fo. 41; A.12/8, George Simpson to W.G. Smith, 10 Jan. 1857, fo. 36d.
120. HBCA, A.6/28, A. Barclay to James Douglas, 17 Dec. 1849, fo. 91.
121. John E. Foster, 'The Country-born in the Red River Settlement: 1820–50', Ph.D. dissertation (University of Alberta, 1973), 96–102.
122. HBCA, A.6/23, London committee to George Simpson, 4 Mar. 1835, par. 6.
123. HBCA, B.135/k/1, minutes of the council of the Southern Department, 1822–75, 3 May 1836, fo. 75.
124. HBCA, B.135/k/1, minutes of the council of the Southern Department, 1822–75, 7 Aug. 1843, fo. 123; B.239/k/28, Standing Rules and Regulations, 1843–75, par. 60.
125. Great Britain, House of Commons, Report of the Select Committee, 1857, testimony of George Simpson, 94–5.
126. HBCA, A.6/35, London committee to George Simpson and councils, 18 Apr. 1860, fo. 67d.
127. HBCA, A.6/32, W.G. Smith to George Simpson, 30 Jan. 1857, fo. 118d.
128. HBCA, B.239/k/3, minutes of the council of the Northern Department, 1851–70, 23 June 1862, 259; A.6/38, London committee to A.G. Dallas, 15 Apr. 1863, fo. 74.
129. HBCA, A.6/20, London committee to George Simpson, 13 Mar. 1823, fos. 71–2.
130. HBCA, B.239/c/5, London committee to George Simpson, 4 Apr. 1849, fos. 95d–96; Simpson to James Hargrave, 28 June 1849, fo. 92d.
131. HBCA, B.153/c/1, George Simpson to William Nourse, 1 Mar. 1844, fo. 67.
132. HBCA, A.6/26, London committee to George Simpson, 4 Mar. 1844, fos. 107–107d; B.135/k/1, minutes of the council of the Southern Department, 1822–75, No. 52; B.239/k/2, minutes of the council of the Northern Department, 1832–50, fo. 168; B.239/k/28, Standing Rules and Regulations, 1843–75, No. 74.
133. HBCA, A.5/13, W.G. Smith to Edward Clouston, 1 Apr. 1840, 45–6; Smith to Thomas Crosse, 30 April 1840, 59; Smith to Clouston, 6 May 1840, 63–4; Smith to Clouston, 22 May 1840, 71.
134. HBCA, A.5/20, W.G. Smith to Edward Clouston, 12 Feb. 1856, 11.
135. HBCA, A.10/30, William Ross to Archibald Barclay, 25 Oct. 1851, fo. 739; doctor's certificate, 25 Oct. 1851, fo. 740; Ross to Barclay, 17 Nov. 1851, fo. 793.
136. HBCA, A.5/13, W.G. Smith to David Robertson, 2 Sept. 1840, 99; A.10/30, petition of David Robertson, 29 Oct. 1851, fo. 749; doctor's certificate, 30 Oct. 1851, fo. 750.

137. HBCA, A.5/24, Thomas Fraser to Rev. John McRae, 12 Feb. 1861, 172.
138. NAC, MG19 A21, Hargrave Correspondence, Edward Clouston to James Hargrave, 16 Feb. 1844, 2822–3.
139. HBCA, A.10/49, George Pierce to W.G. Smith, 14 Jan. 1861, fo. 46; A.10/80, Kemball Cook to London committee, May 1870, fos. 619–619d; A.10/48, William Parrer to the governor, deputy governor, and committee, 9 Aug. 1860, fo. 159.
140. HBCA, F.27/1, International Financial Society circular, 1863, fos. 94–94d.
141. Duane C. Tway, 'The Wintering Partners and the Hudson's Bay Company, 1863 to 1871', *Canadian Historical Review* 33 (Mar. 1952), 50–63; Tway, 'The Wintering Partners and the Hudson's Bay Company, 1867–1879', *Canadian Historical Review* (Sept. 1960), 215–18; Arthur J. Ray, *The Canadian Fur Trade in the Industrial Age* (Toronto, 1990), 8, 15.
142. HBCA, A.6/39, Thomas Fraser to James R. Clare, 25 June 1864, fo. 108d.
143. HBCA, A.32/60, contract of Sinclair Young, 1870, fo. 21.

Chapter 3

1. 'Report to the Governor and Committee by John Nixon 1682', in Rich, ed., *Minutes of the Hudson's Bay Company 1679–1684: First Part, 1679–82,* 251, 277.
2. Ibid., *Second Part, 1682–84,* 16 Mar. 1683, 86; ibid., 14 Jan. 1683, 189; 9 Apr. 1684, 222–3; 7 May 1684, 239.
3. Richard Grassby, 'Social Mobility and Business Enterprise in Seventeenth-century England', in Donald Pennington and Keith Thomas, eds, *Puritans and Revolutionaries: Essays in Seventeenth-Century History Presented to Christopher Hill* (Oxford, 1978), 374–5; Stanley D. Chapman, *The Early Factory Masters: The Transition to the Factory System in the Midlands Textile Industry* (Newton Abbot, 1967), 169–70.
4. See M. Dorothy George, *London Life in the Eighteenth Century* (Chicago, 1965), 216–61; Hugh Cunningham, 'The Employment and Unemployment of Children in England, c. 1680–1851', *Past & Present* 126 (Feb. 1990), 131–3.
5. Richard I. Ruggles, 'Hospital Boys of the Bay', *The Beaver* Outfit 308 (Autumn 1977), 14–21.
6. HBCA, A.5/2, secretary of the London committee to William Wales, 26 Mar. 1778, fo. 32.
7. Davies, ed., *Letters from Hudson Bay 1703–40,* 33, 63, 76, 79, 88–9, 123, 152, 233–4, 289.

8. Steven R. Smith, 'The London Apprentices as Seventeenth-Century Adolescents', *Past & Present* 61 (Nov. 1973), 149–61; Geoffrey Pearson, *Hooligan: A History of Respectable Fears* (London, 1983), 190–7.
9. Michael Hechter, *Internal Colonialism: The Celtic Fringe in British National Development 1536–1966* (Berkeley, 1975), 9, 30–3, 73; James D. Young, *The Rousing of the Scottish Working Class* (London, 1979), 19, 165–6; Hugh Trevor-Roper, 'The Invention of Tradition: The Highland Tradition of Scotland', in Eric Hobsbawm and Terence Ranger, eds, *The Invention of Tradition* (Cambridge, 1983), 25.
10. Richard Glover, Introduction to *Cumberland House Journals and Inland Journals, 1775–82, Second Series, 1779–82*, eds E.E. Rich and A.M. Johnson (London, 1952), xxxvii.
11. J. Storer Clouston, 'Orkney and the Hudson's Bay Company', *The Beaver* Outfit 268, 1 (Mar. 1937), 43.
12. Laslett, *The World We Have Lost*, 4.
13. Robert A. Dodghson, *Land and Society in Early Scotland* (Oxford, 1981), 301–4; Frances J. Shaw, *The Northern and Western Islands of Scotland: Their Economy and Society in the Seventeenth Century* (Edinburgh, 1980), 75, 77, 113–14, 122–3, 128, 150, 167, 199–201; Alexander Fenton, *The Northern Isles: Orkney and Shetland* (Edinburgh, 1978), 61, 571–5; James R. Hunter, *The Making of the Crofting Community* (Edinburgh, 1976), 16–18, 34–5.
14. Francis, *Battle for the West*, 61.
15. J. Storer Clouston, 'Orkney and the Hudson's Bay Company', *The Beaver* Outfit 267 (Dec. 1936), 6–8.
16. Edward Umfreville, *The Present State of Hudson's Bay Containing a Full Description of that Settlement, and the Adjacent Country . . .*, ed. W.S. Wallace (Toronto, 1954 [London, 1790]), 109.
17. John Nicks, 'Orkneymen in the HBC 1780–1821', in Carol M. Judd and Arthur J. Ray, eds, *Old Trails and New Directions: Papers of the Third North American Fur Trade Conference* (Toronto, 1980), 106–7, 112, 113, 116, 122; Payne, 'Daily Life on Western Hudson Bay 1714 to 1870', 33.
18. Nicks, 'Orkneymen in the HBC 1780–1821', 119–23.
19. HBCA, A.1/146, Standing Rules, 1796–1805, fo. 10; A.6/16, London committee to John Hodgson, 28 May 1800, fo. 111; A.5/4, A. Lean to William Jefferson, 13 Apr. 1802, fo. 94d; A.5/5, Lean to D. Geddes, 8 Dec. 1810, fos. 31–31d.
20. HBCA, A.11/116, William Tomison to London committee, 19 July 1788, fo. 21d.
21. HBCA, B.3/b/27, Joseph Colen to John McNab, 10 Mar. 1790, fos. 62–62d.

22. HBCA, B.135/c/1, London Committee to John Thomas and council at Moose Factory, May 1791, fo. 212d; NAC, MG 31 G4, 'David Geddes, Whom You Pronounced a Dunce . . .', typescript, 1970, 95–6.
23. Allan Greer, 'Fur-Trade Labour and Lower Canadian Agrarian Structures', *Canadian Historical Association Historical Papers* (1981), 197–214.
24. HBCA, B.3/a/79, Albany journal, 1780–1, May 1781, fo. 4.
25. HBCA, B.211/a/1, Sturgeon Lake journal, 1779–80, 31 July 1779, fo. 1d; 2 Aug. 1779, fo. 2; 3 Aug. 1779, fo. 2; 12 Aug. 1779, fo. 3; 19 Aug. 1779, fo. 4; 14 Sept. 1779, fo. 10; 31 Dec. 1779, fos. 22d–24d; 31 Jan. 1780, fos. 31d–33.
26. HBCA, B.42/b/44, London committee to council at Churchill, 27 May 1789, fo. 33d; A.5/2, committee to Edward Jarvis, 28 May 1787, fo. 161d.
27. HBCA, B.135/c/1, London committee to John Thomas and council, Moose Factory, 16 May 1787, fo. 187d; A.6/14, committee to Edward Jarvis and council, Albany, 21 May 1788, fos. 28–28d.
28. HBCA, A.6/15, London committee to officers at Albany, 29 May 1794, fos. 98–98d.
29. HBCA, A.11/117, Joseph Colen to London committee, 29 Aug. 1788, fo. 24d; officers at York to committee, 26 Sept. 1791, fos. 118–19d.
30. HBCA, A.11/117, Joseph Colen to London committee, 7 Sept. 1789, fo. 31.
31. See, for example, the criticisms of William Walker, HBCA, B.121/a/4, Manchester House journal, 1789–90, 17 Sept. 1789, fo. 11d; and the complaints by Donald MacKay, a former Nor'wester, regarding the hostility towards Canadians among the HBC's officers, B.3/100, Albany journal, 1796–7, 20 Oct. 1796, fo. 6; 29. Jan. 1797, fo. 7; 5 Feb. 1797, fos. 18d–19; 18 Feb. 1797, fo. 19d.
32. HBCA, A.5/3, Rev. William Clouston to David Geddes, 27 May 1794, fos. 139d–140.
33. Clouston, 'Orkney and the Hudson's Bay Company', 43.
34. HBCA, A.6/15, London committee to officers at Albany, 29 May 1794, fo. 98d.
35. HBCA, A.6/16, London committee to Capt. John Richards, June 1797, fo. 35; B.135/b/25, William Bolland to John Thomas, 18 Sept. 1798, fo. 4.
36. See, for example, HBCA, B.3/a/102, Albany Factory journal, 1798–9, 14 Oct. 1798, fo. 3d; 5 Sept. 1799, fo. 32; 8 Sept. 1799, fo. 32d; 10 Sept. 1799, fo. 33; 18 Sept. 1799, fo. 32d; B.3/a/103, Albany Factory journal, 1799–1800, 15 June 1800, fo. 25; 9 July 1800, fo. 43d; 29 Aug. 1800, fos. 32d–33; B.239/b/63, John Ballenden to Thomas Stayner, 3 Mar. 1800, fo. 21; B.42/b/42, Thomas Stayner to John Ballenden, 18 Mar. 1800, 26–7; B.42/b/43, Stayner to Ballenden, 19 Sept. 1800, 6.

37. HBCA, A.5.3, Alexander Lean to David Geddes, 2 Feb. 1795, fo. 146; A.5/4, Lean to Geddes, 1 Dec. 1802, fo. 102d, 20 Apr. 1803, fo. 112.
38. HBCA, B.49/a/31, Cumberland House journal, 1801–2, William Tomison to John Ballenden, 6 June 1802, fos. 29d–30.
39. HBCA, B.42/f/2, Servants' Resolves, 1804, fo. 9; NAC, MG 31 G4, 'David Geddes, Whom You Pronounced a Dunce. . . . ', 95.
40. HBCA, A.6/17, London committee to council, Albany, 31 May 1805, fos. 29, 32d; A.5/4, Alexander Lean to William Auld, 14 Mar. 1805, fo. 138; Archibald Barclay to Donald McKay, 1 May 1805, fo. 143d; Barclay to David Geddes, 1 May 1805, fo. 144; Barclay to Francis Heddle, 1 May 1805, fos. 144–144d; B.123/a/10, Martins Fall journal, 1805–6, letter from John Hodgson, 11 Sept. 1805, fos. 1d–2d.
41. HBCA, A.5/4, Alexander Lean to David Geddes, 22 Jan. 1806, fos. 156–156d, 15 Mar. 1807, fos. 170d–171; A.6/17, London committee to council, Albany, 31 May 1807, fo. 94, 20 May 1808, fos. 124d–125.
42. HBCA, A.6/17, London committee to Thomas Vincent and council, Albany, 20 May 1808, fo. 125; committee to John McNab and council, York Factory, 25 May 1808, fo. 140.
43. HBCA, A.5/5, Alexander Lean to David Geddes, 8 Dec. 1810, fo. 31.
44. HBCA, A.5/4, Alexander Lean to Jean Henry De Saulles, 10 July 1804, fos. 129d–130; A.10/1, Colin Robertson to London committee, 17 Jan. 1810, fos. 89–90d; PP–1810–1, Instructions for Conducting the Trade in Hudson's Bay, 31 May 1810, 9.
45. HBCA, A.5/5, HBC secretary to Charles McLean, 4 Dec. 1810, fo. 31d; J.M. Bumsted, 'The Affair at Stornoway, 1811', *The Beaver* Outfit 312, 4 (Spring 1982), 53, 55; HBCA, B.42/b/57, Miles Macdonell to William Auld, 25 Mar. 1811, fo. 15.
46. HBCA, A.1/49, minutes of the governor and committee, 1805–10, 21 Feb. 1810, fo. 114; A.5/5, secretary to Charles McLean, 4 Dec. 1810, fos. 32–32d, 10 Jan. 1811, fo. 35d.
47. Bumsted, 'The Affair at Stornoway, 1811', 53–8; NAC, MG19 A23, John McLeod Papers, autobiographical fragment, 1; HBCA, B.42/b/57, Miles Macdonell to William Auld, 25 Mar. 1811, fo. 15.
48. HBCA, B.42/b/57, William Auld to Miles Macdonell, 16 Oct. 1811, fos. 2–2d.
49. HBCA, B.42/b/57, Miles Macdonell to William Auld, 25 Dec. 1811, fos. 16d–17.
50. HBCA, B.42/b/57, remarks on letters from William Hillier and Miles Macdonell, fos. 20d–21; William Auld to William Hemmings Cook, 18 Mar. 1812, fos. 23–4; Auld to Macdonell, 30 Apr. 1812, fos. 35–35d.
51. Malcolm I. Thomis and Peter Holt, *Threats of Revolution in Britain 1789–1848* (Hamden, Conn., 1977), 30–1.

52. See Young, *The Rousing of the Scottish Working Class,* 12–59; Thomis and Holt, *Threats of Revolution,* 1–82; C.H.E. Philpin, ed., *Nationalism and Popular Protest in Ireland* (Cambridge, 1987).
53. HBCA, B.42/b/57, complaint of William Hillier before Miles Macdonell, fo. 30; Macdonell to William Auld, 3 May 1812, fo. 40; Hillier to Auld, 12 May 1812, fo. 42d.
54. Rich, *History of the Hudson's Bay Company,* II, 304; John P. Pritchett, *The Red River Valley 1811–1849: A Regional Study* (New York, 1942; 1970), 68, 93–8; Marcus Rediker, *Between the Devil and the Deep Blue Sea: Merchant Seamen, Pirates, and the Anglo-American Maritime World, 1700–1750* (Cambridge, 1987), 205–53.
55. HBCA, A.10/1, B.H. Everard to Edward Roberts, 23 Dec. 1815, fo. 364.
56. HBCA, A.5/5, Alexander Lean to Auldjo, Maitland & Co., 1 Jan. 1812, fos. 52d–53d; B.239/b/83, William Hillier to William Auld, 4 Dec. 1812, fo. 1.
57. HBCA, B.239/b/85, Thomas Thomas to Peter Fidler, 8 Sept. 1814, fo. 1; A.30/14, Servants' List, 1814–15, fos. 21d–22, 32d–33, 37d–38, 50d–51.
58. HBCA, B.239/b/85, Thomas Thomas to Enner Holte, 25 Mar. 1815, fo. 39d. This must be the basis for the notion that Norwegian convicts built Norway House, although references to it have been misleading. Richard Glover suggested that the story indicates that the HBC might have sent agents to get men from 'foreign jails'. Glover, 'The Difficulties of the Hudson's Bay Company's Penetration of the West', *Canadian Historical Review* 29 (Sept. 1948), 251. More recently, Glenn Makahonuk refers to the HBC's resorting even to the 'jails of Norway' in its search for workers to replace the increasingly unsatisfactory Orkneymen. Makahonuk, 'Wage-Labour in the Northwest Fur Trade Economy, 1760–1849', *Saskatchewan History* 41 (Winter 1988), 7. His source is Glover's article and Glover gives no source at all, although it might have been Morton's *History of the Canadian West to 1870–71.* Morton says that Norwegians, 'apparently ex-convicts', were brought out to build the posts along the winter road and that they built Norway House to be the depot on Lake Winnipeg. Actually, it is unlikely that it was they who completed the job. The ill-fated Robert Semple, second governor of the colony, had planned to hire some settlers to carry out the company's plans for a permanent post and 'decent settlement' at Norwegian Point, as it was known. After the Métis drove the settlers from the colony in the summer of 1816, Colin Robertson and Semple's successor, Alexander MacDonell, decided to carry out the plan as a way of employing the 'principal settlers' and inducing them to stay, thereby influencing others to remain as well, besides making it unnecessary to

take men from the fur trade to do the work. (B.60/a/15, Edmonton House journal, 1815–16, 9 Aug. 1816, fos. 51d–52.) Morton gave no source for his information. Although perhaps insignificant in the grand scheme of things, this inaccuracy is irritating and reflects the condescension with which fur trade historians frequently view the servants. Labelling the Norwegians 'gaolbirds' (Glover, 251) suggests that they had no valid reason for misbehaviour other than the bad characters that led them into crime in the first place, while Makahonuk's allegation that the HBC recruited Norwegian criminals implies that the company was utterly desperate and its hiring policy entirely bankrupt. Glover even speculates that the company searched foreign jails because the army and navy were bribing English convicts into their services by offering them pardons, thereby depriving the HBC of this source of manpower. These suggestions are illogical. The committee was always too concerned that it hire only men of good character to have recruited criminals, foreign or otherwise.

59. M. Drake, *Population and Society in Norway, 1735–1865* (Cambridge, 1977), 29–40.
60. HBCA, A.6/18, London committee to Alexander Christie, 25 May 1814, 217–18; A.30/14, Servants' List, 1814–15, fos. 35d–37, 51d–53.
61. HBCA, B.239/b/85, James Sutherland to Thomas Thomas, 28 Feb. 1815, fos. 29d–30; Enner Holte to Thomas, 28 Feb. 1815, fos. 29d–30; Thomas to Holte, 25 Mar. 1815, fo. 39d.
62. HBCA, B.239/b/85, Thomas Thomas to Miles Macdonell, 25 Mar. 1815, fo. 38d; A.30/16, Servants' List, 1819, fos. 36d–37, 51d–52. Only one Dane and one Norwegian appear in this list.
63. HBCA, A.6/19, London committee to James Bird, 20 May 1818, fo. 48d.
64. HBCA, A.5/5, Alexander Lean to Donald MacKenzie Jr, 17 Jan. 1816, fo. 115.
65. HBCA, B.39/a/6, Fort Chipewyan journal, 1815–16, 14 Aug. 1815, fos. 5d–6; 18 Dec. 1815, fo. 35.
66. HBCA, A.6/18, London committee to Robert Semple, 27 Mar. 1816, 333.
67. HBCA, A.5/5, Alexander Lean to Maitland, Garden & Auldjo, 24 Jan. 1816, fo. 116; Lean to Auldjo, Maitland & Co., 1 Jan. 1812, fo. 52d.
68. HBCA, B.60/a/15, Edmonton House journal, 1815–16, 16 July 1816, fo. 46d.
69. HBCA, B.105/e/1, Lac La Pluie report, 1816–18, fo. 9d.
70. HBCA, A.5/5, Alexander Lean to Maitland, Garden & Auldjo, 24 Jan. 1816, fo. 116.
71. HBCA, A.5/5, Alexander Lean to Maitland, Garden & Auldjo, 18 June 1817, fos. 147d–150.

72. HBCA, D.1/1, William Williams to Maitland, Garden & Auldjo, 2 Jan. 1819, 15.
73. HBCA, A.6/19, London committee to William Williams, 3 Feb. 1819, fo. 68.
74. HBCA, B.105/a/7, Lac La Pluie journal, 1819–20.
75. HBCA, D.1/13, Colin Robertson to William Williams, 25 Jan. 1820, fos. 12d–13, 16 Feb. 1820, fos. 21–21d.
76. HBCA, A.5/6, William Smith to Maitland, Garden, & Auldjo, 29 Oct. 1819, fo. 72d; D.1/3, William Williams to Maitland, Garden & Auldjo, 23 July 1820, fo. 28.
77. HBCA, D.2/1, London committee to William Williams, 25 May 1820, 7.
78. HBCA, A.5/6, William Smith to Maitland & Co., 28 Oct. 1820, fo. 121.
79. These figures were calculated by analysing several of the pre-1821 servants' lists: HBCA, A.30/6, 10, 11, 14, 16, *Names &c of the Company's Servants at Hudson's Bay,* 1794–5, 1800–1, 1811–12, 1814–15, and 1818–19.
80. HBCA, D.1/11, John McDonald to William Williams, 10 June 1819, fo. 24d.
81. HBCA, A.6/19, London committee to William Williams, 3 Feb. 1819, fo. 70; D.1/3, Williams to Sutherland, 11 Mar. 1820, fo. 17.
82. HBCA, B.135/k/1, minutes of the council of the Southern Department, 1822–75, 8 Aug. 1839.
83. HBCA, D.2/1, London committee to William Williams, 26 Feb. 1821, fos. 18–19.
84. HBCA, A.6/6, William Smith to John Rae, 22 Jan. 1820, fo. 87d.
85. HBCA, A.6/20, London committee to George Simpson, 27 Feb. 1822, fo. 16.
86. HBCA, B.239/b/87b, Summary of letter, probably George Simpson to London committee, 31 July 1822, fos. 4–5d.
87. HBCA, A.12/1, George Simpson to London committee, 1 Aug. 1823, fos. 14d–16d, 24d.
88. HBCA, D.2/1, London committee to William Williams, 12 Mar. 1824, fo. 57.
89. HBCA, A.12/1, George Simpson to London committee, 10 Aug. 1824, fos. 76d–77; D.2/1, committee to William Williams, 11 Mar. 1825, fo. 61.
90. HBCA, B.239/c/1, William McGillivray to J.G. McTavish, 24 Apr. 1825, fo. 186; B.134/c/1, William Smith to McGillivrays, Thain and Co., 6 May 1825, fo. 113d.
91. HBCA, A.12/1, George Simpson to London committee, Aug. 1825, fos. 104d, 158–158d, 177–8.
92. HBCA, B.235/e/3, Red River District Report, 1826–7, fos. 6–6d.

93. HBCA, A.12/1, George Simpson to London committee, 20 Aug. 1826, fos. 247–8.
94. HBCA, B.22/a/22, Brandon House journal, 1828–9, 2.
95. HBCA, B.22/a/23, Brandon House journal, 1829–30, 13 Nov. 1829, fo. 9.
96. Frederick Merk, ed., *Fur Trade and Empire: George Simpson's Journal Entitled Remarks Connected with the Fur Trade in the Course of Voyage from York Factory to Fort George and Back to York Factory 1824–25*, rev. ed. (Cambridge, Mass., 1968), 91; Alexander Ross, *Fur Hunters of the Far West*, ed. Kenneth A. Spaulding (Norman, Okla., 1956 [1855]), 192–3.
97. HBCA, A.12/12, George Simpson to London committee, 25 July 1827, 162.
98. HBCA, B.134/c/7, François Boucher to James Keith, 14 June 1830, fo. 353; John Crebassa to Keith, 18 Jan. 1830, fo. 26.
99. HBCA, A.6/23, HBC secretary to James Keith, 11 Dec. 1833, fo. 52d.
100. HBCA, B.223/c/1, George Simpson to John McLoughlin Sr, 21 June 1843, fo. 196.
101. HBCA, A.12/2, George Simpson to London committee, 7 Feb. 1844, fo. 332d.
102. HBCA, A.12/12, George Simpson to London committee, 5 Sept. 1827, 193; A.12/1, Simpson to committee, 31 July 1830, fos. 368–9, 18 July 1831, fo. 416d, 10 Aug. 1832, fo. 419d; Philip Goldring, 'Lewis and the Hudson's Bay Company in the Nineteenth Century', *Scottish Studies* 24 (1980), 23, 27; HBCA, A.10/8, Edward Clouston to William Smith, 24 June 1839, fo. 405; A.10/10, Clouston to Smith, 21 Mar. 1840, fos. 225–225d, 15 Apr. 1840, fo. 286, 24 Apr. 1840, fo. 300.
103. HBCA, B.235/c/1, London committee to Duncan Finlayson, 3 June 1840, fos. 57d–58.
104. HBCA, A.10/11, Edward Clouston to William Smith, 27 Oct. 1840, fos. 265–265d, 18 Nov. 1840, fos. 342–342d; A.10/12, Clouston to George Simpson, 16 Feb. 1841, fos. 124d–125; Clouston to Smith, 1 Mar. 1841, fos. 173–173d; A.10/12, Gilbert Craigie to Clouston, 10 Feb. 1841, fo. 126; Clouston to Smith, 13 Mar. 1841, fo. 204, 17 Apr. 1841, fo. 314; A.10/12, Clouston to Smith, 7 May 1841, fo. 374; B.235/c/1, London committee to Duncan Finlayson and councils of the Northern and Southern departments, 2 June 1841, fos. 68–68d.
105. HBCA, B.239/b/94, James Hargrave to W. and R. Morrison, 9 Sept. 1841, fo. 18; B.235/c/1, London committee to Duncan Finlayson and councils of the Northern and Southern departments, 1 June 1842, fo. 101; Goldring, 'Lewis and the Hudson's Bay Company in the Nineteenth Century', 26–7; HBCA, B.239/b/103, James Hargrave to Archibald Barclay, 23 Aug. 1850, fo. 65.

106. Hunter, *The Making of the Crofting Community*, 43–87; H. Jones, 'Population Patterns and Processes from c. 1600', in G. Whittington and I.D. Whyte, eds, *An Historical Geography of Scotland* (London, 1983), 105–6.
107. HBCA, A.6/26, Alexander Barclay to William Rouse, 19 May 1845, fo. 163d.
108. HBCA, B.153/c/1, Alexander Barclay to William Nourse, 3 June 1847, fos. 133–133d.
109. HBCA, A.10/28, John Cowie to Archibald Barclay, 26 Jan. 1850, fos. 232–232d; A. Duncan to Cowie, 31 Jan. 1850, fos. 267–8; Cowie to Barclay, 19 March 1850, fo. 370d; A.5/16, Barclay to Cowie, 26 May 1849, 132, 22 May 1850, 264.
110. HBCA, A.10/30, Edward Clouston to Archibald Barclay, 4 Nov. 1851, fos. 764–764d; A. Bain to Clouston, 1 Nov. 1851, fos. 766–766d.
111. HBCA, A.10/30, Edward Clouston to Archibald Barclay, 21 Nov. 1851, fos. 803–803d; A.5/18, Barclay to Clouston, 21 Apr. 1853, 96.
112. HBCA, A.6/30, Archibald Barclay to George Simpson, 6 Oct. 1852, fos. 25–25d, 32d; A.12/5, George Simpson to London committee, 1 May 1851, fo. 401, 1 Nov. 1851, fo. 546; A.12/6, George Simpson to Archibald Barclay, 25 Oct. 1852, fos. 244–244d.
113. Drake, *Population and Society in Norway 1735–1865*, 81–2.
114. HBCA, A.5/17, George Simpson to J.R. Crowe, 6 Nov. 1852, 353–5; A.6/30, Archibald Barclay to Simpson, 12 Nov. 1852, fo. 36.
115. HBCA, A.6/30, Archibald Barclay to George Simpson, 18 Mar. 1853, fo. 75d; A.5/18, Barclay to J.R. Crowe, 20 May 1853, 117; Barclay to Edward Clouston, 16 June 1853, 135.
116. HBCA, A.5/18, W.G. Smith to A. de C. Crowe, 2 May 1854, 306; C.1/242, log of the *Colinda*, 1853; A.5/18, Smith to David Landale, 23 May 1854, 324–5; A.5/19, Archibald Barclay to John Hay, 18 July 1854, 32, 5 Aug. 1854, 40.
117. HBCA, C.1/242, log of the *Colinda*, 4 Aug. 1853, 1; 5 Sept., 27–8; 6 Sept., 28; A.5/19, W.G. Smith to A. de C. Crowe, 13 Mar. 1855, 132.
118. HBCA, A.5/18, Archibald Barclay to J.R. Crowe, 14 Mar. 1854, 280; A.5/19, W.G. Smith to A. de C. Crowe, 12 June 1855, 195; B.239/c/8, Smith to William Mactavish, 21 June 1855, fos. 118d–119.
119. HBCA, A.12/8, George Simpson to William Smith, 25 Feb. 1856, fo. 40d; B.239/c/8, Smith to William Mactavish, 21 June 1856, fos. 327–327d.
120. HBCA, A.12/7, George Simpson to London committee, 29 June 1855, fos. 457d–458; A.12/8, Simpson to committee, 26 June 1856, fos. 125, 130.

121. HBCA, A.12/8, George Simpson to London committee, 30 June 1857, fos. 486–486d; Drake, *Population and Society in Norway 1735–1865*, 24–5.
122. HBCA, A.12/7, 'Translated Copy of a Letter from six Norwegian Servants of the Hudson Bay Company to HW Crowe Esq dated Moosefactory Hudson's Bay Sept. 10, 1854', fos. 521–521d.
123. HBCA, A.12/8, George Simpson to London committee, 30 June 1857, fos. 490d–492.
124. HBCA, A.12/8, George Simpson to William Smith, 10 Jan. 1857, fos. 361–361d.
125. NAC, MG19 A21, Series 1, Hargrave Papers, Edward Clouston to James Hargrave, 23 Mar. 1857, 6189; HBCA, A.5/20, W.G. Smith to Clouston, 28 Jan. 1857, 254; A.12/9, George Simpson to Smith, 22 March 1858, fo. 113d; A.11/46, Donald MacKenzie to Smith, 20 Aug. 1857, fo. 228; A.5/22, Thomas Fraser to A. de C. Crowe, 4 Nov. 1858, 150; A.5/20, Smith to A. de C. Crowe, 24 Apr. 1857, 301, 12 May 1857, 13.
126. HBCA, A.5/21, W.G. Smith to A. de C. Crowe, 24 Mar. 1858, 237–8, 8 Apr. 1858, 244, 19 May 1858, 286–7; Smith to Edward Clouston, 3 May 1858, 277.
127. HBCA, B.239/b/105, James Hargrave to William Smith, 12 Sept. 1857, fo. 43d; Hargrave to Rev. E.A. Watkins, 1 Dec. 1857, fo. 62; post mortem of Andreas Johannisen, fos. 72–3; Hargrave to George Simpson, 27 Feb. 1858, fo. 77d; James R. Clare to Simpson, 16 Aug. 1858, fo. 103; B.239/c/10, Robert Wilson to Hargrave, 11 March 1858, fo. 34d; A.12/9, Simpson to London committee, 24 June 1858, fos. 154–156d.
128. HBCA, B.239/b/105, James Hargrave to George Simpson, 27 Aug. 1858; C.7/132, Miscellaneous Papers—*Prince of Wales* (II), 1866–86. Declaration by Norwegians, 14 Aug. 1858, fo. 1.
129. HBCA, B.3/c/2, J. Mackenzie to Richard Hardisty, 3 Jan. 1859, fo. 333, 9 July 1859, fo. 360d; A.5/22, Thomas Fraser to A. de C. Crowe, 4 Apr. 1859, 278–9; A.12/10, Petition from Norwegian Servants, 9 Jan. 1859; A.5/22, Fraser to Crowe, 17 Feb. 1859, 222.
130. HBCA, B.239/c/11, Thomas Fraser to James R. Clare, 24 June 1859, fo. 95d.
131. HBCA, PP 1859–1, Engagement of Mechanics, 22 Nov. 1859; PP 1859–2, Engagement of Labourers, 22 Nov. 1859.
132. HBCA, B.239/b/104b, William Mactavish to A. Barclay, 15 Sept. 1854, fo. 65; A.12/10, George Simpson to London committee, 21 June 1859, fo. 175.
133. HBCA, A.12/10, George Simpson to Thomas Fraser, 10 Jan. 1859, 14 Feb. 1859, fos. 52–52d.

134. HBCA, A.10/45, Duncan Mactavish to secretary, 4 Mar. 1859, fos. 181–182d.
135. HBCA, A.10/45, Duncan Mactavish to Thomas Fraser, 16 June 1859, fos. 609–609d, 22 June 1859, fo. 641, 29 June 1859, fos. 653d–654, 11 Aug. 1859, fos. 162–3; MacPherson and MacAndrew to Mactavish, 10 July 1859, fos. 164–165d; Edward Clouston to Mactavish, 19 Aug. 1859, fos. 206–206d; Mactavish to Fraser, 24 Aug. 1859, fos. 222–222d, 22 Sept. 1859, fos. 326–326a; Clive Emsley, *Crime and Society in England 1750–1900* (London, 1987), 115, 157.
136. HBCA, A.6/36, Thomas Fraser to E.M. Hopkins, 20 June 1861, fo. 109.
137. NAC, MG19 A21, Series 1, Hargrave Papers, Edward Clouston to James Hargrave, 6 Jan. 1858, 6944–5; HBCA, A.10/47, Duncan Mactavish to Thomas Fraser, 8 Mar. 1860, fos. 431–431d, 22 June 1860, fos. 655–655a, 25 June 1860, fo. 664d; A.10/47, W. and R. Morrison to Fraser, 25 June 1860, fo. 663; A.10/48, Clouston to Fraser, 3 July 1860, fos. 12–12d; A.6/36, Fraser to Edward M. Hopkins, 20 Feb. 1861, fo. 33, 10 Apr. 1861, fo. 52.
138. HBCA, A.6/38, Thomas Fraser to A.G. Dallas, 15 Jan. 1863, fo. 14d; A.6/39, Fraser to James R. Clare, 25 June 1864, fos. 107d–108; B.239/c/16, Fraser to J.W. Wilson, 27 June 1866, fos. 196d–197.
139. HBCA, A.12/44, William Mactavish to Thomas Fraser, 16 Oct. 1866, fos. 192d–193; A.6/41, Fraser to Mactavish, 17 Nov. 1866, fo. 10d.
140. HBCA, A.10/81, John Stanger to secretary, 3 July 1870, fo. 12.
141. HBCA, B.239/c/13, James A. Graham to officers of the Northern Department, 26 Dec. 1862, fos. 212d–213.
142. HBCA, A.6/44, W.G. Smith to Donald A. Smith, 1 Nov. 1870, fos. 91–92d.
143. HBCA, A.6/44, W.G. Smith to Donald A. Smith, 13 Jan. 1871, fo. 117.
144. NAC, MG19 A44, Charles McKenzie and Hector Aeneas McKenzie Correspondence, 1828–55, C. McKenzie to H.A. McKenzie, 1 May 1854.

Chapter 4

1. HBCA, B.239/a/79, York Factory journal, 1780–1, 5 Dec. 1780, fos. 12d–13; 18 Dec. 1780, fo. 14d; 1 Sept. 1781, fo. 54d.
2. HBCA, B.239/a/65, York Factory journal, 1770–1, 17 Aug. 1771, fo. 47.
3. HBCA, B.99/a/15, Kenogamissi journal, 1813–14, 16 Nov. 1813, fo. 3d; B.99/e/1, Kenogamissi report, 1813–14, fos. 3d–5; B.145/a/42, New Brunswick journal, 1820–1, 8 Oct. 1820, fo. 12.
4. HBCA, B.39/a/17, Fort Chipewyan journal, Feb. 1821 to May 1821, 18 Apr. fo. 19.

5. HBCA, B.155/a/79, Osnaburgh House journal, 1870–1, 27 Dec. 1870, fo. 17.
6. HBCA, B.239/a/78, York Factory journal, 1779–80, 4 Jan. 1780, fos. 15–15d.
7. See Frits Pannekoek, ' "Corruption" at Moose', *The Beaver* Outfit 309, 4 (Spring 1979), 4–11; Ens, 'The Political Economy of the "Private Trade" on Hudson Bay', 382–410.
8. E.E. Rich, ed., *Journal of Occurrences in the Athabaska Department by George Simpson, 1820–21, and Report* (Toronto, 1938), 51, 278; HBCA, B.39/a/16, Fort Chipewyan journal, June 1820 to Feb. 1821; B.39/a/17, Fort Chipewyan journal, Feb. 1821 to May 1821.
9. HBCA, B.5/a/10, Fort Alexandria journal, 1858–64, 17 Dec. 1860, fo. 48.
10. HBCA, B.198/a/24, Severn House journal, 1779–80, 25 May 1780, fos. 39d–40, 27 May 1780, fos. 40–40d; B.198/a/26, Severn House journal, 1780–1, 25 Aug. 1780, fo. 4d.
11. HBCA, B.162/a/11, Pic journal, 1840–1, 3 June 1840, fo. 2.
12. HBCA, B.49/a/36, Cumberland House journal, 1820–1, 22 Nov. 1820, fo. 19.
13. HBCA, B.59/a/67, Eastmain journal, 1790–1, 28 Dec. 1790–1 Jan. 1791, fos. 10d–11; 2 Mar. 1791, fo. 17; 5 Mar. 1791, fo. 17d.
14. HBCA, B. 154/a/51, Norway House journal, 1848–50, 15, 16 Mar. 1850, fo. 81d, 8 Apr. 1850, fo. 84a; B.154/a/52, Norway House journal, 1850–1, 3 June 1850, fo. 2d, 19 June 1850, fo. 5; A.5/17, A. Barclay to W. and R. Morrison, 30 Oct. 1850, 34.
15. Rediker, *Between the Devil and the Deep Blue Sea,* 166.
16. HBCA, B.42/b/42, Thomas Stayner to John Ballenden, 10 Mar. 1800, 26–7; B.60/e/4, Edmonton report, 1820–1, fo. 3; B.109/a/4, La Cloche journal, 1830–1, John McBean to George Simpson, 8 Sept. 1830, n. p.
17. Rule, *The Labouring Classes in Early Industrial England,* 259.
18. HBCA, B.198/a/60, Severn journal, 20 May 1821, fo. 29; B.149/a/23, Nipigon journal, 1870–6, 18 Dec. 1870, fo. 2.
19. See E.P. Thompson, 'Time, Work-Discipline, and Industrial Capitalism', in F.W. Flinn and T.C. Smout, eds, *Essays in Social History* (Oxford, 1974), 39–77.
20. Ginzburg, *The Cheese and the Worms,* xiv–xv, xxiii–xxiv.
21. Ibid., xxi.
22. Margaret MacLeod, ed., *The Letters of Letitia Hargrave* (Toronto, 1947), Letitia Hargrave to Mrs Dugald Mactavish Sr, 30 Oct. 1849, 246.
23. Brown, *Strangers in Blood,* xxi, 80, 131.
24. HBCA, B.3/a/124, Albany journal, 1819–20, Joseph Beioley to Jacob Corrigal, 29 Sept. 1819, fo. 6d.

25. HBCA, A.10/45, Catherine Narquay to HBC, 21 May 1859, fos. 477–477ad.
26. HBCA, A.10/79, Margaret Sutherland to HBC, 31 Aug. 1869, fo. 238.
27. HBCA, E.31/2, B. McCarthy to John Bracebridge, 31 Oct. 1849; Adam Buck to Jonathan Buck, 6 Sept. 1844; John Spence to Joseph Spence, 17 Sept. 1835.
28. HBCA, B.198/a/60, Severn journal, 1820–1, 22 Sept. 1820, fos. 12–12d; B.201/a/7, Fort Simpson journal, 1852–3, 26 Dec. 1852, fo. 46; E.E. Rich, ed., *The Letters of John McLoughlin From Fort Vancouver to the Governor and Committee, Second Series: 1839–44* (Toronto, 1943), McLoughlin to London committee, 7 July 1842, 60.
29. HBCA, B.38/a/1, Fort Chimo journal, 1830–3, 12 Nov. 1831, fo. 38; B.3/c/2, George McPherson to James Watt, 21 Aug. 1856, fo. 259d.
30. HBCA, B.135/a/90, Moose Factory journal, 1802–3, David Robertson to John Thomas, 3 Apr. 1803, 72; B.135/f/1, Moose Factory servants' resolves, 1803, fos. 2d–3.
31. HBCA, B.3/b/66, George Barnston to Joseph Beioley, 4 Jan. 1841, fo. 6d.
32. HBCA, B.3/c/1, Charles McKenzie to Thomas Corcoran, 20 Apr. 1847, fo. 28d.
33. HBCA, B.239/c/6, W.J. Christie to W. Mactavish, 11 Aug. 1851, fo. 179d.
34. HBCA, B.239/c/6, W.H. Watt to W. Mactavish, 4 Mar. 1853, fo. 304.
35. HBCA, B.141/a/6, Nelson House journal, 1812–13, 6 Sept. 1812, fo. 4d.
36. HBCA, B.77/c/1, G.J. McTavish to Gilbert Hackland, 3 Jan. 1868, fo. 34d, 7 Mar. 1868, fo. 36.
37. HBCA, B.239/c/6, John Cromartie to James Hargrave, 3 Mar. 1851, fo. 17.
38. HBCA, B.60/a/30, Edmonton journal, 1858–60, 11 Nov. 1858, fo. 8d.
39. HBCA, B.39/b/11, William Shaw to Alexander Fisher, 24 Sept. 1840, fo. 5d, 22 Nov. 1840, fo. 7d.
40. See Jeffrey Weeks, *Sex, Politics and Society: The Regulation of Sexuality since 1800* (London, 1981), 24–33.
41. NAC, MG19 A21, George Barnston to James Hargrave, 15 Mar. 1862.
42. NAC, MG19 A21, James Hargrave to Richard Grant, 5 Dec. 1826.
43. HBCA, A.11/46, James Anderson to A.G. Dallas, 8 Sept. 1862, fos. 419d–420.
44. Brian Gallagher, 'Re-examination of Race, Class and Society in Red River', *Native Studies Review* 4, 1 and 2 (1988), 25–65.
45. Van Kirk, *'Many Tender Ties'*, 235–6; Van Kirk, '"What if Mama is an Indian?": The Cultural Ambivalence of the Alexander Ross Family', in Jacqueline Peterson and Jennifer S.H. Brown, eds, *The New Peoples: Being and Becoming Métis in North America* (Winnipeg, 1985), 211.

46. See Weeks, *Sex, Politics and History,* 99–121; Arthur N. Gilbert, 'Buggery and the British Navy, 1700–1861', *Journal of Social History* 10, 1 (Fall 1976), 72–98.
47. See B.R. Burg, *Sodomy and the Perception of Evil: English Sea Rovers in the 17th Century Caribbean* (New York, 1983).
48. HBCA, A.11/43, George Howy and Richard Staunton to London committee, 1 Aug. 1738, fo. 14. To 'ride up Holborn Hill' was one of many slang expressions for hanging. Holborn was one of the districts through which the procession taking a condemned criminal travelled on its way to the scaffold at Tyburn until 1783, when the site of executions was moved behind the walls of Newgate Prison and processions were prohibited because of the disorder that accompanied them. The 'cart' was pulled away by a horse to remove the support under the man's feet prior to the introduction of the trap door. See Peter Linebaugh, 'The Tyburn Riot Against the Surgeons', in Douglas Hay et al., *Albion's Fatal Tree: Crime and Society in Eighteenth-Century England* (New York, 1975), 66–7.
49. Payne, 'Daily Life on Western Hudson Bay 1714 to 1870', 120–1.
50. HBCA, B.135/a/91, Moose Factory journal, 1803–4, 30 Dec. 1803, fo. 11, 31 Dec. 1803, fo. 11, 1 Apr. 1804, fo. 20, 4 Apr. 1804, fos. 20–20d, 23 July 1804, 9 Aug. 1804, fo. 38; B.135/f/2, Moose Factory servants' resolves, 1804, fo. 1.
51. HBCA, B.77/a/14, Fort George journal, 1839–40, 7–8 May 1840, 63–5; B.135/a/144, Moose Factory journal, 1839–40, 8–9 Aug. 1839, fos. 10d–11d; *The Shorter Oxford English Dictionary on Historical Principles,* I, 751.
52. Pannekoek, '"Corruption" at Moose', 5; Michael Payne, *'The Most Respectable Place in the Territory': Everyday Life in Hudson's Bay Company Service York Factory, 1788–1870,* Studies in Archaeology, Architecture and History, National Historic Parks and Sites, Canadian Parks Service, Environment Canada (Ottawa, 1989), 98–9.
53. See, for example, B.42/a/129, Churchill journal, 1803–4, Oct. 1803, fo. 2d; B.86/a/17, Henley House journal, 1770–1, *passim;* B.105/a/4, Lac La Pluie journal, 1796–7, 22 Aug. 1796, fo. 2; B.117/a/1, Long Lake journal, 1815–16, 16 Feb. 1816, fo. 20; B.135/a/94, Moose Factory journal, 1806–7, 20 June 1807, fo. 44; B.135/a/103, Moose Factory journal, 1812–13, 21 Apr. 1813, fo. 22d; B.155/a/15, Osnaburgh House journal, 1799–1800, 1 Mar. 1800, fo. 19; B.177/a/1, Red Lake journal, 1790–1, 1 Aug. 1790, fo. 2d.
54. HBCA, B.239/a/90, York Factory journal, 1789–90, 31 Mar. 1790, fo. 31; 21 Apr. 1790, fo. 37d.
55. HBCA, B.3/a/74, Albany journal, 1777–8, 26 Dec. 1777, fo. 9d; B.3/a/77a, Albany journal, 1779–80, 24 Apr. 1780, fo. 20d; B.3/a/92,

Albany journal, 27 Dec. 1790, fo. 10d; B.59/a/86, Eastmain journal, 1808–9, 29 Apr. 1829, fo. 27d; B.3/a/134, Albany journal, 1829–30, 25 Dec. 1829, fos. 25–25d, 1 Jan. 1830, fo. 26; B.8/a/1, Assiniboine journal, 1828–9, 23 Jan. 1829, fo. 10; B.45/a/1, Fort Colvile journal, 1830–1, 25 Dec. 1830, fo. 27d; B.117/a/8, Long Lake journal, 1831–2, 1–2 Jan. 1832, fo. 8d; B.129/a/15, Michipicoten journal, 1830–1, 25 Dec. 1830, fo. 15; B.162/a/3, Pic journal, 1829–30, 1 Jan. 1830, fo. 15; B.159/a/11, Fort Pelly journal, 1829–30, 1 Jan. 1830, fo. 21d; B.201, Fort Simpson journal, 1838–40, 1 Nov. 1838, fo. 61d; B.5/a/10, Fort Alexandria journal, 1858–64, 1 Jan. 1861, fo. 51; B.39/a/6, Fort Chipewyan journal, 1815–16, 1 Nov. 1815, fo. 26; B.181/a/2, Fort Resolution journal, 1819–20, 1 Nov. 1819, 24; B.201/a/4, Fort Simpson journal, 1 Nov. 1838, fo. 61d; B.235/c/1, George Barnston to James Hargrave, 1 Feb. 1823, fo. 4.
56. HBCA, B.42/a/80, Churchill journal, 1770–1, 22 Apr. 1771, fo. 53; B.107/a/9, Lac Seul journal, 1830–1, 13 Oct. 1830, fo. 8; B.22/a/10, Brandon House journal, 1802–3, 14 Nov. 1802, fo. 5d; B.8/a/1, Assiniboine journal, 1828–9, 23 Jan. 1829, fo. 10; B.129/a/22, Michipicoten journal, 1840–1, 1 Jan. 1841, fo. 16; B.129/a/14, Michipicoten journal, 1829–30, 17 May 1830, fo. 21d; 19 June 1830, fo. 2; B.60/a/30, Edmonton journal, 1858–60, 27 Oct. 1858, fo. 6d; 12 Dec. 1859, fo. 87d; B.22/a/1, Brandon House journal, 1793–4, 9 Sept. 1793, fo. 3. See also B.181/a/1, Fort Resolution journal, 1818–19, 26 Aug. 1818, fo. 5; Rich, ed., *Journal of Occurrences in the Athabaska Department*, 13 Sept. 1820, 37; Rediker, *Between the Devil and the Deep Blue Sea*, 186–9.
57. HBCA, B.115/a/5, Lesser Slave Lake journal, 1821–2, 5 Jan. 1822, fo. 17.
58. HBCA, B.5/a/10, Fort Alexandria journal, 1858–64, 1 Jan. 1861, fo. 51.
59. HBCA, B.39/a/15, Fort Chipewyan journal, 1819–20, 16 Nov. 1819, fo. 11.
60. HBCA, B.22/a/4, Brandon House journal, 1796–7, 7 Sept. 1796, fo. 11, 27 Jan. 1797, fo. 34.
61. HBCA, B.3/a/115, Fort Albany journal, 1811–12, 17 Apr. 1812, fo. 8.
62. See Robert W. Malcolmson, *Popular Recreations in English Society 1700–1850* (Cambridge, 1973),118–71; Bushaway, *By Rite*, 231–74; Underdown, *Revel, Riot, and Rebellion*, 44–72, 239–91.
63. HBCA, B.3/a/134, Albany journal, 1829–30, 25 Dec. 1829, fo. 25.
64. HBCA, B.135/k/1, minutes of the council of the Southern Department, 1822–75, 8 Aug. 1839, fo. 96d.
65. HBCA, B.129/a/22, Michipicoten journal, 1840–1, 25 Dec. 1840, fos. 15–15d; B.123/a/43, Martins Fall journal, 1840–1, 25 Dec. 1840, fo. 14d.

66. HBCA, B.3/b/66, Joseph Beioley to George Barnston, 2 Feb. 1841, fo. 31.
67. Rich, ed., *Letters of John McLoughlin . . . Second Series*, McLoughlin to London committee, 31 Oct. 1842, 71, George Simpson to McLoughlin, 13 May 1842, 72 n; HBCA, B.223/c/1, committee to McLoughlin, 27 Apr. 1843, fo. 216.
68. HBCA, B.226/b/3, James Douglas to Richard Blanchard, 2 Feb. 1851, fos. 46–46d; B.201/a/8, Fort Simpson journal, 1855–9, 20 Nov. 1855, fo. 25.
69. HBCA, E.61/5, McMurray correspondence, John Macaulay to William McMurray, 23 May 1859, fo. 18d.
70. HBCA, B.239/b/107, James R. Clare to William Mactavish, 14 Aug. 1862, fo. 142; B.49/z/1, Governor Dallas to H.H. Berens, 7 Feb. 1863, fo. 132.
71. HBCA, B.226/b/1, Roderick Finlayson to John McLoughlin, 11 Jan. 1845, fo. 14d; B.220/a/41, Trout Lake journal, 1870–2, 31 Dec. 1870, fo. 20, 1 Jan. 1871, fo. 20.
72. HBCA, B.239/c/7, George Simpson to William Mactavish, 18 June 1853, fo. 103d; Simpson to Mactavish, 1 July 1853, fo. 128; Simpson to Mactavish, 1 Dec. 1853, fo. 213; John Black to Mactavish, 8 Dec. 1853, fos. 221–221d; A.12/6, 1852–3, Simpson to London committee, 2 July 1853, fos. 418–418d; B.239/b/97a, James Hargrave to Alexander Christie, 29 Aug. 1845, fos. 16–16d.
73. HBCA, B.239/b/104b, W. Mactavish to John Ballenden, 4 Sept. 1854, fo. 60; B.239/c/10, George Simpson to officer in charge of York Factory, 21 June 1858, fo. 106; B.239/c/14, James A. Graham to James Clare, 26 June 1863, fo. 183; B.303/a/1, Lower Fort Garry journal, 1868–74, 3 Oct. 1868, fo. 1d; B.239/b/110, William Parson to Robert Hamilton, 11 Sept. 1870, fo. 80.
74. See, for example, HBCA, A.12/10, George Simpson to London committee, 21 June 1859, fos. 180–180d; B.3/a/77a, Albany journal, 1779–80, 4 Jan. 1780, fo. 11; B.3/a/105, Albany journal, 1802–3, 19 Oct. 1802, fo. 7d; B.3/a/110, Albany journal, 1807–8, 16 July 1808, fo. 16; B.3/a/115, Albany journal, 1811–12, 30 Mar. 1812, fo. 7; B.3/a/116, Albany journal, 1812–13, 5 Aug. 1813, fo. 16d; B.19/a/1, Big Lake journal, 1818–19, 24 Sept. 1818, fo. 4; B.22/a/20, Brandon House journal, 1817–18, 1 Dec. 1817, fo. 23; B.42/a/101, Charlotte Sloop journal, 1779–80, 23 June 1780, fo. 18; B.60, Edmonton journal, 1815–16, James Sutherland to James Bird, 7 Aug. 1816, fo. 51; B.123/b/3, John Davis to Thomas Vincent, n.d., 1821, fos. 24d–25; B.186/e/4, Ruperts River report, 1820–1, fos. 3–4; B.198/a/39, Severn journal, 1789–90, 'Particulars respecting the murder of William

Appleby late Master of the Moose Shalop at Hannah Bay the 18th Octr 1788', fo. 38d; B.198/a/40, Severn journal, 1790–1, 23 Dec. 1790, fo. 13d; B.239/a/90, York Factory journal, 1789–90, 26 Apr. 1790, fo. 38d; B.226/b/11, James Douglas to Archibald Barclay, 3 Jan. 1855, fos. 92d–93; B.226/c/2, W.G. Smith to William F. Tolmie and Board of Management, 21 May 1869, fo. 455; B.239/k/3, minutes of the council of the Northern Department, 1851–70, 3 July 1870, 450–1; D.1/4, Thomas Vincent, John Davis, Alexander Christie, Joseph Beioley, and Angus Bethune to London committee, 10 Sept. 1822, fos. 26–26d.

75. HBCA, B.3/a/46, Fort Albany journal, 1809–10, George Budge, George Grot, and Samuel Harvey to John Hodgson, 8 Oct. 1809, fo. 9d.
76. HBCA, B.3/c/2, William Lane to Robert Miles, 24 Mar. 1844, 'Extract verbatim from a letter to John Rae Esq Surgeon Moose from one of the Servants at Ruperts House', fos. 160–1.
77. HBCA, B.239/a/90, York Factory journal, 1789–90, 4 Jan. 1790, fo. 18, 1 July 1791, fo. 27; B.239/f/1, York Factory servants' resolves, 1783–95, fo. 53d.
78. HBCA, B.177/a/1, Red Lake journal, 1790–1, 15 Sept. 1790, fo. 8; B.22/a/1, Brandon House journal, 1793–4, 18 Nov. 1793, fo. 11d; B.22/a/2, Brandon House journal, 1794–5, 22 Oct. 1794, fo. 7d, 29 Nov. 1794, fo. 9d; B.22/a/5, Brandon House journal, 1797–8, 4–5 Nov. 1797, fos. 15d–16.
79. HBCA, C.1/243, log of the *Columbia*, 1835–7, 19 July 1836, fo. 131d, 25 July 1836, fos. 132d–33, 26 July 1836, fo. 133d, 24 Dec. 1836, fo. 176, 27–30 Dec., fos. 176–176d, 5–6 Jan. 1837, fos. 177d–178. See also HBCA, C.1/981, log of the *Princess Royal*, 1859–65, 28 Feb.–14 Mar. 1860, fos. 77d–80d, 17 Jan. 1861, fo. 205d, 5 Feb. 1861, fo. 211a, 16 Feb. 1861, fo. 211b, 12 Feb. 1861, fo. 211bd; C.1/721, log of the *Prince Arthur*, 1860, 15 Oct. 1860, fo. 55d; C.1/499, log of the *Lady Lampson*, 1870–1, 16 Jan. 1871, fo. 28.
80. HBCA, B.198/a/59, Severn House journal, 1819–20, 10–11 Aug. 1819, 7–8.
81. HBCA, B.22/a/16, Brandon House journal, 1808–9, 27 July 1808, fo. 2.
82. HBCA, B.44/a/1, Colvile journal, 1818–19, 5 Sept. 1818, fos. 6d–7; B.64/a/7, Escabitchewan journal, 1818–19, 20 July 1818, fo. 1d; B.99/e/2, Kenogamissi report, 1814–15, fo. 1d.
83. HBCA, B.154/a/69, Norway House journal, 1869–72, 20 Aug. 1870, fo. 42d–43; B.239/b/105, James Hargrave, York, to E.A. Watkins, RRS, 1 Dec. 1857, fo. 62.
84. HBCA, B.135/a/104, Moose Factory journal, 1813–14, 17 July 1814, fo. 17.

85. HBCA, B.143/a/15, Neoskweskau journal, 1815–16, 24 May 1816, fos. 18d–20.
86. HBCA, B.209/a/1, Fort Stikine journal, 5 Oct. 1841, fo. 53d.
87. HBCA, A.12/44, 'Swan River District Report Outfit 1866' by Robert Campbell, fos. 358–358d; B.239/c/17, William J. Christie to officers of the Northern Department, 2 Jan. 1867, fos. 9–9d.
88. Hartwell Bowsfield, ed., *Fort Victoria Letters, 1846–51* (Winnipeg, 1979), James Douglas to Archibald Barclay, 15 May 1850, 88.
89. HBCA, A.11/77, A.G. Dallas to Thomas Fraser, 12 Sept. 1860, fo. 713; B.113/b/2, Ovid Allard to Board of Management, 1 Sept. 1868, fo. 44.
90. HBCA, B.3/a/79/, abstract of Albany journal, 1780–1, 1 Oct. 1780, fos. 1–1d; B.59/a/86/, Eastmain journal, 1808–9, 10 Mar. 1809, fo. 21d; B.3/a/128, Albany journal, 1822–3, 29 Dec. 1822, fo. 13; B.134/c/8, James Keith to James Keith, 12 Aug. 1830, fos. 95–95d.
91. See, for example, HBCA, B.3/a/99, Albany journal, 1794–7, 8 June 1795, fo. 10; B.188/a/14, Fort St James journal, 1829–30, 8 Apr. 1829, fo. 13d; B.188/a/16, Fort St James journal, 19 Apr. 1831, fo. 22, 20 April 1830, fo. 22; B.188/a/19, Fort St James journal, 1840–6, 4 Mar. 1841, fo. 24d; B.198/a/114, Severn journal, 1860–1, 19 July 1860, fo. 6d.
92. HBCA, B.86/a/61, Henley House journal, 1809–10, 31 Sept. 1809, fo. 6.
93. HBCA, B.145/a/42, New Brunswick journal, 1820–1, 23 Aug. 1820, fo. 6, 25 Aug. 1820, fo. 6d, 2 Dec. 1820, fo. 19d, 13 Dec. 1820, fo. 20d, 5 Feb. 1821, fos. 28, 29, 30 Mar. 1821, fos. 37–37d.
94. See HBCA, A.11/118, declaration by James Anderson (a) and Alexander Mackenzie (c) witnessed by James Grahame at Norway House, 17 Aug. 1864, fo. 462; B.3/a/99, Albany journal, 1794–7, 20 June 1795, fo. 12; B.3/a/102, Albany journal, 1798–9, 10 Sept. 1799, fo. 33; B.3/a/117a, Albany journal, 1813–14, 18 Aug. 1813, fo. 1; B.22/a/19, Brandon House journal, 1815–16, 16 Mar. 1816, fo. 22; B.35/a/17, Fort Chipewyan, 1821, 28 Mar. 1821, fo. 12; B.42/a/140, Churchill journal, 1813–14, 29 June 1814, fo. 29; B.59/a/83, Eastmain journal, 1805–6, 22 Sept. 1805, fo. 2d; B.60/a/30, Edmonton journal, 1858–60, 11 Nov. 1858, fo. 8d; B.77/a/3, Fort George journal, 1816–17, 20 Sept. 1816, fo. 1d; B.117/a/4, Long Lake journal, 1818–19, 28 Nov. 1818, fo. 13; B.123/b/2, John James Smith to John Davis, 27 Mar. 1820, fo. 16; B.135/b/26, John Mannall to George Gladman, 2 Feb. 1801, fo. 13d; B.135/a/94, Moose Factory journal, 1806–7, 19 Jan. 1807, fo. 19; B.135/a/108, Moose Factory journal, 1815, 12 June 1815, fo. 33; B.145/b/2, John Murphy to Thomas Vincent, 27 Mar. 1818, 47; B.145/a/15, New Brunswick journal, 1800–1, 28 Oct. 1800, fo. 4d; B.149/a/23, Nipigon journal, 1870–6, 18 Feb. 1871, fo. 7d; B.155/a/27, Osnaburgh House journal, 1814–15, 25 Mar. 1815, fo. 8d; B.155/a/52,

Osnaburgh House journal, 1840–1, 21 Jan. 1841, fo. 17d; B.162/a/11, Pic journal, 1840–1, 3 June 1840, fo. 2; B.188/a/19, Fort St James journal, 1840–6, 5 Dec. 1840, fo. 10, 5 Apr. 1841, fo. 33; B.180/a/20, Fort St James journal, 1846–51, 27 May 1850, fo. 100; B.190/a/1, Fort St Mary journal, 1818–19, 23 Feb. 1819, fo. 41; B.201/a/7, Fort Simpson journal, 1852–3, 25 Mar. 1853, fo. 59; B.239/b/93, report on Donald Smith, fos. 26d–27; B.239/b/108, J.W. Wilson to Thomas Fraser, 25 Sept. 1866, fo. 585; E.61/12, McMurray correspondence, 1866, 15 Dec. 1866, fo. 33.
95. HBCA, B.105/a/7, Lac La Pluie journal, 1819–20, 17 Nov. 1819, fo. 49.
96. See, for example, HBCA, B.10/a/2, Attawapiscat journal, 1814–15, 6 Jan. 1815, fo. 11d; B.27/a/8, Carlton House journal, 1818–19, 14 Jan. 1819, fo. 20; B.39/a/3, Fort Chipewyan journal, 1803–4, Thomas Swain to Peter Fidler, 10 April 1804, fo. 18; B.49/a/32a, Cumberland House journal, 1802–3, 5 Mar. 1802, fo. 24d; B.60/a/31, Edmonton journal, 1860–1, 1 Feb. 1861, fo. 63; B.108/a/1, Lac Travers journal, 1819–20, *passim*; B.121/a/4, Manchester House journal, 1 July 1790, fo. 60d; B.133/a/24, Mistassini journal, 1840–1, 10 Mar. 1841, fo. 20; B.135/a/61, Moose Factory journal, 1779–80, 25 Feb. 1780, fo. 17d; B.181/a/2, Fort Resolution journal, 1819–20, 7 Jan. 1820, 60; B.190/a/3, Fort St Mary journal, 1820–1, 29 Oct. 1820, fo. 6; B.239/a/79, York Factory journal, 5 Dec. 1780, fo. 12d; B.39/c/1, George Simpson to Edward Smith, 8 Feb. 1823, fo. 2; B.239/c/10, R. Wilson to James R. Clare, 29 Aug. 1858, fo. 220.
97. See, for example, HBCA, B.10/a/2, Atttawapiscat journal, 1814–15, 6 Jan. 1815, fo. 11d; B.22/a/1, Brandon House journal, 1793–4, 8 Dec. 1793, fo. 12d; B.22/a/19, Brandon House journal, 1815–16, 23 Feb. 1816, fo. 18d; B.39/a/16, Fort Chipewyan journal, 1820–1, 13 Nov. 1820, fo. 38; B.121/a/4, Manchester House journal, 1789–90, William Walker to Mitchel Oman, 11 Dec. 1789, fo. 32; B.78/a/24, Gloucester journal, 1815–16, 1 Dec. 1815, fo. 9; B.93/a/1, Island Lake journal, 1818–19, 24 Mar. 1819, fo. 19d; B.122/e/1, Manitoba District report, 1818–19, fo. 2; B.123/a/86, Martins Fall journal, 1869–70, 22–3 June 1870, fos. 22d–23; B.135/a/94, Moose Factory journal, 1806–7, 8–9 Dec. 1806, fo. 12d, 10 Mar. 1807, fo. 28d; B.135/b/41, John Murphy to Thomas Vincent, 3 July 1821, 53–4; B.145/a/41, New Brunswick journal, 1819–20, 13 Jan. 1820, fo. 11; B.155/a/29, Osnaburgh House journal, 1816–17, 20 Mar. 1817, fo. 20d; B.155/a/79, Osnaburgh House journal, 1870–1, 22 Sept. 1870, fo. 8; B.188/a/19, Fort St James journal, 1840–1, 6 Dec. 1840, fo. 10d; B.190/a/1, Fort St Mary journal, 1818–19, 1 Apr. 1819, fo. 45d; B.209/a/1, Fort Stikine journal, 1840–2, 13 Jan. 1841, fo. 24d; B.224/a/7, Fort Vermilion journal, 1840, 27 June

1840, fo. 1; B.240/a/4, Fort Yukon journal, 1850–1, 28 Aug. 1850, fo. 8d.
98. HBCA, B.59/a/101, Eastmain journal, 1818–19, 14–15 Aug. 1818, fos. 1–1d; B.59/e/6, Eastmain report, 1819, fo. 3d.
99. HBCA, B.60/a/30, Edmonton journal, 1858–60, 31 Oct. 1859, fos. 78–78d.
100. HBCA, B.123/a/86, Martins Fall journal, 1869–70, 29 Apr. 1869, fo. 14.
101. Payne, 'Daily Life on Western Hudson Bay 1714 to 1870', 68–9; HBCA, A.11/14, Moses Norton to London committee, 5 Sept. 1770, fo. 129.
102. HBCA, B.154/c/1, James Anderson to George Barnston, 27 Nov. 1857, fo. 141d; B.239/k/3, minutes of the council of the Northern Department, 1851–70, 23 June 1862, 239; A.6/38, London committee to A.G. Dallas and councils of the Northern and Southern departments, 15 Apr. 1863, fo. 74.
103. See Geoffrey Crossick, *An Artisan Elite in Victorian Society: Kentish London 1840–1880* (London, 1978), 134–64; Robert Q. Gray, *The Labour Aristocracy in Victorian Edinburgh* (Oxford, 1976), 91–143.
104. HBCA, B.129/b/10, Thomas Vincent to Andrew Stewart, 7 July 1819, fo. 10d.
105. Crossick, *An Artisan Elite in Victorian Society,* 77–81; HBCA, B.223/c/1, London committee to John McLoughlin, 31 Dec. 1839, fos. 137–137d; A.6/33, W.S. Smith to Board of Management, Victoria, 11 Oct. 1858, fo. 170d.
106. HBCA, B.113/c/1, James Fitz Hams to James M. Yale, 22 Aug. 1858, fo. 133.
107. HBCA, B.239/b/105, James Hargrave to George Simpson, 26 May 1858, fos. 91–91d; James R. Clare to Simpson, 16 Aug. 1858, fo. 102.
108. HBCA, A.12/7, George Simpson to W.S. Smith, 17 Mar. 1855, fos. 395–395d; 'Translated Copy of a Letter from six Norwegians Servants of the Hudson Bay Company to H W Crowe Esq dated Moosefactory Hudson's Bay Sept 10, 1854', fo. 521.
109. HBCA, B.239/b/40, Humphrey Marten to Walter Bigger, 24 Sept. 1779, fos. 3–3d.
110. HBCA, B.239/a/78, York Factory journal, 1779–80, 9 Mar. 1780, fo. 23; B.239/a/79, York Factory journal, 1780–1, 2 June 1781, fo. 36d; 6 Sept. 1781, fo. 68d.
111. HBCA, B.59/a/79, Eastmain journal, 1801–2, 24 Aug. 1802, fo. 30d.
112. HBCA, B.3/a/127, Albany journal, 7 Dec. 1822, fo. 6d.
113. HBCA, A.10, James Hargrave to ?, 28 Jan. 1859, fo. 69.
114. HBCA, B.153/a/20, North West River journal, 1868–70, 5 June 1860, fo. 18d.

115. Ens, 'The Political Economy of the "Private Trade" on Hudson Bay', 387; Andrew Graham, *Observations on Hudson's Bay, 1767–91,* ed. Glyndwr Williams (London, 1969), 282–4.
116. HBCA, A.6/11, London committee to John Garbut and council, 20 May 1772, fos. 144–144d.
117. HBCA, B.42/b/44, London committee to Samuel Hearne and council, 24 May 1786, fo. 19d; A.1/46, minutes of governor and committee, 12 Apr. 1786; William Christopher, Joshua Tunstall, and John Richards to committee, 15 Mar. 1786, fo. 82d.
118. HBCA, A.5/4, Alex Lean to David Geddes, 17 Dec. 1800, fo. 66.
119. HBCA, B.42/b/44, council at Churchill to London committee, n.d. Aug. 1786, fo. 22.
120. R. Harvey Fleming, ed., *Minutes of the Council of Northern Department of Rupert [sic] Land, 1821–31* (Toronto, 1940), 8 July 1822, 25; HBCA, B.39/z/1, 'Mema Notes of Replies to Mr Fortescues letters from York factory 12th & 15th Augt, & 6th Dec', from Alex Christie, 12 May 1864, fo. 116d; B.235/c/1, London committee to Duncan Finlayson, 4 Mar. 1840, fo. 40d.
121. NAC, MG19 A21, Hargrave Family Papers, Series 4, extract of letter from George Simpson to Donald Ross, 20 Dec. 1843, 2766–7; Fleming, ed., *Minutes of the Council of Northern Department,* 10 July 1824, 87; 1 July 1825, 124; HBCA, B.239/k/28, Standing Rules and Regulations, Northern Department, 1843–75, Nos 32, 66; HBCA, B.39/b/12, James Anderson to Messrs Shaw and Boucher, circular, 27 Dec. 1850, fo. 75.
122. Fleming, ed., *Minutes of the Council of Northern Department,* 10 July 1824, 87; HBCA, B.239/k/28, Standing Rules and Regulations, Northern Department, 1843–75, resolutions, Nos 123, 124; A.12/7, George Simpson to London committee, 29 June 1855, fo. 452.
123. HBCA, B.218/c/1, Johnson G. King to James Cameron, 1 Sept. 1850, fos. 9, 12d.
124. HBCA, B.223/c/2, George Simpson to the Board of Management, 18 June 1853, fos. 66–67d.
125. HBCA, A.11/62, Arthur Bates to Archibald Barclay, 29 Oct. 1850, fos. 520–521d; deposition of George Pelly, 29 Oct. 1850, fo. 532; Bates to Barclay, 1 Nov. 1850, fos. 529–529d.
126. HBCA, B.42/a/136a, 'Mr Aulds Memorandum Book', 1810–11, fo. 29d; B.59/b/30, Thomas Thomas to George Gladman, 20 Apr. 1811, 5; A.6/18, London committee to Thomas, 26 May 1813, 98.
127. HBCA, B.42/b/55, William Auld to James Bird, 8 Mar. 1811, fo. 5.
128. HBCA, A.6/15, London committee to officers at Moose Factory, 29 May 1794, fo. 101d; A.6/14, committee to Edward Jarvis and council, 21 May 1788, fo. 29d.

129. HBCA, B.60/a/9, Edmonton journal, 1810–11; B.60/d/2a, Edmonton account book, 1810–11, fos. 23d–24. Account books generally recorded the fines imposed for misbehaviour. A.30/14, servants' list, 1814–15, fos. 5d–6.
130. John E. Foster, 'James Bird', *Dictionary of Canadian Biography,* VIII, 90–1.
131. Shirlee Anne Smith, 'James Sutherland', *Dictionary of Canadian Biography,* IV (Toronto, 1979), 727–8; HBCA, B.22/a/4, Brandon House journal, 1796–7, 18 Nov. 1796, fo. 19, 20 Nov. 1796, fo. 19d; A.6/15, London committee to officers at Albany, 30 May 1795, fo. 128d.
132. See Emsley, *Crime and Society in England,* 103–28.
133. Dobson, *Masters and Journeymen,* 60–73, 154–70; HBCA, B.59/a/81, Eastmain journal, 1803–4, 25 Oct. 1803, fos. 5–5d; 24 Nov. 1803, fos. 8d–9; 10 Dec. 1803, fo. 10; 12 Dec. 1803, fo. 10d; 21 Dec. 1803, fo. 11d; 7 Feb. 1804, fo. 15; 8 Feb. 1804, fo. 15d; 10 Feb. 1804, fos. 15d–16; 15 Feb. 1804, fo. 16; 14 Mar. 1804, fo. 18; 15 Mar. 1804, fos. 18–18d; 19 Mar. 1804, fo. 18d; 22 Mar. 1804, fos. 18d–19; 26 July 1804, fo. 27d; 26 Aug. 1804, fo. 29; 31 Aug. 1804, fo. 20d; B.59/f/1, Eastmain servants' resolves, 1804, fo. 2d; B.59/f/2, Eastmain servants' resolves, 1805, fos. 3d–5.
134. HBCA, B.135/c/1, London committee to officers at Moose Factory, [1771], fo. 93; A.5/1, committee to Humphrey Marten, 8 May 1770, fos. 105d–106.
135. HBCA, B.3/b/7, orders to Thomas Powell, master at Henley, fos. 3–3d; B.3/a/65, Albany journal, 1772–3, 2, 4 Jan. 1773, fos. 19–19d.
136. HBCA, B.60/a/18, Edmonton House journal, 1819–20, 13 Jan. 1820, fo. 17.
137. HBCA, E.31/2, James Gunn to George Gunn, n.d. [1840].
138. HBCA, B.42/f/3, Churchill servants' resolves, 1805, fos. 4d–5. Until 1812, none of these lists record anything other than satisfactory behaviour on Taylor's part. Nor was his transgression mentioned in the column set aside for reporting on the men's characters in the large list of 1812, A.30/11, fos. 46d–47; B.42/f/7, Churchill servants' resolves, 1812, fos. 5d–6.
139. It was customary in the HBC to auction off the effects of deceased co-workers and send the proceeds to their families. This practice was also a seafaring tradition and perhaps derived from the large contingent of seamen in the service during its earliest years and from the maritime experiences of the Orcadians, who for many years comprised the majority of the HBC's employees. Such auctions are occasionally mentioned in the company's records. For example: HBCA, B.239/a/65, York Factory journal, 1770–1, 26 Dec. 1770, fo. 16d; B.135/a/113a, Moose

Factory journal, 1816–17, 7 Sept. 1816, fo. 9; B.135/a/116, Moose Factory journal, 1817–18, 3 June 1818, fo. 50d; B.3/a/129, Albany journal, 1824–5, 8 Mar. 1825, fo. 25; B.218/c/1, Johnson G. King to James Cameron, 1 Sept. 1850; B.46/z/1, extract of letter from Angus McDonald, Flathead Post, 7 Mar. 1852, fo. 4. See Rediker, *Between the Devil and the Deep Blue Sea,* 197–8.
140. HBCA, B.42/a/137, Churchill journal, 1811–12, 15 Jan. 1812, fos. 5–6.
141. Emsley, *Crime and Society in England,* 113.
142. HBCA, A.11/3, officers to London committee, 3 Sept. 1770, fo. 148d.
143. HBCA, B.3/a/145, Albany journal, 1839–40, 5 Mar. 1840, fos. 20d–21d.
144. HBCA, B.239/c/17, W.J. Christie to J.W. Wilson, 1 May 1867, fos. 62d–63.
145. Ens, 'The Political Economy of the "Private Trade" on Hudson Bay', 397–401.
146. See, for example, HBCA, B.59/a/81, Eastmain journal, 1803–4, 26 July 1804, fo. 27d; B.3/b/46, John Eunson to John Hodgson, 20 Jan. 1810, fos. 14d–15; B.3/a/116, Albany journal, 1812–13, 23 Jan. 1813, fo. 7d; B.22/a/4, Brandon House journal, 14 Nov. 1796, fo. 17d; B.39/a/3, Fort Chipewyan, 1803–4, Thomas Swain to Peter Fidler, 10 April 1804, fo. 18; B.42/a/136b, Churchill journal, 1810–11, 4 July 1811, fo. 6; B.84/a/2, Green Lake journal, 1801–2, 27 July 1801, fo. 1d, 13–19 Sept. 1801, fo. 3; B.135/a/91, Moose Factory journal, 1803–4, David Robertson to John Thomas, 5 June 1804, fo. 29d.
147. HBCA, B.22/a/4, Brandon House journal, 1796–7, 20 Apr. 1797, fo. 35d; 14, 16, 19 Nov. 1796, fos. 17d–19d.
148. HBCA, B.145/b/1, Thomas Vincent to William Thomas, 17 Sept. 1816, 1.
149. HBCA, B.39/a/6, Fort Chipewyan journal, 1815–16, 13 Dec. 1815, fo. 35, 21 Dec. 1815, fo. 35d; B.89/a/3, Ile a la Crosse journal, 1815–16, 28 Dec. 1815, fo. 10, 15 April 1816, fo. 18.
150. See, for example, HBCA, B.49/a/35, Cumberland House journal, 1819–20, 7 July 1819, fo. 12; B.49/a/36, Cumberland House journal, 1820–1, 14 June 1820, fo. 3; B.105/a/6, Lac La Pluie journal, 1818–19, 19 May 1819, fo. 27; B.105/a/7, Lac La Pluie journal, 1819–20, 18 May 1819, fo. 4; B.115/a/2, Lesser Slave Lake journal, 1818–19, 24 Aug. 1818, fo. 10; B.117/a/1, Long Lake journal, 1815–16, 29 Aug. 1815, fo. 1d, 23 Dec. 1815, fos. 13–13d; B.133/a/1, Mistassini journal, 1814–15, 19–20 Jan. 1815, fos. 6–6d, 30 Jan. 1815, fo. 7.
151. HBCA, B.218/c/1, James Cameron to John Sievright, 19 Jan. 1844, fos. 1–2; A.11/28, Duncan Finlayson to W.S. Smith, 24 May 1858, fo. 776.
152. Bowsfield, ed., James Douglas to Archibald Barclay, 3 Sept. 1849, 47–8; Douglas to London committee, 27 Oct. 1849, 34; Douglas to Archibald Barclay, 3 April 1850, 76.

153. Ibid., James Douglas to Archibald Barclay, 13 June 1850, 100. HBCA, A.10/28, Alexander John Weynton to Barclay, 21 Jan. 1850, fo. 226.
154. HBCA, A.12/4, George Simpson to London committee, 30 June 1849, fo. 542d; B.218/c/1, Johnson G. King to James Cameron, 1 Sept. 1850, fo. 12d; B.5/b/1, John Saunders to P.S. Ogden, 6 Mar. 1861, fo. 8d; Saunders to Board of Management, 2 April 1861, fo. 9d; Saunders to P.H. Rind, 27 Apr. 1861, fos. 10d–11d.
155. HBCA, B.239/c/1, Robert Campbell to Joseph Fortescue, 9 Feb. 1867, fo. 20d; A.12/42, W. Mactavish to Thomas Fraser, 20 Nov. 1861, fo. 162; B.239/c/17, W.J. Christie to J.W. Wilson, 1 May 1867, fo. 62d.

Chapter 5

1. HBCA, B.121/a/4, Manchester House journal, 1789–90, 22 Oct. 1789, fo. 17.
2. H. Clare Pentland, *Labour and Capital in Canada 1650–1860,* ed. and with an intro. by Paul Phillips (Toronto, 1981), 31.
3. HBCA, B.121/a/4, Manchester House journal, 1789–90, 19 Oct. 1789, fo. 23d; 21 Oct. 1789, fo. 24; William Walker to Mitchel Oman, 11 Dec. 1789, fo. 32; 19 Apr. 1790, fo. 51; 4 May 1790, fo. 52d; 22 June 1790, fo. 59d; 1 July 1790, fo. 60d; B.121/a/6, Manchester House journal, 1790–1, Walker to Thomas Stayner, 2 Mar. 1791, fos. 26d–27.
4. See Shirlee Anne Smith, 'William Walker', *Dictionary of Canadian Biography,* IV, 760–1.
5. HBCA, B.135/b/41, John Murphy to Thomas Vincent, 3 July 1821, 54.
6. HBCA, B.135/a/50, Moose Factory journal, 1770–1, 27 July 1771, fo. 41.
7. HBCA, B.22/a/4, Brandon House journal, 1796–7, 12 Nov. 1796, fo. 17d.
8. HBCA, B.42/a/123, Churchill journal, 1796–7, 26 Oct. 1796, fo. 4d; 9 Dec. 1796, fo. 6d; 3 Apr. 1797, fo. 9d; B.42/a/124, Churchill journal, 1797–8, 24 Oct. 1797, fo. 5d.
9. HBCA, B.59/a/79, Eastmain journal, 1801–2, 25 June 1802, fos. 23d–24; 28 June 1802, fo. 24; 30 June 1802, fo. 24d.
10. HBCA, B.60/z/3, 'Report of the Disobedience of Samuel Flaws, Laborer, at Moose Factory', 24–25 Aug. 1812, fos. 231–231d.
11. HBCA, B.239/c/4, Laurence Robertson to William Mactavish, 1 June 1847, fos. 12–14d.
12. HBCA, B.240/a/4, Yukon journal, 1850–1, 28 Aug. 1850, fos. 8d–9; 29 Aug. 1850, fo. 9; 31 Aug. 1850, fo. 9d.
13. HBCA, B.188/a/20, Fort St James journal, 1846–51, 16 May 1851, fo. 137d.
14. HBCA, B.60/a/37, Edmonton journal, 1869–71, 17 Aug. 1870, fo. 77.

15. See HBCA, B.28/a/1, Carlton House journal, 1795–6, 10 Jan. 1796, fo. 14; B.42/a/126, Churchill journal, 1801–2, 13 June 1802, fo. 5d, 7 July 1802, fo. 6d; B.135/a/92, Moose Factory journal, 1804–5, 26 Apr. 1805, fo. 31; B.135/a/114, Moose Factory journal, 1817, 15 June 1817, fo. 16; B.115/a/2, Lesser Slave Lake journal, 1818–19, 7 Mar. 1819, fo. 26d; B.154/c/1, Robert Cummings to George Barnston, 16 Mar. 1852, fo. 107; C.1/998, log of the *Princess Royal*, 1870, 3–4 July 1870, fos. 52–52d.
16. HBCA, B.3/a/113, Albany journal, 1809–10, 26 Aug. 1810, fo. 19d.
17. See, for example, HBCA, B.135/a/50, Moose Factory journal, 1770–1, 23 Dec. 1770, fo. 14d; 31 Mar. 1771, fo. 55d; 21 Apr. 1771, fo. 29; B.135/a/89, Moose Factory journal, 1801–2, 3 Jan. 1802, fo. 7d; B.135/a/91, Moose Factory journal, 1803–4, *passim;* B.135/a/92, Moose Factory journal, 1804–5, 24 Mar. 1805, fo. 25; B.135/a/100, Moose Factory journal, 1811–12, 1 Dec. 1811, fo. 7d; B.135/a/128, Moose Factory journal, 1825–6, 5 Feb. 1826, fo. 26d; 6 Aug. 1826, fo. 47; B.166/a/1, Portage de l'Ile journal, 2 Mar. 1794, fo. 16; B.239/a/66, York Factory journal, 1771–2, 19 Apr. 1772, fos. 42d–43; B.239/c/3, George Simpson to James Hargrave, 18 June 1841, fo. 225.
18. HBCA, A.10/79, R. Cowie to W. Armit, 24 Nov. 1869, fo. 547d.
19. Ron G. Bourgeault, 'The Indian, the Métis and the Fur Trade: Class, Sexism and Racism in the Transition from "Communism" to Capitalism', *Studies in Political Economy* 12 (Fall 1983), 69.
20. HBCA, B.42/a/126, Churchill journal, 1801–2, 7 July 1802, fo. 6d.
21. HBCA, A.10/41, 'Deposition of John MacIver', 16 Dec. 1857, fo. 8; A.67/1, statement of Murdo Macleod, 30 Nov. 1857, fo. 398d; B.135/c/2, George Barnley to Robert Miles, 19 Jan. 1847; B.154/c/1, Robert Cummings to George Barnston, 16 Mar. 1852, fo. 107. See Frits Pannekoek, 'The Rev. James Evans and the Social Antagonisms of the Fur Trade Society, 1840–1846', in Richard Allen, ed., *Canadian Plains Studies 3: Religion and Society in the Prairie West* (Regina, 1974), 9–12.
22. For other examples, HBCA, see B.3/a/101, Fort Albany journal, 1797–8, 21 Oct. 1797, fo. 4d; 3 July 1798, fo. 38; B.10/a/2, Attawapiscat journal, 1814–15, 24 June 1815, fo. 23d; B.42/a/122, Churchill journal, 1795–6, 30 June, 1–3 July 1796, fos. 14d–15; B.59/a/94, Eastmain journal, 1815–16, 21 Aug. 1815, fo. 6; B.104/a/1, Lac La Biche journal, 1799–1800, 6 Oct. 1799, fo. 15; B.239/b/63, J. Rowse, Peter Fidler, James Bird, and Henry Hallet to John Ballenden, 5 Aug. 1799, fo. 13; B.239/b/108, J.W. Wilson to Thomas Fraser, 23 Sept. 1865, fos. 450–2; B.239/c/15, J.A. Grahame to James R. Clare, 23 July 1864, fos. 108d–109; B.239/c/16, Wilson to officers of the Northern Department, 1 Dec. 1865, fos. 106d–107.

23. Great Britain, *Journals of the House of Commons* XXV, 'Report from the Committee appointed to inquire into the State and Condition of the Countries Adjoining to Hudson's Bay and of the Trade carried on there (24 April 1749)', London committee to Henry Sargeant, 22 May 1685, 274; Sargeant to committee, 24 Aug. 1685, 274.
24. Morton, *A History of the Canadian West*, 272–90.
25. HBCA, B.3/a/71, Fort Albany journal, 1776–7, 13 Aug. 1777, fo. 27d; B.78/a/3, Gloucester House journal, Aug. to Dec. 1777, 12–13 Nov. 1777, fo. 7d; B.3/a/74, Fort Albany journal, 1777–8, 16 June 1778, fo. 24d.
26. HBCA, B.3/a/73, Fort Albany journal, 1777–8, 'Tenting with the Indians', 20 June 1777–27 June 1778; B.211/a/1, Sturgeon Lake journal, 1779–80, 31 July 1779, fo. 1d; 2 Oct. 1779, fo. 15d; 31 Dec. 1779, fos. 22–22d; A.11/4, Thomas Hutchins to London committee, 14 Sept. 1780, fo. 121d; B.3/a/77, Albany journal, 1779–80, 21 June 1780, fo. 27d.
27. HBCA, B.239/a/38, York Factory journal, 1779–80, 5 July 1780, fo. 38.
28. HBCA, B.3/a/79, abstract of Fort Albany journal, 1780–1, May 1781, fos. 3–3d; B.59/a/56, Eastmain journal, 1780–1, 27 May 1781, fo. 28d.
29. HBCA, B.3/b/18, Germain Maugenest to Thomas Hutchins, 9 June 1781, fo. 32.
30. HBCA, B.239/a/90, York Factory journal, 1789–90, 12 July 1790, fo. 55.
31. HBCA, A.11/44, E.B. Kitchen to London committee, 19 Sept. 1779, fo. 93.
32. HBCA, B.42/b/44, London committee to Samuel Hearne and council, 19 May 1784, fo. 6; Churchill council to committee, Aug. 1786, fo. 22d.
33. HBCA, B.42/b/44, London committee to council at Churchill, 31 May 1799, fo. 68.
34. See B.3/a/74, Fort Albany journal, 1777–8, 16 June 1778, fo. 24d; B.3/a/102, Fort Albany journal, 1798–9, 8 July 1799, fo. 43; B.3/a/103, Fort Albany journal, 1799–1800, 9 July 1800, fo. 43d; B.49/a/31, Cumberland House journal, 1801–2, William Tomison to John Ballenden, 18 July 1801, fo. 2; B.239/a/91, York Factory journal, 1790–1, 23 July 1791, fo. 31d.
35. HBCA, B.64/e/1, Escabitchewan district report, 1819, fos. 1–1d.
36. HBCA, B.239/a/91, York Factory journal, 1790–1, 24 July 1791, fo. 32.
37. HBCA, B.59/a/79, Eastmain journal, 1801–2, fo. 27d; A.30/10, servants' list, 1800, fos. 19d–20.
38. HBCA, B.3/a/103, Fort Albany journal, 1799–1800, 29 Aug. 1800, fos. 32d–33; 20 Sept. 1800, fo. 35; 25–27 Sept. 1800, fos. 35d–36; B.3/a/104, Fort Albany journal, 1800–1, 28 Sept. 1800, fo. 1; 7 July 1801, fo. 44.

39. HBCA, B.14/a/1, Bedford House journal, 1796–7, 20 Nov. 1796, fo. 16d. See also HBCA, B.39/a/4, Fort Chipewyan journal, 1804–5, T. Swain to Peter Fidler, 23 Mar. 1805, fo. 14d; B.44/a/1, Fort Colvile journal, 1818–19, 29 Nov. 1818, fo. 12d; 12 Jan. 1819, fo. 14; 4 Feb. 1819, fo. 15, 9 Feb. 1819, fo. 15d; B.122/a/2, Manitoba District journal, 1818–19, 19 Dec. 1818, fo. 6d.
40. HBCA, B.231/a/4, Point Meuron journal, 1818–19, 8 Jan. 1819, fo. 17; 16 Jan. 1819, fo. 18; 13 Feb. 1819, fo. 21.
41. HBCA, B.149/a/9, Nipigon House journal, 1802–3, 30 Jan. 1803, fo. 5d; 25 Feb. 1803, fo. 5; 27 Feb. 1803, fos. 5 d–6.
42. HBCA, B.105/a/6, Lac La Pluie journal, 1818–19, 20 Apr. 1819, fo. 24.
43. HBCA, B.135/a/100, Moose Factory journal, 1811–12, 16–18 Jan. 1812, fo. 11.
44. HBCA, B.78/e/7, Gloucester House report, 1817–18, fo. 2d; A.30/16, servants' list, fos. 53d–54, 54d–55.
45. See HBCA, B.22/a/4, Brandon House journal, 1796–7, 19 Dec. 1796, fo. 23d; B.28/a/1, Carlton House, 1795–6, 10 Jan. 1796, fo. 14; B.39/a/5, Fort Chipewyan journal, 1805–6, 8 Dec. 1805, fo. 8; B.39/a/16, Fort Chipewyan journal, 1820–1, 29 June 1820, fo. 5d, 18 Aug. 1820, fo. 16d, 8 Sept. 1820, fo. 22d; Rich, ed., *Journal of Occurrences in the Athabaska Department,* 16 Oct. 1820, 82, 15 Nov. 1820, 109, 13 Apr. 1821, 319; B.39/a/17, Fort Chipewyan journal, 1821, 16 Feb. 1821, fo. 3d; B.42/a/134, Churchill journal, 1808–9, 19 July 1809, fo. 11; B.59/a/82, Eastmain journal, 1804–5, 13 June 1805, fo. 17d; B.155/a/33, Osnaburgh House journal, 13 Apr. 1821, fo. 17; B.155/a/79, Osnaburgh House journal, 1870–1, 27 Dec. 1870, fo. 17; 31 Dec. 1870, fo. 17.
46. HBCA, B.3/a/160, Fort Albany journal, 1850–1, 2 July 1850, fo. 4d; 16 July 1850, fo. 5d; B.3/b/81, Thomas Corcoran to Robert Miles, 29 June 1850, 11.
47. HBCA, A.12/8, George Simpson to London committee, 30 June 1857, fos. 491d–492; A.67/1, Norwegians' complaints, 1858, fo. 409; A.11/46, J.C. Arnesen to W.G. Smith, Sept. 1859, fos. 315–16.
48. HBCA, B.239/c/11, William Sinclair to James R. Clare, 21 June 1860, fos. 388d–389.
49. HBCA, A.11/18, Samuel McKenzie to Thomas Fraser, 31 July 1864, fos. 451–451d.
50. HBCA, B.239/c/16, J.W. Wilson to officers of the Northern Department, 1 Dec. 1865, fo. 106d; A.67/8, Characters of Servants Retiring to Europe P. Ships, 1865, fos. 44–5.
51. HBCA, A.11/116, Robert Davey, William Lewtit, Mitchell Oman, Magnus Twatt, Nicol Wishart, James Sandison, James Tate, Magnus Annal,

Charles Isham, James Spence, Edward Wishart, Thomas Johnston, William Folster, Thomas Tate, and John Irvine to William Tomison, 23 May 1781, fo. 83.

52. HBCA, A.11/116, Humphrey Marten and council to London committee, 1 Sept. 1781, fo. 92.

53. HBCA, A.6/15, London committee to council at Albany, 29 May 1794; B.22/a/1, Brandon House journal, 1793–4, *passim*; B.3/a99, Fort Albany journal, 1794–7, 1, 3 July 1796, fo. 25d; B.3/a/100, Fort Albany journal, 1796–7; B.155/a/12, Osnaburgh House, 1796–7, 11 June 1797, fos. 37d–38.

54. T.R. McLoy, 'John McKay', *Dictionary of Canadian Biography,* V (Toronto, 1983), 534–5; HBCA, B.3/a/104, 14 May 1801, fo. 15; B.155/a/15, Osnaburgh House journal, 1799–1800, 1 Dec. 1799, fo. 13d; 24 Dec. 1799, fo. 15; 25–27 Dec. 1799, fo. 15; B.123/a/10, Martins Fall journal, 23 July 1806, fo. 15d.

55. HBCA, B.42/a/124, Fort Churchill journal, 1797–8, 5 July 1798, fo. 19d; Glyndwr Williams, ed., *Hudson Bay Miscellany 1670–1870* (Winnipeg, 1975), 173.

56. HBCA, B.64/a/7, Escabitchewan journal, 1818–19, 31 July 1818, fo. 2; 11 Aug. 1818, fos. 2d–3; 14 Aug. 1818, fo. 3; 15 Aug. 1818, fos. 3–3d; B.64/e/1, Escabitchewan report, 1819, fos. 1d–2; B.105/a/6, Lac La Pluie journal, 1818–19, 5–6 Nov. 1818, fos. 8–8d.

57. HBCA, B.27/a/6, Carlton House (Saskatchewan) journal, 1816–17, 'Deposition of Thomas Costello', 8 Jan. 1817, fos. 11d–15; B.155/a/29, Osnaburgh House journal, 1816–17, fos. 2–9.

58. HBCA, A.5/2, London committee to John Thomas, 24 May 1786, fo. 142d.

59. See, for example, B.59/a/79, Eastmain journal, 1801–2, 25 June 1802, fo. 24; 24 Aug. 1802, fo. 30d; B.86/a/62, Henley House journal, 1812–13, 13 May 1813, 13; B.99/e/2, Kenogamissi report, 1814–15, fo. 1d; B.105/a/7, Lac La Pluie journal, 1819–20, 11 Jan. 1820, fo. 60; B.116/a/8, Fort Liard journal, 1829–30, 10 June 1829, fo. 1d; B.133/a/2, Mistassini journal, 1820–1, 29 Jan. 1821, fo. 11d; B.239/a/65, York Factory journal, 17 Aug. 1771, fo. 47; B.239/a/68, York Factory journal, 1772–3, 22 Feb. 1773, fo. 25d; B.239/c/1, George Simpson to George McTavish, 1 Jan. 1822, fo. 66; B.239/c/6, William H. Watt to William McTavish, 4 Mar. 1852, fos. 304–5.

60. J.M. Beattie, *Crime and the Courts in England 1660–1800* (Princeton, N.J., 1986), 461–4, 614.

61. E.P. Thompson, *The Making of the English Working Class* (Harmondsworth, 1968), 662 n.; Christopher Hill, 'Pottage for Freeborn Englishmen: Attitudes to Wage Labour in the Sixteenth and Seventeenth Centuries', in C.H. Feinstein, ed., *Socialism, Capitalism and*

Economic Growth: Essays Presented to Maurice Dobb (Cambridge, 1967), 343. See J.R. Dinwiddy, 'The Early Nineteenth-century Campaign against Flogging in the Army', *English Historical Review* 97, 383 (Apr. 1982), 308–31; E.E. Steiner, 'Separating the Soldier from the Citizen: Ideology and Criticism of Corporal Punishment in the British Armies, 1790–1815', *Social History* 8, 1 (June 1983), 19–35.

62. HBCA, B.42/b/44, London committee to council at Churchill, 25 May 1792, fos. 43–43d.
63. Payne, *'The Most Respectable Place in the Territory'*, 38–9; HBCA, B.42/a/124, Churchill journal, 1797–8, 12 Aug. 1798, fo. 22d.
64. See HBCA, B.117/a/4, Long Lake journal, 1818–19, 19 Aug. 1818, 5; B.145/e/11, New Brunswick report, 1820–1, fo. 11.
65. N.A.M. Rodgers, *The Wooden World: An Anatomy of the Georgian Navy* (Glasgow, 1986), 227; HBCA, B.154/a/5, Norway House journal, 1812–13, 5–6 Oct. 1812, fo. 3; William Auld to William Sinclair, 28 Jan. 1813, fos. 17–17d.
66. HBCA, B.223/c/1, William Burris to William Smith, 9 June 1836, fos. 100–1; London committee to James Douglas, 15 Nov. 1837, fos. 95d–96; 1826–50, Edward Clouston to committee, 8 Nov. 1837, fo. 102; Rich, ed. *Letters of John McLoughlin . . . Second Series,* McLoughlin to committee, 8 July 1839, 1–3; excerpt from letter from Douglas to committee, 16 Oct. 1838 (B.223/b/21, fos. 14–15), 2 n.; excerpt from letter from committee to Douglas, 15 Nov. 1840 (A.6/25, fo. 99d), 2 n.; HBCA, A.10/10, 'Unto the Governor and Directors of the Hnble Hudsons Bay Company the Petition of William Brown in Sandwick Orkney', 1840, fos. 124–124d.
67. Barry Cooper, *Alexander Kennedy Isbister: A Respectable Critic of the Honourable Company* (Ottawa, 1988), 111–14; Thomas E. Jessett, *Reports and Letters of Herbert Beaver, 1836–1838* (Portland, 1959), Beaver to Harrison, 15 Nov. 1836, 20; Beaver to Harrison, 10 Mar. 1837, 36–7; Beaver to Harrison, 19 Mar. 1838, 86–7; Beaver to Harrison, 19 Mar. 1838, 87–8; HBCA, A.11/69, declaration by James Logie and statement by Herbert Beaver, 19 Nov. 1836, fos. 35d–36; A.10/10, Beaver to William Brown, 5 Feb. 1840, fos. 127–128d.
68. W. Kaye Lamb, Introduction to *The Letters of John McLoughlin from Fort Vancouver to the Governor and Committee, First Series, 1825–38,* ed. E.E. Rich (Toronto, 1941), xxii–xxx.
69. HBCA, B.209/a/1, Fort Stikine journal, 1840–2, 17 Mar. 1741, fos. 29d–30; 29 Mar. 1841, fo. 31; 4 Sept. 1841, fo. 49.
70. HBCA, B.201/c/1, John McLoughlin Jr to Roderick Finlayson, 2 Dec. 1841, fo. 1; 14 Feb. 1842, fos. 3–3d; 26 Feb. 1842, fo. 5d.

71. HBCA, B.209/a/1, Fort Stikine journal, 1840–2, 20–1 April 1842, fos. 17d–18.
72. Glyndwr Williams, ed., *London Correspondence Inward from Sir George Simpson 1841–42* (London, 1973), Simpson to London committee, 6 July 1842, 161–2; Rich, ed., *Letters of John McLoughlin . . . Second Series*, McLoughlin Sr to committee, 24 June 1842, 43.
73. Rich, ed., *Letters of John McLoughlin . . . Second Series,* McLoughlin to London committee, 7 July 1842, 60–1; HBCA, A.12/2, George Simpson to committee, 28 July 1843, fo. 211; E.31/1, John McLoughlin Jr Papers, 1842–3, deposition of Thomas McPherson, 20 Aug. 1842, fos. 2–4; deposition of Kanakanui, 24 Aug. 1842, fo. 7; deposition of Powhow, Aug. 1842, fo. 9; deposition of Louis Leclaire, Aug. 1842, fo. 12.
74. W. Kaye Lamb concluded that the conspiracy existed because, although only Kanaquassé claimed there was a plot, he had apparently tried to shoot McLoughlin Jr before. Moreover, Lamb thought that McLoughlin Sr knew the men involved better than Simpson did and, therefore, was in a better position to judge. Lamb believed Kanaquassé's testimony and the depositions of Aug. 1842 and concluded that all punishments were deserved. He failed, however, to take into account the fact that McLoughlin Sr was, naturally enough, determined to clear his son's name, that, if Kanaquassé really was a scoundrel, his testimony might have been worthless, and that the depositions do not provide unequivocal support for Kanaquassé's allegations. It is, in fact, impossible to determine what actually happened, but given the tendency of fur trade historians to adopt the views of the officers, it is not surprising that Lamb would come down on McLoughlin Sr's side. See Lamb, Introduction to *Letters of John McLoughlin . . . First Series,* xxxiv–xli. At least Lamb did not, as Peter C. Newman did, describe how Pierre Kanaquassé 'produced a written pact, signed by all but one of Fort Stikine's staff members, swearing to murder McLoughlin and cover up the crime.' Peter C. Newman, *Caesars of the Wilderness, Company of Adventurers,* II (Markham, Ont., 1987), 294.
75. Van Kirk, *'Many Tender Ties',* 31.
76. HBCA, B.223/c/1, William Glen Rae to John McLoughlin, 18 Apr. 1843, fos. 190–190d; 20 Apr. 1843, fo. 194; E.13/a/1, John McLoughlin Jr Papers, 1842–3, 'Questions put to Mr Rodk Finlayson'.
77. HBCA, A.6/26, London committee to George Simpson, 1 June 1843, fo. 67; A.12/2, Simpson to committee, 28 July 1843, fos. 210d–211d; Rich, ed., *Letters of John McLoughlin . . . Second Series,* committee to John McLoughlin Sr, 27 Sept. 1843, 310–12.

78. MacLeod, ed., *Letters of Letitia Hargrave,* Letitia Hargrave to Dugald Mactavish Sr, 9 Sept. 1843, 149.
79. HBCA, B.47/z/1, depositions of Hilair Gibeault and Narcisse Forcier, 30 July 1842, fos. 1–2; Rich, ed., *Letters of John McLoughlin . . . Second Series,* 19 Aug. 1842, 66–7.
80. MacLeod, ed., *Letters of Letitia Hargrave,* Letitia Hargrave to Mrs. Dugald Mactavish, 10 Apr. 1843, 145–6.
81. HBCA, A.5/13, W. Smith to Edward Clouston, 20 Feb. 1840, 28.
82. Glyndwr Williams, 'Peter Skene Ogden', *Dictionary of Canadian Biography,* VII (Toronto, 1985), 660–2; Kenneth L. Holmes, 'Donald Manson', *Dictionary of Canadian Biography,* X (Toronto, 1972), 495–6; HBCA, B.188/c/1, George Simpson to Donald Manson, 18 June 1853, fo. 2; A.67/1, statement of Murdo Macleod, 26 Nov. 1857, fo. 397; 30 Nov. 1857, fos. 398–9.
83. Paul Kane, *Wanderings of an Artist among the Indians of North America From Canada to Vancouver's Island and Oregon through the Hudson's Bay Company's Territory and Back Again,* quoted in Mary Cullen, 'Outfitting New Caledonia 1821–58', in Carol M. Judd and Arthur J. Ray, eds, *Old Trails and New Directions: Papers of the Third North American Fur Trade Conference* (Toronto, 1980), 239.
84. HBCA, B.223/c/1, George Simpson to John McLoughlin Sr, 21 June 1843, fo. 196; Rich, ed., *Letters of John McLoughlin . . . Second Series,* McLoughlin to London committee, 18 Nov. 1843, 175–6.
85. HBCA, B.218/c/1, Johnson G. King to James Cameron, 1 Sept. 1850, fo. 5d.
86. HBCA, A.12/1, George Simpson to London committee, 1 Aug. 1823, fo. 25d. Historians have tended to accept Simpson's view. See, for example, John E. Foster, 'The Origins of the Mixed Bloods in the Canadian West', in R. Douglas Francis and Howard Palmer, eds, *The Prairie West: Historical Readings* (Edmonton, 1985), 92.
87. Rich, ed., *Letters of John McLoughlin . . . Second Series,* London committee to McLoughlin, 27 Sept. 1843, 307–8; HBCA, B.188/c/1, George Simpson to Donald Manson, 18 June 1853, fo. 1d–2d.
88. See HBCA, A.67/1, statement of John McIvor, 16 Dec. 1857, fo. 400; statement of Murdo Macdonald, n.d. Dec. 1857, fo. 400d; A.6/38, Thomas Fraser to A.G. Dallas, 24 Oct. 1863, fo. 186; William Christie to Fraser, 20 Feb. 1864, fo. 3; statement of Malcolm Groat, steward at Edmonton House, 14 Mar. 1864, fo. 6; deposition of Donald McDonald, clerk, 8 Mar. 1864, fos. 7–7d; deposition of Peter C. Pambrun, clerk, 4 Mar. 1864, fos. 8–8d; deposition of Louis Chastellain, clerk, 21 Mar. 1864, fos. 9–9d; statement of William Christie, 24 Feb. 1864, fos. 10–12; A.11/118, Christie to James R. Clare, 28 June 1864, fos.

458–61; A.12/43, Roderick McKenzie to A.G. Dallas, 18 Jan. 1864, fos. 191–191d.
89. HBCA, B.135/a/108, Moose Factory journal, 1815, 24–25 Apr. 1815, fos. 23–23d; Apr. 1815, fo. 25d; 6 May 1815, fo. 27; B.135/a/111, Moose Factory journal, 1815–16, 15 Dec. 1815, fo. 9; A.30/14, servants' list, 1814–15, fos. 51d–52; A.6/18, London committee to Thomas Thomas, 9 Apr. 1814, 164.
90. HBCA, A.10/5, 'The Memorial of Charles Marshall of No 5 Philpot Gt Commercial Road', 8 Nov. 1837, fos. 304d–305. Marshall was petitioning for payment of wages from 2 June until 15 Sept. because he had continued to perform his tin work.
91. HBCA, B.201/a/8, Fort Simpson journal, 1855–9, 23 Nov. 1855, fo. 25d; 26 Nov. 1855, fo. 25d.
92. HBCA, B.135/a/100, Moose Factory journal, 1811–12, 6 Mar. 1812, fo. 16; 9 Mar. 1812, fo. 16d; 30 Mar. 1812, fo. 18d; 8 Apr. 1812, fo. 19d.
93. HBCA, B.201/a/3, Fort Simpson journal, 1834–8, 31 May 1837, fos. 108–108d; 3 June 1837, fo. 110d.
94. HBCA, B.5/b/1, John Saunders to Peter Ogden, 11 Mar. 1862, fo. 18.
95. HBCA, B.125/a/116, Moose Factory journal, 1817–18, 27 June 1817, fo. 1d.
96. HBCA, B.153/a/4, North West River journal, 1840–1, 5 Aug. 1840, fo. 3.
97. HBCA, B.201/a/7, Fort Simpson journal, 1852–3, 2 June 1852, fo. 25.
98. HBCA, B.123/a/18, Martins Fall journal, 1819–20, 3–4 Aug. 1819, fo. 3d; 6 Aug. 1819, fo. 3d; 9–11 Aug. 1819, fos. 4–4d.
99. HBCA, B.235/a/3, Winnipeg journal, 1814–15, 20 Sept. 1814, fo. 8d.
100. HBCA, B.22/a/19, Brandon House journal, 1815–16, 15–16 Jan. 1816, fos. 14–14d; 23 Feb. 1816, fo. 19; 24 Feb. 1816, fo. 19.
101. HBCA, B.27/a/8, Carlton District journal, 1818–19, 1 Dec. 1818, fo. 14d; 26 Dec. 1818, fo. 18; 1 Jan. 1819, fo. 19; 14 Jan. 1819, fos. 20–20d; 25–26 Jan. 1819, fos. 21d–22; 8 Feb. 1819, fo. 27; 27 Feb. 1819, fo. 27; 19–20 Mar. 1819, fo. 29d.
102. Aboard ships the day was divided into six watches of four hours each. At the beginning of a voyage, the crew was divided into two groups, also called watches, which took their names from the side of the ship where they bunked and which worked around the clock in shifts. While one group was on deck, the other had watch below.
103. HBCA, C.1/613, log of the *Norman Morison,* 1849–51, 15 Nov. 1849, fo. 13; enclosure, 27 Nov. 1849; enclosure, 10 Feb. 1850; enclosure, 13 Feb. 1850; 14 Feb. 1840, fo. 58d; 17 Feb. 1850, fo. 60; enclosure, 24 Feb. 1850.
104. HBCA, B.201/a/7, Fort Simpson journal, 1852–3, 13 April 1853, fo. 62d; 15 Apr. 1853, fo. 63; 17 Apr. 1853, fo. 63d.

105. HBCA, B.3/c/3, Charles Savage to Alex MacDonald, 30 June 1866, fo. 254d.
106. Bryan D. Palmer, *Working-Class Experience: Rethinking the History of Canadian Labour 1800–1991* (Toronto, 1992), 42.

Chapter 6

1. HBCA, B.145/e/10, New Brunswick report, 1819–20, fo. 3d.
2. HBCA, A.6/20, London committee to George Simpson, 13 Mar. 1823, fo. 72d.
3. HBCA, A.11/118, William Auld to London committee, 26 Sept. 1811, fo. 29d.
4. NAC, MG19 A21, Donald Ross to James Hargrave, 7 Feb. 1844, 2812.
5. HBCA, A.12/1, George Simpson to London committee, 31 July 1830, fo. 368d.
6. HBCA, B.22/c/1, James Sutherland to Peter Fidler, 28 Mar 1816, fo. 2.
7. HBCA, A.12/1, George Simpson to London committee, 10 Aug. 1832, fo. 419d.
8. Ibid., 1 Aug. 1823, fos. 16–16d.
9. HBCA, D.1/10, William Williams to London committee, 10 Sept. 1823, fo. 11d.
10. HBCA, A.10/30, Edward Ellice to A. Barclay, 23 May 1851, fo. 415.
11. HBCA, B.239/c/10, George Simpson to officer in charge at York Factory, 21 June 1858, fo. 105.
12. HBCA, A.12/8, George Simpson to London committee, 26 June 1856, fos. 125, 130.
13. HBCA, B.135/a/174, Moose Factory journal, 1859–60, 2 June 1859, 1–2.
14. Reinhard Bendix, *Work and Authority in Industry: Ideologies of Management in the Course of Industrialization* (New York, 1956), xxi.
15. Robert W. Malcolmson, 'Workers' Combinations in Eighteenth-Century England', in Margaret C. Jacob and James R. Jacob, eds, *The Origins of Anglo-American Radicalism* (Atlantic Highlands, N.J., 1991), 170–1; E.J. Hobsbawm, 'Custom, Wages, and Work-Load in Nineteenth-Century Industry', in Asa Briggs and John Saville, eds, *Essays in Labour History* (London, 1960), 113–20; K.D.M. Snell, *Annals of the Labouring Poor: Social Change and Agrarian England, 1660–1900* (Cambridge, 1985), 10–14, 122–4, 168–70, 215; Hill, 'Pottage for Freeborn Englishmen', 340–4; A. Kussmaul, *Servants in Husbandry in Early Modern England* (Cambridge, 1981), 34–7.
16. Rediker, *Between the Devil and the Deep Blue Sea*, 150–1.
17. HBCA, A.67/1, statement of Murdo Macleod, 26 Nov. 1857, fo. 397d; A.11/46, J.C. Arnesen to W.G. Smith, Sept. 1859, fo. 315.

18. See Underdown, *Revel, Riot, and Rebellion*, 116–19; Rodger, *The Wooden World*, 229–35; G.E. Manwaring and Bonamy Dobrée, *Mutiny: The Floating Republic* (London, 1935), 8–11.
19. HBCA, A.6/12, London committee to Humphrey Marten, 13 May 1778, fo. 107d.
20. HBCA, B.239/a/38, York Factory journal, 1779–80, 5–6 July 1780, fo. 38.
21. HBCA, A.11/116, William Tomison to London committee, 16 July 1787, fo. 187; A.11/117, Tomison to committee, 10 July 1788, fo. 21d; B.239/a/91, York Factory journal, 1790–1, 7 July 1791, fo. 28; 23 July 1791, fo. 31d.
22. HBCA, B.60/a/5, Edmonton House journal, 1799–1800, in Alice M. Johnson, ed., *Saskatchewan Journals and Correspondence: Edmonton House, 1800–1902* (London, 1967), 1 Aug. 1799, 196–7; 3 Aug. 1799, 197; 5 Aug. 1799, 197; 6 Aug. 1799, 197–9; 18 Aug. 1799, 203–4; James Bird to Peter Fidler, 30 Aug. 1799, 206; 204 n. B.239/b/63, James Bird to James Bird, 4 Aug. 1799, fos. 17–17d.
23. HBCA, B.3/a/103, Fort Albany journal, 1799–1800, 9 July 1800; B.42/b/42, John Ballenden to Thomas Stayner, 4 Mar. 1800, 19–22; Stayner to Ballenden, 18 Mar. 1800, 26–7.
24. HBCA, B.49/a/31, Cumberland House journal, 1801–2, William Tomison to John Ballenden, 18 July 1801, fos. 2–2d; 8 Aug. 1801, fos. 5–5d.
25. HBCA, B.39/a/1, Fort Chipewyan journal, 1802–3, 7 Aug. 1802, fo. 1; 16 Mar. 1803, fo. 24; B.123/a/4, Martins Fall journal, 1797–8, 'Extract from General Letter', 31 May 1797, fo. 18; B.42/b/44, London committee to council at Churchill, 31 May 1799, fos. 68–68d.
26. HBCA, B.3/a/106, Fort Albany journal, 1803–4, 5 Sept. 1803, fo. 1; 18 July 1804, fo. 43d–44.
27. HBCA, B.123/a/10, Martins Fall journal, 1805–6, letter from John Hodgson, 11 Sept. 1805, fos. 1d–2d.
28. HBCA, B.42/a/136b, Churchill journal, 1811, 5–8 July 1811, fos. 6d–7d.
29. HBCA, B.60/a/15, Fort Edmonton journal, 1815–16, 1 Aug. 1816, fos. 49–49d.
30. See HBCA, B.118/a/2, Lesser Slave Lake journal, 1818–19, 30 June–1 July 1818, fo. 5; D.1/13, Colin Robertson to William Williams, 16 Feb. 1820, fos. 21–21d; B.42/a/145, Churchill journal, 1819–20, 1 July 1820, 7; Rich, ed., *Journal of Occurrences in the Athabaska Department*, 18 May 1821, 340.
31. HBCA, B.60/e/4, Fort Edmonton report, 1820–1, fos. 2d–3.
32. HBCA, A.12/9, George Simpson to London committee, 24 June 1858, fo. 146.
33. HBCA, B.109/a/4, John McBean to George Simpson, 8 Sept. 1830, n.p.

34. See HBCA, C.1/293, log of the *Eddystone,* 1810, 'List of officers and men on board'; C.1/312, log of the *Eddystone,* 1820, 'List of the Ship Eddystones Crew'; C.1/408, log of the *King George II,* 1800, 'Ship's Company'; C./981, log of the *Princess Royal,* 1859–65, crew's list; C.7/32, *Colinda*—miscellaneous papers, 1835–50, agreement, 24 Aug. 1835.
35. Eric Sager, *Seafaring Labour: The Merchant Marine of Atlantic Canada, 1820–1914* (Montreal, 1989), 156.
36. HBCA, A.10/28, Capt. Alexander John Weynton to Archibald Barclay, 29 Jan. 1850, fo. 248.
37. Bowsfield, ed., *Fort Victoria Letters, 1846–51,* James Douglas to Archibald Barclay, 27 Oct. 1849, 66–7; Douglas to Barclay, 3 Sept. 1849, 47–8.
38. Ibid., James Douglas to Archibald Barclay, 3 Apr. 1850, 76–8. For details, see HBCA, A.11/62, London correspondence inward—from Sandwich Islands, 1850, fos. 448, 451–7, 472–473d; Capt. A.J. Weynton to Barclay, 24 June 1850, fo. 466.
39. HBCA, C.1/613, log of the *Norman Morison,* 1849–51, 9–10 Apr. 1850, fos. 80–80d; 8 May 1850, fo. 83; 11 May 1850, fo. 83; 13 May 1850, fo. 84; 14 May 1850, fo. 84; B.223/c/2, Archibald Barclay to P.S. Ogden, James Douglas, and John Work, 1 Mar. 1851, fos. 4–4d.
40. HBCA, B.226/c/1, Archibald Barclay to James Douglas, 15 Nov. 1850, fo. 108d.
41. Rodger, *The Wooden World,* 26; HBCA, B.226/b/6, James Douglas to Archibald Barclay, 15 Jan. 1852, 2–3.
42. HBCA, B.226/b/6, James Douglas to Archibald Barclay, 15 Mar. 1853, 192.
43. HBCA, A.10/45, Capt. J.T. Trivett to W.G. Smith, 8 Mar. 1859, fos. 212–212d; A.6/39, Thomas Fraser to William Fraser Tolmie and board of management of the Western Department, 30 Sept. 1864, fo. 154d–155.
44. Alan Campbell and Fred Reid, 'The Independent Collier in Scotland', in Royden Harrison, ed., *Independent Collier: The Coal Miner as Archetypical Proletarian Reconsidered* (New York, 1978), 55–9.
45. Lynne Bowen, 'Independent Colliers at Fort Rupert: Labour Unrest on the West Coast, 1849', *The Beaver* 69, 2 (Mar. 1989), 28; H. Keith Ralston, 'Miners and Managers: The Organization of Coal Production on Vancouver Island by the Hudson's Bay Company, 1848–1862', in E. Blanche Norcross, ed., *The Company on the Coast* (Nanaimo, BC, 1983), 45; HBCA, A.67/1, colliers' indenture, 1850s.
46. Bowen, 'Independent Colliers at Fort Rupert', 29; HBCA, A.11/72, James Douglas to Archibald Barclay, 3 Apr. 1850, fos. 221–221d.

47. HBCA, A.11/72, James Douglas to Archibald Barclay, 8 Apr. 1850, fo. 222; John Muir Jr, Archibald Muir, John McGregor, John Smith, Robert Muir, Andrew Muir, and Michael Muir to Douglas, 27 Mar. 1850, fo. 222d; A.10/28, David Landale to Archibald Barclay, 17 June 1850, fos. 696–7.
48. HBCA, B.226/c/1, London committee to James Douglas, 25 Oct. 1850, fos. 84, 85; 'Extract from a letter from Mr John Muir dated Fort Rupert 2nd July 1850 to Archibald Barclay Esqre', fos. 86–7; Barclay to Muir, 25 Oct. 1850, fos. 112–13.
49. HBCA, A.11/73, James Douglas to Archibald Barclay, 24 Feb. 1851, fos. 72–4; A.6/29, Barclay to Douglas, 15 Nov. 1850, fo. 9d.
50. HBCA, A.11/72, James Douglas to Archibald Barclay, 17 Aug. 1850, fos. 291d–292d; B.226/b/3, Douglas to George Blenkinsop, 29 May 1851, fos. 99d–100; B.223/c/2, Barclay to officers in charge of Vancouver, 13 Dec. 1851, fos. 17–17d; B.226/c/1, Boyd Gilmour to Douglas, 22 Aug. 1851, fo. 165d; A.10/30, Gilmour to Barclay, 23 Aug. 1852, fos. 592–3.
51. HBCA, A/6/30, Archibald Barclay to James Douglas, 18 Nov. 1853, fos. 157d–158; B.226/b/14, Douglas to Barclay, 15 Mar. 1854, fos. 18–18d.
52. HBCA, A.5/18, Archibald Barclay to David Landale, 26 May 1853, 121–2; Barclay to Landale, 9 June 1853, 132–3; A.6/30, secretary to James Douglas, 17 June 1853, fo. 117d; Eric Newsome, *The Coal Coast: The History of Coal Mining in B.C.—1835–1900* (Victoria, 1989), 48.
53. HBCA, A.6/31, W.G. Smith to James Douglas, 21 Apr. 1854, fos. 23–23d; Randolph Sydney Vickers, 'George Robinson: Nanaimo Mine Agent', *The Beaver* Outfit 315, 2 (Nov. 1984), 46–7.
54. HBCA, B.226/b/14, James Douglas to Archibald Barclay, 11 Aug. 1854, fos. 30–30d; Douglas to Barclay, 25 Dec. 1854, fo. 37d; Douglas to Barclay, 22 April 1855, fos. 45–45d; Douglas to W.G. Smith, 24 July 1855, fo. 49d; A.6/31, Smith to Douglas, 31 Dec. 1855, fos. 204–204d; Douglas to Smith, 11 Oct. 1855, fos. 53–53d; A.6/32, Smith to Douglas, 16 May 1856, fos. 48d–49.
55. HBCA, B.226/b/14, James Douglas to W.G. Smith, 19 Dec. 1856, fo. 70; Douglas to Smith, 3 Dec. 1857, fo. 79; Douglas to Smith, 26 July 1858, fo. 86; Douglas to Thomas Fraser, 21 Oct. 1859, fo. 90; B.226/b/20, John Work to Fraser, 23 June 1860, 146; A.11/77, A.G. Dallas to Fraser, 16 Sept. 1860, fos. 715–18.
56. HBCA, B.3/b/28, Donald Mackay to Edward Jarvis, 4 Apr. 1791, fo. 33.
57. See, for example, HBCA, B.59/a/78, Eastmain journal, 1800–1, 11 Oct. 1800, fos. 2d–3; B.105/a/5, Lac La Pluie journal, 1817–18, 30 Mar. 1818, fo. 19; B.113/c/1, James Douglas to J.M. Yale, 27 June 1850, fos. 12d–13; B.115/a/3, Lesser Slave Lake journal, 1819–20; B.132/c/1,

William Gladman to Joseph LaRoque, 8 Mar. 1830, fo. 9d; B.135/a/84, Moose Factory journal, 1796–7, 11 Feb. 1797, fo. 16; 25 Feb. 1797, fo. 17d; B.135/b/25, H. Moze to J. Thomas, 10 Apr. 1800, fo. 61d; B.135/b/26, R. Good to J. Thomas, 11 July 1802, fo. 83; B.159/a/2, Fort Pelly journal, 1795–6, 12 Oct. 1795, fo. 5; B.166/a/1, Portage de l'Ile journal, 1793–4, 20 Apr. 1793, fo. 1d; 26 Oct. 1793, fo. 8; 21 Feb. 1794, fo. 15d; B.198/a/122, Fort Severn journal, 1869–71, 7 June 1869, fo. 1d; B.227/a/1, Waswanipi journal, 1820–1, John Walford to Richard Hardisty, 16 Oct. 1820, fos. 9d–10; B.239/a/67, York Factory journal, 1772–3, 27 May 1773, fo. 39d; B.239/a/90, York Factory journal, 1789–90, 16 Oct. 1789, fo. 7d; 18 Feb. 1790, fo. 23d; 14 Mar. 1790, fos. 27d–28; B.239/a/104, York Factory journal, 30 June 1800, fo. 46; B.239/a/105, York Factory journal, 1800–1, 7 Mar. 1801, fo. 32; B.239/b/105, James Hargrave to George Simpson, 26 May 1858, fo. 91; B.239/c/2, Thomas Spence to 'James Halgrieve', 2 Mar. 1835, fo. 98. Spence, in charge of the sawing tent, also had to put up with the sawyers' grumbling about the 'howers' he made them work.
58. HBCA, B.3/a/101, Fort Albany journal, 4 July 1798, fo. 38. See, for example, HBCA, B.59/a/79, Eastmain journal, 1801–2, 27 Feb. 1802, fo. 14; B.135/a/95, Moose Factory journal, 1807–8, 17 Oct. 1807, fo. 2d; B.135/a/100, Moose Factory journal, 1811–12, 19 Oct. 1811, fo. 3; 2–3 Dec. 1811, fos. 7d–8; 25 Apr. 1812, fo. 21d; B.235/a/3, Winnipeg journal, 1814–15, 8 Aug. 1814, fo. 2; 9 Aug. 1814, fo. 2.
59. HBCA, B.42/b/32, Joseph Colen to Churchill, 12 April 1790, fo. 4d.
60. HBCA, B.49/a/31, Cumberland House journal, 1801–2, 12 Nov. 1802, fos. 14d–15.
61. HBCA, B.85/a/2, Fort Halkett journal, 1830–1, 28 Dec. 1830, fo. 12.
62. HBCA, E.37/1, Chief Factor James Anderson (a) Papers—journey, 1850, 25 June-2 July 1850, fos. 8–8d.
63. HBCA, B.239/c/17, Robert Campbell to J.W. Wilson, 11 Nov. 1867, fo. 221d.
64. HBCA, B.3/a/78, Fort Albany journal, 1780–1, 15 Sept. 1780, fo. 2.
65. HBCA, B.22/a/4, Brandon House journal, 1796–7, 6 Dec. 1796, fo. 22d.
66. HBCA, B.104/a/1, Lac La Biche journal, 1799–1800, 6 Oct. 1799, fo. 15.
67. HBCA, B.22/a/18b, Brandon House journal, 1812, 16 Apr. 1812, fos. 14–14d.
68. HBCA, B.372/a/3, Great Whale River journal, 1815–16, 9 Mar. 1816, fos. 12–12d; 19–20 Apr. 1816, fo. 15d; 29 June 1816, fo. 20d; 5 July 1816, fos. 22d–23.
69. HBCA, B.59/a/94, Eastmain journal, 1815–16, 22 Oct. 1815, fo. 12d; 31 Oct. 1815, fos. 13d–14; 8 Nov. 1815, fos. 16–16d; 12 Jan. 1816, fo. 21d; 13 Jan. 1816, fo. 22; 21 Jan. 1816, fo. 22d; 25 Jan. 1816, fos.

23–23d; 28 Jan. 1816, fos. 23d–24; 3 Feb. 1816, fo. 24d; 16 Feb. 1816, fo. 26; 6 Apr. 1816, fo. 30d; B.59/e/3, Eastmain report, 1815–16, 18 Jan. 1816, fo. 1d; B.145/b/1, Thomas Vincent to Lord Selkirk, 22 Oct. 1816, 8.

70. HBCA, B.59/a/96, Eastmain journal, 1816–17, 23 Oct. 1816, fo. 11d; 25 Jan. 1817, fos. 25d–26; 29 Apr. 1817, fos. 43–4; B.3/a/120, Fort Albany journal, 1816–17, Jacob Corrigal to Joseph Beioley, 16 Nov. 1816, fos. 9–9d; 20 Nov. 1816, fo. 10; 5 Dec. 1816, fo. 12; Mark Prince to Jacob Corrigal, 20 Apr. 1817, fo. 30d; 18 May 1817, fos. 34–34d; B.135/a/113a, Moose Factory journal, 1816–17, 29 Oct. 1816, fo. 15; B.135/a/116, Moose Factory journal, 1817–18, 19 Aug. 1817, fo. 11d; 20 Aug. 1817, fo. 12.

71 See HBCA, B.22/a/19, Brandon House journal, 1815–16, 30 July 1815, fo. 2; B.59/e/4, Eastmain report, 1816–17, fo. 2; B.239/c/3, Robert Harding to John Charles, 27 Mar. 1837, fo. 21d; A.11/70, Peter Skene Ogden and James Douglas to London committee, 28 July 1846, fo. 214.

72. Rich, ed., *Journal of Occurrences in the Athabaska Department*, 27 Sept. 1820, 60; 29 Sept. 1820, 6; Simpson to William Williams, 30 Nov. 1820, 119–20.

73. HBCA, B.134/c/9, C. Cumming to James Keith, 12 Jan. 1831, fo. 24.

74. HBCA, B.201/a/7, Fort Simpson journal, 1852–3, 20 Nov. 1852, fo. 42; 4 July 1853, fos. 74d–75.

75. HBCA, B.5/a/10, Fort Alexandria journal, 1858–60, 18–19 Nov. 1858, fos. 46d–47.

76. HBCA, A.12/43, A.G. Dallas to London committee, 18 Oct. 1862, fo. 27d.

77. HBCA, B.39/c/1, George Simpson to Edward Smith, 1 June 1835, fo. 9; B.3/b/65, Simpson to George Barnston, 1 Mar. 1840, fo. 2. See HBCA, A.12/6, Simpson to London committee, 19 Sept. 1853, fo. 442d; B.39/b/14, Robert Campbell to William Mactavish, 9 July 1857, 11; B.60/a/30, Edmonton journal, 1858–60, 17 Oct. 1858, fos. 4–4d; B.227/a/19, Waswanipi journal, 1840–1, 16 June 1840, fo. 1d; B.239/c/5, William McKay to James Hargrave, 11 Feb. 1849, fos. 8–8d.

78. HBCA, A.12/9, George Simpson to Thomas Fraser, 20 Oct. 1858, fos. 281d–282; E.61/10, McGowan Collection, William McMurray correspondence, 1864, W.I. Christie to William McMurray, 27 Dec. 1864, fo. 29.

79. HBCA, A.11/51, Donald A. Smith to London committee, 1 Aug. 1870, fos. 87d–91; B.239/k/28, Standing Rules and Regulations, 1843–75, Nos. 52, 89, 90.

80. HBCA, B.239/b/105, James Hargrave to George Barnston, 17 Aug. 1857, fo. 41d.

81. HBCA, B.239/c/17, W.L. Hardisty to J.W. Wilson, 18 Aug. 1867, fos. 199–199d.
82. HBCA, B.239/b/104b, William Mactavish to George Simpson, 5 Sept. 1855, fo. 89d.
83. HBCA, B.239/c/16, J.A. Grahame to J.W. Wilson, 23 Aug. 1856, fo. 90.
84. HBCA, B.239/c/9, George Barnston to James Hargrave, 15 Aug. 1857, fo. 261; Barnston to Hargrave, 22 Aug. 1857, fo. 265.
85. HBCA, B.239/b/107, James R. Clare to William Mactavish, 29 Aug. 1862, fo. 144d.
86. HBCA, B.239/c/14, William Mactavish to officers of the Northern Department, 9 Dec. 1863, fo. 322d.
87. HBCA, A.12/44, Mactavish to Thomas Fraser, 19 Sept. 1865, fos. 67–67d; B.239/b/108, J.W. Wilson to James R. Clare, 13 Sept. 1865, fo. 441; B.239/c/16, James A. Graham to officers of the Northern Department, 24 Dec. 1865, fo. 116d.
88. HBCA, B.239/b/108, J.W. Wilson to officers of the Northern Department, 1 Dec. 1867, fo. 783; B.154/c/1, Wilson to J.A. Grahame, 7 Sept. 1866, fo. 164; B.239/c/16, William Mactavish to officers of the Northern Department, 8 Dec. 1866, fos. 267d, 270.
89. HBCA, B.239/c/17, James Stewart to J.W. Wilson, 26 Aug. 1867, fo. 206; Stewart to officers of the Northern Department, Dec. 1867, fos. 236–236d; B.239/c/18, Stewart to officers of the Northern Department, 7 Dec. 1868, fo. 186.
90. HBCA, B.239/c/18, William Cowan to Samuel K. Parsons, 10 Dec. 1868, fo. 188d.
91. HBCA, A.11/51, Donald A. Smith to W.G. Smith, 1 Aug. 1870, fos. 88d–89d; B.239/b/110, W. Parson to Robert Hamilton, 8 Sept. 1870, fo. 78; Parson to Hamilton, 10 Sept. 1870, fo. 79; Parson to Hamilton, 11 Sept. 1870, fo. 80; B.239/c/19, J. Fortescue to officers of the Northern Department, 26 Dec. 1870, fo. 248; Ray, *The Canadian Fur Trade in the Industrial Age,* 18–19.
92. 'Hudson's Bay Company's Code of Penal Laws, Published at Moose Factory, Sept. 1, 1815: Public Notice By Thomas Vincent, Esquire, Governor of the Southern Territories of Rupert's Land', in Oliver, ed., *The Canadian North-West,* II (Ottawa, 1915), 1285–7. Contrary to Oliver's heading, this document does not appear to be a penal code published by the HBC, but rather a notice intended to remind the servants of the laws to which they were subject.
93. See Manwaring and Dobrée, *Mutiny: The Floating Republic.*
94. HBCA, B.22/a/18a, Brandon House journal, 1810–11, 5–6 Nov. 1810, fo. 7d; B.22/z/1, 'Papers relating to the mutiny at Brandon House', 1811, fos. 1–15; B.156/c/1, Hugh Heney to William Sinclair, 21 June 1811, fos. 1–3; B.42/a/136a, 'Mr Aulds Memorandum Book',

1810–11, fo. 31; B.145; A.11/16, William Auld to London committee, Aug. 1811, fos. 5–5d.
95. HBCA, B.22/a/4, Brandon House journal, 1796–7, 19–20 Nov. 1796, fos. 19–19d; 20 Apr. 1797, fos. 35d–36; 22 Apr. 1797, fo. 36; B.22/a/5, Brandon House journal, 1797–8, 1–2 Sept. 1797, fos. 4d–5d; 4–5 Nov. 1797, fos. 15d–17; 23 Nov. 1797, fos. 19–20; A.10/1, 'Copies of Certificates and other Documents referred to In the Petition of William Yorston To the Honble Directors of the Hudsons Bay Compy', fos. 111A–111Dd; A.30/6, servants' list, 1794–5, fos. 47d–48, 52d–53, 54d–55, 56d–57, 57d–58.
96. HBCA, B.239/b/83, William Auld to Hugh Heney, Jan. 1813, fo. 8d.
97. HBCA, B.3/f/4, Albany River servants' resolves, 1806, fo. 3; B.3/f/6, Albany River servants' resolves, 1808, fo. 2.
98. HBCA, B.22/a/18b, Brandon House journal, 1811–12, 5 Jan. 1812, fos. 7d–8; 8 Jan. 1812, fo. 8; B.22/z/1, 'Papers relating to the mutiny at Brandon House', 1811, fo. 8.
99. HBCA, A.10/1, 'Copies of Certificates and other Documents referred to In the Petition of William Yorston To the Honble Directors of the Hudsons Bay Compy', fos. 111Dd–111G, 111Jd.
100. HBCA, B.22/a/18b, Brandon House journal, 1811–12, 1 Apr. 1812, fo. 13d; 8 Jan. 1812, fo. 9.
101. All the insurgents appear in the list of passengers aboard the HBC's vessels in 1811, destined for the Red River Colony. See J.M. Bumsted, *The People's Clearance: Highland Emigration to British North America, 1770–1815* (Winnipeg, 1982), app. B, Passenger List XVII, Red River Settlers, 1811, 281. Whether these men were recruited specifically for the colony, however, is unclear, since it was not until after their arrival at York Factory that Miles Macdonell and William Hillier selected their men, leading to complaints from the latter that Macdonell had left him with 'a parcel of the rubbish' and from William Auld that Macdonell's requirements deprived the HBC of manpower. HBCA, B.42/b/57, Auld to Macdonell, 16 Oct. 1811, fos. 2–2d; Auld to William Hemmings Cook, 19 Nov. 1811, fo. 11.
102. HBCA, B.42/b/57, Miles Macdonell to William Auld, 23 Dec. 1811, fo. 17; Macdonell to Auld, 27 Feb. 1812, fo. 20; B.239/b/82, Macdonell to William Hemmings Cook, 14 Feb. 1812, fos. 18d–19; Cook to Macdonell, 15 Feb. 1812, fo. 19d; Macdonell to Cook, 15 Feb. 1812, fo. 20; Cook to Macdonell, 16 Feb. 1812, fo. 20; Macdonell to Cook, 31 Mar. 1812, fo. 28; Morton, *History of the Canadian West*, 538–9; Oliver, ed., *The Canadian North-West*, I, 176–7.
103. HBCA, B.42/b/57, William Auld to Miles Macdonell, 30 Apr. 1812, fos. 35–35d; William Auld's remarks, fos. 38–9; Macdonell to Auld, 3 May

1812, fo. 39d; Auld to Macdonell, 10 May 1812, fos. 41d–42; B.239/a/118, York Factory journal, 1811–12, 30 Apr. 1812, fos. 11d–12.
104. HBCA, B.42/b/57, remarks by William Auld, fo. 43; Miles Macdonell to Auld, 12 May 1812, fos. 42d–43.
105. HBCA, B.42/b/57, William Auld to Miles Macdonell and William Hillier, 13 May 1812, fos. 44–44d; notification to be read to insurgents, 15 May 1812, fo. 44d.
106. HBCA, B.42/b/57, Miles Macdonell and William Hillier to William Auld, 15 May 1812, fos. 46–46d.
107. HBCA, B.42/b/57, 'From the Men off Duty to Mr Auld, Nelson River 15th May 1812', signed Andrew Mcfarlane, James Robertson, Daniel Campbell, John Chambers, William Brown, John Macintyre, George Merriman, Murdoch Rosie, Peter Barr, William Anderson, James Urie, John Walker, fos. 47–47d; Miles Macdonell to William Auld, 10 Apr. 1812, fo. 31; Auld to Macdonell, 30 Apr. 1812, fos. 34d–35; remarks by Auld, fos. 58–58d.
108. HBCA, B.42/b/57, William Hillier to William Auld, 15 May 1812, fo. 45; Miles Macdonell to Auld, 15 May 1812, fo. 45d; Auld to Macdonell and Hillier, 16 May 1812, fos. 46d–48.
109. HBCA, B.42/b/57, Miles Macdonell to William Auld, 22 May 1812, fo. 51d; Macdonell to Auld, 24 May, 1812, fo. 52d; remarks by Auld on Macdonell's letter, fos. 52d–53; B.239/a/118, York Factory journal, 1811–12, 24–25 May 1812, fo. 14; 13 June 1812, fo. 16; B.239/b/82, William Hemmings Cook to Mr Swain, 20 July 1812, fo. 36d; A.30/14, servants' list, 1814–15, Andrew McFarlin, fos. 2d–3; Hugh Carswell, fos. 5d–6; John McIntyre, Murdoch Rossie, fos. 7d–8; Peter Spence, George Merriman, fos. 14d–15; James Robertson, fos. 25d–26; William Brown, fos. 30d–31. Brown was now a trader. B.60/a/15, Edmonton journal, 1815–16, 7 Aug. 1816, fo. 51.
110. HBCA, B.42/b/57, William Auld to Thomas Thomas, 10 June 1812, fos. 57–57d; remarks by William Auld, fos. 58–58d.
111. HBCA, B.42/b/57, William Hemmings Cook to William Auld, 23 Dec. 1811, fo. 14.
112. Rich, ed., *Letters of John McLoughlin . . . First Series,* James Douglas to London committee, 10 Oct. 1838, 247.
113. Rich, ed., *Letters of John McLoughlin . . . First Series,* McLoughlin to London committee, 26 Oct. 1837, 190–3; James Douglas to George Simpson, 18 Mar. 1838, 274–6.
114. G.R. Newell, 'William Henry McNeill', *Dictionary of Canadian Biography,* X, 484–5; HBCA, E.31/2, A. Randall to George Gordon, 22 Oct. 1838.

115. Milton Rugoff, Afterword to William Bligh, *The Mutiny on Board the H.M.S. Bounty* (New York, 1961), 228, 231, 233; Richard Henry Dana Jr, *Two Years before the Mast and Twenty-Four Years After* (New York, 1909), 104–9, 374–7.
116. Rediker, *Between the Devil and the Deep Blue Sea,* 205–53.
117. HBCA, B.201/a/3, Fort Simpson journal, 1834–8, 26–31 Jan. 1838, fos. 166d–70.
118. Ibid., 31 May 1837, fos. 108–108d; 3 June 1837, fo. 110d; B.201/z/1, deposition of Capt. W.H. McNeill, 19 Aug. 1839, fos. 2d–4; deposition of Peter Duncan, fos. 7–7d.
119. HBCA, A.10/8, James Starling, George Gordon, and William Willson to London committee, n.d., received 13 May 1839, fos. 309–309d; A.6/25, committee to James Douglas, 31 Oct. 1838, fo. 11; B.223/c/1, committee to John McLoughlin Sr, 14 Sept. 1839, fos. 130d–131.
120. HBCA, A.12/2, Simpson to London committee, 20 June 1845, fos. 532–532d.
121. HBCA, A.11/70, Peter Skene Ogden and James Douglas to London committee, 20 Sept. 1847, fos. 268d–269.
122. HBCA, B.226/b/13, James Douglas to W.G. Smith, 27 Dec. 1855, fo. 35d; Douglas to Smith, 14 Feb. 1856, fos. 41–41d.
123. See Marcus Rediker, '"Under the Banner of King Death": The Social World of Anglo-American Pirates, 1716 to 1726', *William and Mary Quarterly* 3rd ser., 38 (Apr. 1981), 203–27.

Index

Aboriginals. *See* Native peoples
Aborigines' Protection Society, 179
Absent without leave, 113, 120, 144, 153–5
Adams, Joseph, 66
Aitkin, Alexander, 152
Alder, Thomas, 215
All Saints' Day, 13
American army, 175
American collieries, 211
American Revolution, 83
American traders, 6, 94, 102, 183
Antler Creek, 155
Apprentices and apprenticeship, 25, 49, 54, 65–7, 90–1, 128, 142, 176, 205
Arnesen, J.C., 170, 199
Arthur, Peter, 241, 242
Artisanal culture, 42–3, 140–1, 148, 159, 186–7
Artisans and craftsmen, 27, 82, 140–1, 148, 186, 198, 223. *See also* Tradesmen
Assiniboia, 94
Assiniboine River, 225
Athabasca district, 85, 92, 218
Athabaska River, 8
Auld, William, 82, 147, 158, 173, 176, 194, 225, 228, 229, 231–8 *passim*
Australia, 96, 103, 105

Authority, 2, 11, 14, 15, 18, 19, 21, 23, 26, 29, 33, 34, 174, 193, 199, 247; indifference to, 110, 157

Baikie, Peter, 176
Bain, A., 99
Bain, Laurence, 161
Barnston, George, 49, 124, 126, 131, 220
Bates, Arthur, 146–7
Beads, Charles, 112
Beatings, 179, 183, 184, 185. *See also* Discipline, physical
Beaver, 112, 141, 177, 188, 203, 239, 241
Beaver, Rev. Herbert, 178–9
Beaver Lake House, 35
Beaver River, 200
Beioley, Joseph, 187, 216
Bellingham Bay, 211
Bendix, Reinhard, 196
Bews, William, 59, 124
Bigger, Walter, 143
Bird, James, 38, 147, 202, 237
Bird, Thomas, 66
Black, John, 135
Black Island, 131
Blanshard, Richard, 205
Blenkinsop, George, 180, 209, 210

Bligh, Capt. William, 225, 240
Boats, 89, 91–2, 130, 137, 141, 142, 174, 200, 201, 203, 219, 220, 221, 222, 223
Bolland, William, 143, 159, 166
Bonuses, 5, 32, 44–5, 46, 55, 78, 79–80, 165, 166, 208, 210, 251
Botany Bay, 176
Boucher, François, 95
Boulton, Watt and Co., 141
Bounties. *See* Bonuses
Bounty, HMS, 224, 225
Bourgeault, Ron, 161
Brandon House, 94, 131, 132, 136, 137, 158, 172, 173, 214, 225, 228, 229
Brandon House mutiny, 18, 111–12, 115–16, 225–32, 238
Brazil, 22
Bright, William, 65
British army, 4, 33, 78, 175, 223, 224, 236
British navy, 4, 33, 78, 128, 164, 203, 205, 223, 224–5, 236, 238
Brown, James, 188
Brown, Jennifer, 123
Brown, William (officer), 115
Brown, William (servant), 178, 179, 248
Brown, William (servant), 235
Buchan, John, 164
Budge, Gilbert, 147
Burg, B.R., 128–9
Burris, William, 177, 178, 242

California, 154–5, 179, 203, 204, 210, 212
Cameron, Hugh, 174
Cameron, John Dugald, 95
Campbell, Robert, 49, 155, 214
Canada, 5, 54, 58, 74, 92, 93, 96, 97, 100, 101, 103, 145, 183
Canada Jurisdiction Act (1803), 232
Canadians, 4, 8, 13, 27, 35, 39, 54, 74–8, 80, 81, 85–96 *passim*, 100, 102, 118, 129, 136, 149, 154, 163, 164, 167, 173, 174, 184, 195, 196, 202, 214, 227, 228, 229, 236; traders, 138, 148, 151, 162, 163
Canoes, 75, 76, 77, 85, 87, 92, 96, 138, 145, 157, 200, 206, 217
Cape Horn, 6
Capitalist system, 197
Capusco, 216
Carless, Joseph, 141
Carr, Thomas, 129
Carswell, Hugh, 237
Cartwright, John, 29, 175, 224
Cat-o'-nine-tails, 150, 175, 182, 239
Cavinough (Cavinor), Patrick, 174
Cedar Lake, 218
Celebrations, 13, 76, 123, 131
'Celtic Fringe' of England, 67
Celts, 195
Certificates of good character, 74
Charity schools, 65, 66
Charles, John, 173
Charlton Island, 215
Christie, Alexander, 47, 85
Christie, W.J., 124, 152, 218
Christmas, 13, 20, 30, 76, 123 132, 133, 134, 181, 189, 213
Christ's Hospital, London (Blue Coat School), 66
Churchill River, 219
Clapham sect, 179
Clare, James R., 62
Clark, George, 31
Clarke, John, 38–9, 87
Class, 15, 67, 71, 90, 93, 100, 122–3, 127, 141, 155, 161, 175, 244; middle class, 48, 125–6; working class, 12, 21, 161, 244
Clergy, 102; Roman Catholic, 134
Clouston, Edward, 59, 60, 96–7, 99, 106, 107, 178
Clouston, James, 137–8
Clouston, John, 194
Clouston, Rev. William, 78, 79, 178
Clowes, William, 66
Coalmining and coalminers, 7, 13, 47, 101, 118, 152, 197, 203, 207–12, 243, 246

Cole, Capt., 182
Colen, Joseph, 74, 77, 164, 213
Colinda, 101, 211
Collective action. *See* Combination
Columbia, 136, 204, 242
Columbia Department, 6, 7, 59, 60, 95–6, 146, 169
Columbia district, 6, 177, 183
Columbia River, 6, 205
Combination, 31, 79, 102, 113, 120, 195–224 *passim*, 244
Combination Acts (1799, 1800), 120, 196
'Commercial aristocracy of Montreal', 48
Competition, 4, 5, 26, 35, 48, 73, 118, 157, 162, 200
Contracts of employment, 15, 16, 26, 27, 28–9, 34, 35, 42, 44, 62–3, 73, 77, 78, 86, 89, 98–107 *passim*, 111, 120, 131, 141, 144, 150, 153, 155, 159, 163, 170, 187, 192, 194, 199, 200, 202, 203, 209, 211, 223, 245, 246, 247, 251
Cook, William Hemmings, 233, 237
Cooper, John, 125
Corcoran, Thomas, 130
Corporal punishment, 151, 174–5, 176, 178, 184–5, 224, 239; as deterrent, 175, 217. *See also* Discipline; Flogging
Corrigal, Jacob, 152, 216
Corrigal, James, 174
Corrigal, Jasper, 172–3
Corrigal, William, 168
Corston, James, 167–8
Cowie, John, 99
Cowie, Robert, 135
Cowlitz, 154, 204, 205
Cowlitz Farm, 182
Crebassa, John, 95
Cromartie, John (officer), 125
Cromartie, John (servant), 32
Cromartie, John (servant), 137, 216
Crouch, Henry, 65
Crowe, H.W., 102, 104

Crowe, J.R., 100
Culture, 12, 122, 123, 136, 148, 155, 246, 255 n.7
Cumberland House, 3, 36, 91, 200, 201, 219, 221
Cunningham, Richard, 198
Curry, Archibald, 188–9
Customs and customary practice, 42, 123, 131–2, 133, 134, 144, 162, 198, 213, 218. *See also* Celebrations

Dallas, Alexander Grant, 218
Dana, Richard Henry, Jr, 240
Daniel, John, 168
Davis Strait fisheries, 92
Dearness, William, 130
Debtors' prison, 99, 187
Deed Poll, 49, 53–4, 61
Deers Lake, 125
Denial of duty, 18, 156–92. *See also* Refusal to do as ordered
Denmark and Danes, 85, 86, 100
Desertion and deserters, 17, 58, 63, 94, 101, 105, 106–7, 113, 119, 125, 144, 145, 149, 153–5, 158, 174, 192, 203–7, 212, 220, 223, 224
Destitute Sailors' Asylum, 60
Dickson, James, 179
Director, HMS, 225
Discipline, 40, 62, 104, 115, 157, 158, 176, 240, 243; military, 224; physical, 14, 112, 129, 137, 143, 149, 172, 174, 175, 179, 180, 181, 182, 183, 192, 217, 231, 240, 242–3. *See also* Fines; Half-allowance
Dogs, 114, 121, 145, 153, 164, 166, 186, 189
Donald, John, 241
Douglas, James, 133, 177, 179, 181, 204–6, 209, 210, 211, 212, 238, 243
Down, Joseph, 32
Drinking and drunkenness, 11, 17, 30, 42, 58, 76, 82, 83, 88, 101, 104, 109, 110, 112, 113, 114, 115, 117, 118, 120, 124, 130, 131–9, 143, 145, 153, 155, 171, 174, 177, 180,

182, 194, 204, 222, 226, 227, 229, 240, 243
Drowning, 138, 183
Dudley, Robert, 168
Duffle, William, 117, 175
Duncan, Peter, 242
Dunch, Thomas, 109–10, 117

Easter, John, 229
East India Company, 256 n.15
Eastmain, 36, 117, 137, 138, 140, 148, 158, 166, 168, 215, 216
Eddystone, 215
Edmonton district, 237
Edmonton House, 125, 140, 201
Edward & Anne, 81
Edwards, Edward, 205
Élite, 3, 10, 19, 21, 24, 34, 50, 60, 67, 71, 121, 127, 196, 199
Embezzlement, 147, 153
Emerald, 216
Emigration Advances Act (1851), 98
England, 2, 85, 101, 148, 191, 223, 236
England, 138, 210
English colliers, 211
English River district, 170
Ens, Gerhard, 154
Equipments, 26, 27, 41, 91, 92
Esquimalt, 208
Ethnicity and racial stereotypes, 11–13, 16, 47, 67–8, 70, 77–8, 92, 93, 96, 102, 112, 127, 136, 176, 809, 186, 194–6, 244, 246
Ewing, John, 150, 160–1, 175
Explorers, 1, 162

Favel, John, 189
Favel, Thomas, 230
Fidler, Peter, 188–9, 201, 214
Fighting, 35, 82, 104, 117, 131, 132, 137, 145, 152, 159, 176, 177, 196
Filpt, William, 29, 175, 224
Fines, 23, 33–4, 93, 99, 112, 124, 130, 146, 151, 158, 159, 166, 168, 175–6, 184, 189, 195, 201, 209, 217, 224, 229, 242; for singing, 173

Finlay, William, 83, 232–3, 236, 237, 242
Finlayson, Roderick, 180, 182
Finns, 100
Fisheries, 92, 97, 98
Fishing. *See* Hunting and fishing
Fitz Hams, James, 141
Flaws, Samuel, 159
Flett, John, 189
Flett, William, 137–8
Flogging, 29, 117, 150, 174, 175, 176, 177, 178, 179, 180, 181, 182, 184, 185, 224, 239, 240
Folster, Hugh, 124
Food. *See* Provisions
Forrest, Charles, 182–3
Fort Albany, 29, 30, 31–2, 36, 37, 66, 76, 114, 123, 124, 132, 133, 138–9, 143, 150, 151–2, 161, 164, 166, 167, 171, 172, 173, 201, 214, 216, 227
Fort Alexandria, 14, 115, 132, 155, 217
Fort Chipewyan, 114, 115, 169, 217
Fort Churchill, 33, 36, 79, 131, 143, 145, 151, 158, 161, 165, 176, 201, 202
Fort Edmonton, 6, 131, 147, 155, 161, 184, 202, 218
Fort Garry, 94, 135
Fort George, 125, 130
Fort Halkett, 215
Fort Hope, 141
Fort Langley, 138, 178
Fort Rupert, 208, 210
Fort St James, 161
Fort Simpson, 134, 180, 187, 188, 192, 217, 239, 240, 242
Fort Stikine, 53, 138, 179, 180, 181, 238
Fort Vancouver, 6, 146, 178, 179, 180, 184, 203, 204, 241, 242
Fort Vermilion, 87, 125
Fort Victoria, 6, 138, 141, 203, 205, 242
Fort Wedderburn, 87
Fort William, 174
Fort Yale, 141

Fort Yukon, 160
France, 2, 26, 29, 78, 79, 158
Francis, Daniel, 11, 15
Fraser, Thomas, 62
Fraser River, 132
Free traders, 96, 102, 138, 153, 169
Freezing and frostbite, 132, 154, 168
French army, 175
French Canada. *See* Canada; Lower Canada
French Canadians. *See* Canadians
French Foreign Legion, 102
French Revolution, 3, 4, 34, 74, 83, 158
French traders, 3
Fund for the Relief of the Destitute Inhabitants (Scottish Highlands), 98
'Fur trade society', 121–30, 155

Gaddy, James, 129–30
Gallagher, Brian, 127
Garrioch, William, 188
Gauls, 195
Gauntlet, running the, 174, 176
Geddes, David, 74, 78, 79–80, 82
Genovese, Eugene, 28
Gibeault, Hilair, 182
Ginzburg, Carlo, 122
Gladman, George, 140
'Glasgow Insurgents', 18, 82–3, 231, 232–8
Gloucester House, 163, 164, 168
Glover, Richard, 269 n.58
Gold fever, strikes, and mining, 154–5, 203, 212
Goldring, Philip, 97
Good, Richard, 112
Goods. *See* Equipments; Trade goods
Gordon, George, 239, 240
Grahame, James A., 220
Grand Rapid, 222
Grand River, 184
Gratuities. *See* Bonuses
Great Britain, 65, 85, 86, 106, 108, 126, 151, 179; social unrest in, 186
Great Lakes, 6
Great Whale River, 215

Green, John, 150
Greenland fisheries, 92, 98
Greenwich House, 214
Greer, Alan, 74
Grey Coat School, Westminster, 66
Groat, John, 60
Gulbransen, Lars, 103
Gunn, James, 150
Gunn, Robert, 170
Guy Fawkes Day, 13

Hadlow, 215
Half-allowance (-rations), 159, 160, 166, 196, 214, 216, 218
'Half-breeds', 90, 93, 94, 102, 105, 108, 112, 127, 140, 152–3, 161, 180, 201, 218, 222
Hall, James, 135–6
Hannah Bay, 124
Hanwell, Capt., 216, 217
Hardisty, William L., 219–20
Hardwick, Guy, 31
Hargrave, James, 97, 104, 125, 126, 141–2, 252
Hargrave, Letitia, 123, 183
Harrison, Benjamin, 179
Hawaii. *See* Sandwich Islands
Hawaiians. *See* Sandwich Islanders
Hay, Honeyman, 188
Hayes River, 232
Hearne, Samuel, 162
Heath, William, 177
Hebrides, the (Western Islands), 80, 97–8; Lewis and Lewismen, 86, 96, 97, 98, 107, 195
Hechter, Michael, 67
Henderson, George, 228
Henderson, Jacob, 158
Heney, Hugh, 225–8, 230, 231
Henley House, 30–2, 139, 163, 164, 171
Henry, Alexander, Sr, 67
Heron, Francis, 94, 202
Hillier, William, 232–6 *passim*
Hinson, John, 66
Hodgson, John, 135, 167, 172, 201

Holborn Hill, 129, 278 n.48
Holmes, J.P., 125
Home, Capt. David, 177, 238–9
Homosexuality, 128–9
Honolulu, 134, 146, 154, 203, 204, 205
Hopkins, Samuel, 66
Houston, James, 167
Hudson Bay, 2, 6, 8, 13, 23, 73, 79, 87, 89, 162, 176, 203, 204, 215, 218, 220
Hudson House, 171
Hudson's Bay Company (HBC): Archives, 172, 249–52; as a business, 1, 172; charter of 1670, 2, 16, 23, 224, 232; coal operations of, 207–12; competition, 4, 5, 26, 35, 48, 73, 118, 157, 162, 200; concern for former servants, 59–60; London committee, 1, 4, 8, 10–11, 12, 14–18, 24, 26, 27, 29–45 *passim*, 47–8, 52, 53, 54, 56, 58–62, 64–9, 72, 73, 74, 76–7, 82, 83, 84, 85, 87, 88, 89, 90, 97, 99, 100, 101, 103, 104, 105–6, 108, 110, 111, 114, 121, 122, 123, 133, 138, 139, 141, 144–5, 148, 153, 156, 158, 163, 165, 170, 171, 174, 175, 177–8, 179, 182, 185, 192, 194, 199, 201, 202, 206, 207, 208, 209, 210, 236, 238, 242, 244, 245, 247, 248; merger with NWC, 5, 6, 48–9, 91, 92, 96, 118, 123, 127, 138, 154, 202, 203; officers, 5, 12, 13, 14–15, 24–5, 29, 33, 34, 35, 36, 38, 39, 40, 43–4, 50, 53, 58, 59, 61, 62, 73, 88, 89, 104, 107, 110, 111, 114, 118, 119, 121, 122–3, 126, 127, 129, 130, 131, 135, 136, 144–8, 150, 171–4, 178, 183–6, 192, 194, 199, 201, 214, 217, 220, 237, 238, 246, 240–50; organization of, 48–9; paternalism of, 2, 57–63, 132, 199, 212, 245; posts, 9, 51; profits, 44, 49, 53, 60, 61; recruitment, 3, 24, 26, 41, 64–5, 67–9, 71, 74–7, 79, 85, 91, 92–3, 96, 100, 103, 107, 108, 207, 209, 247; reports and journals, 36–8, 249–50; shareholders, 25, 61; take-over of, 61; timber business, 45, 46, 47; traditional view of, 1; transfer of lands to Dominion of Canada, 61
Hunting and fishing, 139–40, 168, 201, 220
Hutchins, Thomas, 163, 164
Hutchinson, John, 214

Ile-a-la-Crosse, 219, 221
Imprisonment (in irons), 29, 99, 117, 138, 155, 174, 178, 179, 192, 205, 209, 223, 224, 238
'Indian Territories', 232
Industrialism, 20, 198
Injuries, 59, 60, 168
Inland service, 32, 35, 73, 75–7, 79, 89, 162, 163–4, 165, 167, 169, 200, 214
Insolence, 113, 117, 120, 149, 160, 176, 189
International Financial Society, 61, 222
Interpreters, 54
Inverness Journal, 81
Ireland, 4, 5, 67, 81, 83, 84, 97
Irish, 67, 81, 82–4, 92, 150, 176, 195, 196, 224, 237
Irvine, Sam, 166
Isbister, John, 226
Isbister, William, 32

Jacobs, Ferdinand, 112
James Bay, 2, 6, 30, 130
Jarvis, John, 239
Johnson, Jonathan, 125
Johnston, James, 59–60
Jones, Robert, 173–4
Joyce, Patrick, 20

Kanaquasse, Pierre, 181, 182, 248, 294 n.74
Kane, Paul, 184
Kelsey, Henry, 162
Kennedy, William, 227–8, 230–2
Kenogamissi, 112

INDEX 313

Keveny, Owen, 84, 174, 176
King, Johnson G., 146, 155, 184
King George, 231
Kipling, John, 163
Kitchen, Eusebius Bacchus, 165
Knight, James, 125
Knight, Ralph, 65

Laboucher, 141
Labourers, 1, 3, 5, 6, 10, 13, 21, 22, 26, 28, 29, 46, 47, 58, 78, 82, 90, 91, 94, 104, 134, 141, 146, 179, 187, 198, 201, 208; characterization of, 2
Labour pool, 64
Labour shortages, 26, 33, 73, 78, 80, 158, 167, 170, 200
Labrador, 7, 94, 99, 169
Lachine, Lower Canada (Quebec), 52, 95, 143
Lac La Biche, 214
Lac La Pluie, 140, 166, 173, 175, 214
La Cloche, 14, 203
Lacourse, Francois, 183–4
Lac Seul, 131
Lain, Alexander, 123
Lake Athabasca, 87, 201
Lake La Loche, 219
Lake St Annes, 140
Lake Superior, 3, 141
Lake Winnipeg, 36, 45, 170, 218, 220
La Loche River, 219
Lamb, W. Kaye, 180, 294 n.74
Landale, David, 207, 208, 211
Land grants, 41, 55, 56–7, 81, 82, 103, 107, 247
Langston, Andrew, 84
Language problems, 102, 195
Larkins, Thomas, 136
Laslett, Peter, 69
Lawson, John, 65
Laziness, 157, 192
Lesser Slave Lake, 132
Lesser Slave River, 214
Levellers, the, 175
Liard River, 214
Liddell, Rev. Francis, 42, 78

Linklater, Caesar, 158–9, 162
Linklater, William, 59, 152
Liquor (brandy, grog, rum, whisky), 35, 41, 42, 58, 82, 103, 109, 112, 117, 120, 121, 122, 131–9, 145, 153, 165, 166, 174, 177, 189, 191, 222, 239; abolishment of regular allowances, 133
Literacy, 39
Local Militia Bill, 80
Logan, Robert, 39
Logie, James, 179
London, 3, 13, 52, 73, 148, 150, 203, 227
Long Lake, 124
Longmoor, Robert, 171–2
Lords of the Admiralty, 225
Loutet (Luitet), Ned, 109
Loutit, William, 125
Lower Canada, 6, 26, 88, 95, 145, 232. *See also* Canada
Lucas, John, 239

McAuley, Aulay, 39
McBean, John, 203
Macdonald, Peter, 105–6
McDonald, Roderick, 81
MacDonell, Alexander, 269 n.58
Macdonell, Miles, 82, 84, 232–7 *passim*
MacGillivray, Simon, 81
McGillivrays, Thain and Co., 92
McGregor, John, 209, 210
Mackay, Donald, 131, 172, 213
McKay, John, 172–3, 225, 227, 228–9, 239
McKenzie, Charles, 49, 108, 124
Mackenzie, Donald, 81–2
Mackenzie, John, 105
Mackenzie, Murdoch, 70, 71, 93
McKenzie, Robert, 55
McKenzie, Roderick, 88–9, 93
McKenzie, Samuel, 170
Mackenzie River district, 7, 8, 103, 146, 170, 177, 218, 219, 221, 222
McKinnon, John, 117–18
Maclean, Donald, 14

McLean, John, 53
MacLeod, Donald, 28
McLeod, John, 60
Macleod, Murdo, 14, 184, 199
McLeod, Peggy, 60
McLoughlin, John, Jr, 53, 112, 179–83, 185, 238, 251, 294 n.74
McLoughlin, John, Sr, 133, 178, 179, 181, 182–3, 184, 238–40, 242, 294 n.74
McNab, John, 172
McNeill, Capt. William Henry, 134, 188, 209, 239–42
McPherson, Murdoch, 146
McPherson, Thomas, 180, 181
MacPherson and MacAndrew (law firm), 106
Mactavish, Duncan, 105–7
McTavish, Frobisher and Company, 49
Mactavish, William, 50, 133
Made Beaver, 36
Maitland, Garden and Auldjo, 85
Makahonuk, Glenn, 269 n.58
Malcolm, John, 168
Malingering, 115, 120. *See also* Neglect of duty
Malthus, Thomas, 85
Manchester House, 162, 171
Manitoba, 5
Mannal, John, 38
Mannall, John, 148–9
Manson, Donald, 14, 181, 182, 183–4, 241
Market economy, 198
Marriage, 41, 50, 52, 55, 122, 123, 125–7; common law, 126; middle-class model, 125–6; refusal of by officer, 181
Marshall, Charles, 187
Marten, Humphrey, 31–2, 109–10, 117, 143, 157
Martins Fall, 140, 167, 170, 172, 173, 188, 201
Mary Dare, 204, 205, 243
Mason, Archibald, 226–9, 238, 242
Mason, Thomas, 225

Master and Servant Act (1823), 106
Master-servant relationship, 20–9, 63, 83, 144, 199, 223, 245
Mentalite, 122
Merchant Shipping Act, 207
Methye Portage, 8
Métis, 11–12, 49, 93, 269 n.58. *See also* 'Half-breeds'
Miles, John, 158
Millar, Roderick, 107
Miller, Thomas, 229
Miller, William (consul general), 205
Miller, William (servant), 28
Minnesota, 5
Missionaries, Methodist, 161
Moad, George, 137
Moar, George, 124
Moar, John, 141–2
Monopoly. *See* Trade monopoly
Montreal, 3, 52, 80, 85, 86, 87, 88, 89, 90, 94, 145
Montreal Department, 6, 7, 52, 96, 217
Moose Factory, 30, 33, 36, 45, 102, 104, 114, 124, 129, 130, 135, 137, 142, 152, 158, 159, 168, 187, 195–6, 217
'Moral economy', 10, 244
Morantz, Toby, 15
Morison, W. and R. (recruitment agents), 96, 107
Morrison, James, 123, 152
Morton, A.S., 52, 270 n.58
Mousette, Narcisse, 182
Muir, Andrew, 209, 210
Muir, John, 207, 208, 209, 210, 248
Murder, 30, 31, 53, 103, 136, 174, 179–83, 238, 251
Murphy, John, 112, 139, 158, 194
Murray, Alexander Hunter, 111, 160–1
Murray, Magnus, 229
Mutiny, 18, 29, 84, 91, 101, 104, 112, 131, 151, 174, 199, 205, 217, 222–42; definition of, 223; naval, 224–5

Nanaimo, 211, 212
Nance, Jacques, 139

Napoleonic Wars, 74
Narquay, Catherine, 123
Native-born servants, 8, 107, 112, 118, 119, 145, 168. *See also* 'Half-breeds'
Native peoples, 1, 3, 4, 6, 13, 15, 24, 35, 36, 41, 47, 66, 75, 87, 94, 105, 112, 117, 121, 122, 125, 130, 135, 136, 138, 139, 147, 151, 152, 153, 157, 159, 162, 163–4, 165, 167–8, 173, 200, 201, 211, 215, 231; Christianized, 161, 222; corruption of, 179; fear of, 208, 209, 210; hostile, 30, 31, 94, 104, 180, 183; hunters and trappers, 10, 112; languages of, 54, 163, 230; tripmen, 7, 218; traders, 2, 3, 15, 35, 38, 150, 155, 163, 192, 239, 249; wintering with, 169; women as wives, 24, 48, 50, 52, 55, 124, 125–6, 153, 159, 181, 251
Neglect of duty, 17, 27, 63, 110, 113, 115, 117, 119, 139–44, 153, 155, 158, 224, 243
Negligence. *See* Neglect of duty
Nelson House, 125
Nereide, 177, 238, 239
Nesquiscow, 137
New Brunswick House, 139
New Caledonia district, 6, 14, 177, 183, 184, 185, 199
Newell, G.R., 239
Newgate Prison, 278 n.48
Newton, Sir Isaac, 172
New Year's Eve/Day, 13, 82, 104, 117, 123, 131, 132, 133, 134, 176, 189
New Zealand, 105
Nicks, John, 72
Nipigon House, 121, 167, 168
Nixon, John, 64, 65, 67, 108
Norman Morison, 138, 190, 205, 206, 207, 210
Norn, John, 137–8
North Dakota, 5
Northern Department, 6, 7, 8, 27, 36, 52, 55, 59, 82, 89–90, 91, 96, 99, 101, 108, 134, 141, 145, 146, 176, 219
North Saskatchewan River, 162, 171
North West Company (NWC), 5, 6, 35, 36, 48, 49, 52, 53, 75, 77, 81, 87, 88, 89, 90, 95, 112, 114, 124, 154, 174, 200, 202, 203, 225, 230
North West River, 143, 188
Norway, 8, 85, 100, 102, 103, 107
Norway House, 7, 14, 28, 86, 103, 117, 183, 218, 219, 220, 221, 222, 298 n.58
Norwegians, 46, 47, 85–6, 92, 100, 101, 102–3, 104, 142, 170, 187, 195–6, 224, 269 n.58

Ogden, Peter Skene, 183
Orcadians, 3, 4, 5, 6, 8, 10, 12, 41, 47, 54, 67–9, 70–2, 74, 77, 78, 79, 80, 81, 82, 83, 86, 90, 91, 93, 95, 96–7, 99, 101, 102, 104, 107, 108, 123, 129, 147, 150, 166, 176, 196, 202, 226, 228, 229, 231, 232, 237, 238, 269 n.58, 286 n.139; stereotype of, 4, 11, 70, 92, 194–5
Ordinance of Labourers (1349), 22
Oregon, 61, 154, 212
Orkney Islands, 24, 59, 60, 67–72, 74, 75, 78, 85, 90, 92, 93, 97, 142, 150, 178, 179, 201–2; Orphir parish, 72; recruitment in, 2–3, 54, 65, 79, 96, 107, 124, 178; traditional society of, 3, 68–9, 70
Orkneymen. *See* Orcadians
Osnaburgh House, 135, 137, 172, 174, 192
Outfit, definition of, 13
Oxford House, 14, 104, 159, 160, 219

Pace of work, 139, 157, 186–92
Pacific Northwest, 203
Packers, 155
Paine, William, 148–50, 248
Palmer, Bryan, 193
Pannekoek, Frits, 131, 138
Parson, William, 222

Passengers' Act, 81
Paternalism, 2, 19, 20, 22, 24, 28–9, 57–63, 132, 193, 199, 212, 243, 245
Pauper children, 65, 91
Paupers and vagrants, 198
Payne, Michael, 131
Peace River, 87, 217
Pearson, Peter, 124
Pelly, George, 146–7
Pembina, 226, 227
Pemmican, 41, 219
Pensions, 59
Pentland, H. Clare, 156
Perquisites of employment, 42, 144, 148
Petitions, 104, 170, 199, 215, 233, 240, 242
Petty, William, 190
Pic, 115
Piece-work and piece-rates, 45, 46–7, 55, 207, 208, 212
Pirates, 84, 128–9, 243
Plowman, William, 227
Point Meuron, 167
Point of the Marsh, 130
Pollard, Sidney, 45
Poor Law, 65, 98
Portage La Loche, 161, 221, 222
Portage La Loche brigade, 8, 9, 134, 218–22
Prayers. *See* Sunday
Pre-industrial (traditional) society and workers, 2, 10, 21, 41, 56, 69, 70, 121, 139, 198, 244, 246, 254 n.2
Prejudice. *See* Ethnicity and racial stereotypes
Press gang, 175
Prince of Wales, 144, 216, 217
Princess Royal, 243
Prisoners of war, 85, 86, 100
Prisons, 50
Pritchett, J.P., 84
Private trade, 17, 24, 65, 113, 114, 118, 120, 130, 138, 144–53, 154, 155, 158, 165, 169, 256 n.15; ammunition, 151, 152; livestock, 145–6; supplies, 146
Profits, 4, 5, 44, 49, 53, 60, 61, 213
Promotion, 38, 39, 48, 123, 127
Provencher, Bishop, 134
Provisions, 4, 41, 45, 86, 87, 89, 90, 100, 101, 104–5, 117, 142, 147, 149, 153, 155, 164, 170, 171, 176, 189, 190, 191, 200, 201, 211, 213–18, 219, 233, 234, 246, 247
Pruden, John Peter, 189–90
Prussian army, 175
Puget's Sound Agricultural Company, 7

Qu'appelle River, 189

Race. *See* Ethnicity and racial stereotypes
Rae, William Glen, 179, 180, 181, 182
Ralston, Keith, 207
Rations. *See* Provisions
Recruitment, 3, 24, 41, 54, 64–108 *passim*, 247; agents, 28, 59, 74, 75, 76, 79, 80–8 *passim*, 90, 92, 95, 96, 99, 102, 105, 107, 108, 178, 192, 207; of Canadians, 85–96; of coalminers, 207, 211–12; of seamen, 203; of tripmen, 221–2
Rediker, Marcus, 120, 198
Red River, 134, 174, 188, 225, 228
Red River Colony and settlers, 5, 6, 7, 8, 41, 46, 50, 53, 93, 94, 96, 101, 102, 103, 125, 145, 152, 153, 155, 169, 179, 202–3, 212, 218, 219, 220, 221, 222, 228, 232, 247; retirement to colony, 55–6, 81, 82, 84, 90
Red River district, 228
Red River Rebellion (1869–70), 222, 223
Refusal to do as ordered, 31, 63, 110, 113, 114, 115–17, 119, 142, 143, 149, 161, 162, 167, 168–9, 170, 171, 186, 189, 190–1, 197, 204, 205, 218, 222, 225, 243, 246
Regales, 134, 222
Reid, Robert, 123
Religion, 24
Retirement, 55, 59

'Retrenching System', 5, 35, 36–44, 80, 202, 225, 237
Rich, E.E., 48
Richards, John, 228–9
Richards, Capt. John, 136, 144
Richards, Thomas, 167
Richards, William, 30, 37
Rites of passage, 131–2
Roadbuilding, 45–6
Robertson, Colin, 80, 87, 89, 268 n.58
Robertson, David, 60
Robertson, Laurence, 159–60
Robertson, Peter, 105
Robert Taylor, 84, 174
Ross, Donald, 195
Ross, James, 127
Ross, Malcolm, 164
Ross, William, 60
Rowland, John, 28
Royal African Company, 256 n.15
Royal Foundation of Queen Anne, 66
Rule, John, 45
Rupert's House, 169
Rupert's Land, 2, 4, 6, 8, 13, 25, 26, 36, 48, 50, 59, 61, 66, 79, 88, 89, 94, 97, 107, 108, 120, 122, 126, 127, 154, 155, 174, 232, 236; sold to Canadian government, 222
Rupert's River, 135
Rushworth, George, 31, 171
Russell, James, 215–16
Russian traders, 6, 94, 183

Sabbatarianism, 161. *See also* Sunday
Sailors. *See* Seamen
Sailors' Home (Dover, Eng.), 101
St George's Day, 13, 42, 123
St Lawrence River, 7
St Peter's, 222
Sandwich Islanders (Hawaiians), 58, 95, 136, 146, 179, 181, 182, 184, 195, 204, 205, 209
Sandwich Islands (Hawaii), 7, 205
San Francisco, 203, 204
Saskatchewan, 5
Saskatchewan brigade, 103

Saskatchewan district, 7, 36, 41, 102, 142, 152, 153
Saskatchewan River, 218, 222
Sault Ste Marie, 14, 145
Sault Ste Marie district, 203
Saunders, John, 155
Saunders, Palm, 159–60, 248
Saunders, William, 216
Scandinavia, 85
Scandinavians, 85
Scarborough, James, 242
Scotland, 5, 8, 41, 67, 80–1, 82–3, 90, 98, 101, 103, 105, 107, 161, 205; Highlands and Highlanders, 4, 67–8, 81, 92, 98, 195
Scots, 1, 7, 47, 65, 67, 84, 90, 92, 101, 103, 104, 107, 108, 195; coalminers, 207, 211; women, 127
Scott, John, 49
Scottish Court of Session, 83
Scurvy, 215
Seaman's Hospital Society, 60
Seamen, 118, 129, 136, 154, 161, 177, 179, 187, 188, 190–1, 197, 199, 203–7, 214, 216, 223, 224–5, 238–43, 250; culture of, 243, 246; stereotype of, 217
Selkirk, Earl of, 5, 81, 84
Semple, Robert, 269 n.58
Servants' list, 112
Settlement. *See* Red River Colony
Seven Years' War, 3
Severn House, 35, 82, 115, 121, 137
Sexual assault, 124
Sexual relations, 123–9, 159, 179
Seymour, Charles, 158
Shaw, William, 125
Shetland Islands and Shetlanders, 79, 83, 96, 97, 99, 101, 107
Ship Master's Assistant, 242
Ships and shipping, 95, 108, 124, 132, 136, 147, 154, 187, 199, 203, 250, 296 n.102; mutiny, 238–43
Ships' captains, 25, 74, 128, 129, 132, 136, 144, 199, 215, 216, 217, 224–5, 238–43 *passim*, 255 n.15

Shoe allowance, 145
Short, George, 157
Simpson, George, 49, 54, 55, 57, 87, 91–2, 93, 94, 95–6, 100, 101–5, 108, 115, 126, 127, 131, 133, 134, 141–3, 145, 146, 155, 178, 179–80, 181, 182, 184–5, 195, 203, 217, 218, 243, 248, 251, 294 n.74; as manager, 48, 50, 52–3, 58; 'Character Book', 173; character of, 52, 53; lack of understanding, 143; personal life, 48
Simpson, Wemyss, 52
Sinclair, Charles, 32
Sinclair, William, 170
Skinner, John, 117
Slavery, 29, 179
Small Debt Act, 106
Smith, Donald A., 108
Smith, Johannes, 187
Smith, John (miner), 207
Smith, John (servant), 192
Smith, Jno, 129
Snoddy, Francois, 161
Social reformers, 50, 126, 128, 175
Sodomy, 128–30
Songs and singing, 173, 191
Sorel, Lower Canada (Quebec), 74–5, 95
Southern Department, 6, 7, 36, 46, 52, 55, 56, 91, 96, 99, 101, 133, 145, 154, 215, 223
Spence, John, 32
Split Lake, 49
Squatters, 56, 138
Starling, James, 240, 242
Starvation, 14, 87, 154, 164, 167, 177, 184, 185, 187, 215–16, 217, 218
Statute of Labourers (1351), 22
Steamboats, 108, 141, 222
Stereotypes. *See* Ethnicity and racial bias; names of ethnic and national groups
Stewart, James, 221
Strikes, 103, 210, 210, 217, 223, 238, 241. *See also* Combination

Stuart's Lake, 14
Sturgeon Lake, 75
Sturgeon-Weir River, 219
Sunday (the Sabbath), 13, 14, 24, 76, 121, 138, 161–2, 190, 191
Sutherland, George, 75–6, 163–4
Sutherland, James, 86, 148, 154, 195, 214, 229
Sutherland, John, 34
Swain, James, 35
Swainson, Hendrich, 188
Swan River district, 102, 166, 232
Sweden and Swedes, 85, 100, 103
'Systematic management', 38

Tate, Thomas, 32
Taylor, Edward, 141
Taylor, Frederick, 43
Taylor, Samuel, 150–1, 286 n.138
Teach, Edward (Blackbeard), 129
Thames Church Missionary Society, 60
Theft, 103, 117, 120, 136, 138, 151, 166, 175, 176, 180, 182, 236
The Pas, Manitoba, 3
Thomas, John, 129, 174, 187
Thomas, Thomas, 46, 86
Thompson, David, 162, 248
Thompson, E.P., 3, 22, 175
Thomson, James, 32
Tilloch, William, 79
Timber industry, 95
Todd, Robert, 14, 184
Todd, William, 131
Tomison, William (officer), 73, 79, 171, 201, 213
Tomison, William (servant), 59
Topping, Thomas, 151
Trade goods, 2, 4, 12, 13, 89, 165, 214
Trade monopoly, 91, 203
Tradesmen, 1, 3, 46, 91, 101, 104, 141–3, 148, 188, 207, 223. *See also* Artisans and craftsmen
Traditional social relations, 64
Trapping, 150
Tripmen, 6, 7, 13, 18, 108, 118, 137, 145, 197, 218, 219, 223, 246, 247

United States, 155
United States government, 61
Upper Canada, 232
Upper Fraser River, 6

Valparaiso, Chile, 101, 211
Vancouver, 243
Vancouver Island, 6, 7, 47, 101, 123, 138, 197, 205, 207, 211
Venereal disease, 192
Vincent, Thomas, 154, 173, 215, 223, 224, 228
Virago, 217
Voyageurs, 1, 3, 11, 80, 85, 161, 218

Wages and salaries, 3, 10, 11, 12, 15, 18, 19–20, 21, 26, 27, 32, 42, 43, 44–7, 49, 54–5, 56, 57–8, 63, 64, 68–9, 70, 73, 75, 77, 78, 79, 80, 81, 89, 90, 91, 92, 95, 96–7, 100, 101, 103, 104, 106, 107, 110, 120, 122, 141, 142, 148, 154, 155, 163, 164, 165, 167, 187, 196–214, 220, 229, 242, 244, 246, 247, 251
Wales, 67
Walker, John, 235
Walker, William, 156–7, 162, 171
War, 3, 29, 73, 74, 86, 200
Watt, William, 124
Weavers, 83
Wedderburn (Colvile), Andrew, 5
Wellington, Duke of, 175

Western Department, 185
Weymontachingue, 139
Weynton, Capt., 154, 204, 205
Whaling, 96, 97
Whipping. *See* Cat-o'-nine-tails; Flogging
White-collar workers, 48, 50
Wiegand, Thomas, 27–8
Williams, William, 55, 88, 89, 90, 91
Willson, William, 188, 240–2
Wilson, Robert, 104
Winnipeg district, 36, 41
Winter stations, 87, 137, 157, 162
Wishart, Capt., 190–1, 205
Women: British, 50, 126, 127; in fur trade society, 1, 28, 123–7; Native women as wives, 24, 48, 50, 52, 55, 124, 125–6, 153, 159, 181, 251
Work, John, 137, 240–1
Workplace, transformation of, 19–20

Yeats, William, 184
York Factory, 6, 7, 8, 9, 14, 32, 36, 45, 46, 73, 74, 77, 82, 86, 89, 94, 103, 107, 109, 111, 114, 117, 123, 129, 131, 134, 135, 141, 143, 150, 151, 157, 164, 170, 171, 172, 176, 183, 200, 201, 202, 213, 214, 218, 219, 220, 221, 222, 225, 227, 228, 232, 233, 234, 237, 241, 252
Yorston, William, 225–31, 248

THE CANADIAN SOCIAL HISTORY SERIES

Terry Copp,
The Anatomy of Poverty:
The Condition of the Working Class
in Montreal, 1897–1929, 1974.
ISBN 0-7710-2252-2

Alison Prentice,
The School Promoters:
Education and Social Class in
Mid-Nineteenth Century
Upper Canada, 1977.
ISBN 0-7710-7181-7

John Herd Thompson,
The Harvests of War:
The Prairie West, 1914–1918, 1978.
ISBN 0-7710-8560-5

Joy Parr, Editor,
Childhood and Family in Canadian
History, 1982.
ISBN 0-7710-6938-3

Alison Prentice and
Susan Mann Trofimenkoff, Editors,
The Neglected Majority:
Essays in Canadian Women's History,
Volume 2, 1985.
ISBN 0-7710-8583-4

Angus McLaren and
Arlene Tigar McLaren,
The Bedroom and the State: The
Changing Practices and Politics of
Contraception and Abortion in Canada,
1880–1980, 1986.
ISBN 0-19-541262-1

Ruth Roach Pierson,
"They're Still Women After All":
The Second World War and
Canadian Womanhood, 1986.
ISBN 0-7710-6958-8

Bryan D. Palmer,
The Character of Class Struggle:
Essays in Canadian Working Class
History, 1850–1985, 1986.
ISBN 0-7710-6946-4

Alan Metcalfe,
Canada Learns to Play:
The Emergence of Organized Sport,
1807–1914, 1987.
ISBN 0-19-541304-0

Marta Danylewycz,
Taking the Veil:
An Alternative to Marriage,
Motherhood, and Spinsterhood in
Quebec, 1840–1920, 1987.
ISBN 0-7710-2550-5

Craig Heron,
Working in Steel: The Early Years in
Canada, 1883–1935, 1988.
ISBN 0-7710-4086-5

Wendy Mitchinson and
Janice Dickin McGinnis, Editors,
Essays in the History of
Canadian Medicine, 1988.
ISBN 0-7710-6063-7

Joan Sangster,
Dreams of Equality: Women on the
Canadian Left, 1920–1950, 1989.
ISBN 0-7710-7946-X

Angus McLaren,
Our Own Master Race: Eugenics in
Canada, 1885–1945, 1990.
ISBN 0-7710-5544-7

Bruno Ramirez,
On the Move:
French-Canadian and Italian Migrants
in the North Atlantic Economy,
1860–1914, 1991.
ISBN 0-7710-7283-X

Mariana Valverde,
"The Age of Light, Soap and Water":
Moral Reform in English Canada,
1885–1925, 1991.
ISBN 0-7710-8689-X

Bettina Bradbury,
Working Families:
Age, Gender, and Daily Survival in
Industrializing Montreal, 1993.
ISBN 0–19–541211–7

Andrée Lévesque,
Making and Breaking the Rules:
Women in Quebec, 1919–1939, 1994.
ISBN 0–7710–5283–9

Cecilia Danysk,
Hired Hands: Labour and the
Development of Prairie Agriculture,
1880–1930, 1995.
ISBN 0–7710–2552–1

Kathryn McPherson,
Bedside Matters: The Transformation
of Canadian Nursing, 1900–1990, 1996.
ISBN 0–19–541219–2

Edith Burley,
Servants of the Honourable Company:
Work, Discipline, and Conflict in the
Hudson's Bay Company, 1770–1879,
1997.
ISBN 0–19–541296–6

Mercedes Steedman,
Angels of the Workplace: Constructing
Gender Inequality in the Canadian
Needle Trade, 1890 to 1940, 1997.
ISBN 0–19–541308–3